EASTERN EUROPE

Other Titles of Interest

Russia and the Former Soviet Union: A Bibliographic Guide to English Language Publications, 1986-1991. By Helen F. Sullivan and Robert H. Burger. 1994.

Ukraine: A Bibliographic Guide to English-Language Publications. By Bohdan S. Wynar. 1990.

EASTERN EUROPE
A Bibliographic Guide to
English Language Publications,
1986-1993

Robert H. Burger
and
Helen F. Sullivan

Slavic and East European Library
University of Illinois at Urbana-Champaign

With the assistance of Lisa Radloff

1995
LIBRARIES UNLIMITED, INC.
Englewood, Colorado

Copyright © 1995 Robert H. Burger and Helen F. Sullivan
All Rights Reserved
Printed in the United States of America

No part of this publication may be reproduced, stored in a retrieval system, or transmitted in any form or by any means, electronic, mechanical, photocopying, recording, or otherwise, without the prior written permission of the publisher.

LIBRARIES UNLIMITED, INC.
P.O. Box 6633
Englewood, CO 80155-6633
1-800-237-6124

Library of Congress Cataloging-in-Publication Data

Burger, Robert H. (Robert Harold), 1947-
    Eastern Europe : a bibliographic guide to English language publications, 1986-1993 / Robert H. Burger and Helen F. Sullivan.
      xii, 254p. 17x25 cm.
      Includes bibliographical references and index.
      ISBN 1-56308-047-8
      1. Europe, Eastern--Bibliography. 2. English imprints.
I. Sullivan, Helen F. II. Title.
Z2483.B89   1995
[DJK9]
016.947085' 4--dc20   95-33592
                                                                                                   CIP

"Remember that it was of your parents you were born; how can you repay what they have given to you?"

Ecclesiasticus 7:28

*For
Marceline K.
and
Bernard J. Sullivan
with
gratitude*

CONTENTS

INTRODUCTION xi

1-EASTERN EUROPE 1
   General Reference Works 1
   Bibliography 5
   History 6
   Government, Politics and Law 13
   Foreign Relations 19
   Communism 27
   Economics, Trade & Business 31
   Language and Literature 57
   National Minorities 59
   Holocaust 63
   Dissident Movements 68
   The Society, Sociology 69
   The Arts and Culture 73
   Science and Technology 75
   The Downfall of Communism 77

2-ALBANIA 83

3-BULGARIA 85
   General Reference Works 85
   History 85
   Economics, Trade and Business 86
   Language and literature 88
   Government, Politics and Law 89
   The Society, Sociology 90

4-CZECHOSLOVAKIA 91
   General Reference Works 91
   History 92
   Government, Politics and Law 95
   Communism 98
   Language and Literature 99
   Individual Authors 101
   National Minorities 105
   Arts and Culture 106
   Dissident Movement 106
   Velvet Revolution 107
   Economics, Business and Trade 108

5-GERMAN DEMOCRATIC REPUBLIC ... 110

General Reference Works ... 110
History ... 110
Government, Politics and Law ... 112
Economics, Business and Trade ... 115
Language and Literature ... 116
Individual Authors ... 117
The Society, Sociology ... 118
Reunification ... 120

6-HUNGARY ... 123

General Reference Works ... 123
History ... 124
Government, Politics and Law ... 128
Foreign Relations ... 131
Economics, Business and Trade ... 131
Language and Literature ... 136
Individual Authors ... 137
The Society, Sociology ... 138
National Minorities ... 141
The Arts and Culture ... 142

7-POLAND ... 144

General Reference Works ... 144
History ... 145
Government, Politics and Law ... 153
Foreign Relations ... 159
Economics, Business and Trade ... 161
Language ... 165
Literature ... 166
Individual Authors ... 167
The Society, Sociology ... 174
Religion ... 178
Dissident Movements ... 179
National Minorities ... 182
Crash Course in Capitalism ... 186
Arts and Culture ... 187

8-ROMANIA ... 190

General Reference Works ... 190
History ... 190
Government, Politics and Trade ... 194
Foreign Relations ... 196
Economics, Business and Law ... 197
Language and Literature ... 198
Individual Authors ... 198
The Society, Sociology ... 199
National Minorities ... 201

9-YUGOSLAVIA 203
General Reference Works 203
History 205
Government, Politics and Law 210
Foreign Relations 214
Economics, Business and Trade 214
The Society, Sociology 218
Language and Literature 219
Individual Authors 221
Arts and Culture 222
Dissident Movements 223
National Minorities 223
Civil War 223

AUTHOR INDEX 227
SUBJECT INDEX 239

INTRODUCTION

This volume both continues and expands on an earlier work by Stephen Horak titled *Russia, the USSR and Eastern Europe*. His base volume, covering items in English from 1900 to 1975, was supplemented by two five-year supplements, the last one appearing just before his death in 1986. The purpose of those volumes, as well as this one, is to provide students and researchers of all kinds with an annotated guide to major publications in the field.

Because of the momentous changes that have taken place in Eastern Europe and the former Soviet Union in the past few years there has been an avalanche of materials in English that focus on that part of the world. In a companion volume, published in the spring of 1994, Helen Sullivan and I covered books in English published between 1986 and 1991 that were concerned with Russia and the Soviet Union. This volume covers the Eastern European countries of Albania, Bulgaria, Czechoslovakia, the German Democratic Republic, Hungary, Poland, Romania, and Yugoslavia. Some of these countries no longer exist at the time of this writing. Czechoslovakia has split into the Czech and Slovak Republics, the GDR has reunited with the Federal Republic of Germany, and Yugoslavia has disintegrated into warring and independent factions and countries. Even in some circles, Eastern Europe is now being called Central Europe. In this volume, we have continued to refer to these geographic and political entities by their former names. Because of this, our book represents the last bibliographical vestiges of a former political world.

As with our companion volume, this bibliography is a representative selection of titles as opposed to a comprehensive listing. The titles were selected from two sources, the *American Bibliography of Slavic and East European Studies* and *Books in Print*. English language titles published from 1986 to 1993 made up the pool from which we selected. Certain categories of material were excluded: serials, occasional papers, juvenile literature, most publications under fifty pages, locally published genealogies, gallery guides, most U.S. government publications, reprints of materials published outside the chronological scope, and books not readily available to the compilers. The test for this last category of materials was the availability of the book in the Illinois interlibrary loan network (ILLINET). Some seminal publications under fifty pages were included. Although of importance, we reluctantly had to exclude publications such as *Rand Notes*, *Carl Beck Papers*, and materials dealing with East European immigration in the United States.

As with all bibliographies attempting a representative selection rather than comprehensive coverage, some titles were not selected that technically fell within our scope. The compilers believed their first responsibility was to include all major works on the area. The importance of the works was determined either by critical acclaim and coverage, uniqueness of subject matter or perspective, or significance of the author. There will, no doubt, be some omissions because of oversight and lack of time. We apologize for these omissions. The attentive scholar will also discover that items on Eastern Europe in general that appeared in our companion volume also appear here in a similar section. This was by design.

We have tried to maintain an arrangement similar to Horak's volume. Titles are arranged in sections by country, and further subdivided by subject area. The titles are consecutively numbered throughout. Within each section entries are arranged alphabetically by author, or lacking an author, by editor, or, lacking both of these by title. Each entry includes complete bibliographic information, a descriptive annotation, and information, if available, on where the book was reviewed. The bibliographic description of each title includes full author, title, dates, place of publication, publisher, extent, ISBN, and series information. Volumes published as part of a series are accessible through the individual volume title. Earlier volumes in this series often included quotations from book reviews. While we have abandoned that practice, citations to book reviews are provided when available. Because of the delay in publishing reviews of current books and other time constraints placed upon us, no reviews are listed for 1992 and 1993 titles. Citations for book reviews were taken from the *American Bibliography of Slavic and East European Studies*.

The annotations included here are descriptive rather than critical. They are intended to assist the student and researcher in choosing individual works on a topic of interest by describing the topic, arrangement, bias, intended audience, and special features of each book. Since both compilers contributed annotations, and we each have different areas of expertise, the annotations necessarily vary in emphasis and detail. Further, some works did not readily lend themselves to such straightforward description (for example, novels). In some cases, the best descriptions of the book were found in the introduction and conclusion. Those quotations are included in the annotations with appropriate attribution.

Access is provided through the general subject arrangement and the author and subject indexes. While the author index is self-explanatory, a word on the compilation of the subject index might be helpful. The subject headings are based on the Library of Congress usage, with some additions for more specific access. Unless otherwise indicated, all headings refer to Eastern Europe in general. Other headings are qualified by the specific country to which they refer. The numbers after each heading refer to individual citations in the main bibliography. While we tried to make the headings as specific as we deemed useful, certain headings still had an extremely large number of entries.

Procite was used to organize all the data for this bibliography and to generate the indexes, with further modification using Microsoft Word.

As with most books, this one could not have been completed without the assistance or forbearance of many people. We wish to gratefully acknowledge the excellent editorial support of Bohdan Wynar and the monetary support provided by the University of Illinois Research Board.

Aaron Trehub has been unusually generous with his time and resources, both with this volume and its companion, in providing us with machine-readable citations and book review information from the *American Bibliography of Slavic and East European Studies*. Lisa Radloff, Alexa Sennyey, and Meg Burger tolerated our terrible handwriting to retrieve, organize, and input our citations. Our respective spouses, Ann Burger and Chuck Mode, have been unusually patient in suffering our inattention and clutter. Finally, the staff of the Slavic and

East European Library have made this burden easier by virtue of their support and good cheer.

Finally I owe a great deal of gratitude to Helen Sullivan, my coauthor. During the period that we produced these two volumes Helen gave birth to a daughter and managed, with husband Chuck, to raise her for the first two years of life. In spite of these familial burdens and joys, she has always provided support and encouragement to me personally and also managed to stay sane in the process.

EASTERN EUROPE
A Bibliographic Guide to
English Language Publications,
1986-1993

- Eastern Europe
- Albania
- Bulgaria
- Czechoslovakia
- German Democratic Republic
- Hungary
- Poland
- Romania
- Yugoslavia

Chapter 1
EASTERN EUROPE

GENERAL REFERENCE WORKS

1. **Russia in the Twentieth Century: The Catalog of the Bakhmeteff Archive of Russia and East European History and Culture, the Rare Book and Manuscript Library, Columbia University**. Boston: G. K. Hall, 1987. xi, 187 p. ISBN: 081610462X. Includes index.

The Bakhmeteff Archive at Columbia University has four focal areas: (1) materials pertaining to prominent literary figures of the Russian emigration; (2) archives of institutions and organizations, worthy émigré benevolent and professional organizations, church organizations, and some political parties of revolutionary and prerevolutionary Russia; (3) historical materials that lay at the origin of the Russian immigration; and (4) materials pertaining to Eastern Europe. The catalog is arranged alphabetically by name of organization. Each entry includes a physical description as well as a summary of the holdings. An index of names and subjects facilitates access to the main listing.

2. Goldman, Minton F., **Global Studies. The Soviet Union and Eastern Europe**. Guilford, Conn.: The Dushkin Pub. Group, 1990. xii, 212 p. ISBN: 0879678607. Includes index.

This volume is one in the series entitled *Global Studies*. The aim of the series is to provide the reader with basic background information on a particular area within the global context. In this volume the author "covers the Soviet Union and the eight countries of Eastern Europe—Albania, Bulgaria, Czechoslovakia, East Germany, Hungary, Poland, Romania and Yugoslavia." For the Soviet Union and Eastern European region, the author/editor has written narrative essays focusing on the cultural, sociopolitical and economic differences and similarities of the countries and people in the region.

Accompanying the regional essays are full-page maps showing the political boundaries of each of the countries within the regions." (p. viii) A country report on each nation is also included providing a summary of statistical data, an essay on historical, geographical, political, cultural and economic conditions, a historical timeline of major events and four graphic indicators with brief statements on development, freedom, health/welfare and achievements. An appendix on governmental structure and a glossary of terms is provided. Many of the articles in the volume are reprinted from newspapers and journals.

3. Hale, Keith, **In the Land of Alexander: Gay Travels, with History and Politics in Hungary, Yugoslavia, Turkey, and Greece**. Boston, MA: Alyson Publications, 1990. 286 p. ISBN: 1555831680. Includes bibliographical references (p. 285-286).

"In the summer of 1989, Keith Hale set out to discover the gay life, culture, and history of Eastern Europe, a region not known for its gay movement. He sometimes found more than he expected, sometimes less. This unusual travelogue combines historical and cultural insights, useful travel tips, and first-person experiences." (cover)

4. Howard, A. E. Dick, **Democracy's Dawn: A Directory of American Initiatives on Constitutionalism, Democracy, and the Rule of Law in Central and Eastern Europe**. Charlottesville, Va.: University Press of Virginia for the United States Institute of Peace, 1991. 225 p. ISBN: 0813913527. Includes index.

"The present study seeks to inventory those initiatives, public and private, being undertaken in the United States to assist the countries of Central and Eastern Europe with respect to bringing about democracy, constitutionalism, and the role of law. Thus the report's emphasis is on subjects touching the constitutional, political, and legal aspects of society" (p. 11)

5. Kulikowski, Mark, **A Bibliography of Slavic Mythology**. Columbus, Ohio: Slavica, 1989. 137 p. ISBN: 0893572039.

Kulikowski's bibliography is divided into two parts: primary sources and secondary sources. Within each part items are listed alphabetically by author. A brief subject index facilitates access to the entries. Each annotation includes location symbols of libraries that hold the cited work.

6. Lazic, Branko M., **Biographical Dictionary of the Comintern; in collaboration with Milorad M. Drachkovitch**. New, rev., and expanded. Stanford, Calif.: Hoover Institution Press, 1986. iv, 532 p. ISBN: 0817984011. Bibliography (p.xxii-xxiii).

This expanded edition now includes 753 biographies and 435 pseudonyms. Two hundred twenty-nine biographies from the original edition have been corrected or additional information supplied to them. Individuals were included if they were part of the Comintern's overall directorate, people who spoke at Comintern Congresses from 1919 to 1935 or were delegates to the enlarged plenary meetings of the Executive Committee from 1922 to 1933, members of the Comintern "apparatus" (secret emissaries, etc.), leaders of the international organizations and graduates of the four principal Comintern schools.

7. **Fodor's 90 Eastern Europe**. New York: Fodor's Travel Publications, 1990. vi, 466 p. ISBN: 0679017623. Includes index.

Fodor's guide covers Bulgaria, Czechoslovakia, East Germany, Hungary, Poland and Romania. An introductory section to the volume gives tips in such matters as tours, travel documents, insurance, money, photography, and other relevant details. Each country section includes "Facts at Your Fingertips"—tours, visas, money, climate, special events, etc., a short essay on the history, politics and culture of the region, characteristic food and drink, and prominent cities and areas of the country. A six page atlas of Eastern Europe complements city and other local maps found throughout the text.

8. **The Soviet Union and Eastern Europe,** edited by George Schopflin, rev. and updated ed. New York: Facts on File, 1986. xvii, 637 p. *Handbooks to the Modern World*, ISBN: 0816012601. Includes bibliographies and index.

A handbook covering historical, political, economic and social developments in the Soviet Union and Eastern Europe since World War II. This second edition was prompted by the increasing amount of information and analysis of events. The volume is divided into broad subject categories: historical, political, economic, social, each made up of essays on various topics. The opening section is comprised of introductory essays on each country including biographical sketches on major political figures and a section on comparative statistics for the region. Each of the latter essays includes a brief bibliography of materials for further reading. In the sections on historical, economic and social aspects there are no essays on specific East European countries, rather topical essays deal with the entire area. There are a number of essays on the situation in the Soviet Union.

9. Simmons, P. J., **Archival Research on the Cold War Era: A Report from Budapest, Prague and Warsaw**. Washington, D.C.: Cold War International History Project, Woodrow Wilson International Center for Scholars, 1992. 103 p. Includes bibliographical references.

"This report presents findings of a four-week investigation of Hungarian, Czechoslovak and Polish archives from the years 1945 to the present. During trips to Budapest, Prague and Warsaw in October and November 1991, I met with the directors of major archives and with scholars and institutes conducting archival research on Cold War-related topics." (p. 1) The book is divided into five sections, one on each country's archives and research conditions, conclusion and appendixes. The sections on the individual country's include lists of scholars working on topics related to the Cold War. The appendixes comprise half of the volume and describe some of the archives and new publications on the Cold War.

10. Stanley, David, **Eastern Europe on a Shoestring**. Berkeley, Calif.: Lonely Planet Pub., 1989. 667 p. ISBN: 0864420080 (pbk).

This highly detailed and informative travel guide covers East Germany, Poland, Czechoslovakia, Hungary, Romania, Bulgaria, Yugoslavia, Albania, and the former Soviet Union. Each country section includes general facts about the country, facts for the visitor (visas, money, climate, etc.) getting there and away, and getting around within the country. Maps are plentiful.

BIBLIOGRAPHY

11. Horak, Stephan M., **Russia, the USSR, and Eastern Europe: A Bibliographic Guide to English Language Publications, 1981-1985**. Littleton, Colo.: Libraries Unlimited, 1987. 273 p. ISBN: 087287561X. Includes indexes.

This work is the culmination of the late Stephen Horak's bibliographic tour de force of the Soviet Union and Eastern Europe. The present volume is a supplement to his earlier works covering the same area for the years 1964 to 1974 and 1975 to 1980. Like his earlier bibliographies, this work is divided into three parts: general and interrelated themes; Russian Empire to 1917 and USSR, non-Russian republics, Jews, and others; and, third, Eastern Europe. Coverage is, again, selective. Each entry consists of a bibliographic citation, with price when available, plus a brief but informative critical abstract usually based on a cited review of the book. Access to the bibliography is facilitated by a detailed table of contents and author-title and subject indexes. Reviews: *Slavic Review* 47, no.4 (Winter 1988): 784. *Polish Review* 33, no.3 (1988): 363-365.

12. Jessup, John E., **Balkan Military History: A Bibliography**. New York: Garland Pub., 1986. xii, 478 p. *Garland Reference Library of Social Science, vol.234, Military History Bibliographies, vol. 8*, ISBN: 0824089634. Includes index.

This book covers the Balkan's military history from earliest times to 1984. Each chronological section begins with an essay on the period and then turns to a discussion, in essay form, of works on the period beginning with general histories and then describing specialized works. A bibliographic listing ends each chapter. A list of abbreviations, subject and author index are included. The author has not attempted to be comprehensive but does cover a wide range of materials. The works included are in numerous languages.

13. **Church and State in Postwar Eastern Europe: A Bibliographical Survey,** compiled by Paul Mojzes, G. E. Gorman advisory editor. New York: Greenwood Press, 1987. xi, 109 p. *Bibliographies and Indexes in Religious Studies, 0742-6836, no. 11*, ISBN: 0313240027. Includes indexes.

A bibliography of titles on the relationship between Church and State in Eastern Europe and the Soviet Union since 1945. The volume includes an introductory survey supplying a context for the reader. The compiler is interested in the attitudes of the various churches toward their societies and vice-versa. The bibliographic section lists books and articles covering the area in general and then categorizes titles by individual countries. The work is not intended to be comprehensive. Annotations are not fully critical. Author, title, and subject indexes are included. Review: *Slavic Review* 47, no.3 (Fall 1988): 561-562.

HISTORY

14. **From the Baltic to the Black Sea: Studies in Medieval Archeology,** edited by David Austin and Leslie Alcock. Boston: Unwin Hyman, 1990. xxii, 322 p. *One World Archeology, 18.*

These studies are the result of papers presented at the World Archeological Congress in 1986. The papers are arranged in five sections: objectives of medieval archeology, early state and ethnic formations, population, rural settlement, and urban development. The papers focus an "how far 'cultural-historical' description based in an unquestioned set of assumptions about the uniqueness of a so-called European tradition is really appropriate." (p.xii)

15. Bailey, J. Martin, **The Spring of Nations: Churches in the Rebirth of Eastern Europe.** New York: Friendship Press, 1991. 166 p. ISBN: 0377002240. Includes index.

Organized religion in Eastern Europe has been repressed for many years under the Communist regime. Since the reforms of the late 1980s churches have begun to reemerge. This book takes a brief look at the role of religion in the reforms—that is, both in the destruction of the old political system and the creation of a new one. It is divided into three parts. The first provides a background for the reader, discussing the relationship of the Communist governments of Eastern Europe to organized religions. Part two is divided into six chapters each devoted to the role of the churches in a specific country. The final part discusses the future of religion in Eastern Europe. The author draws his information from interviews with church leaders and political figures.

16. Berend, Ivan T., **The Crisis Zone of Europe: An Interpretation of East-Central European History in the First Half of the Twentieth Century.** Cambridge: Cambridge University Press, 1986. viii, 106 p. ISBN: 0521320895. Includes bibliographical notes and index.

This short study is based on a lecture series presented by the author at Cambridge University in the autumn of 1984. The discussion centers on the successes and failures of East-Central Europe's attempts at modernization at the turn of the century. The author looks at economic, social and cultural aspects of this period. Reviews: *Slavic Review* 48, no.3 (Fall 1989): 514-16. *Canadian-American Slavic Studies* 22, no.1 (Spring 1989): 126-27.

17. Biro, Sandor, **The Nationalities Problem in Transylvania, 1867-1940: A Social History of the Romanian Minority Under Hungarian Rule, 1867-1918 and of the Hungarian Minority Under Romanian Rule, 1918-1940,** translated from the Hungarian original by Mario D. Fenyo. Boulder, Colo.: Social Sciences Monographs, 1992. xix, 744 p. *East European Monographs; no. 333*, ISBN: 088033228X. Includes bibliographical references (p. 673-684) and indexes.

With a view to dissolving the hatred that exists between Hungarians and Romanians in Transylvania, the author sought to reveal "those actual living conditions which best describe the Romanians of Transylvania in the period of the Dual Monarchy, and the Hungarians in the period of Romanian rule between 1918 and 1940." (p. xix) The author touches on various cultural institutions and societal aspects such as means of livelihood, language policy, the church, education, civil rights, and the economic situation.

18. Bogdan, Henry, **From Warsaw to Sofia: A History of Eastern Europe,** edited by Istvan Fehervary. Santa Fe, N.M., USA: Pro Libertate Pub., 1989. 442 p. ISBN: 0962204900. Translation of: De Varsovie a Sofia.

This book, originally written in French, provides a comprehensive history of Eastern Europe. The time period covered is from the 10th century to Gorbachev. The book proceeds in chronological sequence. Its 27 chapters are divided into four parts: the weight of the past, the awakening of nationalism, an era of confrontation, and in the shadow of Moscow. Two appendices provide statistical material on the countries and portraits of famous East Europeans.

19. Bridge, F. R., **The Habsburg Monarchy Among the Great Powers, 1815-1918.** New York: St Martin's Press, 1990. viii, 417 p. ISBN: 0854963073. Includes bibliographical references (p. 392-402) and indexes.

The decline of the Austro-Hungarian Empire is the subject of this study. The author focuses on the role of the monarchy in foreign policy particularly. The tension between the Empire and its Eastern neighbors is of particular importance and there are lengthy discussions on Serbia, Romania, Bosnia, Bulgaria. The book includes maps and appendices with translations of various treaties affecting the position of the Austro-Hungarian Empire. The author believes the empire was weak at the beginning of the nineteenth century and was drawing heavily for support on its conquered territories. By the end of the century it was at the mercy of its stronger allies. Review: *East-Central Europe* 18, no.1 (1991): 102-105.

20. Brogan, Patrick, **The Captive Nations: Eastern Europe, 1945-1990**. New York: Avon Books, 1990. 281 p. ISBN: 0380763044. Includes bibliographical references (p.265-269).

This volume is a brief survey history of each of the countries that make up the East European bloc. Rather than focusing on communism in Eastern Europe, the author examines more long-standing historical problems such as nationalism. Each country has one chapter devoted to it. The book includes a chronology of the downfall of communism and a bibliography of English language sources on each country.

21. Castellan, Georges, **History of the Balkans: From Mohammed the Conqueror to Stalin,** translated by Nicholas Bradley. Boulder: East European Monographs, 1992. vii, 493 p. *East European Monographs; cccxxv*, ISBN: 0880332220. Includes bibliographical references.

After a brief introduction to the Balkans in which he describes its countries, peoples and the region as a whole, Castellan traces the history of the Balkans from the Hellenic Period, the conquest by the Ottomans, the upheavals caused by the Hapsburgs and Napoleon, continuing in the nineteenth century with the Serbian and Greek revolts, the Eastern Question crises, the rivalries between the various Christian states in the latter part of the nineteenth century, the Balkans as a source of conflicts in Europe, the interwar period and ending at the conclusion of World War II.

22. **The Byzantine Legacy in Eastern Europe,** edited by Lowell Clucas. New York: Columbia University Press, 1988. xiv, 295 p. *East European Monographs, no. 230*, ISBN: 0880331275. Includes bibliographies.

Twelve essays on various aspects of Byzantine influence in Eastern Europe are collected in this volume. The essays are grouped into four sections: "the early post-Byzantine period"; "the Byzantine legacy in the Balkans under Ottoman rule"; "the Byzantine legacy in Russia and Romania"; "the Byzantine legacy in Eastern Europe in the twentieth century". The papers collected here originated from a conference on the subject.

23. Fine, John Van Antwerp, **The Late Medieval Balkans: A Critical Survey from the Late Twelfth Century to the Ottoman Conquest**. Michigan: University of Michigan Press, 1987. xvi, 683 p. ISBN: 0472100793. Includes bibliography (p. 633-643) and index.

This is the second volume of Professor Fine's study of early Balkan history. The earlier volume covers Balkan history from the sixth to the twelfth centuries. Like the previous volume this work is based on Professor Fine's lectures. The volume is arranged chronologically and includes discussions of the role of the Church in the region, national groups in the Balkans and their interactions, relations between the Balkan states and discussions of the success of the Ottomans, among many other topics. This work fills a gap in the historical literature. It includes a glossary of terms, an appendix on medieval rulers and a guide to authors of the sources referred to in the text.

24. **Essays on War and Society in East Central Europe, 1740-1920,** edited by Stephen Fischer-Galati and Bela K. Kiraly. New York: Columbia University Press, 1987. ix, 274 p. *War and Society in East Central Europe, v.22, Atlantic Studies on Society in Change, no. 41, East European Monographs, no. 233*, ISBN: 0880331305. Includes bibliographical references.

This is one in a series of volumes that constitute a comprehensive history of war in East Central Europe. "This volume concentrates upon the era of the dawn of modern, and subsequently, total wars." (p. ix) The volume is divided into five parts: 1) generalizations; 2) the armed forces; 3) the home front; 4) the armed forces; and 5) cultural life.

25. Hamann, Brigitte, **The Reluctant Empress: Elisabeth of Austria**. New York, N.Y.: Knopf, 1986. xii, 410 p. ISBN: 0394537173. Translation of: Elisabeth, Kaiserin wider Willen.

This is the biography of Elisabeth, Empress of Austria and Queen of Hungary and Bohemia. The author focuses on Elisabeth's strong democratic and antimonarchist ideals—the book also includes a discussion of Elisabeth's poetic works.

26. **The Columbia History of Eastern Europe in the Twentieth Century,** edited by Joseph Held. New York: Columbia University Press, 1992. lxix, 435 p. ISBN: 0231076967. Includes bibliographical references (p. 405-416) and index.

This is a general history of Eastern Europe describing its changes through the tumultuous twentieth century. The contributors are experts in their fields. Each chapter discusses one country's development from 1918 through 1990. A chronology of events and a bibliography of sources are included.

27. Heller, Agnes, and Ferenc Feher, **From Yalta to Glasnost: the Dismantling of Stalin's Empire**. Cambridge, Mass.: B. Blackwell, 1991. vii, 288 p. ISBN: 0631177728. Includes bibliographical references and index.

The essays contained here were originally written between 1979 and 1989 to chronicle what the authors term "Eastern Europe's long revolution against Yalta." The eleven essays are divided into five parts: Introduction; The First Assault: Hungary, 1956; After the Historic Year 1956; Soviet Strategy before Gorbachev; and Gorbachev's long March. Reviews: *Orbis* 35, no.2 (Spring 1991): 307. *Reason* 22, no.11 (April 1991): 49-51. *Political Science Quarterly* 106, no.4 (Winter 1991-92): 751-752.

28. **The East Central European Officer Corps 1740-1920s: Social Origins, Selection, Education, and Training,** edited by Bela K. Kiraly and Walter Scott Dillard. New York: Columbia University Press, 1988. xi, 241 p. *East European Monographs, no. 241, War and Society in East Central Europe, v. 24, Atlantic Studies*

on Society in Change, no. 43, ISBN: 0880331380. Includes bibliographical references and index.

One volume in the series on War and Society in East Central Europe, this is a collection of essays. The essays in this volume are grouped into five sections: generalizations, extraterritorial patterns, the Habsburg Imperial system, national patterns and paramilitary officers' training. The contributors believe a multidisciplinary approach is most useful in their study. Papers were selected from those presented at a series of conferences by the Program on Society in Change.

29. **East Central European Society and the Balkan Wars,** edited by Bela K. Kiraly and Dimitrije Djordjevic. New York: Columbia University Press, 1986. xii, 434 p. *East European Monographs, no. 215, War and Society in East Central Europe, v. 18, Atlantic Studies on Society in Change, no. 37*, ISBN: 0880330996. Includes bibliographies and biographical index.

A collection of essays all dealing with the "Balkan upheaval" of the 1870s. The essays are grouped into six sections: a general introduction, discussions of the military and its operations, society, economy and diplomacy; great power involvement in the Balkan Wars; the effects of the wars and documents on the wars. A biographical index is included. "The volumes [of this series] deal with the peoples whose homelands lie between the Germans and the West, the Russians to the East and North and the Black Mediterranean and Adriatic Seas to the South." (p.xi) Review: *Canadian Slavonic Papers* 30, no.3 (September 1988): 416-416.

30. Kula, Witold, **Measures and Men,** translated by R. Szreter. Princeton: Princeton University Press, 1986. x, 386 p. ISBN: 0691054460. Translation of: Miary i ludzie. Includes bibliography (p. 339-373) and index.

This translated volume is a history of weights and measures by a noted Polish economic historian. It is divided into four sections. Part one is a general discussion of weights and measures and who invented them, beliefs associated with them, types of measures, standards of measure, the function of measure in a pre-capitalist society, etc. Part two looks at measures in Poland. Part three turns to weights and measures in France. The final section returns to the general theme of the role of weights and measures in history. Reviews: *American History Review* 92, no.5 (December 1987): 1193-94. *Slavic Review* 46, no.2 (Summer 1987): 357-58.

31. McLaughlin, R. Emmet, **Caspar Schwenckfeld, Reluctant Radical: His Life to 1540**. New Haven: Yale University Press, 1986. xii, 250 p. *Yale Historical Publications. Miscellany. 134*, ISBN: 0300033672. Includes index and bibliography (p.229-243).

A biography of the Christian reformation figure Schwenckfeld, who was born in Silesia in 1469.

32. Michta, Andrew A., **East Central Europe After the Warsaw Pact: Security Dilemmas in the 1990s,** foreword by Vojtech Mastny. New York: Greenwood Press, 1992. xv, 192 p. ISBN: 0313278865. Includes bibliographical references (p. 177-185) and index.

"This book examines the emerging national security environment in East Central Europe based on the following propositions. First, changes in the region's security framework are directly a function of the Soviet Union's rethinking of the very concept of war in Europe,... Second, small-scale, low-intensity military conflict along the East Central European periphery is today and will remain for the rest of the decade a distinct possibility.... Third, the Western European and ultimately the pan-European orientation of the three East Central European states is dictated by the need for economic modernization and development." (pp. 9-10) Michta begins by placing East Central European history in context as it developed through the twentieth century. He then turns to an analysis of the national and regional security policies of Poland, Czechoslovakia and Hungary.

33. Narkiewicz, Olga A., **Eastern Europe 1968-1984**. Totowa, N.J.: Barnes & Noble, 1986. 273 p. ISBN: 0389206075. Includes index and bibliography (p. 270-71).

Narkiewicz's surveys and analyzes events in Bulgaria, Czechoslovakia, Hungary, East Germany, Poland, and Romania over the period 1968-1984. She examines their bilateral relations, their economic and political relations with the Soviet Union and the non-socialist world as well as their particular internal administrative, economic and ideological difficulties. She hopes to have demonstrated that "conflicts do not arise solely out of inherent tensions, but also because of sudden changes of course." Reviews: *Perspective: Reviews of New Books* 15:4:122 (July-August 1986). *American Academy of Political and Social Sciences Annals* 493 (September 1987): 198-99. *Slavic Review* 46, no.1 (Spring 1987): 169-70.

34. Okey, Robin, **Eastern Europe, 1740-1985: Feudalism to Communism**. 2nd ed. Minneapolis: University of Minnesota Press, 1986. 283 p. ISBN: 0816615616. Includes index and bibliography (p. 255-271).

A general history of Eastern Europe from the eighteenth to the twentieth century. This is the second edition of this work and it contains an updated bibliography and chronology and additions to the final chapter to cover events through 1985. "From the mid-eighteenth century on, in Okey's view, Eastern Europe was a region struggling to achieve the modernity that seemed embodied in its western neighbors. His book traces the effort of East Europeans to overcome a legacy of underdevelopment and dependence from the era of the Enlightenment through the liberal and nationalist movements of the nineteenth century down through the postwar years of the twentieth." (back cover) The book is chronologically and topically arranged covering the Enlightenment, liberalism, the rise of nationalism, economics, and political development. The bibliography is arranged to coincide with topics covered in each chapter and consists of English language publications.

35. **Historians and the History of Transylvania,** edited by Laszlo Peter. Boulder, Colo.: East European Monographs, 1992. ix, 254 p. *East European Monographs; no. 332*, ISBN: 0880332298. Includes bibliographical references and index.

This book contains essays by scholars largely from the staff of the School of Slavonic and East European Studies at the University of London. Topics covered include Historians and Transylvania, Ethnos and Mythos in the History of Transylvania; Voivode and Regnum, the Portrayal of the Transylvanian Romanian in Saxon Historical Writings between the Fifteenth and Eighteenth Centuries; Hungarian Cultural Tradition in Transylvania; The Past in Contemporary Romania; Nicolae Iorga's conception of Transylvanian Romanian History in 1915; and Bad Blood in Transylvania (clash between Romanian and Hungarian versions of Transylvania's history).

36. Simocatta, Theophylactus, **The History of Theophylact Simocatta, an English translation with Introduction and notes by Michael and Mary Whitby**. New York: Oxford University Press, 1986. xxx, 258 p. ISBN: 019822799X. Includes bibliography (p. 256-258) and index.

Simocatta wrote in the early seventh century during the reign of Heraclius (610-41). This is a translation of the history of the twenty year reign of Maurice. The major topic is the warfare in the Balkans against the Slavs and Avars and Persians. The translation is fully annotated. A chronological table of events, a gazetteer, an index of names and maps help to make the history more understandable.

37. Simons, Thomas W., **Eastern Europe in the Postwar World**. New York: St. Martin's Press, 1991. ix, 246 p. ISBN: 0312061684; 0312061692. Includes bibliographical references and index.

Based on lectures given at Brown University in 1989-1990, this book is "an attempt at exploration of events in Eastern Europe in the half-century that ended in 1989." (p.vii) Review: *Foreign Affairs* 70, no.5 (winter 1991-92): 198.

38. Sked, Alan, **The Decline and Fall of the Habsburg Empire, 1815-1918**. New York: Longman, 1989. 295 p. ISBN: 0582025311 (pbk); 0582025303. Includes bibliographies and index.

The Austro-Hungarian Empire was perhaps Europe's greatest supra-national empire. While this is not a comprehensive history of the Empire this chronologically arranged study does attempt a discussion of the major themes. The basic question this study poses is at what point did the fall of the Habsburg Empire become inevitable and could it have been avoided. Three appendices are included: a chronology of events, a list of Habsburg foreign ministers and statistics on population and nationalities of the Empire. Review: *East-Central Europe* 18, no.1 (1991): 101-102.

39. **Scholar, Patriot, Mentor: Historical Essays in Honor of Dimitrije Djordjevic**, edited by Richard B. Spence, Linda Nelson. Boulder: East European Monographs, 1992. xi, 422 p. ISBN: 0880332174. Includes bibliographical references.

This collection of essays marked the retirement of historian Dimitrije Djordjevic, a scholar of Balkan history. While the majority of the essays focus on the Balkans there are a few on other areas. The first section is devoted to the background and publications of Djordjevic. Parts two through four include essays on Balkan history of various periods. The final section is made up of essays by scholars from other fields. A bibliography of Djordjevic's publications is included in part one.

40. Subtelny, Orest, **Domination of Eastern Europe: Native Nobilities and Foreign Absolutism, 1500-1715**. Gloucester (Eng.): Alan Sutton, 1986. xii, 270 p. ISBN: 0773504389. Bibliographical notes (p.218-256) and indexes.

This book is a history of foreign domination in Eastern Europe in the late seventeenth and early eighteenth centuries. Focusing on Hungary, Moldavia, Ukraine, Livonia and Poland and Lithuania, the author demonstrates that the domination of strong nobilities in these countries prevented the rise of absolute monarchies domestically, but could not prevent the encroachment of foreign monarchies. The author believes there is a cultural commonalty that justifies treating these nations together. The scope of this analysis is broad. "By identifying the basic similarities among the East European societies, we hope to make a particularly complex aspect of the area's past more comprehensible to students of West European as well as of East European history." (p. x) The five chapters provide a survey of East European development, a discussion of the character of the nobility, a description of the penetration of foreign powers, the relationship between the domestic nobilities and foreign powers and political émigrés. A chronology and bibliographical essay are included. Reviews: *American Historical Review* 92, no.1 (February 1987): 167. *International History Review* 9, no.3 (August 1987): 496-98.

41. Turnock, David, **Eastern Europe: An Historical Geography, 1815-1945**. New York: Routledge, 1989. ix, 357 p. ISBN: 0415012694. Includes bibliography (p.330-339) and index.

"This volume together with its companion *The Making of Eastern Europe: from Earliest Times to 1815* traces the historical geography of Eastern Europe from earliest times to the present day. The frequency with which political boundaries and other patterns have changed in this area makes the picture that emerges very complex. The region has never achieved political unity and the author accounts for this in terms of internal political, geographical and cultural division and of the importance of external influences and forces at key historical moments." (p. i) The book is divided into two parts: the first on what Turnock terms the "century of Peace" from 1815-1914. The second part follows the history of the two world wars in the twentieth century. In both parts there is extensive discussion of the political geography, economic development and settlement geography in the area. A bibliography of English language sources is included.

42. ———, **The Making of Eastern Europe: From the Earliest Times to 1815**. New York: Routledge, 1988. ix, 326 p. ISBN: 0415012678. Includes bibliography (p. 306-310) and index.

"This volume together with its companion, *Eastern Europe: An Historical Geography, 1815-1945*, traces the historical geography of Eastern Europe from earliest times to the present day. It draws on indigenous sources which have not been widely studied in the West but provide a wealth of detail about the development of landscape, settlement patterns, towns, political units and economic behavior and about their interrelationship. The region has never achieved political unity and the author accounts for this in terms of internal political, geographical and cultural divisions and of the importance of external influences and forces at key historical moments." (p. i) The book is chronologically arranged in three parts and includes a bibliography of English language sources that supplement the notes at the end of each chapter.

43. **Louis the Great: King of Hungary and Poland,** edited by S. B. Vardy, Geza Grosschmid and Leslie S. Domonkos. New York: Columbia University Press, 1986. xvi, 534 p. *East European Monographs, no. 194*, ISBN: 0880330872. Bibliography (p. 493-525).

A collection of essays in various languages on one of Hungary's most beloved monarchs Louis the Great, marking the 600th anniversary of his death. The essays are grouped into five sections on the people and period, Louis the Great, Poland and the South Slavic Lands, art and culture of the time, portrayals of Louis the Great in literature and those discussing the decretum of 1351. Appendices are provided on the genealogy of the House of Anjou, the changing geographic border of Louis the Great's kingdom and a critical bibliography on Anjevin Rule in Croatia.

44. Walters, E. Garrison, **The Other Europe: Eastern Europe to 1945**. New York: Syracuse University Press, 1988. xiii, 430 p. ISBN: 0815624123. Includes index.

This volume is intended as an introduction to those unfamiliar with Eastern Europe and its history. Although the title indicates a very broad time coverage, the focus tends to be on the interwar years. For these years there are individual chapters on Poland, Czechoslovakia, Hungary, Romania, Yugoslavia, Bulgaria and Albania along with an overview of the period. For all other cases one chapter is devoted to each time period. There is an opening chapter on the geography and resources of the area. The book contains numerous historical maps and a bibliography of sources in West European languages.

45. World Congress for Soviet and East European Studies (3rd: 1985: Washington, D. C.), **East European History: Selected Papers of the Third World Congress for Soviet and East European Studies,** edited by Stanislav J. Kirschbaum. Columbus, Ohio: Slavica Publishers, 1988. 183 p. ISBN: 0893571938. Includes bibliographies.

The third World Congress of Soviet and East European Studies held in 1985 sponsors this volume of essays on topics in East European history. While the topics covered in the papers are diverse, all the authors are reexamining the accepted views on their topics. The volume is divided into two parts: the first on historiography, the second on history. The first three essays discuss themes in southeast European and Romanian historiography and Hellenism in Soviet history. Five essays make up the second part. They cover such topics as Polish Radical Ideology in the nineteenth century; agricultural productivity under the Ottomans in Bulgaria in the same period; popular democracy in nineteenth century Czechoslovakia; "Srpski Knjivzevni Glasnik and the Yugoslav Idea, 1901-1914" and "Red Unions" and the Czech Communist Party of the 1920s.

46. Cohen, Yohanan, **Small Nations in Times of Crisis and Confrontation,** translated from Hebrew by Naftali Greenwood. Albany: State University of New York Press, 1988. xiv, 399 p. ISBN: 0791400190 (pbk); 0791400182. Translation of: Umot-be-mivhan. Includes bibliography (p. 379-387) and index.

This study considers how three small nations, Czechoslovakia, Poland and Finland, deal with crisis situations. The years of World War II are the focus. "The crisis that beset them during that period; their confrontation with enemies of superior strength; their disappointment caused by a lack of support from faraway friends; the wars into which they were thrust—these are the central themes of this book." (p.1) The book is divided into three parts, one devoted to the experiences of each country. This work originally appeared in Hebrew in 1986.

47. **From Stalinism to Pluralism: A Documentary History of Eastern Europe Since 1945,** edited by Gale Stokes. New York: Oxford University Press, 1991. xi, 267 p. ISBN: 0195063821 (pbk); 0195063813 (alk. paper).

The documents compiled in this volume are intended to guide the reader through the events of the last forty years that led Eastern Europe from Stalinist dictatorship to pluralism. No attempt to be comprehensive was made. The documents are grouped chronologically into four parts: "The Stalinist Moment," The Marxist Critique," "Antipolitics and the Retreat to Ethics" and "The Return of Politics." There are textual discussions of the documents preceding each, recreating the historical context for the reader.

48. Williamson, Samuel R., **Austria-Hungary and the Origins of the First World-War.** New York: St. Martin's Press, 1991. xviii, 272 p. *Making of the 20th Century,* ISBN: 0312052391. Includes bibliographical references (p.249-264) and index.

In this monograph Williamson seeks to answer several questions, among them: "What led the decision makers in Vienna to conclude that war would resolve the problem posed by greater Serbian nationalism? How did the tensions of the Balkan Wars of 1912-1913 contribute to a set of perceptions that rendered a military solution preferable to further diplomatic efforts." (p. 1) In short, he examines the "unspoken assumptions" of a nation state that propel it toward war. Review: *East-Central Europe* 18, no.1 (1991): 102-105.

GOVERNMENT, POLITICS AND LAW

49. **The Soviet-East European Relationship in the Gorbachev Era: The Prospects for Adaptation,** edited by Aurel Braun. Boulder, Colo.: Westview Press, 1990. 249 p. *Westview Special Studies on the Soviet Union & Eastern Europe, 0163-6057,* ISBN: 0813377994 (pbk). Includes bibliographical references.

The contributors to this volume attempt to identify trends in the Gorbachev government as seen from both the Soviet Union and Eastern Europe. The essays focus on political and ideological problems, reforms in the USSR and their effect on Eastern Europe, the military, and cultural identity in Eastern Europe. A separate section is devoted to the changes in the USSR. The contributors to the volume are largely scholars specializing in political studies of the Soviet Union and Eastern Europe.

50. Brown, James F., **Nationalism, Democracy, and Security in the Balkans**. Brookfield, Vt.: Dartmouth Pub. Co., 1992. x, 205 p. ISBN: 1855213168. Includes bibliographical references (p. 189-195) and index.

"This book is about six Balkan countries and their relationships with each other: Albania, Bulgaria, Greece, Romania, Turkey and Yugoslavia. This book discusses the strength of nationalism in these countries, its impact on their stability and security, and the relative weakness of the liberal democratic tradition." (p. ix) Brown has divided the volume into two parts. The first describes the Balkans in general, i.e. the political and historical context, emphasizing the relationship between nationalism and democracy in each country. Part II focuses on the "crisis areas of the Balkans." Brown suggests possible Western responses to these problems.

51. **Legal Aspects of Doing Business in Eastern Europe and the Soviet Union,** edited by Dennis Campbell. St. Paul Minn.: Distribution in USA and Canada, Kluwer Law and Taxation Publishers, 1986. vii, 298 p. *International Business Series, v. 8*, ISBN: 9065442634. Includes index.

This 1986 guide was intended as a practical resource for lawyers, academicians, scholars, businessmen and political scientists. The book contains one chapter on each country devoted to the economic system of that country as it applies to law. The chapters were contributed by different individuals and tend to cover somewhat different subject matter. Some of the chapters provide extensive information on the economic relations with foreign countries. The book supplies what is now interesting historical information on the legal business climate in Eastern Europe in the mid-1980s.

52. **Towards Greater Europe?: A Continent Without an Iron Curtain,** edited by Colin Crouch and David Marquand. Oxford, UK: Blackwell Publishers, 1992. 174 p. ISBN: 0631185518. Includes bibliographical references and index.

"The contributors to this volume address the issues raised by the extraordinary changes now in progress. David Reynolds explores links between the emerging new Europe and that before the Cold War. William Wallace and Stephen George, in separate chapters, look forward to the possibility of a European Community of twenty four states. Patrizio Bianchi considers likely economic scenarios for the 1990s. Roger Morgan examines the position of Germany and Tony Judt discusses the lessons from the 1989 uprisings." (back cover) Other essays focus on Poland, Finland, ethnic tensions and regionalism in Europe. These papers resulted from a symposium held in Oxford in 1991 and sponsored by the *Political Quarterly*.

53. Cviic, Christopher, **Remaking the Balkans**. London: Royal Institute of International Affairs, 1991. viii, 113 p. *Chatham House Papers*, ISBN: 0861870867(pbk); 0861870859(cased). Includes bibliographical references (p. 111-113).

Cviic maintains that the upheavals occurring in the Balkans are the result of internal pressure, not external forces. He analyses some of these changes and suggests what direction these countries may go. He only deals with Albania, Bulgaria, Romania, and Yugoslavia, countries that have been dominated by communism since World War II.

54. Dahrendorf, Ralf, **Reflections on the Revolution in Europe: In a Letter Intended to Have Been Sent to a Gentleman in Warsaw**. New York: Times Books, 1990. 163 p. ISBN: 0812918835.

An explanation of Poland's revolution in 1989 by an Oxford sociologist. The work is presented in the form of a letter to a friend and gives a general discussion of the East European revolution of the late 1980s. Review: *National Review* 42, no.20 (October 15, 1990): 84-85.

55. **Conflict in Urban Development: A Comparison Between East and West Europe,** Arie Dekker et al. Brookfield, Vt.: Ashgate, 1992. xi, 181 p. ISBN: 1857420403. Includes bibliographical references.

This volume contains three pairs of case studies dealing with physical planning and the attendant problems under different political systems. In these case studies, which were carried out in Poland and the Netherlands, "the conflict solving process was examined. As part of that, the formal and informal means that the parties used in the course of the conflict were studied. The cases deal with the location of a large waste disposal site, urban development in the environmental shadow of an industrial plant, and urban expansion in a metropolitan region." (p. viii) The period covered is 1970-1989.

56. Fodor, Neil, **The Warsaw Treaty Organization: A Political and Organizational Analysis**. New York: St. Martin's Press, 1990. xv, 235 p. ISBN: 0312046227. Includes bibliographical references (p. 212-224) and index.

The author has attempted a practical guide to the Warsaw Treaty Organization. The study is arranged topically beginning with the earliest post war period and discusses the origins of the Warsaw Treaty at some length. This is followed by a discussion of the structural development of the WTO. The author then analyzes some of the most important documents related to the WTO written from 1955 to 1985. Finally the author discusses the role of the WTO in the period of the Gorbachev reforms. There are several appendices including documents, a chronology of meetings, a documentary history, and bilateral treaties among others.

57. **Labyrinth of Nationalism: Complexities of Diplomacy: Essays in Honor of Charles and Barbara Jelavich,** edited by Richard Frucht. Columbus, OH: Slavica Publishers, 1992. 377 p. ISBN: 0893572330. Includes bibliographical references.

This festschrift in honor of Charles and Barbara Jelavich contains essays by their former students on nationalism and diplomacy. Individual essays explore these two themes in most of the East European countries. In addition to these contributions, the volume also contains a bibliographical essay on the work of these two scholars as well as an enumerative bibliography of their publications.

58. **Diverse Paths to Modernity in Southeastern Europe: Essays in National Development,** edited by Augustinos Gerasimos. New York: Greenwood Press, 1991. 176 p. *Contributions to the Study of World History, no. 20*, ISBN: 0313266700. Includes bibliographical references and index.

The contributors to this volume explore the various ways the individual Balkan states have developed in the modern world and "consider how development has been affected by the historically specific and problematic social and economic context." (p.2) Special emphasis is given to nationalism and socialism as potent ideologies that have influenced each country's developmental path. Review: *Journal of Baltic Studies* 22, no.4 (Winter 1991): 374-376.

59. Liska, George, **Fallen Dominions, Reviving Powers**. Washington D.C.: Johns Hopkins Foreign Policy Institute, 1990. iii, 63 p. ISBN: 0941700682.

Three lectures by Professor George Liska are collected in this volume. All three deal with relations between the East European countries. Professor Liska served in the General Secretariat of the Czechoslovak Ministry of Foreign Affairs making him particularly well qualified to write on the topic. Review: *Foreign Affairs* 70, no.2 (Spring 1991): 193-194.

60. Lovenduski, Joni, and Jean Woodall, **Politics and Society in Eastern Europe**. Bloomington, IN: Indiana University Press, 1987. xiii, 474 p. ISBN: 0253286034 (pbk); 0253345464. Includes bibliography (p.433-455).

The authors' purpose in writing this book "has been to provide students with a systematically comparative study of the politics of the state socialist systems of Eastern Europe which points out not only the differences but also the similarities between these and other European states." (p. 1-2) After an introductory chapter on "How we know what we know about Eastern Europe," the authors cover interwar Eastern Europe, war communism and Stalinism, centrally planned economies and reform, equality and the social order, party rule, political participation, social welfare and educational policy and foreign relations. Review: *Canadian Slavonic Papers* 30, no.2 (June 1988): 292-93.

61. **Soviet-East European Survey, 1986-1987: A Selected Research and Analysis from Radio Free Europe/Radio Liberty,** edited by Vojtech Mastny. Boulder, Colo.: Westview Press, 1988. xii, 470 p. ISBN: 0813374774. Includes index.

In this volume, selected essays from Radio Free Europe / Radio Liberty Research reports have been collected. These essays discuss the most important events of the period of Gorbachev's reforms: glasnost, drug abuse, health services, the failing economy of the Soviet Union, reform on Czechoslovakia, Hungary, dissidents in Yugoslavia, the situation in Poland in 1986, the place of religion in Polish society, COMECON and the common market. The essays are by specialists in East European studies. They provide the reader with in-depth analyses of the events of the period.

62. Nelson, Daniel N., **Balkan Imbroglio: Politics and Security in Southeastern Europe**. Boulder: Westview Press, 1991. viii, 136 p. ISBN: 0813379563. Includes index.

Nelson "examines principal domestic, regional and international dynamics affecting the Balkan prognoses for the 1990s and beyond." (p. 5) In his first chapter he explores regional security issues and then devotes chapters to Yugoslavia, Bulgaria, Romania and Greece. An underlying question that informs his work is: "What are the chances that the peoples and states of the Balkans can indeed, arrive at a stable, secure and prosperous future?" (p.5) Review: *Foreign Affairs* 70, no.5 (Winter 1991-92): 184-185.

63. Pilon, Juliana Geran, **The Bloody Flag: Post-Communist Nationalism in Eastern Europe: Spotlight on Romania; with a foreword by Robert Conquest**. New Brunswick: Transaction Publishers, 1992. xi, 126 p. *Studies in Social Philosophy & Policy; no. 16*, ISBN: 156000620X. Includes bibliographical references (p. 107-118) and index.

Pilon's book "presents the philosophical and the historical basis for nationalism in general, for the specific types of nationalism to be seen in the area, and also for the characteristics they have in common." The work has four chapters: ch. 1, Some basic philosophical categories; ch. 2, The East-Central European Context: Post-Communist trauma; ch. 3, Spotlight on Romania; and ch. 4, Some Notes on Harmony. It also contains an essay as an afterword entitled *Subterranean Societies* by Vasile Popovici and an appendix presenting the Copenhagen Document, an agreement that focuses on human rights issues.

64. **Eastern Europe: Opposing Viewpoints, Janelle Rohr, book editor**. San Diego, CA: Greenhaven Press, 1990. 288 p. *Opposing Viewpoints Series*, ISBN: 0899084559 (pap.); 089908480X (lib.). Includes bibliographical references and index.

This volume contains essays that present opposing viewpoints on the division of Europe, the effects of recent revolutions in Eastern Europe, the economic policies Eastern European countries should adopt, the impact of German unification, and the possibility of a united Europe.

65. Rollo, J. M. C., **The New Eastern Europe: Western Responses, with Judy Batt, Brigitte Granville and Neil Malcolm**. New York: Council On Foreign Relations Press, 1990. 137 p. *Chatham House Papers*, ISBN: 0876090854. Includes bibliographical references.

In the wake of the overthrow of communism in Eastern Europe many questions have arisen regarding proper Western responses. "This survey attempts to answer these questions by examining why change has occurred in Eastern Europe at this juncture, why the previous system failed, what the East Europeans are proposing to put in its place, what policy instruments in the hands of the West may help, and what has been done and what more needs to be done." (p. 1) Review: *Foreign Affairs* 69, no.4 (Fall 1990): 192-193.

66. Roskin, Michael G., **The Rebirth of East Europe**. Englewood Cliffs, N.J.: Prentice Hall, 1991. 208 p. ISBN: 0137634420. Includes bibliographical references and index.

This is a text written to be used in a basic comparative politics course. Its ten chapters include an introductory section on the history of late nineteenth, early twentieth century Eastern Europe, and other chapters on the interwar years, East Europe and World War II, the communist takeovers, the entrenchment of the regimes, the decay of communism, the Gorbachev factor, the elections of 1989 and 1990, and prospects for the future.

67. **Quantitative Analyses of Law: A Comparative Empirical Study: Sources of Law in Eastern and Western Europe,** by Heinz Schaffer, Attila Racz, in collaboration with Barbara Rhode. Budapest: Akademia Kiado, 1990. 404 p. ISBN: 9630556731. Includes bibliographical references.

"The international comparative research project launched by the European Coordination Centre for Research and Documentation in the Social Sciences has focused on the investigation of a very important field, that of the legal normative systems. In the course of this, legal and sociological methods, qualitative and quantitative analyses have been combined in studying the dynamic of the systems of sources of law in Eastern and Western countries." (back cover) The book is organized in two parts and a general introduction which discusses the sources of law in general and structure methodology of the research project. Part one contains country reports, each of which includes a dynamic analysis of state and federal law as well as a static analysis of state and federal law. Reports an Austria, France, the GDR, the Federal Republic of Germany, Hungary, Norway, Poland and Switzerland are included. Part two is a comparison of the sources of law in Western and socialist countries. This is a highly specialized work but it does contain general information on laws and the legislative process for each country studied.

68. Schopflin, George, **Politics in Eastern Europe, 1945-1992**. Oxford, UK: Blackwell, 1993. 327 p. ISBN: 0631147241. Includes bibliographical references and index.

Schopflin has attempted an analysis of the changes in Eastern Europe and their underlying causes. The analysis is framed in terms of political science. The volume is arranged chronologically but it is largely a topical treatment of the subject discussing first the political traditions of the region and the establishment of communism in the region and its development from the reforms of the 60s to its collapse in the 80s. The book ends with a discussion of pre-communist Eastern Europe. The book is directed at both the university student and the general reader.

69. Seligman, A., **The Idea of Civil Society**. New York: Free Press, 1992. xii, 241 p. ISBN: 0029233159. Includes bibliographical references (p. 207-234) and index.

In this work Adam Seligman analyzes the "ethical ideal of social order" embodied by the concept of Civil society. While he discusses the concept in broad terms he is interested in differences in interpretation in Eastern and Western Europe. The first three chapters discuss the historical evolution of the idea of the civil society. The final chapter is devoted to a comparison of its development in the West and in East-Central Europe.

70. Sipkov, Ivan, **The Codified Statutes on Private International Law of the East European Countries: A Comparative Study**. Washington, D.C.: Law Library, Library of Congress, 1986. 55 p. Includes bibliography (p.52-55).

Sipkov compares the private international law of the East European countries that were under the control of the Soviet Union immediately after World War II. Private international law "is an independent and separate branch of law within the international sector of the municipal law of a state." After a brief discussion of the science of private international law and sources and codification of private international law, Sipkov then examines conflicts of law rules among the various states; these include general rules as well as rules relating to legal capacity, property, contracts, family law, succession, civil law, copyright, and inventions and international transport, and limitations of claims.

71. Staar, Richard Felix, **Communist Regimes in Eastern Europe**. Stanford, Calif.: Hoover Institution Press, 1988. xiv, 369 p. *Hoover Press Publication, no. 381*, ISBN: 0817988122. Includes bibliography (p.337-363) and index.

The first eight chapters of this handbook cover the eight East European countries. Each one "includes the constitutional framework and the electoral system; the ruling party, which is called variously a communist, socialist, or workers' movement; domestic policies; and foreign relations." (p.xiii) The last three chapters cover, respectively, the Warsaw Part and the CMEA as well as intrabloc political relations.

72. **Handbook of Political Science Research on the USSR and Eastern Europe: Trends from the 1950s to the 1990s,** edited by Raymond C. Taras. Westport, Conn.: Greenwood Press, 1992. vi, 345 p. ISBN: 0313274665. Includes bibliographical references and indexes.

"Each of the chapters in this book has two principal objectives: (1) to review research trends in the period from the 1950s to 1990s; and (2) to evaluate the scholarship of individual specialists. The handbook asks, then: over some forty years, how accurately did Western scholars—and the most prominent Soviet and East European political scientists—portray politics in the USSR and Eastern Europe? Which approaches provided the greatest explanatory power? Which scholarship was most incisive, proved to be ahead of its time, anticipated later developments, and perhaps influenced thinking in U.S. governmental circles?" (p. 4-5).

73. Tomaszewski, Jerzy, **The Socialist Regimes of East Central Europe: Their Establishment and Consolidation, 1944-1967,** translated by Jolanta Krauze. London: Routledge, 1989. 305 p. ISBN: 0415020271. Includes bibliographical references and index.

A study of East Central European political development from 1945 to 1967 "Beginning with an account of the social and political situation in East Central Europe at the end of the Second World War, Professor Tomaszewski discusses political changes in East Central European countries under the impact both of internal struggles and the influence of the Great Powers. In particular, he sheds new light on British policy in the area. He describes the establishment and development of the socialist states.. Once in power the new governments faced the considerable task of reforming society, the economy and the political system along socialist lines. Tomaszewski traces the process of Stalinization after 1948, through the Hungarian struggle and the political crisis in Poland in 1956 and on to the limited reform which took place in the period 1960-67." (frontispiece) The three sections of the book follow a largely chronological scheme. The author is a Professor of Political Science at Warsaw University. Review: *Foreign Affairs* 69, no.4 (Fall 1990): 193.

74. Turnley, David C., **Moments of Revolution: Photographs of Eastern Europe by David and Peter Turnley,** text by Mort Rosenblum. New York: Distributed by Workman Pub., 1990. 183 p. ISBN: 1556701683. After an introduction to the East European revolution by Mort Rosenblum, the rest of the book contains photographs

by David and Peter Turnley that capture scenes and emotions that were part of these turbulent times.

75. Volgyes, Ivan, **Politics in Eastern Europe**. Chicago, Ill: Dorsey Press, 1986. xvii, 368 p. ISBN: 0256031444. Includes bibliography (p.359-368) and index.

This textbook in comparative politics covers Albania, Bulgaria, Czechoslovakia, East Germany, Hungary, Poland, Romania and Yugoslavia. Its fourteen chapters are divided into five parts: Part one examines the people, the land and the history of Eastern Europe. Part two analyzes the structure of power and part three the issues of politics. Part four dissects the various aspects of political values and part five describes foreign policy and the future of Eastern Europe.

76. **Bound to Change: Consolidating Democracy in East Central Europe,** edited by Peter M. E. Volten. New York: Institute for EastWest Studies, 1992. vii, 240 p. ISBN: 0813387043. Includes bibliographical references.

At the time of the publication of this work the Soviet Union was still a force to be considered as a possible obstacle to the development of democratic systems. It seemed a particular threat to the newly emerging democratic states of Eastern Europe. This collection of essays is divided into two sections. The first includes essays comparing the problems of several emerging democracies with particular attention to nationalism, various types of democracies and activist states in historical perspective. In part two five case studies are presented focusing on transformation of bureaucracies, assessing democratic progress, election procedures, privatization, and economic reform.

77. **Communist Politics: A Reader,** edited by Stephen White and Daniel N. Nelson. London: Macmillan Education, 1986. xii, 416 p. ISBN: 0333414071 (pbk); 0333414063 (cased). Includes bibliography (p. 380-410) and index.

Examples of what the editors consider a fair representation of some of the best work on communist politics appear in this reader. The nineteen essays are arranged in five parts. Part 1 (chapter 1) describes the historical origins of the communist movement; Part 2 (chapters 2-6) deal with structures of government and elections, especially in the USSR, Poland, Yugoslavia and China. Part 3 (chapters 7-10) explore various facets of the communist party by examining it in the USRR, Poland, Cuba and China. Part 4 (chapters 11-15) evaluate the policy process and the groups that formulate and implement policies. Finally, Part 5 (chapters 16-19) examine policy outcomes and provide comparative perspectives between East and West.

FOREIGN RELATIONS

78. **In from the Cold: Germany, Russia and the Future of Europe,** edited by Vladimir Baranovsky and Hans-Joachim Spanger; foreword by Eduard Shevardnadze. Boulder, Colo.: Westview Press, 1992. xxv, 321 p. ISBN: 0813386241. Includes bibliographical references.

"In this timeless book, distinguished scholars from the Peace Research Institute in Frankfurt and institutes of the Russian Academy of Sciences in Moscow take up the challenge passionately articulated by Eduard Shevardnadze considering the unprecedented opportunities for unifying a region split into antagonistic blocs for more than forty years, they explore the rapidly shifting context for cooperation in Europe." (p. 323) The essays are arranged into four parts: "Continuity and Change," "Security and the Future Architecture of Europe," "Germany—a European Problem?," and "Europe on the Way to Integration." The contributors are united in their belief that Western support is essential for success.

79. Barnett, Thomas P. M., **Romanian and East German Policies in the Third World: Comparing the Strategies of Ceausescu and Honecker**. Westport, Conn.: Praeger, 1992. xx, 173 p. ISBN: 0275941175. Includes bibliographical references (p. 161-164) and index.

"This study examines the special places occupied by Romania and East Germany within the Warsaw Pact's relations with the Third World in the 1970s and 1980s. As part of this effort, an attempt is made to conceptualize the historical dynamics of the Warsaw Pact's division of labor in the Third World. While previous Western studies have noted Moscow's tendency to assign particular foreign policy tasks to its junior allies, there has been little analysis in terms of how and why this division occurred in relations with the Third World. In part, this lack of understanding stemmed from sometimes crude assumptions about the Kremlin's ability to force the East Europeans into supporting its global strategy. Western studies in the 1980s on the reliability of East European armies threw a much needed light on this question with regard to East-West military relations. This study seeks to do much the same in terms of the East-West rivalry in the Third World. By measuring and analyzing the varying levels of activity by pact members, it is possible to hypothesize the complex causality behind the formation of the division of labor—in other words, why certain nations were sought by Moscow for more prominent roles while others were not." (p. xvii)

80. Brown, James F., **Western Approaches to Eastern Europe,** Robert D. Hormats, William H. Luers; edited by Ivo John Lederer. New York: Council on Foreign Relations Press, 1992. ix, 107 p. ISBN: 0876091303. Includes bibliographical references (p. 14-15).

The essays in this volume were originally written for a symposium held in New York in September of 1991 which was entitled "The United States and Eastern Europe." The four papers are intended for policy makers and the general reader interested in the transformation of Eastern Europe politically and economically. The essays focus on the historical context of the region, the East European view of the future, the U.S. interests in the region and how Eastern Europe and the U.S. can work to better secure the future.

81. Byrnes, Robert Francis, **U.S. Policy Toward Eastern Europe and the Soviet Union**. Boulder, Colorado: Westview Press, 1989. 218 p. ISBN: 0813309522. Includes bibliographical references.

Byrnes examines U.S. policy towards the Soviet Union and Eastern Europe over four decades. His book is divided into two parts. In part one Byrnes treats U.S. and Soviet policy toward Eastern Europe. This includes chapters devoted to the triumph of containment, Soviet and Chinese communist relations with Yugoslavia the insecure hegemony of the Soviet Union in Eastern Europe, U.S. policy in Eastern Europe before and after Helsinski and a concluding chapter on the present situation and current trends. In part two he deals with the Soviet Union and the West. Here individual chapters concern Russian and Soviet attitudes toward the West, post-Stalinist policy toward Western Europe, scholarly exchange with the Soviet Union, and the use of trade restrictions to influence Soviet policy. He concludes by offering suggestions how the West and East could bring about the "break-up or gradual mellowing" of the Soviet system.

82. **Continuity and Change in Soviet-East European Relations: Implications for the West,** edited by Marco Carnovale and William C. Potter. Boulder, Colorado: Westview Press, 1989. viii, 238 p. *Studies in International and Strategic Affairs Series of the Center for International and Strategic Affairs, University of California, Los Angeles*, ISBN: 0813375266.

The book is the result of a conference on Soviet-East relations held in 1985. The essays analyze the topic from various points of view. The contributors include Andrzej Korbonski, William C. Potter, Wolfgang Pfeiler, Eberhard Schulz, Keith Crane, Donato Di Gaetano, Marco Carnovale, Joachim Krause, Wolfgang Berner. The book is directed at anyone interested in how Soviet-East European relations have developed and what possibilities are on the horizon. Topics covered include German-Soviet foreign relations, East-West German relations, Soviet-East European economic policy, the role of the West in Soviet and East European economic reform, the future of the Warsaw Pact, Soviet-East-European military aid to third world countries and the past effects and future of Comecon. There is no index.

83. Dawisha, Karen, **Eastern Europe, Gorbachev, and Reform: The Great Challenge,** 2nd ed. Cambridge: Cambridge University Press, 1990. xv, 268 p. ISBN: 0521356636(pbk); 0521355605. Includes bibliographical references.

The second edition of Dawisha's book updates the earlier edition by including changes to the spring of 1990. In other respects the book remains essentially the same. The work is divided into two parts with an introduction. Part one (ch. 2-4) gives an historical perspective of Soviet-East European relations over the past 45 years by examining political, economic, cultural and military factors. Part two (ch. 5-8) focuses on meeting the challenges that lie ahead. In this part she analyses the reaction of East European leaders to the challenges facing their regimes, the short-term policy agenda in the political, economic and social spheres and how they all can move beyond the threat of a use of force by the Soviet Union. Effects on the West and influences from the West are also taken into account. Several useful appendixes are included covering a chronology of East European events from Feb. 1945 to April,1990, Soviet and East European leadership successors 1945-1990, East European Communist Parties, successors, leaders and East European Elections and major contenders, 1990. Reviews: *Problems of Communication* 39, no.3 (May-June 1990): 99-103. *Conflict* 10, no.3 (July-September 1990): 275-277. *Current History* 89, no.551 (December 1990): 425. *Canadian Slavonic Papers* 32, no.4 (December 1990): 528-529. *Canadian-American Slavic Studies* 24, no.4 (Winter 1990): 493-495.

84. De Nevers, Renee, **The Soviet Union and Eastern Europe: The End of an Era**. London: Brassey's for the International Institute for Strategic Studies, 1990. 95 p. *Adelphi Papers, 0567-932x, 249*. Includes bibliographical references (p. 84-95).

After a brief overview of Soviet-East European relations from 1945 to 1985, the author sets out to meet three objectives: 1) "to analyse the changes in Soviet policy toward Eastern Europe that made recent developments possible, concentrating on the evolution of Soviet policy since 1985, when Mikhail Gorbachev came to power; 2) to analyse the origins of East European political and economic reforms, focusing on the catalytic role played by Gorbachev's new thinking; (p. 4) and 3) to outline some possibilities for the years ahead.

85. Dean, Jonathan, **Meeting Gorbachev's Challenge: How to Build the NATO-Warsaw Pact Confrontation**. New York: St. Martin's Press, 1989. xviii, 445 p. ISBN: 0312032668; 0312032676 (pbk). Includes bibliographical references and index.

An arms control adviser gives his view on how disarmament can proceed in Europe. Specifically, the author deals with how C.F.E. negotiators can proceed with the then ongoing task at the Vienna meetings. How both sides could cut back, which weapons and the problem of verification are all dealt with. Another theme of the book is the defense of Europe after such a cutback. The author foresees future policy of the Warsaw Pact and NATO organization as continuing. Other related topics such as the INF treaty, existing relations between East and West, and Gorbachev's reforms make up a large part of the discussion. The book also includes several appendices providing data published by the alliances, data published by the Institute of Strategic Studies, air strength, ground forces, unilateral withdrawals from Eastern Europe, documents from various meetings of the two alliances, and a table of reductions proposed in this book. A detailed study of a complex topic.

86. **European Detente: Case Studies of the Politics of East-West Relations,** edited by Kenneth Dyson. London: Pinter, 1986. xi, 279 p. ISBN: 0861875575. Includes bibliographical references and index.

These eleven essays are from an Anglo-German conference held at the University of Brodford. The overall purpose of the volume is to place European detente in its historical context and then to draw conclusions about the proper conduct of East-West relations from this analysis. In examining detente—easing the strained relations between states—Germany has been and continues to be a key element. Three of the eleven essays focus on Germany. Other topics include the Conference on Security and Cooperation in Europe and the Helsinki Final Act, the Soviet Union and European detente, national independence and Atlanticism and the dialectic of French policies, and British and European political cooperation. Dyson concludes the volume with his three-dimensional view of East-West relations.

87. **The Warsaw Pact and Balkans: Moscow's Southern Flank,** edited by Jonathan Eyal. New York: St. Martin's Press, 1989. xvi, 246 p. ISBN: 0312031513. Includes index.

The essays in this book attempt to examine the way in which Moscow has responded to problems associated with the Balkans. Specifically the authors examine Moscow's changing relationships with Hungary, Romania, Bulgaria, Yugoslavia and Albania in light of growing nationalism in these countries and increasing economic problems. Each author looks at the military's role in the country he examines as it has affected Soviet security. Along with a general introduction to the area the book is divided into five others chapters each devoted to one of the Balkan countries.

88. Garrett, Stephen A., **From Potsdam to Poland: American Policy Toward Eastern Europe**. New York: Praeger, 1986. ix, 237 p. ISBN: 0275923215. Includes bibliography (p.221-232) and index.

Stephen Garrett sets out to challenge some of the more conventional beliefs about American foreign policy toward Eastern Europe in this study. The three parts of the work reflect three of the more commonly held views with which he takes issue: I East European émigré groups in the U.S. pressure the U.S. government into certain policy decisions; II American trade can be used effectively to pressure East European governments; III Americans have played a major role in humanitarian efforts in Eastern Europe. The author is not attempting a negative, revisionist approach. Rather he believes that U.S. foreign policy needs change to be effective in this area of the world.

89. Gati, Charles, **The Bloc That Failed: Soviet-East European Relations in Transition**. Bloomington: Indiana University Press, 1990. xiv, 226 p. *Midland Book, MB561*, ISBN: 0253205611 (pbk); 0253325315 (alk. paper). Includes bibliography (p.220-222) and index.

The author analyzes the changes in relation between the Soviet Union and Eastern Europe by focusing on a number of questions. First the author considers those factors related to Soviet policy in Eastern Europe. Specifically, such questions as how Moscow will define the limits of its tolerance for East European reform; what influence will Moscow be able to exert on East Europe; will changes in East Europe create a demand for greater reform in the Soviet Union; will the reform fail if Gorbachev fails? The author then turns his attention to the question related to the prospect for Eastern Europe. Here he focuses on the following problems: 1) the possibility of the resurgence of the KGB in Eastern Europe; 2) problems in the success of the emerging economies; 3) the possibility of old national rivalries resurfacing; 4) the effects of the breakdown of the Warsaw Pact. Finally the author will also consider the role of the West in security, economically and specifically as it relates to the reunification of Germany. The book is divided into three sections. The first deals with past East European-Soviet relations from Stalin to Chernenko. Part two focuses on the early years of reform 1985-1988. Part three deals with the revolutions in Eastern Europe. The volume includes an appendix with a statement of Moscow's policy on East Europe. There is also a bibliographic essay with suggested readings. Reviews: *Soviet Union/Union Sovietique* 17, no.1-2 (1990): 135-136. *Foreign Affairs* 69, no.4 (Fall 1990): 192. *Current History* 89, no.551 (December 1990): 425.

90. Gordon, Lincoln, **Eroding Empire: Western Relations with Eastern Europe**. Washington, D.C.: Brookings Institution, 1987. xv, 359 p. ISBN: 0815732147; 0815732139 (pbk). Includes bibliographical references and index.

The Brookings Institution policy study "reviews the attitudes, interests, and policies of the major Western countries toward Eastern Europe since World War II.... The study recommends that Western nations seek greater agreement on objectives and more flexible orchestration of methods used to achieve them. They should not miss opportunities for promoting constructive change and should not allow serious discord in this area to weaken a Western alliance already under severe strain." (p. IX)

91. **Central and Eastern Europe: The Opening Curtain?**, edited by William E. Griffith. Boulder, Colo.: Westview Press, 1989. xix, 458 p. ISBN: 0813307732 (alk. paper); 0813307740 (pbk.: alk. paper). Includes index.

Because Eastern Europe has lain at the heart of East-West relations for over forty years and because of the political flux and change evident there, Eastern Europe posed one of the greatest policy challenges to Gorbachev's perestroika. The purpose of these eighteen essays is to describe and analyze the political and economic conditions that support current policy in East European states. The essays are focused on various aspects of the problems confronted by these regimes, such as economic growth and development, technology transfer, human rights, and nationalism. Some essays encompass several countries while others limit their discussion to only one.

92. Harbutt, Fraser J., **The Iron Curtain: Churchill, America and the Origins of the Cold War**. New York: Oxford University Press, 1986. xiv, 370 p. ISBN: 019503877. Includes bibliography (p. 341-353) and index.

Harbutt portrays Churchill in his role "as the most active protagonist of a joint Anglo-American political front against the Soviet Union during and immediately after World War II." (p. xi) The book also examines the place of the Eastern European countries in the intense postwar diplomacy that culminated in the cold war.

93. Jelavich, Barbara, **Russia's Balkan Entanglements, 1806-1914**. New York: Cambridge University Press, 1991. xi, 292 p. ISBN: 0521401267. Includes bibliographical references (p. 277-284) and index.

"The purpose of this study is to examine reasons for the Russian involvement in the Balkan Peninsula and to attempt at least partially to explain the connections that drew the Russian government into entanglements that were not very often in contradiction with its great-power interests, but contained emotional commitments that were difficult to control. The emphasis is on the unique relationship that many Russian statesmen felt that they had with the Orthodox Balkan people, one that they believed was shared by no other state, at the same time an explanation is offered about why Balkan national leaderships did not reciprocate their feelings but were extremely happy to exploit Russian willingness to come to their assistance." (p. ix)

94. **East-West Relations and Divided Nation Problems in the Gorbachev Era: German and Korean Perspectives,** edited by Dalchoong Kim, Werner Gumpel and Gottfried-Karl Kindermann. Seoul: Institute of East and West Studies, Yonsei University, 1988. xiv, 441 p. *East-West Studies Series, 4*. Includes bibliographical references and index.

This collection of 22 essays is an outgrowth of the 3rd and 4th Korean-German conferences. Its focus is the understanding of factors that lead to understanding a crisis, which arise from conflicts of interests among nations. The essays are grouped in four sections. Section one (1-6) examines security issues in global and regional contexts. Section II (7-11) focuses on the role of the Soviet Union in Eastern Europe and Asia and the possible change in Soviet policy under Gorbachev. Section III (12-16) analyzes East-West economic relations. Korean-Hungarian economic relations are the subject of two of these five essays. Section IV (17-22) looks at the various issues surrounding inter-relations of Germany and Korea and speculations regarding their future courses.

95. **The Uncertain Future: Gorbachev's Eastern Bloc,** edited by Nicholas N. Kittrie and Ivan Volgyes. New York: Paragon House Publishers, 1988. iii, 281 p. ISBN: 0943852617; 0943852625 (pbk). Includes bibliography (p. 271-277) and index.

In the light of improved relations between the super powers, this volume was "undertaken to record and realistically review the historical as well as contemporary forces within the Eastern bloc countries." (p. 7) Individual essays explore political reform, the decreasing importance of ideology, economic conditions and policy, human rights, the effect of reforms, the Warsaw Pact and changes in the military balance, and U.S. policy toward Eastern Europe.

96. Kovrig, Bennett, **Of Walls and Bridges: The United States and Eastern Europe**. New York: New York University Press, 1991. xiii, 425 p. ISBN: 0814746136 (pbk); 0814746128. Includes bibliographical references (p. 365-410) and index.

"This book aims to trace the historical elements of continuity and flexibility in the pursuit of America's interests in Eastern Europe. The first three chapters give a chronological overview of relevant policies and actions from the Roosevelt to the Bush administrations.... The remaining three chapters focus more narrowly on the themes of human rights and democratization, the application of economic leverage, and European security, looking back to prior experiences with these issues and forward to the tasks that face Washington's policymakers." (p. 2)

97. Nelson, Daniel N., **Alliance Behavior in the Warsaw Pact**. Boulder, Colo.: Westview Press, 1986. xvii, 134 p. *Westview Special Studies on the Soviet Union & Eastern Europe, 0163-6057*, ISBN: 0813372240. Includes bibliography (p.123-127) and index.

"How do alliances, in the aggregate, 'behave'? What explains the actions and performance of alliances? Within alliances, how do members' actions and performance vary, and what explains that variance? This book addresses these questions with respect to one of the world's principal alliances of the late twentieth century, the Warsaw Treaty Organization (WTO), also known as the Warsaw Pact. The author argues that though we understand a great deal about the military hardware of the Warsaw Pact, little is known about its cohesiveness, and the distribution of the military burden within it—all key variables, he argues, in influencing change in alliance behavior. In each chapter he offers a new way to measure one of these variables and suggests possible explanations for variance. In addition, he examines the effect East-West relations have on cohesion and how Warsaw Pact allies have distributed the defense effort in the past. A concluding chapter is devoted to an empirical assessment of Warsaw Pact alliance behavior, combining indicators of cohesion, reliability, and burden-sharing in a general portrait of the WTO as a collective actor in international politics." (frontispiece)

98. ———, **Elite-Mass Relations in Communist Systems**. Basingstoke: Macmillan, 1988. x, 217 p. ISBN: 0333428218. Includes bibliography (p. 191-202) and index.

As Nelson states in his introduction, the study of communist politics requires more attention to the "base" of such systems rather than to their apex (p. 1). His goal is to develop the means for gauging change in elite-mass relationships. The when, how and to what extent people will challenge the legitimacy of party values and how, when and to what extent their leaders will respond. Nelson's focus on this type of analysis is the changing relationship between the party and people and institutions at the local level. Seven of the eight chapters were previously published in journals in slightly altered forms. He has provided an introduction and conclusion to make these essays cohere into a unified theme. Topics covered include vertical integration and political control, women in local communist politics in Poland and Romania, leadership, public opinion and public policy, Leninists and political inequalities and workers and political alienation.

99. Ozinga, James R., **The Rapacki Plan: The 1957 Proposal to Denuclearize Central Europe, and an Analysis of Its Rejection**. Jefferson, N.C.: McFarland & Co., 1989. v, 193 p. ISBN: 0899504450. Includes bibliographical references (p. 179-187) and index.

This early denuclearization plan, the Rapacki plan, is discussed against the backdrop of current arms limitations negotiations between the east and west. The author believes that both the terms of the plan, making Germany (East and West), Poland and Czechoslovakia a denuclearized zone, and the circumstances of its failure in 1957 have lessons pertinent to the current situation. The book is arranged topically first presenting the historical context in which the plan was put forth, then turning to the terms of the plan itself, problems created by the cold war, and West Germany's role in the failure of the plan. Several appendices are included.

100. Ploss, Sidney I., **Moscow and the Polish Crisis: An Interpretation of Soviet Policies and Intentions**. Boulder, CO: Westview Press, 1986. ix, 182 p. *Westview Special Studies on the Soviet Union & Eastern Europe, 0163-6057*, ISBN: 0813303516. Includes bibliographical references and index.

In 1980, in the midst of the Polish crisis, the West was uncertain about the Soviet's response to unrest. When martial law was declared, Secretary of State Alexander Haig declared that it came without warning. Ploss, however, says that it was clear from analysis of the Soviet press what could happen. Using propaganda analysis Ploss shows how the press was the best source for tracing policy decisions and leadership debates.

101. **The End of the Outer Empire: Soviet-East European Relations in Transition, 1985-1990,** edited by Alex Pravda. London: SAGE Publications, 1992. 238 p. ISBN: 0803987234. Includes bibliographical references and index.

"This volume examines the changes in relations in the second half of the 1980s. Chapter 1 looks at the evolution of Soviet policy towards the region, assessing the Gorbachev leadership's perspectives and the way these affected strategy at various stages. Chapters 2 and 3 examine changes in the Warsaw Pact and Council for Mutual Economic Assistance (CMEA) to early 1990, while Chapter 9 analyses the final decline and demise of these multilateral organizations over the subsequent year. The chapters in between (4-8) look at developments in bilateral relations in five of the most important states in the region." (p. x)

102. Roberts, Ian W., **Nicholas I and the Russian Intervention in Hungary**. New York: St. Martin's Press, 1991. xi, 301 p. ISBN: 0312048971. Includes bibliographical references (p. 277-285) and index.

The present work is an attempt to give an account of Russian foreign policy during the revolutionary years 1848 and 1849 which culminated in Nicholas I's decision to respond to an appeal of Francis Joseph for aid in restoring order in Hungary. It is based on a study of material from diplomatic archives (published and unpublished) and makes extensive use of the memoirs written by Russian officers who took part in the campaign in 1849." (p. ix)

103. **Problems of Balkan Security: Southeastern Europe in the 1990**, Paul S. Shoup, editor, George W. Hoffman, project director. Washington D.C.: Wilson Center Press, 1990. xii, 286 p. ISBN: 0943875218 (pbk); 0943875226. Includes bibliographical references.

A collection of essays examining the rise of domestic problems and national tensions as the Soviet Union withdraws its control of the Balkans. The essays are divided into three sections reflecting three different perspectives: historical, area wide security, and external influences, in particular U.S. and Soviet relations with the countries of the area. "[The contributors] have drawn on their scholarly expertise to address contemporary issues of great importance to U.S. and Western interests. Their thoughts and conclusions are relevant to the policy makers charged with protecting those interests." (back cover).

104. **East-West Tensions in the Third World,** edited by Marshall D. Shulman. New York: W.W. Norton, 1986. 243 p. ISBN: 0393023109. Includes index.

These seven essays formed the background papers for the Seventieth American Assembly held in November 1985. The Final Report of the Assembly has been included as an appendix. For the most part the authors of these papers reject the two usual methods of dealing with conflict in the third world. The sphere of influence approach and code of conduct approach, whereby rules for competition have been worked out have given way to an establishment of specific limitations on the kind and degree of intervention in local and regional situations. After an overview of the problem, contributions explore US-Soviet rivalry in the Middle East, Latin America, Asia and Africa. Two final essays focus on economic and military competition in the third world in general.

105. **Security Implications of Nationalism in Eastern Europe,** edited by Jeffrey Simon and Trond Gilberg. Boulder: Westview Press, 1986. xvi, 327 p. *US Army War College Series on Contemporary Strategic Issues*, ISBN: 0813370477. Includes bibliographical references and index.

Suggesting that events in Poland during 1980-1981 represent the tip of an iceberg, the contributors examine the rise of nationalism in Eastern Europe and its potential consequences for European security. They analyze developing problems and trends in the region, including the cooling of relations between the USSR and individual countries in Eastern Europe, the continuing economic crisis, changing social structures, the influence of the intelligentsia, and the eroding importance of ideology as a key part of Eastern Europe's political culture. The second half of the book focuses on the impact of these shifts on political and military relations between the USSR and Eastern European countries and on the efficient functioning of the Warsaw Pact. (frontispiece).

106. **Dominant Powers and Subordinate States: The United States in Latin America and the Soviet Union in Eastern Europe,** edited by Jan F. Triska. Durham, N.C.: Duke University Press, 1986. xi, 504 p. *Duke Press Policy Studies, 0020-6555*, ISBN: 0822306867 (alk. paper); 0822307480 (pbk). Includes bibliography (p.471-498) and index.

These papers were originally presented at a seminar at Stanford University in January 1986. Their purpose is to compare the United States and the USSR as regional powers, the former in Latin America, the latter in Eastern Europe. The essays are grouped into five parts. After a lengthy introduction Part one examines the history of the two regimes and provides justification for comparative analysis. Part two lays out various concepts and theories concerned with dominant-subordinate relationships, sphere of interest behavior and bargaining. Part three explores behavior of dominant powers in general, including strategy and military behavior. Part four turns to similar themes in subordinate states. Part five analyzes the evolution of spheres of influence and the future of dominant-subordinate systems.

107. United States. Congress. House. Committee on Foreign Affairs, Subcommittee on International Operations, **United States Public Diplomacy in Eastern Europe and the Soviet Union: Hearing Before the Subcommittee on International Operations of the Committee on Foreign Affairs, House of Representatives, One Hundred Second Congress, First Session, July 30, 1991.** Washington: Supt. of Docs., Congressional Sales Office, 1991. 169 p. ISBN: 0160355737.

In the face of the drastic changes taking place in Eastern Europe and the Soviet Union other nations must revamp their foreign policies. In this publication the reader is made privy to some of the information that affects the formation of foreign policy in Eastern Europe. The USIA, the Divisory Commission on U.S. Public Diplomacy and the National Endowment for Democracy all testify on their activities in the region. This type of publication is of interest to anyone examining questions of U.S. foreign policy and the changes it has undergone as a result of the changes in Eastern Europe.

108. Wandycz, Piotr Stefan, **The Twilight of French Eastern Alliances, 1926-1936: French-Czechoslovak-Polish Relations from Locarno to the Remilitarization of the Rhineland.** Princeton, N.J.: Princeton University Press, 1988. ISBN: 0691055289. Includes bibliographical references and index.

This book is a sequel to the author's *France and Her Eastern Allies 1919-1925* (1962). The present work concentrates in the mutual relations of France with Poland and Czechoslovakia between 1926 and 1936. The thirteen chapters are divided into three parts. Part one (ch. 1-5) deals with Post-Locarno diplomacy, part two (ch. 6-8) focuses on the depression, and part three (ch. 9-13) examines the responses to Hitler. Several appendices provide additional data, excerpts from treaties. Reviews: *Slavic Review* 49, no.3 (fall 1990): 480-481. *American Historical Review* 95, no.3 (June 1990): 812-813.

109. World Congress for Soviet and East European Studies (4th: 1990: Harrogate, England, **Eastern Europe and the West: Selected Papers from the Fourth World Congress for Soviet and East European Studies, Harrogate, 1990,** edited by John Morrison. New York: St. Martin's Press, 1992. 271 p. ISBN: 0312080409. Includes bibliographical references and index.

These essays demonstrate those relations between East and West that go beyond the diplomatic or military. They are grouped into six sections. In Part one Polish émigré diplomacy in the nineteenth and early twentieth century is examined. Part two focuses on the history of Hungary's relations with the West. In Part three foreign intervention in the Balkans is examined. In Part five the history of Polish migration from the eighteenth through the twentieth centuries is discussed. All papers were originally prepared for the World Congress for Soviet and East European Studies held in 1990.

COMMUNISM

110. Barnard, Frederick M., **Pluralism, Socialism, and Political Legitimacy: Reflections on Opening Up Communism.** New York: Cambridge University Press, 1991. xii, 189 p. ISBN: 0521402522. Includes bibliographical references and index.

As political pluralism develops, Professor F. M. Barnard examines the process, focusing on how it can evolve without destabilizing and crippling the nations involved. He is particularly interested in developments in Czechoslovakia, Poland and Yugoslavia. "Throughout the book, the author explores the political-philosophical as well as the procedural-democratic problems involved in legitimizing socialism as a pluralist political system, and in so doing, also throws new light on central concerns in Western political debate." (p.i) The book is intended for political philosophers and scholars and students of East European political theory. It is arranged topically and includes an appendix on the problem of elections in pluralist democracies as seen by a Czech writer after the Soviet intervention of 1968.

111. Brown, James F., **Eastern Europe and Communist Rule**. Durham: Duke University Press, 1988. xii, 562 p. ISBN: 082230841X (pbk); 082230810X. Includes bibliography (p. 543-553) and index.

A retrospective study of Eastern Europe during its forty years of Communist rule. The author looks at political development in general, Soviet-East-European relations, relations with the West and provides an economic and social overview. Separate chapters on each country, Poland, Hungary, East Germany, Romania, Czechoslovakia, Bulgaria, Yugoslavia and Albania, discuss aspects of communist control specific to those countries. Ten motifs are emphasized: 1) The distinctiveness of each nation; 2) nationalism; 3) "spontaneity" as a threat to the system; 4) the impact of the invasion of Czechoslovakia; 5) the effect of detente in the 1970s; 6) economic and ecological decline; 7) "incompatibilities" in East European politics; 8) the reemergence of a class system; 9) Soviet dilemma in Eastern Europe; 10) systemic change and the effect it would have on the existing system. Three appendices are included: a chronology of events, biographical sketches, and selected social demographic and economic data. Reviews: *Problems of Communism* 39, no.3 (May-June 1990): 99-103. *Studies in Comparative Communism* 23, no.1 (Spring 1990): 101-108. *Canadian-American Slavic Studies* 24, no.3 (Fall 1990): 382-383. *Canadian Slavonic Papers* 30, no.4 (December 1988): 493-95. *Slavic Review* 48, no.3 (Fall 1989): 513-14. *Fletcher Forum* 13, no.1 (Winter 1989): 149-51.

112. Callinicos, Alex, **The Revenge of History: Marxism and the East European Revolutions**. University Park, Pa.: Pennsylvania State University Press, 1991. x, 159 p. ISBN: 0271007680 (pbk); 0271007672 (alk. paper). Includes bibliographical references (p. 137-152) and index.

"*The Revenge of History* is a frontal assault on the widely accepted idea that the East European revolutions of 1989 mark the death of socialism. Alex Callinicos seeks to vindicate the classical Marxist tradition by arguing that socialism in this tradition can only come from below, through the self-activity of the working class.... Callinicos argues that the collapse of Stalinism at the end of the 1980s is one aspect of a world-wide transition from nationally organized to globally integrated capitalism. The result is likely to be greater economic and political instability." (back cover) The author concludes that the changes in Eastern Europe may be the prelude to socialism as opposed to its failure. The book is topically arranged discussing the question of socialism's decline in general and then turning to the specific problems the East European situation presents for Marxist regimes.

113. Daniels, Anthony, **Utopias Elsewhere: Journeys in a Vanishing World**. 1st American ed. New York: Crown Pub., 1991. 202 p. ISBN: 0517585480. Includes index.

Daniels reports his impressions and experiences from countries "in the periphery of the communist world"—Albania, North Korea, Romania, Vietnam and Cuba.

114. **Religion and Nationalism in Eastern Europe and the Soviet Union,** edited by Dennis J. Dunn. Boulder, Colo.: Lynne Rienner, 1987. xi, 128 p. ISBN: 1555870694.

A selection of papers originally presented at the Third World Congress of Soviet and East European Studies (1985) are collected in this volume. The purpose of this collection is to "open the debate on the relationship between religion and nationalism in the Slavic world." These phenomena are, in many regions, inextricably linked and a thorough examination would produce insight into such questions as the resurgence of Islam, the phenomenal growth of religion in the Soviet Union... and certainly the unrest and future direction of events in Eastern Europe." (p.x) The essays in this volume are by six experts in the field. They are not united by a common theoretical approach or subject emphasis. The opening essay presents general questions on the study of nationalism and religion in Eastern Europe. The next two essays deal with the relations between Jews in Eastern Europe and other ethnic groups. These are followed by a discussion of the Russian Orthodox response to the Catholics of Germany from 1870-1905. The relationship between Croat Catholics and the Yugoslav Communist Party is the subject of the next essay. Finally, a paper on the suppression of the Ukrainian Greek Catholic Church closes out the volume.

115. Gzowski, Alison, **Facing Freedom: The Children of Eastern Europe**. Toronto, Ont.: Viking, 1992. 285 p. ISBN: 0670844241.

Alison Gzowski has been a writer and producer for programs broadcast on CBL radio. In this, her first book, she explores the effects of the downfall of the East European totalitarian regimes on teenagers. "Now as their countries reinvent themselves, all of these teenagers are in the process of discovering their own truths. This book is not intended to be comprehensive; it's a glimpse into a few lives." (p. 17) Gzowski talks with sixteen people from Czechoslovakia, Poland, Eastern Germany, Latvia and Russia. The interviews provide the Western reader with a unique perspective on the tremendous changes to their societies.

116. Jowitt, Kenneth, **New World Disorder: The Leninist Extinction**. Berkeley: University of California Press, 1992. ix, 342 p. ISBN: 0520077628. Includes index.

These essays, all of which have been published elsewhere, explore the legacy of the Leninist phenomenon. He does this by using "a theoretical perspective and conceptual language that takes Lenin's contention that he had created a 'party of a new type' seriously, and [by situating] the Leninist phenomenon in comparative terms." (p. viii)

117. Mihalyi, Peter, **Socialist Investment Cycles: Analysis in Retrospect**. Boston: Kluwer Academic Publishers, 1992. xvi, 233 p. ISBN: 0792319737. Includes bibliographical references (p. 205-224) and index.

"*Socialist Investment Cycles* is the first monograph in English on investment fluctuations in planned economies. While providing a broad overview of the literature on socialist investment cycles, as well as a quantitative description of the actual processes, the author puts forth a new framework for understanding investment fluctuations... *Socialist Investment Cycles* encompasses all 35 countries which were ruled by communism and is the first study to penetrate deeply into the data problem, country by country, and series by series." (back cover) The first appendix includes two case studies on Hungary and the second, basic data on some of the nations being discussed. This technical and scholarly study included an extensive bibliography on the subject.

118. Murphy, Kenneth, **Retreat from the Finland Station: Moral Odysseys in the Breakdown of Communism**. New York: Free Press, 1992. xv, 415 p. ISBN: 0029223156. Includes bibliographical references (p. 383-403) and index.

Murphy's book takes as its title a rephrasing of Edmund Wilson's famous work *To the Finland Station*, which traced the idea of socialism to its actual manifestation in Lenin's revolution. Murphy chronicles the decline of this idea to its last gasp in the tumultuous events of 1989-1991 in the Soviet Union and Eastern Europe. His selection of topics was based on the criterion "that each must be truly both representative of and engaged in the disillusion that brought about, step by step, socialism's downfall as an idea." (p. xv)

119. Prychitko, David L., **Marxism and Workers' Self-Management: The Essential Tension**. New York: Greenwood Press, 1991. xvii, 153 p. *Contributions in Economics and Economic History, 0084-9235, no. 123*, ISBN: 0313278547. Includes bibliographical references (p. 123-138) and index.

The reforms of Mikhail Gorbachev have led Marxists to once again examine the works of Karl Marx. In this work David Prychitko takes another look at Marx's writings to see if he can find a theoretical base to support a system of worker managed firms in a market economy. The author begins with a discussion of utopian socialism and its influence on Marx's writings. He then demonstrates that Marx "foresaw the possibility of a nonalienated socialist future." (p. xiii) Prychitko discusses contemporary neoclassical economic theory. Next he examines the situation in Yugoslavia and the problems with self-managed socialism that have appeared there. Next he turns to American cooperatives as examples of worker-managed firms. Finally, he discusses the future of workers' self-management in the "post-Marxist" era (post-1989).

120. Satterwhite, James H., **Varieties of Marxist Humanism: Philosophical Revision in Postwar Eastern Europe**. Pittsburgh, Pa.: University of Pittsburgh Press, 1992. vi, 255 p. *Series in Russian and East European Studies: no. 17*, ISBN: 0822937115. Includes bibliographical references (p. 223-252) and index.

"The aim of this study is to trace the development of Marxist humanism in Eastern Europe through a presentation of some of the key concepts as they were formulated by the various thinkers at different stages in their own intellectual growth, in the context of the historical changes that took place in each country. In addition to following the development of the approach through its various representatives, this study has as its primary purpose the task of showing the fundamental unity underlying the efforts of those from all four of these countries." (p. 11) Each chapter is devoted to one of the East European countries; Poland, Hungary, Czechoslovakia and Yugoslavia. An extensive bibliography is included on each country and its development of Marxist philosophy.

121. Staniszkis, Jadwiga, **The Ontology of Socialism,** edited and translated by Peggy Watson. Oxford: Clarendon Press, 1992. viii, 191 p. ISBN: 0198275986. Translation of: Ontologia socjalizmu. Includes bibliographical references (p. 167-179) and index.

This volume is a translation of Professor Staniszkis' Polish language study of the development of socialism in Eastern Europe. It is a highly theoretical analysis of great interest to those studying Marxist theory as it is applied in Eastern Europe.

122. Stern, Geoffrey, **The Rise and Decline of International Communism**. Brookfield, Vt.: Gower Pub. Co., 1990. xv, 269 p. ISBN: 1852780428. Includes bibliographical references and indexes.

Stern traces the history of communism from its Marxist core to the downfall of communism in Eastern Europe in 1989. The thirteen chapters are divided into three sections: laying the foundations, the use of international communism, and the decline of international communism. A final chapter raises the question of communism's future.

123. **Uprooting Leninism, Cultivating Liberty,** edited by Vladimir Tismaneanu and Patrick Clawson. Lanham: University Press of America, 1992. xiv, 87 p. ISBN: 0819187305.

The Foreign Policy Research Institute has held several conferences on the rapidly changing situation in Eastern Europe. In this volume the conferences held in 1991 which focused on transition are summarized. The volume is divided into two parts. The first half reports on the conference convened in Timisoara in March 1991. "The conference dealt with 'Power and Opposition in Post-Communist Societies: Foundations of Pluralism in East-Central Europe,' and had four goals: to assess progress toward democracy; consider the obstacles of democracy; formulate specific strategies of democratization; and assess how the West can best assist the process of democratization." (p. vii) In part two economic issues were the focus of a series of workshops organized in conjunction with the Kennan Institute. Participants were particularly interested in the process of creating free markets in Eastern Europe.

ECONOMICS, TRADE & BUSINESS

124. **The Path of Reform in Central and Eastern Europe**. Brussels, Luxembourg: Directorate-General for Economic and Financial Affairs, 1991. xi, 306 p. *European Economy*.

This volume is based on papers commissioned by the directorate-General for Economic and Financial Affairs when the program of assistance in Poland and Hungary was extended to Bulgaria, the CSFR, Yugoslavia and Romania. The papers are intended to assist the directors of the European Communities in policy making. They deal with a variety of topics including currency convertibility, economic stability in the CSFR, restructuring industry and trade, privatization and debt payment plans. Each essay has its own table of contents, statistical data and references.

125. **Pressures for Reform in the East European Economies: Study Papers, Submitted to the Joint Economic Committee, Congress of the United States**. Washington: Congressional Sales office, U.S. G.P.O., 1989. ISBN: Includes bibliographical references.

This two volume collection of articles was prepared at the request of the Joint Economic Committee of the U.S. Congress. Experts from many universities and private organizations were asked to contribute. "The study examines recent economic performance and prospects in the East European Countries, the pressures for fundamental reform and the steps that have been taken in each country to facilitate or frustrate change. In addition, there are analyses of the problems of measuring economic performance in those countries, and assessments of their defense sectors and foreign commercial relations." (p. iii) In volume one the essays are grouped topically under headings covering international economy, defense and agriculture. Volume two begins with country studies, then turns to various aspects of trade: finance, the CMEA and US trade policy.

126. **Economic Reforms and Welfare Systems in the USSR, Poland and Hungary: Social Contract in Transformation,** edited by Jan Adam. New York: St. Martin's Press, 1991. xv, 182 p. ISBN: 0312062192. Includes bibliographical references and index.

"The purpose of this book is to examine how recent systemic changes in Poland and Hungary, and expected changes in the USSR, affected and will affect the welfare system. This means examining what impact the transition to a market economy, and a democratisation of the political have and will have on the social contract." (p.xiii) Individual essays cover the social contract in general, housing policy, health care, economic reform and welfare policy.

127. Adam, Jan, **Economic Reforms in the Soviet Union and Eastern Europe Since the 1960's**. New York: St. Martin's Press, 1989. xvi, 264 p. ISBN: 0312020848. Includes bibliography (p. 243-255) and index.

Adam's book is essentially an examination of changes in the system of management in the Soviet Union, Czechoslovakia, Hungary and Poland. An appendix chapter by Horst Betz covers the GDR; Romania and Bulgaria are excluded. His monograph is divided into three parts with a total of eleven chapters. Part one describes the traditional Soviet system of management of the economy and uses this description as a sort of archetypical paradigm of the centrally planned economy. Part two, consisting of five chapters, examines the common and contrasting features of reforms of the 1960s for the countries studied. Subsequent chapters in this part each cover a specific country's reform activity during that decade. Part three is structured in a similar way with the same number and type of chapters. The focus throughout is on industrial reform; agriculture is excluded from analysis. Review: *Slavic Review* 49, no.2 (Summer 1990): 296.

128. **Market Socialism or the Restoration of Capitalism?**, edited by Anders Aslund. Cambridge: Cambridge University Press, 1992. x, 215 p. ISBN: 0521411939. Includes bibliographical references and index.

The papers in this volume were originally written for the World Congress for Soviet and East European Studies held in Harrogate in 1990. All of the essays deal in some way with the efficacy of restoring capitalism in Eastern Europe. The papers are grouped into three parts. "The first part considers what remains of market socialism and what this means to the principal direction of events. The second part poses the questions concerning changes in economic thinking and economic policy making. The third part looks into some particular effects of perestroika in the USSR." (p. 2) Although many essays in this volume are limited to considering the Soviet Union, general discussion of the region and of Poland and Hungary are included.

129. Assetto, Valerie J., **The Soviet Bloc in the IMF and the IBRD**. Boulder, Colo.: Westview Press, 1987. xi, 208 p. *Westview Special Studies in International Economics*, ISBN: 0813372364. Includes bibliography (p. 195-202) and index.

"The purpose of this study is to examine the impact of political, non-economic factors in IMF and IBRD operations and decisions to lend using the Eastern European members of both organizations as case studies." (p.1) The study was motivated by claims that political factors play a large role in the so-called technical decisions of the Bank and Fund.

130. Atkinson, A. B., and John Micklewright, **Economic Transformation in Eastern Europe and the Distribution of Income.** New York: Cambridge University Press, 1992. xvi, 448 p. ISBN: 0521438829. Includes bibliographical references (p. 421-434) and indexes.

By focusing on the pattern of distribution of income Atkinson and Micklewright hope to discover who benefits and who suffers as a result of Eastern Europe's economic transformation. "The book contains extensive statistical evidence that has not previously been assembled on a comparative basis, and takes the story right up to the end of communism. The findings bring out the differences in experience between countries under communism: between Central Europe and the former union, between Czechoslovakia, Hungary and Poland, and between the newly independent states of the former Soviet Union." (p. i) The statistical data comprise over 100 pages of the volume which also includes a detailed discussion of statistical sources and methods.

131. **Privatization Processes in Eastern Europe: Theoretical Foundations and Empirical Results,** edited by Mario Baldassarri, Luigi Paganetto, and Edmund S. Phelps. New York: St. Martin's Press, 1993. 281 p. *Central Issues in Contemporary Economic Theory and Policy,*.

These essays concentrate on the privatization of industrial corporations in Eastern Europe. Part one is an overview of on-going and proposed processes. Part two focuses on the theoretical foundations of privatization processes such as financial markets, industrial relations and foreign trade. The third and final part contains two essays giving an overall evaluation of the privatization processes in Eastern Europe.

132. Batt, Judy, **East Central Europe: From Reform to Transformation**. New York: Council on Foreign Relations Press, 1991. 129 p. *Chatham House Papers*, ISBN: 0876091060. Includes bibliographical references (p.105-116).

Batt deals with the interaction between politics and economics in Poland, Hungary and Czechoslovakia. Topics covered include: economic reform in the crisis of communist rule; the end of communist rule; the emergence of pluralist politics, and the politics of economic transformation. An appendix includes summaries of the electoral system in each country, as well as the results of recent elections.

133. ———, **Economic Reform and Political Change in Eastern Europe: A Comparison of the Czechoslovak and Hungarian Experiences**. University of Birmingham, 1988. viii, 353 p. *Studies in Soviet History and Society*, ISBN: 0333444566. Includes bibliography (p. 326-346) and index.

Batt examines the relationship between economic reform and political stability in Hungary and Czechoslovakia. In the first part of the book, covering two chapters, she examines general aspects of planning markets and political systems. In the second part, consisting of five chapters, she analyzes the politics of reform in Hungary and Czechoslovakia through 1978. Reviews: *Problems of Communism* 39, no.3 (May-June 1990): 89-94. *East European Quarterly* 24, no.4 (Winter 1990): 539-540. *Slavic Review* 49, no.3 (Fall 1990): 476-477.

134. Bergson, Abram, **Planning and Performance in Socialist Economies: The USSR and Eastern Europe**. Boston: Unwin Hyman, 1988. xii, 304 p. ISBN: 0044451156. Includes index.

These previously published essays by Bergson all concentrate on the relative economic merit of the socialist and capitalist systems. His conclusion is that "socialist economic performance tends to be undistinguished by Western standards." (p. 1) The thirteen essays are divided into four parts: 1) productivity and welfare, 2) growth, 3) planning, and 4) problems of measurement. Review: *Comparative Economic Studies* 32, no.4 (Winter 1990): 107-109.

135. **Reform in Eastern Europe,** Oliver Blanchard et al. Cambridge, Mass.: MIT Press, 1991. xxiii, 98 p. ISBN: 0262023288. Includes bibliographical references.

This study, undertaken by the World Institute for Development Economics Research, focuses on stabilization and price liberalization, privatization, and restructuring. "The authors argue that stabilization, price liberalization, and privatization must proceed rapidly, whereas restructuring will take a decade or more." (p. viii) This latter process promises to be "long and painful, requiring entire parts of the economy to disappear, causing unemployment and potential social unrest."

136. Bleaney, M. F., **Do Socialist Economies Work?: The Soviet and East European Experience**. Oxford: B. Blackwell, 1988. xii, 171 p. ISBN: 0631153063. Includes bibliography (p.162-168) and index.

Bleaney wishes to place emphasis not on the details of the planning mechanism itself but rather on the economic behavior underlying such a system of central planning. He focuses, therefore, on the responses of enterprises to the economic environment in which they must act, the actions of planners within such a system and the ways in which political leaders attempt to influence the process. His book's first two chapters provide a historical introduction to the formation of the Soviet economic system and economic growth, investment cycles and agriculture in the USSR and Eastern Europe since 1945. Chapters 3 and 4 discuss the planning mechanism and the various actors within this system. Chapters 5, 6 and 8 deal with planning in Poland, Hungary and Yugoslavia. Chapter 7 provides a comparison between East and West and chapter 9 an assessment and answer posed by his title.

137. Boyd, Michael L., **Organization, Performance, and System Choice: East European Agricultural Development**. Boulder, Colo.: Westview Press, 1991. 181 p. ISBN: 0813311306. Includes bibliographical references and index.

Case studies on agricultural development in Yugoslavia, Poland and Bulgaria are presented in this work. It is of interest to scholars of development and Eastern Europe. "The economic success of the fledgling democracies of Eastern Europe, so crucial to their political viability, will depend to a great extent on their agricultural sectors. And the success of East European agriculture will hinge on how East Europeans manage both their economies at large and, more particularly, the organization of agricultural production.... Professor Boyd's research throws special light on how agricultural organization affects development and on how private and socialized forms of agriculture operate within different economic systems." (back cover) The book is divided into seven topical chapters on economic organization; agriculture's role in development; agriculture in Yugoslavia, Bulgaria and Poland; lessons from East European organization; and conclusions to be drawn from the evidence presented here. Two appendices with statistical data on agriculture in the three countries are included.

138. Brabant, Jozef M. van, **Adjustment, Structural Change, and Economic Efficiency: Aspects of Monetary Cooperation in Eastern Europe**. New York: Cambridge University Press, 1987. xviii, 480 p. *Soviet and East European Studies*, ISBN: 0521334551. Includes bibliography, p. 447-468.

This work focuses on how planned economies could have faster output growth by extending their involvement in the world economy through indirect coordination instruments. The chapters are divided into two parts. Part one presents the historical context in which the planned economies of the Soviet Union, Hungary, Bulgaria, Czechoslovakia, the German Democratic Republic, Poland and Romania, have developed. The remaining chapters present the analysis of socialist coordination instruments and supporting institutions. The discussion focuses on trade prices, domestic prices and pricing policies, foreign prices and pricing policies, the East European monetary system, banking systems and convertibility of funds. The author assumes that socialist economic integration is a goal of the planned economies and that socialist integration problems are affected by external factors. This is a highly detailed analysis for the student of economics.

139. ———, **Economic Integration in Eastern Europe: A Handbook**. New York: Routledge, 1989. xxiii, 452 p. ISBN: 0415902355. Includes bibliographical references and index.

Jozef van Brabant has long been interested in the integration of the economies in Eastern Europe. This work is intended as an introduction to the topic for the non-specialist. Four broad headings subsume the numerous topics discussed in this volume. First van Brabant discusses the origins of the CMEA. Next he introduces the reader to the organizational and institutional structure of the CMEA. The author then discusses how the economic policies of centrally planned economies can be "harmonized" with other countries including those with market economies. Finally, the author looks at those topics related to socialist economic integration in general. The study does not attempt to be comprehensive. "In summary, this monograph is primarily about the economies of international relations within the context of the CMEA as the regional organization of the majority of CPEs [centrally planned economies]. But the horizon will not necessarily blur types of economic cooperation among the members that are initiated, guided, regulated and controlled by forces other than those available to the organization." (p. xxiii) Appendixes list dates and location of CMEA Summit meetings.

140. ———, **Integrating Eastern Europe into the Global Economy: Convertibility through a Payments Union**. Dordrecht: Kluwer Academic, 1991. xv, 262 p. *International Studies in Economics and Econometrics, v.25*, ISBN: 0792313526. Includes bibliographical references (p. 237-249) and index.

Van Brabant intends this book to be "a modest contribution into the ongoing deliberations about how to ease the fairly tight constraints on the external payments of many countries of the eastern part of Europe."(p. vii) In doing so he explains several angles. 1)"The disintegration of the postwar framework for economic cooperation"; 2) The disarray brought about by incisive economic transposition"; and 3) "Various national, regional, and international interest groups" at work there. (p. vii) He covers the prevailing socioeconomic situation, the collapse and dissolution of the CMEA, economic union in Eastern Europe, paths to convertibility, technical aspects of a payment union, macroeconomic surveillance and the transition, downside risks of a payments union, and enlarging the European economic space.

141. ———, **The Planned Economies and International Economic Organizations.** Cambridge: Cambridge University Press, 1991. xv, 318 p. *Soviet and East European Studies, 77*, ISBN: 0521383501. Includes bibliographical references (p. 284-300) and index.

Van Brabant's monograph is an inquiry into the desirability and feasibility of finding a way to enable centrally planned economies (CPE) around the world, Asian as well as European, to became more closely associated with the world economies, trading, monetary and financial frameworks. The book is divided into five chapters. Chapter one examines the period 1941-1947 and the war time planning for a new economic order. Chapter two reviews the basic features of the CPEs, their economic organization and management. Chapter three reviews the key features of international monetary arrangements and zeroes in on Eastern Europe in particular. Chapter four summarizes the role that CPEs have and have not played in the international trading system, especially GATT. The final (fifth) chapter makes recommendations for reform and reconstruction of international economic relations.

142. ———, **Remaking Eastern Europe: On the Political Economy of Transition.** Dordrecht: Kluwer Academic Publishers, 1990. xiv, 223 p. *International Studies in Economics and Econometrics, v. 23*, ISBN: 0792309553. Includes bibliographical references (p. 201-210) and index.

Van Brabant presents a detailed analysis of the state of Eastern Europe economic affairs for the period of 1985-1990. He maintains that recent political and economic events have created a framework within which the centrally planned economies of Eastern Europe could be analyzed. He tries to answer the difficult question of how these countries can solicit and manage regional and international support for abandoning centrally planned economies. His study is not confined to the economics of such a transition, but to the politics of transition as well. The author, with some recognition of irony, suggests that the CMEA itself can be a vehicle for helping these countries make this difficult transition. The CMEA, after all, is a regional cooperative. Van Brabant examines realistically the past difficulties of CMEA cooperation, the various reform proposals that have been offered, the possibilities for east-west assistance, the idea of a Marshall Plan for Eastern Europe, the crucial issue of property rights and privatization, the possible remaking of the CMEA, and the relation of these economies to the global economic system.

143. **Economic Adjustment and Reform in Eastern Europe and the Soviet Union: Essays in Honor of Franklyn D. Holzman,** edited by Josef C. Brada, Ed A. Hewett and Thomas A. Wolf. Durham, N.C.: Duke University Press, 1988. xxv, 428 p. *Duke Press Policy Studies, 0020-6555*, ISBN: 0822308525. Includes bibliography (p. 401-417) and index.

This festschrift for Franklyn D. Holzman consists of fifteen essays in five parts. The entire work deals in one way or another with economic reform in the Soviet Union and Eastern Europe and the prospect for the integration of these centrally planned economies with the larger varied economy. Part one is an overview of economic stabilization, structural adjustment and economic reform in this area. Part two describes macroeconomic stabilization, especially in Hungary and Yugoslavia. Part three deals with structural adjustment and intra-CMEA economic relations. Part four focuses on the role of the centrally planned economies in the IMF, the World Bank and GATT. Finally part five gives more detailed views of economic systems and reforms, especially in Hungary, Poland and the Soviet Union. A bibliography of the works of Franklyn D. Holzman is included in the volume.

144. **Socialist Agriculture in Transition: Organizational Response to Failing Performance,** edited by Josef C. Brada and Karl-Eugen Wadekin. Boulder, Colo.: Westview Press, 1988. ix, 445 p. *Westview Special Studies on the Soviet Union and Eastern Europe, 0163-6057*, ISBN: 0813373441. Includes bibliographies.

A collection of essays on agriculture in socialist countries around the world. The volume includes sections on Poland, Hungary, East Germany, Yugoslavia, China and the USSR with general discussion on the future of agriculture, international trade, and resource allocation in agricultural development. "Because of altered investment priorities, policymakers in socialist countries can no longer increase the resources devoted to agriculture as they have in the past. One approach has been to change the structure of socialist agriculture and to foster organizational changes within agricultural units. The contributors to this volume evaluate such reforms and weigh their implications for agricultural output and trade." (iii)

145. Brus, Wlodzimierz, and Kazimierz Laski, **From Marx to Market: Socialism in Search of an Economic System**. New York: Oxford University Press, 1989. 177 p. ISBN: 0198233027. Includes bibliographical references (p. 153-168) and index.

In this book the authors reappraise their stand with regard to socialism as an economic system. The eleven chapters are arranged in four parts: Marxist socialism—the promise; real socialism—the disappointments; market socialism—the problems so far; and market socialism—the problems ahead.

146. **The Origins of Backwardness in Eastern Europe: Economics and Politics From the Middle Ages Until the Early Twentieth Century,** edited with an introduction by Daniel Chirot. Berkeley: University of California Press, 1988. ix, 260 p. ISBN: 0520064216. Includes bibliographical references.

This volume contains papers of a conference held in 1985 on the causes of backwardness in Eastern Europe. Papers cover such topics as the causes and consequences of backwardness, comparisons with Western Europe, agrarian systems, the Polish economy and evolution of dependency, tradition and rural change in Southeastern Europe, Balkan backwardness, and the social origins of East European politics. Reviews: *Canadian Slavonic Papers* 32, no.1 (March 1990): 102-103. *Journal of Economic History* 50, no.1 (March 1990): 962-963. *American Political Science Review* 84, no.4 (December 1990): 1426-1428. *Journal of Interdisciplinary History* 21, no.2 (Autumn 1990): 337-340.

147. **The Emergence of Market Economies in Eastern Europe,** edited by Christopher Clague and Gordon C. Rausser. Cambridge, Mass.: Blackwell Publishers, 1992. x, 352 p. ISBN: 1557863342. Includes bibliographical references (p. 333-345) and index.

The essays in this volume are the result of a March, 1991 conference held in Prague. The contributors are grouped into five sections focusing on the difficulties of transition, macroeconomic policy, government policy and the private sector, privatization and conclusions. While a variety of topics is discussed, the participants commonly return to a discussion of the value of privatizing large state enterprises. An extensive bibliography is included.

148. **Comrades Go Private: Strategies for Eastern European Privatization,** edited by Michael P. Claudon and Tamar L. Gutner. New York: New York University Press, 1992. x, 179 p. *Geonomics Institute for International Economic Advancement series,* ISBN: 081474595. Includes index.

In addition to dealing with privatization and the reform process in Eastern Europe two other questions are addressed: "To what extent, if at all, does German reunification offer a privatization model for the remainder of Eastern Europe? And why have Poland and Hungary, and to a lesser extent Czechoslovakia, chosen speed over concerns about social justice in the privatization process?" (p. x) The papers are in two parts. Part one contains individual essays on privatization in individual countries. Part two presents working group reports on German reunification, Eastern European reform and the creation of capital markets.

149. Collins, Susan Margaret, and Dani Rodrik, **Eastern Europe and the Soviet Union in the World Economy**. Washington, D.C.: Institute for International Economics, 1991. xiii, 152 p. *Policy Analysis in International Economics, no. 32*, ISBN: 0881321575. Includes bibliography (p. 151-152).

With the countries of Eastern Europe entering the world economy there is an urgent need to evaluate the impact this will have. The present book "assesses the likely effects of the emerging market economies on world trade and capital flows, and through them on such key variables as interest rates and growth in developing countries. Implications are derived for the United States, Germany, the European Community as a whole, Japan, and different sets of developing nations." (p. xi) The authors provide an overview and road map in an introductory chapter and then proceed to evaluate the consequences for international trade, capital flows, and macroeconomic performance. They conclude by speculating on policy implications.

150. **Power, Purpose, and Collective Choice: Economic Strategy in Socialist States,** edited by Ellen Comisso and Laura D'Andrea Tyson. Ithaca, N.Y.: Cornell University Press, 1986. 422 p. *Cornell Studies in Political Economy*, ISBN: 0801419816 (alk. paper); 0801494354 (pbk.: alk. paper). Includes bibliographical references.

Recognizing that the connection between political power and purpose is different from that of the OECD (Organization for Economic Cooperation and Development) states and the NICS (newly industrialized countries) the contributors to this volume proceed to describe analyze and evaluate economic strategy within the European members of the CMEA. Their 14 papers are arranged under four rubrics: Companies' Responses to International Disturbances, Eastern Europe as a Region, Economic Strategy inside the CMEA, and Responding to International Economic Change outside the CMEA. The essays were written based on data available through 1985, thus not privy to the tumultuous changes that would disturb this part of the world in the subsequent half decade. Concluding that economic strategy is related to state structure, but not following it, Comisso states that "even socialism turns out to be much more the governing of men than the administration of things."

151. **Managing Inflation in Socialist Economies in Transition,** edited by Simon Commander. Washington, DC: World Bank, 1991. vii, 271 p. *EDI Seminar Series*, ISBN: 0821317784. Includes bibliographical references and index.

These papers were originally prepared for an Economic Development Institute Senior Policy Seminar in Managing Inflation in Socialist Economies in March of 1990. The authors all recognize that the Central and East Europeans countries have three main tasks: stabilization of their economies, restructuring, and achieving the transition from centrally planned to mixed market economies. The papers focus on the complexity of the interaction between stabilization and economic reform and the role of inflation in that interaction.

152. **Reforming Central and Eastern European Economics; Initial Results and Challenges,** edited by Vittorio Corbo, Fabrizio Coricelli, Jan Bossak. Washington, DC: World Bank, 1991. xiv, 303 p. *A World Bank Symposium*, ISBN: 0821318934. Includes bibliographical references.

Papers presented at the Conference for Adjustment Lending held in Pulutsk, Poland, in October 1990 are collected in this volume. The purpose of the conference was to present examples of the economic development experiences of developing nations that might provide useful information for those trying to deal with the developmental problems in Eastern Europe. "The papers discuss such diverse elements of adjustment as the problems of the macroeconomic stabilization, the development and reform of key markets, and privatization. The book will be of interest to economists, government planners, and policy makers, sociologists, and students of the peoples of Central and Eastern Europe." (back cover) The conference was sponsored by the World Bank.

153. Crane, Keith, **Economic Reform and the Military in Poland, Hungary and China**. Santa Monica, CA: Rand Corporation, 1991. xv, 138 p. *Rand Report, R-3961-PCT*, ISBN: 0833010956. Includes bibliographical references.

"This report is an empirical assessment of the economic reforms of three centrally planned economies: those of Poland, Hungary, and China." (p. iii) All these reforms involved turning from centrally-planned economies to those giving greater emphasis to markets.

154. Csaba, Laszlo, **Eastern Europe in the World Economy**. New York: Cambridge University Press, 1990. 403 p. *Soviet and East European Studies, 68*, ISBN: 0521334268. Includes bibliographical references (p. 375-398) and index.

This volume is a translation, revision and a substantial enlargement of the author's original work published in Hungarian in 1984. "This work—without pretending to be an exclusive or official approach—analyzes the questions of adjustment to the world economy primarily from the point of view of the small nations. It examines the East European countries' external trade policy alternatives and their capability and opportunities for action." (p. 14) The author believes that the Eastern European nations are more vulnerable to economic disturbance caused by market problems arising in the West than in the Soviet Union.

155. **Systemic Change and Stabilization in Eastern Europe,** edited by Laszlo Csaba, with contributions by Anders Aslund et al. Brookfield: Gower, 1991. x, 141 p. ISBN: 1855212048. Includes bibliographical references.

Successful transition strategies were the focus of the papers given at the first international conference of the European Association for Comparative Economic Studies held in Verona in September 1990. Eight of the most significant contributions to that conference are collected in this volume. The contributors have often used the Latin American experience as the model for Eastern Europe. The papers deal with the theoretical issues of the economic problems facing Eastern Europe. Some of the topics covered are currency conversion, sequencing tactics in a transition period, IMF stabilization policies in Latin America and Eastern Europe, Western capital during the transition period and the principles of privatization. This is a theoretical and technical study by a panel of West and East European scholars.

156. **Privatization and Entrepreneurship in Post-Socialist Countries: Economy, Law, and Society,** edited by Bruno Dallago, Gianmaria Ajani, and Bruno Grancelli. New York: St. Martin's, 1992. xiii, 360 p. ISBN: 0312081006. Includes bibliographical references and index.

This discussion of the effects of privatization includes Eastern Europe and Russia. Approximately half the essays focus on Russia, the remainder are devoted to specific problems in Eastern European countries or general problems. Each essay includes a bibliography. The papers were the result of a conference held in Trento Italy in April 1990. The aim of the conference was to compare the experiences of various Eastern European countries. The essays are organized under three headings: "The autonomous sector, entrepreneurship and transition"; "Economic, legal and social problems of ownership transformation"; and "The cooperative movement in the Soviet Union."

157. **Planning in Eastern Europe,** edited by Andrew H. Dawson. New York: St. Martin's Press, 1987. 348 p. *Croom Helm Series in Geography and Environment*, ISBN: 0312614128. Includes bibliographies and index.

This work fills a gap in the literature on Eastern Europe as it describes the achievement of planning the space economy in the countries of the region. The book is of special interest to geographers but is of interest to economists as well. The author does not discuss the mechanics of planning, such as decision making and power structures at length. Dawson focuses on the manner in which spatial problems have been approached. He intends the study to complement other works that have examined the economy in "an spatial manner." He does not concern himself with the politics of the situation. The study begins with a chapter on the economic and political background of the area is then divided into chapters on each country ending with a section on COMECON and the role of planning. Reviews: *Perspective*: R 16, no.3 (May/June/July/August 1987): 81. *Perspective*: R 17, no.1 (Winter 1988): 47.

158. **To Breathe Free: Eastern Europe's Environmental Crisis,** edited by Joan De Bardeleben. Washington, DC: Wilson Center Press, 1991. xiv, 266 p. ISBN: 0943875234 (pbk); 0943875269 (alk. paper). Includes bibliographical references and index.

The papers presented in this volume were originally presented at a conference in 1987. The presenters are environmental specialists from Poland, Czechoslovakia, Hungary, Bulgaria, Yugoslavia, Austria, and West Germany. "They presented papers on the precise extent of air and water pollution in their countries, sometimes also outlining the official policies then in effect to address the grave problems that were apparent even from official East European data." (p. xiii)

159. Dembinski, Pawel H., **The Logic of the Planned Economy: The Seeds of the Collapse,** translated by Kevin Cook. Oxford: Clarendon Press, 1991. x, 249 p. ISBN: 0198286864. Translation of: Les economies planifiees. Includes bibliographical references (p. 235-238) and index.

The purpose of this well organized, clearly written work is to analyze the CPEs (centrally planned economies) from the social science point of view. Dembinski believes it is imperative to conceptualize the "otherness" of such economies, by accurately defining what is meant by such terms as price, money, profit and enterprise within the special environment that the CPEs inhabit. This will remove the "semantic haze" that often obscures western analyses of CPEs. The book's eight chapters are arranged in three sections. The Essence of the System describes how the system works; Internal Dilemmas portrays the role of planning, nature of the enterprise and the function of money. Part 3 External Dilemmas explains the problems of relations in society, the arms race, and trade with the West. Such a structure fulfills the author's two-fold objective of answering the questions: were these inescapable internal contradictions that threatened the system? If the answer were yes then at what critical level would the system collapse? Essentially the author intends to show that there was no way that adherence to Marxist ideology world allow the economic system to reach levels of efficiency necessary to survive the dilemmas identified.

160. Deutsch, Robert, **The Food Revolution in the Soviet Union and Eastern Europe**. Boulder, Colo.: Westview Press, 1986. xxii, 256 p. *Westview Special Studies on the Soviet Union and Eastern Europe, 0163-6057*, ISBN: 0813371619. Includes bibliography (p. 149-241) and indexes.

Besides analyzing the economic performance of the East European socialist economies, Deutsch also examines the ways in which these different economies have attempted to meet the rise in consumer demand, especially for food. In addition to the agricultural economic aspects of the problem, the author also investigates the effect of rising food consumption on international relations.

161. **The Evolution of Economic Systems: Essays in Honour of Ota Sik,** edited by Kurt Dopfer and Karl F. Raible. New York: St. Martin's Press, 1990. xii, 284 p. ISBN: 0312044976. Includes bibliographical references and index.

This festschrift for Ota Sik, a Czechoslovak-born economist who immigrated to the West in the late 1960s, focus on several aspects of economic theory and practice. Individual contributions are grouped in five parts: interdisciplinary views of economic evolution, the evolution of market systems: principal aspects. The evolution of market systems: reproduction, institutions and government planning; the evolution of planning systems: general evolution, and the evolution of planning systems: evolution as reforms in Eastern countries (Russia, Czechoslovakia, Hungary, China).

162. **Privatization in the Transition to a Market Economy: Studies of Preconditions and Policies in Eastern Europe,** edited by John S. Earle, Roman Frydman, and Andrzej Rapaczynski. New York: St. Martin's Press, 1993. vi, 221 p. ISBN: 0312094620. Includes bibliographical references and index.

This collection of essays seeks to familiarize the Western reader with the economic conditions that have hampered and aided in the move to a market economy in Eastern Europe. The contributors attempt to show the differences and similarities between the economies of the East European countries. The essays are grouped into three sections on preconditions, privatization and the stock market. The situations in Hungary, Poland, Czechoslovakia and Romania are discussed.

163. Enderlyn, Allyn, **Cracking Eastern Europe: Everything Marketers Must Know to Sell into the World's Newest Emerging Markets.** Chicago: Probus, 1992. xxi, 385 p. ISBN: 1557382549. Includes bibliographical references and index.

This book is intended for those persons planning to enter the East European marketplace. After a brief introductory chapter on investing in Eastern Europe, individual chapters are devoted to Albania, Bulgaria, Czechoslovakia, Hungary, Poland, Romania, and Yugoslavia, as well as the territory of the former East Germany. Within each chapter information about the geographical and historical background, demographics, the political/institutional infrastructure, trade flows, policies to attract new business, methods of approaching the market, the investment climate, financing and capital markets, licensing, patents, and trademarks, and visiting and locating are given. In addition, names, addresses, telephone numbers and other relevant information is provided for key contacts in each country.

164. Flakierski, Henryk, **Economic Reform & Income Distribution: A Case Study of Hungary and Poland.** New York: M. E. Sharpe, 1986. xi, 194 p. ISBN: 0873323718. Bibliography: p. 165-194.

"In this book the relationship between economic reforms and changes in the degree of inequality will be examined. In particular, the analysis will focus on whether or not the increased use of the market mechanism in some Eastern European countries has changed the pattern of income distribution in those countries." (p. vii) Flakierski focuses on economic conditions in Hungary and Poland from 1965 to 1980 in his study. He hopes to fill a gap in the existing economic literature by examining the situation in these countries which represent extremes on the developmental scale: Hungary with the most advanced market mechanism and Poland with a virtually stagnant market system. The five topical chapters provide a theoretical overview, a discussion of wage differentiation in socialist countries, and a statistical analysis of the dispersion of earnings and household income in Hungary and Poland. Statistical data are provided in the appendices.

165. **The Privatization Process in Central Europe,** Roman Frydman, Andrzej Rapaczynski, John S. Earle, et al. Budapest: Central European University Press, 1993. xiii, 262 p. *CEY Privatization Reports; v. 1,* ISBN: 1858660009.

This volume was issued by the Central European University in Prague. It is one in a series of reports on privatization. The reports aim at exchanging information during this period of economic transformation in the region. This report contains sections on Bulgaria, Czechoslovakia, Hungary, Poland and Romania. Each section contains information on the economic environment, present forms of ownership, privatization and corporatization. The authors present much information formerly unavailable to policy makers and business people. The volume is clearly arranged but does not include an index.

166. **Economic Reforms in Eastern Europe and the Soviet Union,** edited by Hubert Gabrisch. Boulder, CO: Westview Press, 1989. viii, 214 p. *Westview Special Studies in International Economics, Yearbook—Vienna Institute for Comparative Economic Studies, 1-1988*, ISBN: 0813376521. Includes bibliography (p. 166-169).

Aiming to contribute to the assessment of general and national factors that help or hinder the economic transition from a Stalinist to a democratic order, this collection of ten essays focuses on the problems and characteristics of the reform movement that took place from 1981-1988. The book is divided into three parts: I-Basic Thinking about the Problem; II-Comity studies, which examines the Soviet Union, Bulgaria, Czechoslovakia, Hungary and Poland; and III-Special Areas of Reform, i.e. the banking system among CMEA countries and foreign trade and joint ventures. In the 80s the main difference from earlier periods is that the Soviet Union is supporting these reforms. The basic problem is common among these centrally planned economies: how to design a system that is to protect against unemployment and at the same time to bolster the chronically underutilized production capabilities. The theme of this work centers on the problems and characteristics of this latest reform movement.

167. Gelb, Alan H., and Cheryl W. Gray, **The Transformation of Economies in Central and Eastern Europe: Issues, Progress, and Prospects**. Washington, D.C.: World Bank, 1991. v, 74 p. *Policy and Research Series, 1013-3429, 17*, ISBN: 0821318705. Includes bibliographical references (p. 72-74).

This brief study is one in the Policy and Research Series issued by the World Bank. However the authors state in the Introduction that their emphasis is not on the role of the World Bank but on the countries of Central and Eastern Europe. "This paper first reviews the legacies of the previous economic system and analyzes the task of transformation toward a private market economy. Against this backdrop, it then surveys important issues that have arisen and lessons of experience to date in the transformation process. Six annexes explore selected topics—trade, privatization, agriculture, the financial sector, fiscal policy, and poverty and social safety nets—in greater depth. Annex 7 summarizes World Bank Group activities in the CEE countries." (p.1)

168. **Towards a Market Economy in Central and Eastern Europe**, Herbert Giersch, ed. New York: Springer-Verlag, 1991. vii, 168 p. ISBN: 0387539220. Includes bibliographical references and index.

The papers collected in this volume were the result of a conference held in 1990 at the Egon-Sohmen Foundation. The conference participants focused on issues related to the change to a market economy such as the speed at which that change could be accomplished, was the shift to a market economy irreversible, what role does privatization play and how quickly can it be achieved, how long should the transition phase last, should outside aid be accepted? The nine essays in this collection each focus on one of the East European nations and its special problems in the transition.

169. Gomulka, Stanislaw, **Growth, Innovation and Reform in Eastern Europe**. Brighton: Wheatsheaf, 1986. x, 305 p. ISBN: 0745000339. Includes bibliographical references and index.

These essays focus on economic growth, efficiency and innovation in the economies of Eastern Europe and the USSR. The book is in three parts. Part one contains studies on the relationship among socialism, capitalism and innovation. Part two explores industrialization, growth, and growth slowdown. Part three analyzes crisis and reform and is concerned primarily with Poland. Nine of these essays have been published previously.

170. **Finance in Eastern Europe**, edited by D.H. Gowland. Aldershot, England: Ashgate Pub. Co., 1992. ix, 134 p. ISBN: 185521251X. Includes bibliographical references (p. 122-129) and index.

"The purpose of this volume is to analyse the role of the financial system in four economies: Hungary, Poland, Yugoslavia and the former German Democratic Republic (GDR). They have been selected because in these economies and these economies alone, a major attempt has been made at marketisation.... Hence, this book can look at the role of the financial system in a Stalinist economy, during the half-hearted reform of the later Communist period and in the attempts of the new Post-Communist governments." (p. 1-2) In the first chapter the general context of economic change is considered from the Western points of view. The remaining chapters focus on the economic environments of the various countries under consideration. A range of statistical data is provided with each chapter.

171. **Tourism and Economic Development in Eastern Europe and the Soviet Union,** edited by Derek R. Hall. New York: Co-published in the U.S. by Wiley, 1991. xvii, 321 p. ISBN: 0470217588. Includes bibliographical references (p. 296-315) and index.

In the past, there has been little data available to those who wish to compare tourism in the West and in the socialist countries. This collection of essays begins to fill that gap. "It sought to provide both an overview and summary of basic trends within Eastern Europe and the Soviet Union, while also permitting country specialists to undertake a more detailed assessment of tourism and economic development in each of the nine states of the region." (p. xv) The volume is arranged in three parts beginning with a section describing trends in tourism in Eastern Europe and the Soviet Union. The second part consists of country studies by a variety of scholars discussing tourism in each country, statistical data on tourism, domestic and international tourism, environmental impact on tourism, impact of Glasnost on tourism. The final section is a discussion of future trends in the area of tourism.

172. **Red Multinationals or Red Herrings?: The Activities of Enterprises from Socialist Countries in the West,** edited by Geoffrey Hamilton. New York: St. Martin's Press, 1986. xi, 202 p. ISBN: 031266656X. Includes bibliographical references and index.

Since the 1960s there has been a growing number of enterprises of Eastern bloc countries that have undertakings in the West and in developing countries. The essays in this book attempt to describe the nature and the extent of the companies in order to determine whether they are multinational enterprises in the Western sense of the term. After an introduction that discusses the nature of multinationals, there follows several case studies of these enterprises in the United Kingdom, Ireland, Sweden, West Germany, Austria, and in developing countries. In concluding, suggestions for future research are offered.

173. **Planned Economies: Confronting the Challenges of the 1980s,** edited by John P. Hardt and Carl H. McMillan. New York: Cambridge University Press, 1988. xiv, 191 p. ISBN: 0521344611. Includes bibliographical references and index.

These nine essays, all presented at the Third World Congress for Soviet and East European Studies, are arranged in three sections. Section one deals with new conditions of economic management (investment, self-financing, and information and computers). Section two concerns structural changes in the national resource sector (especially energy resources) and section three tackles problems of national and international integration.

174. **Dismantling the Command Economy in Eastern Europe,** edited by Peter Havlik. Boulder, CO: Westview Press, 1991. ix, 280 p. *Vienna Institute for Comparative Economic Studies Yearbook, 3*, ISBN: 0813381371. Includes bibliographical references.

The sixteen essays by various contributors of this volume are divided into three parts: in part one, the general issues section, the two essays deal with various issues in the transition from command economies to market economies and to exchange economies. In part two, selected aspects of transition, the focus is on money and monetary policy, exchange rate policies and convertibility, east-west economic relations, energy prospects, and unemployment and social security measures. Part three, country specific transition policies, covers Bulgaria, Czechoslovakia, GDR, Hungary, Poland, Soviet Union and Yugoslavia. Romania is not examined in part three but is covered under various topics in part two. The material presented in this yearbook offers current data and opinion as of 1991, prior to the collapse of the Soviet Union.

175. **The Transition from Socialism in Eastern Europe: Domestic Restructuring and Foreign Trade,** edited by Arye L. Hillman and Branko Milanovic. Washington: World Bank, 1992. vi, 345 p. *World Bank Regional and Sectoral Studies,* ISBN: 082132148X. Includes bibliographical references.

This publication, issued by the World Bank, contains essays focusing on two arenas of economic change in Eastern Europe: domestic restructuring and foreign trade. The essays are grouped under these two general headings. There are two general conclusions that emerge from the discussions in the first part. The essays on reform in general, employee ownership, China as a model, and the paths taken by Yugoslavia, Hungary and Poland all lead to the conclusion that eliminating central planning is only the first stage of reform. It must be accompanied by privatization on a national scale if these countries are to succeed. In the second part dealing with foreign trade, a variety of topics are discussed including payment plans, and technology transfer. Each essay included a bibliography.

176. Holzman, Franklyn D., **The Economics of Soviet Bloc Trade and Finance.** Boulder: Westview Press, 1987. xi, 215 p. ISBN: 0813372747. Includes bibliographical references and index.

Professor Holzman explores the transition in Soviet bloc economies over the past fifteen years from balanced hard-currency trade to large deficits with the West and the consequent development of a huge hard-currency debt. The author challenges the notion that the USSR is subsidizing trade with its CMEA partners. He also examines the causes and presents possible solutions for the chronic problems related to currency inconvertibility, rigid bilateralism and the inability to use exchange rates.

177. Inotai, Andras, **Regional Integrations in the World Economic Environment,** translated by Karoly Kerepesi. Budapest: Akademia Kiado, 1986. vii, 286 p. ISBN: 9630543532. Includes bibliographical references.

A study of the world economic environment is presented in this volume. While not specifically on Eastern Europe, this analysis is the work of a Hungarian economist, giving a socialist view of world economic development. "It analyzes the dynamic of intraregional trade, the interrelations between common industrial policies and world wide competitiveness, the chances and limitations of monetary cooperation, etc. in order to determine just what position the regional economic integrations really occupy in today's new world economic network, in which the division of labor has become more international than ever before." (back cover)

178. Institute for EastWest Studies. Task Force on Western Assistance to Transition in the Czech and Slovak Federal Republic, Hungary and Poland, **Moving Beyond Assistance: Final Report of the IEWS Task Force on Western Assistance to Transition in the Czech and Slovak Federal Republic, Hungary and Poland,** written by Krzysztof Ners et al. Rev. ed. New York: Institute for EastWest Studies, 1992. v, 80 p. ISBN: 0813386470. Includes bibliographical references.

In this report the Institute for EastWest Studies evaluates the programs of Western assistance to the Czech and Slovak Federal Republic, Hungary and Poland. The purpose of the report is to assess Western assistance programs in terms of the donors, as well as the recipients and make recommendations for the future. The major recommendation of this report was the creation of the Assistance Coordination Council which would coordinate efforts for economic transition in the Czech and Slovak Federal Republic, Hungary and Poland. This brief report, the product of one year of research, presents the reader with one proposal being put forward to smooth the way to transition to a market economy in Central Europe.

179. Jeffries, Ian, **A Guide to the Socialist Economies**. New York: Routledge, 1990. xxii, 322 p. ISBN: 0415007461. Includes bibliographical references and index.

"The basic aim of this book is to give the reader some idea of the rich variety of economic systems to be found among socialist countries today and to highlight and explain some of the major problems facing them." (p. xiii) Since all these economies either adopted or had the Soviet system imposed on them, it starts with an analysis of the Soviet system and proceeds to the communist economies of Eastern Europe and Asia.

180. Johnson, Paul M., **Redesigning the Communist Economy: The Politics of Economic Reform in Eastern Europe**. New York: Columbia University Press, 1989. vi, 281 p. *East European Monographs, no. 270*, ISBN: 0880331674. Includes bibliographical references.

Written before the fall of communism, this book examines the course of economic reform in Eastern Europe from the 1960s through the late 1980s. Topics covered include previous models of socialist economic organization; economic reform, elite conflict and the leadership factor; political impact of the economic reforms, and economic reform in the Gorbachev era. Review: *Journal of Baltic Studies* 21, no.2 (Summer 1990): 164-165.

181. Jonas, Paul, **Essays on the Structure and Reform of Centrally Planned Economic Systems**. Boulder, Colorado: Social Sciences Monographs, Distributed by Columbia University Press, 1990. xx, 211 p. *East European Monographs, no. 275, Atlantic Studies on Society in Change, no. 62*, ISBN: 0880331720.

In these essays, Jonas shows with analytical tools how the Soviet revolutionaries tried to make the ideology of scientific socialism operational. The essays fall into two groups: those concentrating on the structure and growth of the Soviet economic system and those dealing with reform and integration into the world economic system, especially the European Economic Community. Specific topics include examination of the structural price mechanism, the dynamics of the Soviet development path, black market proliferation, interstructural trade and economic integration, joint ventures, economy convertibility and the Gerschenkron effect.

182. **East-West Agricultural Trade,** edited by James R. Jones. Boulder, Colo.: Westview Press, 1986. xvii, 256 p. *Westview Special Studies in International Economics and Business*, ISBN: 081337135X. Includes bibliographies.

This is "the first study of Jones specifically on the economics of agricultural trade issues in centrally planned economies, [and] certain recent findings of economists who have examined the decision making processes and trends that relate to agricultural trade with the West by Eastern Europe, the Soviet Union, and China. Future prospects for agricultural trade with these countries are considered, as are the bilateral trading relations between these countries and the United States." (frontispiece)

183. **Wealth Creation in Eastern Europe: Financial Management Issues and Strategies**. Fred R. Kaen, Ike Mathur, editors. New York: International Business Press, 1992. 128 p. ISBN: 1560243058. Includes bibliographical references and index.

The four papers in this volume were originally published in the *Journal of Multinational Financial Management* (Vol. I, No. 4). All deal with various aspects of the transformation of the East European economies. The first discusses the public cost of German Unifications. The second looks at how privatization has affected the economies of the East European nations. Next, the effects of joint ventures on stock markets are analyzed. The final paper turns to the subject of currency convertibility. While each paper presents a unique perspective on its subject, several common themes can be found in each essay: 1) the difficulty of placing a value on state run enterprises and deciding if they should survive; 2) the need for a legal system that considers the problems of a market economy and private ownership; 3) the absence of "accounting information"; 4) the difficulty in gaining social acceptance of a capitalist system.

184. **Reform in Foreign Economic Relations of Eastern Europe and the Soviet Union: Proceedings of a Symposium Conducted in Association with Osteuropa-Institut, Munich and Sudost-Institut, Munich,** edited by Michael Kaser and Aleksander M. Vacic. New York: United Nations Economic Commission for Europe, 1991. xii, 202 p. *Economic Studies no. 2*, ISBN: 9211165024. Includes bibliographical references.

"This volume contains the papers prepared for or resulting out of the International Symposium on Reforms in Foreign Economic Relations of Eastern Europe and the Soviet Union which took place between 29 August and 2 September 1990 in Wirdbad Kreuth near Munich, Federal Republic of Germany and was organized by the United Economic Commission for Europe." (p. xi) Three topics were the focus of the conference: the institutional framework of foreign economic relations, economic relations with market economies, and economic relations with CMEA countries. These three topics form the three sections of the volume. Each section includes essays on the individual East European countries and Eastern Europe as an economic bloc.

185. **The Road to Capitalism: Economic Transformation in Eastern Europe and the Former Soviet Union,** edited by David Kennett and Marc Lieberman. Fort Worth, TX: The Dryden Press, 1992. xi, 367 p. ISBN: 0030963745. Includes bibliographical references.

This volume "provides a comprehensive overview of economic transformation in Eastern Europe. While media coverage has concentrated on day-to-day events, this reader gives insight into the process of economic change, explaining why central planning failed, why the market may offer a way out, what a successful transformation must accomplish, and how a nation should go about it." The reader contains 37 articles by contemporary scholars.

186. **Trials of Transition: Economic Reform in the Former Communist Bloc,** edited by Michael Keren and Gur Ofer. Boulder, Colo.: Westview Press, 1992. xx, 308 p. ISBN: 0813315654. Includes bibliographical references and indexes.

This collection of essays looks at various aspects of economic transition in the former communist countries of Eastern Europe. Topics include an essay by Joseph Berliner on socialism in the Twenty-First Century, democracy at odds with the market, popular efforts toward self-government, forced savings and monetary overhang, stabilization and restructuring, Polish economic reform, the currency union, privatization, factory ownership, regional economic cooperation, and the transition from the CMEA system of international trade.

187. **From Socialism to Market Economy: The Transition Problem**, William S. Kern. Kalamazoo, MI: Upjohn Institute for Employment Research, 1992. v, 134 p. ISBN: 0880991291. Includes bibliographical references and index.

This collection of six papers originally given as a series of lectures, examines the Soviet economic legacy in Russia and Eastern Europe. The authors discuss obstacles to change, reform under Gorbachev, restructuring the planned economy, Soviet bureaucracy, Soviet economic reform and the economic transformation of Eastern Europe. While the changes in Eastern Europe and Russia have continued since these papers were written, the authors feel they still provide insight into the possible developments of the future.

188. Kiezun, Witold, **Management in Socialist Countries: USRR and Central Europe**. New York: W. de Gruyter, 1991. xiii, 375 p. *De Gruyter Studies in Organization, 27*, ISBN: 3110106701. Includes bibliographical references (p. 341-361) and indexes.

In this book the author intends "to concentrate on a praxiological analysis of management organization in socialist systems. [His] considerations in this field include both historical analysis of the development of socialist organization and management theories and their realization in practice." (p. vii) Special emphasis is given to Poland and the Soviet Union.

189. Kikeri, Sunita, **Privatization: The Lessons of Experience**, Sunita Kikeri, John Nellis, Mary Shirley. Washington, D.C.: World Bank, 1992. iv, 86 p. ISBN: 0821321811. Includes bibliographical references (p. 83-86).

Privatization as an aspect of development has become extremely important for formerly socialist countries. "This book reviews the experience of countries with state-owned enterprises and with the privatization of these enterprises." (p. 1) The book covers the question why privatize, the objectives and strategy for privatization, implementation and a brief examination of privatization performance and continuing obstacles in Eastern Europe and Central Asia.

190. **Socialist Economies in Transition: Appraisals of the Market Mechanism,** edited by Mark Knell and Christine Rider. Brookfield, Vt.: E. Elgar Pub., 1992. ix, 245 p. ISBN: 1852784385. Includes bibliographical references and index.

Instead of relying on the official line from post-communist countries regarding the transition process to market economies, this book takes a more critical approach. In a series of essays by different authors, this volume provides a historical background to the Soviet strategy of economic growth and crisis, theoretical justifications for introducing market-oriented reforms, differences in the ways socialist and capitalist systems operate, the impact of the "shock therapy" program in Poland, privatization, monetary issues, and new planning approaches.

191. Kolodko, Grzegorz W., **Hyperinflation and Stabilization in Postsocialist Economies**, Grzegorz W. Kolodko, Danuta Gotz-Kozierkiewicz, Elzbieta Skrzeszewska-Paczek. Boston: Kluwer Academic Publishers, 1992. xv, 186 p. *International Studies in Economic and Econometrics, v. 26*, ISBN: 0792391799. Includes bibliographical references (p. 179-184).

This is the first book to examine the topic of hyperinflation in the post-socialist economies. "Documented comparative studies go behind political rhetoric to reveal the inner workings of reforms instituted in countries as diverse as Poland, Yugoslavia and Vietnam. Conditions of stabilizing policy are outlined to provide a detailed look at fiscal and monetary programs initiated by different governments." (back cover) After presenting general assumptions about stabilization programs and some background in postsocialist economies the authors examine the problem and its treatment in Yugoslavia, Poland, and Vietnam in separate essays. The final chapter provides comparative analysis. An "annex" presents data on economic stabilization in Israel. While the book lacks an index, it does contain a lengthy bibliography.

192. **Economic Development in the Habsburg Monarchy and in the Successor States: Essays,** edited by John Komlos. New York: Columbia University Press, 1990. vi, 368 p. *East European Monographs, no. 280*, ISBN: 0880331771. Includes bibliographical references (p. 317-367).

The essays gathered here are the second collection of studies on this theme. Contributed papers cover various aspects of economic development.

193. Kornai, Janos, **Contradictions and Dilemmas: Studies on the Socialist Economy and Society,** translated by Ilona Lukacs et al. Cambridge, Mass.: MIT Press, 1986. ix, 165 p. ISBN: 0262111071. Translation of: Ellentmondasok es dilemmak. Includes bibliography (p. 161-165).

The author explores several facets of socialist economies including shortages, hard and soft budget constraints, paternalism, economics and psychology, Hungarian economic reform, socialist ethics, and the health of nations.

194. **Reform and Transformation in Eastern Europe: Soviet-Type Economics on the Threshold of Change,** edited by Janos Matyas Kovacs and Marton Tardos. London: Routledge in association with the Institut fur die Wissenschaften vom Menschen, Vienna, 1992. xix, 345 p. ISBN: 0415066301. Includes bibliographical references and index.

These collected essays are arranged in three parts. Part one contains papers on reform economics and economic theory and the West. Part two looks at reform economics and economic theory and the East: the incomplete separation from Stalinism. Part three focuses on the current state of reform. "The papers in this collection demonstrate not only the cumulative radicalization and professionalization of reform thinking in the past decades but also the seamy side of reform economics, that is, the imperfect understanding on the part of the reformers of modern economic science in the West, the inhibited separation from Stalinism and the built-in obstacles to destroying a sophisticated theory of transformation." (p. xvii)

195. Koves, Andras, **Central and East European Economies in Transition: The International Dimension**. Boulder, Colo.: Westview Press, 1992. xi, 150 p. ISBN: 081331643X. Includes bibliographical references (p. 133-138) and index.

Andras Koves, in this study of economic reform in Eastern Europe, focuses on foreign economic policies which he believes are particularly important given the past isolation of the CMEA states. "He contends that 'Joining Europe' and being integrated into the international economy are pivotal for stabilization and transformation but that inherent structural weaknesses and enormous foreign debt will make economic reorientation an extremely difficult undertaking." (p.139) Koves feels the West must take a central role if the progress is to succeed.

196. Kronenwetter, Michael, **Capitalism vs. Socialism: Economic Policies of the USA and the USSR**. New York: F. Watts, 1986. 103 p. *Economics Impact Book*, ISBN: 0531101525. Includes bibliography (p.97-98).

This book serves as a primer to introduce the two major economic systems in the world today, capitalism and socialism. The author successively gives a brief history of the forerunners of capitalism, its emergence, the response of socialism to it, contrasts between the two systems and a chapter each devoted to a description of two countries where these systems are most highly visible today, the United States and the Soviet Union. A concluding chapter portrays other economic systems and a discussion of the world economy. This book is intended to be only a brief introduction to the topic.

197. **Creating Capital Markets in Eastern Europe,** edited by John R. Lampe. Washington, D.C.: Woodrow Wilson Center Press, 1992. xi, 114 p. *Woodrow Wilson Center Special Studies*, ISBN: 0943875420. Includes bibliographical references and index.

This volume is a collection of papers drawn from a conference of the same title which was held in Bulgaria in 1991. There were four main topics at the conference all of which are represented in the papers of this volume. They are: the pre-1945 financial history of Eastern Europe and the major Western capital markets; the progress of privatization; the role of stock markets; and the structure of commercial and investment banking. All the essays included in this volume support two general conclusions. "First, the slow pace of privatization must be accelerated if the transition to a market economy is to succeed during this decade. Second, a commercial banking system restructured along continental lines offers a better prospect for such an acceleration than do dominant stock markets based on the Anglo-American model." (p. 2)

198. Lavigne, Marie, **International Political Economy and Socialism,** translated by David Lambert. Cambridge, England: Cambridge University Press, 1991. 412 p. ISBN: 0521334276; 0521336635 (pbk). Translation of: Economie internationale des pays socialistes. Includes bibliographical references (p. 394-409) and index.

Lavigne identifies three trading areas: technology, energy and agriculture—upon which depends the future of Eastern Europe in world trade and finance. In nine chapters she then explains whether trade within Comecon will expand or contract, what weight political features will have and other questions relating to these issues. She has added a 1990 postscript in order to try to give the most recent perspectives on the effect of political change in 1989.

199. Lindsay, Margie, **Developing Capital Markets in Eastern Europe: A Business Reference**. New York: New York University Press, 1992. xii, 304 p. ISBN: 0814750672. Includes bibliographical references (p. 302-304).

This source on the economic changes in Eastern Europe is directed at businessmen primarily but may also be of interest to academics. "The book looks at each country in turn, setting into perspective the reform efforts so far. It includes summaries or complete texts of major legislation, and emphasizes the importance privatization plays in the region.

Each chapter summarizes the advancement so far, looking particularly at banking, money and capital markets, insurance, market supervision, emerging stock markets, secondary markets and other relevant topics.

Countries covered include Albania, Bulgaria, Czechoslovakia, Hungary, Poland, Romania and Slovenia" (back cover).

200. **U.S.-East European Trade Directory: An Invaluable Reference for Conducting Business in Poland, Hungary, Czechoslovakia, Yugoslavia, Bulgaria, Romania and Albania**, William S. Loiry editor. Chicago, IL: Probus Pub. Co., 1991. 269 p. ISBN: 1557381917. Includes bibliographical references and index.

"The 1991 *U.S.-East European Trade Directory* is designed to provide American business with the information and contacts needed to successfully enter the East European marketplace. The myriad of consultants, attorneys, government agencies, financing sources, and other resources listed here will help you plot a course for trading victory." (p.11) The book is divided into three main sections. The first, "U.S. Resources," is subdivided into areas of special interest: consultants, law firms, U.S. government resources, financing, advertising, insurance agencies, communications, travel organizations, translators, information sources, research centers, etc. Part two, "East European Resources," is divided by country. Within each country section are listed useful addresses and contacts for establishing and operating a business in that area. The last part, "U.S.-East European Trade Yellow Pages," is an alphabetical list of resources with addresses, phone numbers and when available, fax numbers.

201. **The Second Economy in Marxist States,** edited by Maria Los. New York: St. Martin's Press, 1990. xiv, 240 p. ISBN: 0312031122. Includes bibliographical references.

This is a compendium of studies by different investigators of ten Marxist based economies in a comparative perspective. They seek to determine the conditions that gave rise to the second economy as well as the effects such a phenomenon has on the official economy. Review: *Comparative Economic Studies* 32, no.4 (Winter 1990): 114-116.

202. Macesich, George, **Reform and Market Democracy**. New York: Praeger, 1991. xi, 145 p. ISBN: 0275939898. Includes bibliographical references and index.

This book was issued in honor of the thirtieth anniversary of the Center for Yugoslav-American Studies. "This study argues that market democracy offers an organizing principle for reform of Eastern European and other countries currently searching for a model on which to base their drive to a market economy." (p. ix) The author believes that in order for reform to be successful it must be swift and the elements of any reform program must be interdependent. The book is arranged topically discussing the organization principles of market democracy, its historical underpinnings, the role of money, the problems of nationalism, the place of bureaucracy, property rights, privatization and politics in reform.

203. **Foreign Economic Liberalization: Transformations in Socialist and Market Economies,** edited by Paul Marer and Andras Koves. Boulder, CO: Westview Press, 1991. xii, 288 p. ISBN: 0813381983; 0813381991 (pbk). Includes bibliographical references and index.

About one-half of the essays appearing in this book were originally presented at a conference (1989) in Budapest, on the topic Attempts at Liberalization. The other half of the 22 essays have been added since that conference. The focus of the book is the liberalization of market economies and the possibilities for liberalization of socialist economies. The four divisions are tied together by the editor's introductory essay (Part I) which "contrasts economic liberalization in market economies and in the countries of Central and Eastern Europe." It argues why foreign economic liberalization must be part of the transition from centrally planned to market economies and it describes the different approaches taken by Hungary and Poland in this sphere. Part II (10 essays) describes various market economy experiences around the world. Part III (6 essays) explores Hungary's experiences and policy options. Finally, part IV (5 essays) evaluates liberalization in Central and Eastern Europe and China.

204. **The Challenge of Simultaneous Economic Relations with East and West,** edited by Michael Marrese and Sandor Richter. New York: New York University Press, 1990. xviii, 216 p. ISBN: 0814754538. Includes bibliographical references and index.

Papers resulting from a 1988 conference on the "challenge of simultaneous economic relations with East and West" are published in this volume. The participants focused on Austria, Finland, Hungary and Yugoslavia. "The objective of the conference was to identify the kinds of institutions, methods of settling payments, trade patterns, and so forth that have emerged in these four countries that have 'double attachment' to the OECD and the CMEA. Moreover, the comparison was to serve as a device to understand whether, why, and how much these four countries benefited from 'double attachment'." (p. x) The first eleven essays are published in full, while essays 12 through 18 are reprinted in summary form. Some of the essays deal with theoretical issues, for example the trade approach between a market economy and a centrally planned economy but most deal with specific topics. The contributors were scholars and faculty from institutes all over Europe.

205. McKinnon, Ronald I., **The Order of Economic Liberalization: Financial Control in the Transition to a Market Economy**. Baltimore: Johns Hopkins University Press, 1991. xii, 200 p. *Johns Hopkins Studies in Development*, ISBN: 0801841704. Includes bibliography (p. 187-192) and index.

This study deals with transition problems facing less developed countries attempting to switch to a capitalist system from one characterized by government intervention. Only chapters eleven through thirteen deal specifically with socialist systems. Chapter one discusses "the overall order of liberalization." The remaining essays deal with the experiences of other countries such as Chile, Japan, Taiwan, South Korea and other subject areas, protectionism in foreign trade, exchange rate policies, etc. This is a technical study with essays of interest to the specialist.

206. McMillan, Carl H., **Multinationals from the Second World: Growth of Foreign Investment by Soviet and East European Enterprises**. New York: St. Martin's Press, 1987. xvi, 220 p. ISBN: 031255253X. Includes bibliography (p.203-210) and indexes.

Direct investment by East European countries in the developing countries exceeds that by Western countries. Professor McMillan "assesses the phenomenon, describing its nature, establishing its quantitative dimensions and explaining its motivations and limitations, as well as identifying its more significant directions." (p. xiii) Also included is an appendix on data and methodology, a glossary of terms used, and an index of company names.

207. Murrell, Peter, **The Nature of Socialist Economies: Lessons from Eastern European Foreign Trade**. Princeton, NJ: Princeton University Press, 1990. xiii, 275 p. ISBN: 0691042462. Includes bibliography (p. 255-266) and index.

An attempt to discover if the paradigm of Western economics being applied to the study of East European economic systems is appropriate. "In answering this question, the book develops new methods for analyzing the comparative value of economic systems and presents new evidence on the nature of the differences between capitalist and socialist economies." (p. 4) This highly theoretical work is based on the Schumpeterian theory of economic behavior. The author relies on foreign trade statistics to discover "behavioral regularities" in socialist economic systems. Chapter 1 presents methodological and theoretical backgrounds. Chapter 2 examines the "mirror data" to be used. Chapter 3 looks at various theories relating trade to the domestic economy. Chapter 4 provides summary statistics from the trade data. Chapters 5, 6 and 7 are devoted to examinations of the data. Several appendices are provided.

208. Palankai, Tibor, **The European Community and Central European Integration: The Hungarian Case**. New York: Westview Press, 1991. iii, 79 p. *Occasional Paper Series, 21*, ISBN: 0813382807; 0913449253. Includes bibliographical references.

"In *The European Community and Central European Integration: The Hungarian Case*, Dr. Tibor Palankai argues that the West can best aid the post communist societies by including them in the process of European integration, and by providing them with the greatest financial and political support possible" (p.i) Dr. Palankai believes it is to the advantage of all European states for East and West Europe to loosen economic restrictions. Economic integration is always to be preferred over isolation in his opinion. This brief study suggests some ways in which integration can be achieved and describes its advantages.

209. Petkov, Krusto, and John E. M. Thirkell, **Labour Relations in Eastern Europe**. New York: Routledge, 1991. xx, 235 p. *Social Analysis*, ISBN: 0415001595. Includes bibliographical references and index.

In the 1980s changes were taking place in Bulgaria's economic organization and its labor relations. This is a collaborative study of how those changes were accomplished. A multidisciplinary theoretical approach was used drawing on organization theory, the sociology of work and on labor relations." (p.xvi) The book is organized in three parts. The first discusses the transfer of the Soviet model of labor relations to Bulgaria. Part two examines Bulgarian economic organization in detail. The final part is a comparative analysis of the redesign of labor relations. "It is the view of both authors that the content of this book will facilitate the understanding of further developments in labor relations as they unfold in both Bulgaria and other countries in Eastern Europe." (p. xvi)

210. Pinder, John, **The European Community and Eastern Europe**. New York: Council on Foreign Relations Press, 1991. vii, 118 p. *Chatham House Papers*, ISBN: 0876091125. Includes bibliographical references (p. 109-118).

This book explores the new economic relations between the European Community and Eastern Europe. It includes several chapters outlining the previous history of this relationship and the new possibilities opened up by the Velvet revolution.

211. **Trade Unions in Communist States,** edited by Alex Pravda and Blair A. Ruble. Boston: Allen & Unwin, 1986. xiii, 281 p. ISBN: 0043311083. Includes bibliographies and index.

The editors hope that these eleven essays fill a lacuna in the literature of comparative surveys of trade unions. By and large such surveys ignore communist trade unions, reasoning that they have little in common with their non-communist counterparts. While communist labor unions mobilize rather than defend labor, they also have the potential of becoming mediating organizations in communist states, albeit under party control. The first essay presents the Leninist model of trade unions. The last chapter provides comparisons and contrasts between communist and capitalist trade unions. The intervening chapters are case studies of trade unions in the USSR, China, Poland, Hungary, the GDR, Czechoslovakia, Romania and Yugoslavia.

212. Prybyla, Jan S., **Market and Plan Under Socialism: The Bird in the Cage.** Stanford, Calif.: Hoover Institution Press, Stanford University, 1987. xv, 348 p. *Hoover Press Publication, 335*, ISBN: 081798352X (pbk); 0817983511 (hard). Includes bibliography (p. 317-335) and index.

Prybyla explores the influence of the classical Stalin plan in the Soviet Union, China, Yugoslavia and Hungary. In part one, concepts, the typology of plan models is described as well as the theoretical foundations of the neoclassical offshoots. In part two he examines in more detail the specifics of those plans such as the role of the collective farm, information, coordination, and motivation as key factors in these plans and how the conceptual base in part one has been realized in China, Hungary and Yugoslavia.

213. Przeworski, Adam, **Democracy and the Market: Political and Economic Reforms in Eastern Europe and Latin America.** Cambridge: Cambridge University Press, 1991. xii, 210 p. *Studies in Rationality and Social Change*, ISBN: 0521412250. Includes bibliographical references (p. 193-205) and indexes.

Noting that we have witnessed a radical break with the past as far as politics and economics are concerned, Przeworski analyzes several fairly recent transitions from authoritarian regimes to various forms of democracy and from centrally-planned economies to market economies. The transitions he examines in Latin America, Central America, and Eastern Europe are both radical and interdependent. Przeworski examines these transitions in order to answer questions about conditions that lead to democracy and material prosperity. After a prologue describing the demise of communism, the chapters cover his theory of durable democratic institutions, the choice of institutions during the transition to democracy, the kinds of economic systems most likely to generate growth in a humane way, the political dynamics of economic reforms, and a conclusion detailing the obstacles usually confronted in building a democracy and transforming economies.

214. **East-West Joint Ventures: The New Business Environment,** edited by Evka Razvigorova and Gottfried Wolf-Laudon. Cambridge, Mass: B. Blackwell, 1991. xviii, 327 p. ISBN: 0631180540. Includes bibliographical references (p. 305-312) and index.

The essays in this volume are intended to explore the daily problems of joint ventures. They are divided into three parts. Part one includes introductory material that puts East-West economic relations in perspective. Part two contains essays that cover joint venture problems in specific countries. Part three looks at the promise of joint ventures as a tool for technology transfer and as a bridge between East and West. An appendix includes eleven case studies from the countries covered.

215. Redor, Dominique, **Wage Inequalities in East and West,** translated by Rosemarie Bourgault. Cambridge, England: Cambridge University Press, 1992. xiii, 216 p. ISBN: 2735104486. Translation of: Les inegalites de salaire a l'est et a l'ouest. Includes bibliographical references (p. 205-214) and index.

"This book analyzes wage hierarchy in market and planning theory, and how these theories can be wed as a basis for the comparison of wage structures in Western and Soviet-type systems. The author analyzes statistical data from ten countries in both systems at the beginning of the eighties and attempts to account for wage dispersion by examining such factors as education and training, discrimination against women, and market structure, as well as the influence of systemic factors." (p. iii) Professor Redor finds that the causes of wage inequalities are similar no matter what the political system. The book is divided into two parts. The first compares the features of the wage structures in Eastern and Western economies. Part two analyzes the sources of the similarities between the two. A bibliography and list of statistical sources is included.

216. Reinicke, Wolfgang H., **Building a New Europe: The Challenge of System Transformation and Systemic Reform**. Washington, D.C.: Brookings Institution, 1992. 206 p. ISBN: 0815773919. Includes bibliographical references (p. 167-206).

"In this book, Wolfgang Reinicke examines many of the challenges confronting Europe as it begins a new era. Currently, the countries of Central and Eastern Europe are struggling to build market economies and multiparty democracies, and the European Community is divided on the future courses of integration. Reinicke develops a series of policy recommendations to address these challenges." (back cover) Reinicke discusses the East and West European perspectives in turn and then looks at the prospects for the future. Twenty pages of economic statistics are included in the appendix.

217. Reisinger, William M., **Energy and the Soviet Bloc: Alliance Politics After Stalin**. Ithaca: Cornell University Press, 1992. xiii, 184 p. ISBN: 080142657X. Includes bibliographical references (p. 165-177) and index.

Reisinger uses the analysis of trade in energy resources as a mechanism for studying Soviet-East European relations. His first chapter presents an overview of relations between the East European nations and the Soviet Union and the role of energy policy. Chapter two presents his theoretical approach. In chapter three Professor Reisinger shows how the energy agreements became more complex over time. Chapters four through six provide the reader with statistical data on Soviet exports of fuel to Eastern Europe creating a picture of the pattern of trade relations. In the final chapter, the collapse of the Soviet bloc is discussed. "Energy politics reflected the internal and external changes taking place from the beginning of genuine Soviet-East European relations following Stalin's death to the beginning of the Gorbachev era." (p. xii) Several appendixes of sources and statistical data are included.

218. **The Transition from Command to Market Economies in East-Central Europe,** edited by Sandor Richter. Boulder: Westview Press, 1992. x, 321 p. *The Vienna Institute for Comparative Economic Studies Yearbook; 4,* ISBN: 0813385598.

"The contributors to this volume consider the key factors affecting the economic transition process and analyze strategies for successful reform, especially criticizing the theory and use of 'shock therapy' as a means of accelerating the transition...The authors examine prototypical country-specific problems such as privatization in Hungary, the transformation of the agricultural system in Czechoslovakia, the problems of transition in Bulgaria, and foreign debt in Yugoslavia." (back cover) The volume is dedicated to Kazimierz Laski and a bibliography of his most recent publications is included.

219. **The Role of Competition in Economic Transition,** edited by Christopher T. Saunders. New York: St. Martin's Press, 1993. ix, 245 p. ISBN: 0312091516. Includes bibliographical references and index.

The papers collected in this book are the by-product of a workshop held in April, 1992 and sponsored by the Vienna Institute for Comparative Economic Studies. The essays are grouped under four headings: "Competition: Theories and Conditions," "Eastern Approaches," "Views from the West," and "A Role for International Action." While the subject under review is relevant to all Western economies, the role of competition in Eastern Europe was the focus in light of the degree of change those countries are undergoing. Each part contains a section of comments by participants.

220. Simonovits, Andras, **Cycles and Stagnation in Socialist Economies: A Mathematical Analysis**. Oxford: Blackwell, 1992. xiii, 198 p. ISBN: 0631176799. Includes bibliographical references (p. 185-192) and index.

This macroeconomic study looks at the economic heritage of the socialist nations striving to develop market systems. "In this book I shall examine several macroeconomic problems of the socialist economy from a theoretical point of view. Why and how did investment fluctuate in the 1960s? Why did the growth rate decelerate in the 1970s? What was the reason for stagnation in the 1980s?" (p. vii) The book is divided into two parts: "Investment Cycles" and "Slowdown and Stagnation." While the book does not presume any special knowledge, a familiarity with economic terminology will make it more readily understandable. The author feels that Kornai's book *Growth, Shortage and Efficiency* (1982) was the direct source for this book.

221. **Economic Change in the Balkan States: Albania, Bulgaria, Romania, and Yugoslavia,** edited by Orjan Sjoberg and Michael L. Wyzan. New York: St. Martin's Press, 1991. x, 173 p. ISBN: 0312057350. Includes bibliographical references and index.

These eleven papers are the result of a conference on economic change in the socialist Balkan countries held in June 1990 at the Institute of Soviet and East European Economies, Stockholm School of Economics. All of the authors are of like mind in thinking the Balkans and East Central European countries face similar economic problems. One of the main differences between them however is the prior existence of a civil society in the north, complete with free intellectuals and independent social forces in existence prior to the fall of communism. For real changes to take place in Albania, Bulgaria, and Romania post-totalitarian socialist regimes must also fall. The essays focus on economic conditions and prospects for reform to a market economy in Yugoslavia, Romania, Bulgaria, and Albania.

222. **Labour in Transition: The Labour Process in Eastern Europe and China,** edited by Chris Smith and Paul Thompson. London: Routledge, 1992. ix, 266 p. ISBN: 0415086485. Includes bibliographical references and index.

This collection of essays focuses on labor as it existed in socialist societies, rather than its characterization in socialist literature. The essays are grouped into four sections. The first is a general discussion of the differences between the theory of socialist labor and its real practice in socialist society. The second part describes the differences in labor practice in socialist and capitalist systems. Part three examines labor in Eastern Europe. The final part describes China's labor processes.

223. Sobell, Vladimir, **The CMEA in Crisis: Toward a New European Order?**, foreword by Jan Prybyla. Washington D.C.: Center for Strategic and International Studies, 1990. xiv, 104 p. *Washington Papers, 0278-937x; 145*, ISBN: 0275937313 (pbk); 0275937305 (alk. paper). Includes bibliographical references and index.

The disintegration of the CMEA (Council for Mutual Economic Assistance) and the forces causing its destruction are the subject of this study. The author believes the CMEA was a flawed system from its conception, imposed, in part, on Eastern Europe by Stalin to isolate the Eastern bloc from the West. Thus, Perestroika with its reforms will expose the flawed rationale for the existence of the CMEA, the Soviet satellite system, the effect of Perestroika and possible future trends.

224. **The New European Financial Marketplace,** compiled by Alfred Steinherr. London: Longman, 1992. ix, 298 p. ISBN: 0582089360. Includes bibliographical references and index.

A new challenge to the integration of Europe's financial markets arose with the revolutions in Eastern Europe. While much of this volume discusses the problems facing Europe as a whole, the final part focuses on banking and finance in Eastern Europe. Bankers and academics have contributed to this study of the European financial services industry. The contributors have attempted to use a minimum of mathematics to make the work more accessible to those interested in the research.

225. **Labour Relations in Transition in Eastern Europe**, editor Gyorgy Szell. Berlin: W. de Gruyter, 1992. ix, 369 p. *De Gruyter Studies in Organization; 33*, ISBN: 089925747X. Includes bibliographical references and indexes.

The essays in this volume were originally written in 1989 but have been updated to include events to January of 1991. The essays are organized into six sections: the general framework for restructuring, self-management, new forms of management, changes in trade union structures, legal and political restructuring, and technological changes. The contributors are specialists from the East European countries (including the former Soviet Union). Statistical data is included in most of the discussions.

226. **Fiscal Policies in Economies in Transition,** edited by Vito Tanzi. Washington, D.C.: International Monetary Fund, 1992. v, 359 p. ISBN: 1557751919. Includes bibliographical references and index.

This collection of essays is intended as a comprehensive treatment of fiscal issues in economies in a state of change. The essays were solicited by the editor and they "form a homogenous body." They are divided into three general sections on the general aspects of fiscal policy, revenue and public expenditure. While many nations are included in the discussion a great deal of time is spent on the situation in Eastern Europe. The book should be of interest to anyone interested in the problem of fiscal reform.

227. **Privatization in Europe: West and East Experiences,** edited by Ferdinando Targetti. Brookfield, Vt.: Dartmouth, 1992. xi, 236 p. ISBN: 1855212757. Includes bibliographical references and index.

The majority of the papers collected in this volume were originally given as papers at Trento University's Conference of the European Association for Comparative Economic Systems in March of 1991. Here they are organized into four parts: "General Issues"; "Privatization and Economic Transition to a Market Economy"; "Western Experiences"; and "Eastern Processes."

228. **The Challenge of Free Economic Zones in Central and Eastern Europe: International Perspectives**. New York: United Nations, 1991. xxix, 444 p. ISBN: 9211043581. Includes bibliographical references (p.429-435).

This volume focuses on the role of free economic zones in economic development. Questions about these zones are addressed: "procedures for establishing, regulating and administering such zones; institutional and economic issues related to the zones; domestic and international linkages; alternatives for dealing with foreign exchange in the absence of the convertibility of the ruble; and ways and means of promoting free economic zones to both domestic and foreign investors." (p. vii) Case studies of Ireland, Korea, Hungary, Yugoslavia, Poland, and the United States are presented.

229. Wallace, William V., and Roger A. Clarke, **Comecon, Trade and the West**. New York: St. Martin's Press, 1986. xi, 176 p. ISBN: 0312151047. Includes index and bibliography (p. 170-172).

The authors offer a comprehensive view of COMECON (the Soviet dominated Council for Mutual Economic Assistance) by examining the origins of COMECON and the barriers to co-ordination from Stalin to Brezhnev. Several subsequent chapters then cover further national developments after Brezhnev, including the actions taken at the 27th Party Congress. Various problems facing COMECON, including the economic development of individual CMEA countries, its relations with the EEC, economic reforms and trade are also discussed.

230. Welfens, Paul J. J., **Market-Oriented Systemic Transformations in Eastern Europe: Problems, Theoretical Issues, and Policy Options**. Berlin: Springer-Verlag, 1992. xii, 261 p. ISBN: 3540557938. Includes bibliographical references (p. 243-246) and index.

"This book is a contribution to the theory of systemic transformation and comparative economic systems analysis. [The author examines] the major impulses for the collapse of the socialist economies in Eastern Europe, raise the question which challenges systemic transformation will pose, which issues arise in the context of the prime tasks of organizing privatization and stimulating foreign investment, what foreign economic liberalization could mean for Eastern Europe and finally what some of the global dimensions of the East European transition could be." (p. ix-x)

231. **Joint Ventures and Privatization in Eastern Europe**. New York: Practising Law Institute, 1991. 1040 p. *Commercial Law and Practice Course Handbook Series, no.575, 0548-734x.*

This is a course handbook prepared by the Practising Law Institute and is used for legal instruction. The volume contains a variety of documents and analyses on aspects of privatization and joint ventures. This includes trade law, sources of capital and financing for ventures, treaties, tax considerations, intellectual property, economic reform, and conduct of business.

232. **Currency Convertibility in Eastern Europe,** edited by John Williamson. Washington, DC: Institute for International Economics, 1991. x, 461 p. ISBN: 0881321281; 0881321443. Includes bibliography (p.433-444) and index.

This book "analyzes the external aspects of the economic policies that are being adopted by these emerging market economies. The currency issue is the centerpiece of this dimension of their reforms and is thus the focus of the volume. A cardinal question is whether, and under what circumstances, countries should opt for a 'big bang' strategy as have Poland and Yugoslavia or one of gradualism as did Western Europe after the Second World War." (p. ix) The contents were based on papers delivered at a conference held in Vienna in 1991.

233. Williamson, John, **The Economic Opening of Eastern Europe**. Washington, D.C.: Institute for International Economics, 1991. x, 92 p. *Policy Analyses in International Economics, 31*, ISBN: 0881321869. Includes bibliographical references (p. 91-92).

This book "analyzes the external aspects of the economic policies that are being adopted" by the emerging market economies in Eastern Europe. (p. ix) Sandwiched between an introduction and conclusion are three chapters. One presents the background for the reversal from planned to market economy. A second identifies the salient issues involved, including concepts of convertibility, payments union proposal, trade and exchange rate policy and parallel currencies. A third chapter presents the positions of individual countries on their path to a market economy.

234. Winiecki, Jan, **The Distorted World of Soviet Type Economies**. Pittsburgh, Pa.: University of Pittsburgh Press, 1988. xi, 230 p. *Russian and East European Studies, no. 8*, ISBN: 0822911493. Includes bibliography (p.212-223) and index.

By using the term Soviet type economies to describe those economic systems in Eastern Europe (East Germany, Bulgaria, Poland, Czechoslovakia, Romania, Hungary and the Soviet Union) Winiecki hopes to encompass economic systems excluded by the term centrally planned economies, notably, Hungary. He maintains that Hungary still retains linkages between the political and economic systems that characterize the Soviet system generally. He attempts to point out the links between derivations from Western economic nationality at the behavioral, microeconomic level and resultant economic losses or gains foregone at the aggregate level. The book is divided into three parts. Part one deals with the dynamics of the system—economic growth and prices. Part two explores the structure of the economic system as it is influenced by the dynamics of the system and part three examines the resulting impact of dynamics and structure on foreign trade and technology transfer. A conclusion summarizes his findings.

235. World Congress for Soviet and East European Studies (4th: 1990: Harrogate, England), **The Soviet Union and Eastern Europe in the Global Economy**, edited by Marie Lavigne. Cambridge: Cambridge University Press, 1992. xv, 219 p. ISBN: 0521414172. Includes bibliographical references and index.

The essays in this volume are collected into three sections: integration, growth, and liberalization. The contributors "analyze how the Communist bloc is redirecting its economic relations away from the political privileges of trade and cooperation with the CMEA and the Third World toward the West, in particular Western Europe. Secondly, they examine how the Soviet Union and Eastern Europe are eager to overcome their development lag and implement a restructuring policy, which implies increasing involvement of Western capital. Finally, the authors assess how the transition to the market requires liberalizing foreign trade, introducing convertibility, transforming property structures, all of which are also part of the ongoing domestic reform." (preliminaries)

236. Zloch-Christy, Iliana, **The Debt Problems of Eastern Europe**. New York: Cambridge University Press, 1987. xix, 220 p. *Soviet and East European Studies*, ISBN: 0521335426. Includes bibliography (p.203-212).

The purpose of this book is to analyze the post-1970s development of the Eastern European convertible-currency debt. Five key questions are addressed: 1. What are the main external and internal origins of the indebtedness? 2. Were (and are) convertible-currency debt difficulties inherent in the economic development of Eastern Europe during the 1970s and the 1980s? 3. How has CMEA adjustment to external disturbances affected the national economies? 4. What policies have Western commercial banks, governments, and international financial institutions taken toward resolving Eastern European debt problems? 5. What is the outlook for convertible-currency debt in the late 1980s?" (p. xiii-xiv) Review: *Foreign Affairs* 67, no.1 (Fall 1988): 185.

237. Zwass, Adam, **The Council for Mutual Economic Assistance: The Thorny Path from Political to Economic Integration**. Armonk, NY: Sharpe, 1989. xiii, 269 p. ISBN: 087332496X. Includes bibliographical references.

"The main theme of this book is the chronic conflict between the CMEA's ambitious integration goals and the meager mechanism available for implementing them. This conflict is examined over the most decisive phases of development of the Eastern community, down to the present" (p. xi). Review: *Foreign Affairs* 69, no.2 (Spring 1990): 173.

LANGUAGE AND LITERATURE

238. Carlton, Terence R., **Introduction to the Phonological History of Slavic Languages**. Columbus, Ohio: Slavica Publishers, 1991. 461 p. ISBN: 0893572233. Includes bibliographical references (p. 438-451) and index.

This comprehensive guide to the phonological history of the Slavic languages includes several background chapters on Slavic languages in general, the Slavic writing system, the beginnings of Slavic literacy and Slavic as a member of a larger family of languages. Subsequent chapters then cover the reconstructed phonology of Proto-Indo-European, from Proto-Indo-European to Proto-Slavic, phonological development in the period of disintegration, the prosodic features of late Proto-Slavic, and concludes with a summary of major differences in the individual languages. Several appendices present comparisons of vocabulary, parallel texts, dialect maps and glossaries of Slavic words in the text.

239. Colin, Amy D., **Paul Celan: Holograms of Darkness**. Bloomington, Ind.: Indiana University press, 1991. xxviii, 211 p. *Jewish Literature and Culture*, ISBN: 0253313783. Includes bibliographical references and index.

The works of Jewish-Romanian poet Paul Celan are the subject of this volume of criticism. The author traces Celan's literary roots from his home in Bukovina, through his tortured years during the Holocaust, and the changes in his work in the post war period. "In tracing Celan's early development, his study gradually moves from a panoramic view of his cultural background to textual analysis. These readings attempt to bring out the variety of themes and styles in Celan's early poetry, and become increasingly detailed as they focus on the discrepancies and tensions inherent in his later verses. Yet they continue to draw upon the historical and biographical context of Celan's poetry as well as upon earlier versions of his late poems." (p. xviii) The book includes an index of Celan's prose and poetic works.

240. **Perspectives on Literature and Society in Eastern and Western Europe,** edited by Geoffrey A. Hosking and George F. Cushing. Hampshire: University of London, 1989.

While many observe that censorship and political control have reached an unprecedented level in the societies of Eastern Europe and the Soviet Union, the expected result is that great works of literature will not find the light of day and yet in spite of this repression there are many exceptions to this rule. Recognizing this paradox, the contributors to this volume have attempted to explain it. They hypothesize "that the literary situation of the last 30 years or so in the Soviet Union and Eastern Europe was historically less uncommon than we had been inclined to assume, and that it is usual for good literature to be published only with great difficulty, and with risks for author and publisher alike." (p.1) The essays cover the literary situation in the Soviet Union, Hungary, Romania and Poland. Essays on literature and society, Milton and Voltaire are included for comparative purposes.

241. Kadic, Ante, **Essays in South Slavic Literature**. New Haven, CT: Yale Center for International and Area Studies, 1988. xiv, 260 p. *Yale Russian and East European Publications, no. 10*, ISBN: 0936568109. Includes bibliographical references and index.

Kadic's nineteen essays cover a remarkable range of representatives of South Slavic Literature. He "is interested not merely in literary expression as such: he views a work of literature in its social, historical, and psychological context, he is fascinated by the human qualities it discloses, the political circumstances to which it bears witness." (p. xi)

242. Marcus, Judith, **George Lukacs and Thomas Mann: A Study in the Sociology of Literature**. Amherst: University of Massachusetts Press, 1987. 235 p. ISBN: 0870234862. Translation of: Thomas Mann und Georg Lukacs. Includes bibliography (p. 211-228) and index.

"The aim of this study is to clarify and gain deeper insight into the intricate process of literary interaction between Thomas Mann, the creative artist, and Georg Lukacs, the philosopher and literary critic." (p.8) Marcus has divided her six chapters into two parts. Part one, the author and his critic (chapters 1-2) covers the intellectual and personal relationships of Mann and Lukacs. Part two, *The Magic Mountain* as a "Zeitroman" and a novel of its time (chapters 3-6), focuses on that masterpiece and the physiognomy and personality of the main character, Leo Naphta, for whom Lukacs was supposedly the model.

243. Nobel Symposium (62nd: 1985: Stockholm, Sweden, **The Slavic Literatures and Modernism: A Nobel Symposium, August 5-8 1985**, editor, Nils Ake Nilsson. Stockholm, Sweden: Almqvist & Wiksell International, 1986. 318 p. *Konferenser/Kungl. Vitterhets-, historieoch, antikvitets adademien, 0348-1433, 16*, ISBN: 917402180X. Includes bibliographies.

The symposium's purpose was to bring together scholars to discuss problems that are common to most of the Slavic literatures; Russian, Polish, Czech, Yugoslav and Bulgarian. The focus was on the avant-garde movements of the 1910s and 1920s.

244. Perkowski, Jan Louis, **The Darkling: A Treatise on Slavic Vampirism**. Columbus, Ohio: Slavica Publishers, 1989. 169p. ISBN: 0893572004. Includes bibliography (p.154-169).

Perkowski was often asked at talks and lectures the questions: Are there any real vampires? and Was Dracula a vampire? Seeing that his listeners were dissatisfied with his responses, he attempted to answer these questions more fully in this book. His approach is primary literary and folkloristic. The nine book chapters deal with Dracula the vampire, origins of the European vampire, differences between the Slavic terms used for vampire and werewolf, daemon contamination, testimony from various Slavic folk tales, the English literary vampire and an examination of the psychological underpinnings of vampire beliefs and their mechanisms of transmission. Review: *Slavic and East European Journal* 34, no.4 (Winter 1990): 567-568.

245. Popovic, Tanya, **Prince Marko: The Hero of South Slavic Epics**. Syracuse, N.Y: Syracuse University Press, 1988. xviii, 221 p. ISBN: 0815624441. Includes bibliography (p.203-210) and index.

Prince Marko is a South Slavic folk hero "who protected the South Slavic peoples from injustice and oppression during their long history of hardship" (p. xi). Popovic has provided a detailed study of Marko covering factual and fictional images of him and the interplay of legend and history in epic songs about him. Reviews: *Slavic Review* 49, no.3 (Fall 1990): 493-494. *Canadian-American Slavic Studies* 22, no. 1-4 (Spring/Summer/Fall/Winter 1988): 531-32.

246. Stankiewicz, Edward, **The Slavic Languages: Unity in Diversity**. New York: Mouton de Gruyter, 1986. xv, 472 p. ISBN: 0899252737. Includes bibliographical references and indexes.

A collection of essays by Edward Stankiewicz on a wide range of topics relating to Slavic languages in general. Some essays focus on problems peculiar to Russian such as "The Place and Function of Stress in Russian Nominal Forms with a Zero in the Ending" and "The Accentuation of the Russian Verb." "This volume is a collection of selected papers dealing with comparative and historical problems of Slavic linguistics. Their arrangement reflects, on one hand, the shifting interests of Slavic linguistic scholarship as it has evolved over the last three decades, and, on the other hand, the various phases and facets of my work." (p. vii) References are included at the end of each essay. Review: *Canadian Slavonic Papers* 29, no.2/3 (June/ September 1987): 365-66.

247. Stenberg, Peter, **Journey to Oblivion: The End of the East European Yiddish and German Worlds in the Mirror of Literature.** Toronto: University of Toronto Press, 1991. ix, 213 p. ISBN: 0802058612. Includes bibliographical references (p. 197-203) and index.

Two linguistic communities were, for all intents and purposes, destroyed by the end of the 1940s. These were the Yiddish speakers of East Central Europe and those of the German speaking diaspora in East Europe. The first community was destroyed by the Nazis; the second by the Red Army. Stenberg first examines the historical interdependence of these two communities and then uses prominent works of fiction to explore "the fearful decades" of their destruction. Review: *Journal of Baltic Studies* 22, no.4 (Winter 1991): 379-380.

248. Terry, Garth M., **East European Languages and Literature, v. IV-V: A Subject and Name Index to Articles in English-Language Journals, Festschriften, Conference Proceedings and Collected Papers, 1985-1990**; compiled by Garth M. Terry. Nottingham: Astra Press, 1988-1990. *Astra Soviet and East European Bibliographies, no. 8.* Includes index.

Supplements to the compiler's earlier work *East European Languages and Literatures: A Subject and Name Index to Articles in English Language Journalism, 1900-1977.* These two supplements cover materials published from 1985-1990. Sources for the citations are Festschriften, conference proceedings, collected papers, English language journals, articles omitted from the earlier volumes. Since the volume tries to present a picture of Western scholarship, East European publications are not included. All Slavic languages are covered as well as Hungarian, Romanian and the Baltic languages. Albania, East Germany and Greece are excluded. The entries are arranged by subject. Abbreviations of Festschriften and journals are listed in a table at the beginning of the volume.

249. World Congress for Soviet and East European Studies (3rd: 1985: Washington, D. C.), **Aspects of Modern Russian and Czech Literature: Selected Papers of the Third World Congress for Soviet and East European Studies,** edited by Arnold McMillin. Columbus, OH: Slavica Publishers, 1989. 239 p. ISBN: 0893571946. Includes bibliographical references.

These papers reflect the broad interest of literary scholars who took part in the Third World Congress for Soviet and East European Studies. Most of the articles are on Russian literature, with three on Solzhenitzyn. Three essays are devoted to Czech literature.

250. World Congress for Soviet and East European Studies (4th: 1990: Harrogate, England), **Literature and Politics in Eastern Europe: Selected Papers from the Fourth World Congress for Soviet and East European Studies, Harrogate, 1990,** edited by Celia Hawkesworth. New York: St. Martin's Press, 1992. xi, 169 p. ISBN: 0312079915. Includes bibliographical references and index.

There was no overriding theme to all the papers given at the World Congress for Soviet and East European Studies (1990) on Literature. The editors have tried to select materials that focus on East European literature in the twentieth century. Some of the themes discussed include literature and Serbian politics, the effect of exile on writers from East Europe, portrayals of the past in Hungarian fiction, contemporary Romanian novels, and the modern Bulgarian woman in literature. A few papers were included on more historical topics.

NATIONAL MINORITIES

251. Boyarin, Jonathan, **Polish Jews in Paris: The Ethnography of Memory**. Bloomington: Indiana University Press, 1991. x, 195 p. ISBN: 0253312523. Includes bibliographical references (p.181-191) and index.

This is an ethnographic study of Polish Jews in contemporary Paris. However, unlike most ethnographies, this one has a strong historical element. The author believes the events of the century to be part of the cultural heritage of this community. So much a part of their culture, in fact, that a description of that culture would be incomplete without a discussion of the events of the century. Thus the first part of the book focuses on the element of the past that shaped their culture—their dislocation from Poland, emigration and survival of the Nazi aggression. Part two turns to larger cultural questions such as the integration of the past and present in cyclical celebrations and how to make peace with the past without losing your identity.

252. Brock, Peter, **Folk Cultures and Little Peoples: Aspects of National Awakening in East Central Europe**. Boulder, Colo.: Eastern European Quarterly, 1992. vi, 210 p. ISBN: 0880332433. Includes bibliographical references and index.

As the author states in his preface "The studies in this volume deal with aspects of the movement toward national awakening that swept through East Central Europe during the nineteenth century; a movement which was indeed by no means confined to this area, though it emerged more emphatically in the central and eastern parts of Europe than elsewhere on the continent." (p. v) Each of the case studies presented focuses on specific nationalities, e.g. Polish folklife, Ruthenians, the Kashub question, Lusation Serbs, and Czech and Slovak nationalists.

253. **The Gypsies of Eastern Europe,** edited by David Crowe and John Kolsti. New York: M.E. Sharpe, 1991. vi, 194 p. ISBN: 0873326717. Includes bibliographical references (p. 159-178) and index.

A collection of essays on Gypsies in Germany, Albania, Yugoslavia, Czechoslovakia and Hungary. Several essays deal with the persecution of Gypsies. All of the essays seek to educate the reader about this much misunderstood ethnic minority. The authors hope that by popularizing accurate information about the Gypsies they may help bring them into the mainstream of the various countries in which they live. While the authors sought as much chronological depth in their studies as possible they did have gaps in other areas. Thus, no essays are included on Gypsies of Poland or Bulgaria. The essays focus on the origins of the Gypsies, and their various historical, social and cultural experiences in Eastern Europe from the middle ages on.

254. **A Social and Economic History of Central European Jewry**, Yehuda Don and Victor Karady, editors. New Brunswick, NJ: Transaction Publishers, 1990. viii, 262 p. ISBN: 0887382118. Includes bibliographical references.

A 1986 conference in Paris resulted in eleven of the twelve papers in this book. No single theoretical view unites the essays. Rather, each is an attempt to understand the social-economic development of the Jewish community in the former Austro-Hungarian Empire. Some papers take a regional approach examining the Jews of Vienna, Budapest and Prague, others focus on specific issues such as the Jews in the middle class, patterns of Jewish economic behavior or the ethnic composition of the economic elite of Hungary. Each chapter has a section of notes or, in some cases, suggested readings.

255. Galantai, Jozsef, **Trianon and the Protection of Minorities**. Boulder, Colo.: Social Sciences Monographs, 1992. x, 185 p. *Atlantic Studies on Society in Change; no. 70, East European Monographs; no. 352*, ISBN: 880332492. Includes bibliographical references and index.

Galantai examines the restructuring of the state system of East Central Europe after the dissolution of the Habsburg Empire and minority relations in that area after World War I. He focuses on the importance of the minorities problem in the plans for restructuring, the drafting of the minority protection treaties, the international guarantees in practice and subsequent events. Five appendices contain various documents related to the subject.

256. Grade, Chaim, **My Mother's Sabbath Days: A Memoir**. New York: Knopf, 1986. xvi, 397 p. ISBN: 0394509803. Translation of: Der mames Shabosim.

Chaim Grade describes the Soviet occupation of Vilna in *My Mother's Sabbath Day* and life in that same city before the Soviet takeover. Both the Polish and Russian influences on the city are important in this novel. The study follows Chaim Grade from his experiences as a young writer in Vilna through flight into Russia and back to Vilna after the War. Grade, who died in 1982, is the author of numerous works in Yiddish.

257. **Minority Problems in Eastern Europe Between the World Wars, with Emphasis on the Jewish Minority,** edited by Avraham Greenbaum, introduction Edward Allworth. Jerusalem: Hebrew University of Jerusalem, the Institute for Advanced Studies, 1988. 163 p. Includes bibliographical references.

The Hebrew University in Jerusalem sponsored a seminar during the academic year 1986-1987 that generated the papers collected in this volume. While the focus of the seminar was the Jews of Eastern Europe after 1918 in the context of comparative analysis, the comparative nature of the studies led to examination of other groups. The essays are grouped into three sections. The first discusses "The State of Research," and includes essays on studies of the national question between the World Wars, the historiography of East European Jewry and numerous essays on research in the Soviet Union. Part two includes essays on nationalism policy, economic conditions, and demography. Part three is comprised of essays on culture, religion, and literature.

258. Gruber, Ruth E., **Jewish Heritage Travel: A Guide to Central and Eastern Europe**. New York: Wiley, 1992. xiii, 305 p. ISBN: 0471546127. Includes bibliographical references.

"Part travel guide, part history primer, [this book] is the first work to unveil the rich cultural heritage of European Jewry. In stunning detail, this fascinating guide describes the physical cultural significance of the buildings, towns, and cities from which this world sprang. Rather than focus on places where Jews have died—as books on the Holocaust already do—this guide focuses on the places they lived, uncovering a civilization that was virtually erased within living human memory." (back cover) This volume includes lists of addresses for hotels, restaurants and other detailed travel information for Poland, Czechoslovakia, Hungary, Romania, Yugoslavia, and Bulgaria.

259. Hoffman, Charles, **Gray Dawn: The Jews of Eastern Europe in the Post-Communist Era**. 1st ed. New York: HarperCollins Publishers, 1992. xii, 349 p. ISBN: 0060190035. Includes bibliographical references and index.

As Hoffman says in his introduction "The chapters that follow do not presume to give a detailed, comprehensive report on Jewish life in these countries in the post-communist era. Rather, I have focused on major themes, issues, events, or personalities in these communities that are crucial for understanding the Jewish situation there now and as it may evolve in the future." (p. xi) Countries covered are Czechoslovakia, Hungary, Romania, East Germany, Bulgaria, and Poland.

260. Lederhendler, Eli, **The Road to Modern Jewish Politics: Political Tradition and Political Reconstruction in the Jewish Community of Tsarist Russia**. New York: Oxford University Press, 1989. ix, 240 p. ISBN: 0195058917. Includes bibliography (p. 213-233) and index.

Modern Jewish political development in Eastern Europe is the subject of this study, whose focus is on the period from the 1760s to the late 1870s. It is based on a conceptual analysis of the transition from traditional to modern Jewish politics. Rather than being a definitive history of Russian Jews in the nineteenth century, Lederhendler deals "chiefly with the internal dynamics of Jewish development and the mutual relationship between the Jewish community and the state." (p. 9)

261. McCagg, William O., **A History of Habsburg Jews, 1670-1918**. Bloomington: Indiana University Press, 1989. xi, 289 p. ISBN: 0253331897. Includes bibliography (p. 272-282) and index.

In this work the author seeks to fill the gap in the historical literature on the early history of the East European Jews. He traces the "reintegration" of the Jews into Austrian society after their expulsion in the 1670s. Along with this he also follows the rise of modern anti-Semitism. He follows also the rise of "self-denial" as a part of the assimilation of the Jews and the effect it has had on their culture. This is a social history with some psychological overtones in its analysis. The book contains chronological information on the Jewish population of the period. Reviews: *Canadian Slavonic Papers* 32, no.1 (March 1990): 108-109. *Historian* 52, no.1 (Autumn 1990): 109-110. *German Studies Review* 13, no.1 (February 1990): 140.

262. **East European Jews in Two Worlds: Studies from the YIVO Annual,** edited by Deborah Dash Moore. Evanston, Ill.: Northwestern University Press, 1990. x, 334 p. ISBN: 081010847X.

The fourteen essays published here originally appeared in the YIVO *Annual of Jewish Social Science* from 1944 to 1983. They are authored by some of the most prominent figures in contemporary Jewish scholarship, including Abraham Ain, Abraham Heschel, Horace Kallen, and Dan Miron. They provide a variety of perspectives on modern Jewish life in Eastern Europe such as historical, economic, sociological, psychological, and literary.

263. Wertheimer, Jack, **Unwelcome Strangers: East European Jews in Imperial Germany**. New York: Oxford University Press, 1987. ix, 275 p. *Studies in Jewish History*, ISBN: 0195048938 (alk. paper). Includes bibliography (p. 250-267) and index.

"The present study aims to examine the encounter of German and East European Jews within the context of modern German history. It is predicated on the assumption that this meeting was profoundly conditioned by a specific historical moment, national context and social reality." (p. 5) The arrangement of the book reflects the author's basic assumptions beginning with a description of the German state, then turning to the demographic, economic and organizational activities of the East European Jews. The last section discusses the Jewish community as a whole. More generally, the author is interested in examining Germany's long standing difficulties with aliens and Jews, the self-perception of Jews in pre-Nazi Germany and other broader questions. The work contains a statistical appendix with data on the Jewish populations of many German cities.

264. Winnifrith, Tom, **The Vlachs: The History of a Balkan People**. London: Duckworth, 1987. viii, 180 p. ISBN: 0715621351. Includes bibliography (p. 150-159) and index.

The Vlachs, or Aromanians, are distinguished mainly by their language. The author examines the Vlachs in Greece and the Balkans as well as the relation of Vlachs and the Romans, the Slavs, Byzantines, the Turks and the Great Powers. Several maps are included that indicate current and past locations of Vlachs.

265. Wistrich, Robert S., **The Jews of Vienna in the Age of Franz Joseph**. New York: Oxford University Press, 1989. xiv, 696 p. *Littman Library of Jewish Civilization*, ISBN: 0197100708. Includes bibliography (p. 667-679) and index.

While the Jews of Vienna is the central theme of this work the author is concerned with the cultural mixture of the Jews of the Austro-Hungarian Empire. The author looks particularly at the Galician Jews, Moldavian Jews and Hungarian Jews and the cultures that influenced them. The rise of anti-Semitism is a central focus of the book which is divided into four parts. The first looks at the community in which the Jews were living, their migration, politics, and the effect of liberalism and assimilation. The second section examines the Jews' defense against anti-Semitism. The third section traces the rise of Zionism. Finally the author looks more generally at Jewish culture at the end of the period. A glossary of terms is included.

HOLOCAUST

266. **Lodz Ghetto: Inside a Community Under Siege,** compiled and edited by Alan Adelson and Robert Lapides with annotations and bibliographical notes by Marek Webb. New York: Viking, 1989. xxi, 526 p. ISBN: 0670829838.

This book is the sequel to *The Chronicle of the Lodz Ghetto* published in 1984. The present volume is based on the archive of ghetto materials belonging to Lucjan Dobrodzycki. This archive was composed of writings by residents of the ghetto from all walks of life, of all ages. There are also numerous photographs, including some rare color pictures depicting daily life in the ghetto. "These are the stories of the years of confinement which preceded mass death. People who want to understand why the Jews boarded the trains, people who have become hardened to the loss or who are unable to see heroes or martyrs in the slaughter, who see only victims—all such readers can enter and understand this volume." (p. xii) Review: *New York Times Book Review* (May 6, 1990): 41.

267. Arad, Yitzhak, **Belzec, Sobibor, Treblinka: The Operation Reinhard Death Camps**. Bloomington: Indiana University Press, 1987. viii, 437 p. ISBN: 0253342937. Includes indexes and bibliography (p.401-406).

A study of the Nazi extermination in Poland. These camps were used to destroy Jewish people from Holland, France, Greece, Yugoslavia, Germany, Czechoslovakia, Austria, and the Soviet Union, as well as Poland. This work recounts the building of the camps, their day to day operation, and the brief life of the prisoners brought there for execution. "The book discusses primarily the tragic and cruel events that transpired within these camps; it relates the complete story—from the preparations for construction of the camps at the end of 1941 until their final razing in the autumn of 1943." (p. vii) Two appendices are included, one on the deportation of the Jews and the second on the fate of the perpetrators of Operation Reinhard. The author's parents both died in Treblinka. Review: *International History Review* 11, no.2 (May 1989): 385-87.

268. Bauman, Janina, **Winter in the Morning: A Young Girl's Life in the Warsaw Ghetto and Beyond, 1939-1945**. New York: Free Press, 1986. x, 195 p. ISBN: 0029025303.

The life of a young teenage girl in the Warsaw ghetto from 1939 to 1945 is the subject of this book. The book is recounted from memory many years after the war but attempts to recreate faithfully the life of Jews in the ghetto in those years.

269. **Reflections of the Holocaust in Art and Literature,** edited by Randolph I. Braham. New York: Columbia University Press, 1990. 166 p. *Holocaust Studies Series.*

This collection of essays on the literary and artistic work of the Holocaust is divided into three parts. The first includes critical-literary analyses by writers and covers such authors as Etty Hillesun and Samuel Beckett. The second section includes overview articles. They cover a range of topics from an examination of German-Jewish writers on the pre-Holocaust era to an evaluation of autobiographical accounts by survivors of the Holocaust. The final part contains two essays of reflections on the art of the Holocaust.

270. Browning, Christopher, **The Path to Genocide: Essays on Launching the Final Solution**. New York: Cambridge University press, 1992. xiii, 191 p. ISBN: 0521426952. Includes bibliographical references and index.

Browning has studied the extermination of Jews from three perspectives: policy evolution, historiography, and the "study of the lower- and middle-echelon personnel of what Raul Hilberg has called the 'machinery of destruction'... that in one way or another contributed to carrying out the Final Solution." (p. xii) His book is therefore divided into three sections, each of which focuses on one of these perspectives.

271. Browning, Christopher R., **Fateful Months: Essays on the Emergence of the Final Solution.** Rev. ed. New York: Holmes & Meier, 1991. 113 p. ISBN: 0841912661. Includes bibliographical references (p. 88-107) and index.

Browning intends to make a careful study of events in late 1941 and early 1942 in order "to understand how the Germans took the first step in the Final Solution at the local level." (p. 7) His study focuses on the implementation of the Final Solution among Jews in Serbia during three years.

272. **Dapim: Studies on the Shoah,** edited by Asher Cohen, Yehoyakim Cochavi, Yoav Gelber and Carl Alpert. New York: P. Lang, 1991. 278 p. *Studies in the Shoah, 1.* Translation of a selection of studies previously published in Hebrew in *Dapim.*

These essays cover the Holocaust experience in Poland and its effect on public opinion in Palestine during the war.

273. Dwork, Deborah, **Children with a Star: Jewish Youth in Nazi Europe.** New Haven: Yale University Press, 1991. xlvi, 354 p. ISBN: 0300050542. Includes bibliographical references (p.313-334).

Based on interviews with Holocaust survivors, this book recounts experiences of Jewish children in Nazi Europe during World War II.

274. Edelheit, Hershel, and Abraham J. Edelheit, **A World in Turmoil: An Integrated Chronology of the Holocaust and World War II.** New York: Greenwood Press, 1991. xi, 450 p. *Bibliographies and Indexes in World History, 0742-6852, 22,* ISBN: 0313282188. Includes bibliographical references (p. 405-414) and index.

A chronology of events from January 30, 1938, the date Hitler rose to power to May 14, 1948, the anniversary of the founding of the state of Israel. Emphasis is placed on the events in Europe and the Middle East. The compilers hope to explain how, if not why, the momentous events of those years occurred.

275. Fink, Ida, **A Scrap of Time and Other Stories,** translated from the Polish by Madeline Levine & Francine Prose. New York: Pantheon Books, 1987. 165 p. ISBN: 0394558065. Translation of: Skrawek czasu-opowiadania.

A Polish writer and survivor of the Holocaust recounts some of her memories of life during World War II in these short stories. This volume was published earlier in other languages but was not published in English until 1987. The book was awarded the Ann Frank Prize for Literature in 1985.

276. Gilbert, Martin, **The Holocaust: A History of the Jews of Europe during the Second World War.** New York: Holt, Rinehart, and Winston, 1986. 959 p. ISBN: 0030624169. Includes bibliography (p. 831-896) and index.

The author draws on the account of survivors to tell the horrible tale of those who perished in the Holocaust. The chronological arrangement tells of the indifference of the world to the plight of the Jews as well as of the tremendous anti-Semitism of the time. This detailed study includes numerous sources in the notes. Reviews: *Historian* 50, no.1 (November 1987): 89. *Journal of Modern History* 59, no.4 (December 1987): 826-828.

277. Goldfarb, Aron, **Maybe You Will Survive: A True Story.** New York: Holocaust Library, 1991. 247 p. ISBN: 0896041549 (pbk); 0896041530.

This is the true story of Aron Goldfarb who experienced the invasion of Poland in 1939 while still a young boy. He was imprisoned in a German concentration camp, then fled. He survived the war to tell this story.

278. Gotfryd, Bernard, **Anton, The Dove Fancier: And Other Tales of the Holocaust.** New York: Washington Square Press, 1990. xiii, 175 p. ISBN: 0671691376.

Bernard Gotfryd recounts his experiences of the Holocaust in this collection of stories. "This collection of extraordinary true stories illuminates with understated delicacy the experiences of a young Polish boy before World War II, taking us though the gathering storm of Nazism into the death camps, and to poignant reunions many years later" (back cover). Review: *Nation* 251 (December 31,1990): 849-851.

279. **Nazi Medicine: Doctors, Victims, and Medicine in Auschwitz.** New York: Howard Fertig, 1986. xii, 261, 212, 227 p. ISBN: 0865273510.

The articles that appear in this compilation were originally published in the Polish publication *Przeglad Lekarski* (Medical Review). These writers who were prisoners in Auschwitz-Birkenau, detail their suffering at the hands of Nazi doctors who treated their prisoners as worthless material.

280. Kalib, Goldie Szachter, **The Last Selection: A Child's Journey Through the Holocaust, with Sylvia Kalib and Ken Wachsberger.** Amherst: University of Massachusetts Press, 1991. xx, 266 p. ISBN: 0870237586.

Golda Schachter was seven years old when Germans invaded her native Poland. This is her memoir beginning with those prewar and war years in Poland and ending with her internment and eventual liberation from Bergen-Belsen concentration camp.

281. Kertesz, Imre, **Fateless,** translated by Christopher C. Wilson and Katharina M. Wilson. Evanston, Ill.: Northwestern University Press, 1992. 191 p. ISBN: 0810110490.

Hungarian novelist Imre Kertesz uses the theme of the Holocaust in this 1975 novel, recently translated to English.

282. **"The Good Old Days": The Holocaust As Seen by Its Perpetrators and Bystanders,** edited by Ernst Klee, Willi Dressen and Volker Riess, foreword by Hugh Trevor-Roper, translated by Deborah Burnstone. New York: Free Press, 1991. xxi, 314 p. ISBN: 0029174252. Translation of: Schone Zeiten. Includes bibliographical references and index.

The significance of this book is that the facts are recorded by German participants and bystanders that were responsible for the murder of Jews during World War II. The documents have been translated from German.

283. Krall, Hanna, **The Subtenant: To Outwit God.** Evanston, Ill.: Northwestern University Press, 1992. 247 p. ISBN: 081011075X.

Hanna Krall was a noted Polish journalist and correspondent for *Polityka*. This translation contains two works by the author. The first, "The Subtenant," has also appeared as a film script. The second "To Outwit God," is a record of an interview with one of the leaders of the Warsaw Ghetto Uprising, Marek Edelman.

284. Levin, Nora, **The Holocaust Years: The Nazi Destruction of European Jewry, 1933-1945.** Malabar, Fla.: R. E. Krieger Pub. Co., 1990. x, 373 p. ISBN: 0894642235. Includes bibliographical references (p. 346-351) and index.

A collection of documents supplements this general historical treatment of the Holocaust. The author believes it important that the Holocaust be studied within the discipline of history. She is attempting to provide a useful set of documents to assist others presenting this subject to students. The book is divided into two parts. The first is a brief history of the Holocaust. Part two is the collection of readings which comprises two thirds of the book. The author has also included a list of suggested readings and several maps.

285. Mayer, Arno J., **Why Did the Heavens Not Darken?: The "Final Solution" in History**. New York: Pantheon Books, 1989. xv, 492 p. ISBN: 0394571541. Includes bibliography (p. 451-475) and index.

A reanalysis of the causes of the Holocaust or "Judeocide" as Mayer calls it. The author believes such a reappraisal requires an integrated historical approach drawing on ideology, politics and war. "Three steps can advance this rethinking of the unthinkable: to abandon the vantage point of the Cold War; to place the Judeocide in its pertinent historical setting; and to use an overarching construct to explain the horrors both of the Jewish catastrophe and of the historical circumstances in which it occurred." (p. xiii) Using this method Mayer has arranged the work chronologically in three parts which consider first the nature of the Nazi regime; then, the Eastern campaign and finally Judeocide. Review: *Partisan Review* 57, no.2 (1990): 302-306.

286. Millu, Liana, **Smoke over Birkenau,** translated from the Italian by Lynne Sharon Schwartz. Philadelphia, PA: Jewish Publication Society, 1991. 202 p. ISBN: 0827603983.

This first-person narrative by an Italian prisoner chronicles the imprisonment of Jews, especially women, at the Birkenau concentration camp.

287. Nahon, Marco, **Birkenau: The Camp of Death**. Tuscaloosa: University of Alabama Press, 1989. xvii, 149 p. *Judaic Studies Series*, ISBN: 0817304495. Translation of: Birkenau. Includes bibliography (p.148-149).

Nahon is a Jew of Greek nationality. His memoir of Auschwitz-Birkenau, where his entire family was sent, is a terrifying account of life in the camps. He and his son alone survived. His memoir was originally written in French. An appendix containing the names of the Israelite communities of Dimotika and Orestias, Greece is also included.

288. Patai, Raphael, **Between Budapest and Jerusalem: The Patai Letters, 1933-1938,** selected, translated, and annotated by Raphael Patai. Salt Lake City: University of Utah Press, 1992. xiii, 333 p. ISBN: 0874803845. Includes index. Translated from French, German, Hebrew, and Hungarian.

"This book consists of letters exchanged by members of the Patai family between 1933 and 1938, sent to and from Budapest, Jerusalem, Tel Aviv, Jericho, Zurich, Geneva, and Paris, where they lived or sojourned in those years. Although the letters primarily discuss personal matters, they also tell of the unfolding historical events that the dispersed members of the family witnessed from the inside, in Europe and Palestine, which—we know today—were the prelude to the Nazi Holocaust, on the one hand, and the establishment of the state of Israel, on the other" (p. ix).

289. Patterson, David, **The Shriek of Silence: A Phenomenology of the Holocaust Novel**. Lexington, Ky.: University Press of Kentucky, 1992. 180 p. ISBN: 0813117682. Includes bibliographical references and index.

After an introductory chapter on the theoretical background of the aesthetics of the Holocaust novel, Patterson explores several motifs in a variety of East and Central European writers on the Holocaust.

290. Redlikh, Egon, **The Terezin Diary of Gonda Redlich,** Saul S. Friedman, editor; Laurence Kutler, translator; foreword by Nora Levin. Lexington, KY: University Press of Kentucky, 1992. xiv, 173 p. ISBN: 0813118042. Includes bibliographical references and index.

This book contains the diary of Egon Redlich from January 1, 1942 until October 6, 1944, while he was living in the ghetto/ concentration camp of Terezin (Theresienstadt). "Redlich's diary is unique in the extensive literature we have already have about

Theresienstadt, not only because of his crucial position in the ghetto, but because it unfolds the day-by-day impressions of an acute observer quite fully aware of the historical significance of events he was witnessing and recording." (p. x)

291. **Memory Offended: The Auschwitz Convent Controversy,** edited by Carl Rittner and John K. Roth. New York: Praeger, 1991. xiv, 289 p. ISBN: 0275938484; 0275936066. Includes bibliographical references (p. 271-276) and index.

The essays in this volume focus on the three questions: how does the Auschwitz convent controversy affect Jewish-Christian relations; how can those relations be improved; what can be learned from this controversy. The controversy centers around the presence of a convent of Carmelite nuns on the grounds of the Auschwitz death camp. The essays in this collection are divided into three sections. The first set cover the history of the convent, Auschwitz and the controversy. The second section focuses on the psychological aspects of maintaining the memory of events at Auschwitz for Jews and Christians. The final section examines the theological aspects of memory in Judaism and Christianity. Numerous appendixes are included with documents from both sides of the issue.

292. **The Courage to Care: Rescuers of Jews During the Holocaust**, edited by Carol Rittner and Sondra Myers. New York: New York University Press, 1986. xvii, 157 p. ISBN: 0814773974. Includes index.

This collection of memoirs of survivors of the Holocaust is unique because each one of them was saved by gentiles who risked his or her life to save Jewish men, women and children.

293. Rosenberg, Blanca, **To Tell at Last: Survival Under False Identity, 1941-45**. Urbana, Ill.: University of Chicago Press, 1993. xv, 178 p. ISBN: 0252019989. Includes index.

This is a memoir by a Polish Jew who received false identity papers and eventually managed to escape from occupied Poland during World War II.

294. **Letters from Prague, 1939-1941,** compiled by Raya Czerner Schapiro, Helga Czerner Weinberg. Chicago, IL: Academy Chicago Publishers, 1991. xvii, 218 p. ISBN: 0897333691. Includes bibliographical references and index.

This volume contains letters from a grandmother and an uncle who remained in Prague after the German occupation. They provide a first hand account of the suffering of Jews during the Holocaust. They were both murdered in concentration camps in late 1942 and early 1943.

295. **Secretaries of Death: Accounts by Former Prisoners Who Worked in the Gestapo of Auschwitz,** edited and translated by Lore Shelley. New York: Shengold Publishers, 1986. xviii, 378 p. ISBN: 0884001237. Includes bibliography (p. 377-378).

This is a collection of testimonies of former prisoners of Auschwitz. These people were made to work for the Gestapo in the camp. As the writer of the preface reminds us: "Let there be no mistake about the primary purpose of this book. It is not the work of a person driven to respond to those malicious souls who deny that the Holocaust ever happened. Dr. Shelley is not being dictated to by those who would grant Nazidom a judgmental reprieve. This volume has a far more important stimulus. It is to honor the dead; and as such because of the manner of their deaths, it serves as a warning to the living." (p. xiii)

296. Steinberg, Jonathan, **All or Nothing: The Axis and the Holocaust, 1941-1943**. London: Routledge, 1990. xiv, 320 p. ISBN: 0415007739. Bibliography p.245-260.

"The two Fascist armies in the Second World War treated the Jews quite differently. Jews who fell into the German army ended up in concentration camps; none of those taken by the Italians suffered the same fate. Yet the protectors of the Jews were no philo-Semites, nor were they (often) great respecters of human life. Some of those same officers had sanctioned savage atrocities against Ethiopians and Arabs in the year before the war. Jonathan Steinberg uses this remarkable and poignant story to unravel the motives and forces underpinning both Nazism and Fascism." (back cover) While the book covers the Holocaust in several parts of Europe the first section is devoted to the final solution in the Balkans.

297. Stojka, Karl, **The Story of Karl Stojka: A Childhood in Birkenau: Exhibition at the Embassy of Austria, April 30 to May 29, 1992: Catalogue, by the United States Holocaust Memorial Museum; a project of the United States Holocaust Memorial Council.** Washington, DC: The Council, 1992. 64 p. Includes bibliographical references (p. 63-64).

This is an exhibition catalog of the paintings of Stojka, a Gypsy, who was sent to Birkenau with his family. The paintings here depict life in the camps during the years 1943-1945. Stojka survived and settled in Vienna after the war.

298. Tedeschi Brunelli, Giuliana, **There Is a Place on Earth: A Woman in Birkenau,** translated by Tim Parks. New York: Pantheon Books, 1992. ISBN: 0679403035. Translation of: C'e un punto della terra.

An account of the hellish existence of women in the Nazi concentration camps. Giuliana Tedeschi lost her husband and mother-in-law to the camps.

299. Weil, Jiri, **Life With a Star,** with a preface by Philip Roth, translated from the Czech by Ruzena Kovarikova with Roslyn Schloss. New York: Farrar Straus Giroux, 1989. x, 208 p. ISBN: 0374187371.

The story of life for the Jews in Prague during the Nazi occupation when they were all forced to wear the Star of David. This fictionalized account seems to be drawn largely from Weil's own experience of having had to fake his own suicide and then hide. Weil's writing all displays his intense hatred for the Nazis. Weil was born near Prague in 1900 and studied at Charles University in Prague. His writings were banned by the Communists and many remained unpublished until many years after his death. Review: *World Literature Today* 64, no.2 (Spring 1990): 329.

300. Yahil, Leni, **The Holocaust: The Fate of European Jewry, 1932-1945,** translated from the Hebrew by Ina Friedman and Haya Galai. New York: Oxford University Press, 1990. xviii, 808 p. *Studies in Jewish History*, ISBN: 019504522X. Translation of: ha-Shoah. Includes bibliographical references (p. 753-783) and index.

Yahil attempts "to struggle with the problems and enigmas of the Holocaust." (p. 11) His book, originally published in Hebrew, is in three parts. Part one covers the Jews of Germany during the rise and under the rule of the National Socialists, 1932-September 1939. Part two is the prologue to the final solution, the first phase of World War II, 1939-1941. The third and last part covers the Holocaust itself, from 1941-1945.

DISSIDENT MOVEMENTS

301. Garton Ash, Timothy, **The Uses of Adversity: Essays on the Fate of Central Europe.** New York: Random House, 1989. xi, 335 p. ISBN: 0394575733. Includes bibliographical references and index.

A journalist's impressions of the changes in Eastern Europe are collected in this book. Most of the essays here originally appeared in either *The New York Review of Books* or *The Spectator*. They describe conditions in Poland, Czechoslovakia, East Germany and Hungary during the last ten years. "This book reflects my own interest in ideas rather than armies, cultures rather than economies, nations rather than political systems and, above all, individual men and woman rather than amorphous collectives." (p. vii)

302. MacFarlane, L. J., **Human Rights: Realities and Possibilities: Northern Ireland, the Republic of Ireland, Yugoslavia and Hungary**. New York: St Martin's Press, 1990. xi, 304 p. ISBN: 0312045336. Includes bibliographical references and index.

This work contains four case studies on the difficulties of human rights implementation in four countries: Northern Ireland, the Republic of Ireland, Yugoslavia and Hungary. "My approach to the issue of human rights implementation is based on two precepts. The first is that human rights problems in any society can be understood only in the context of that society. The second is that it is from within this complex of forces, in particular from the government and those capable of exerting pressure on the government that one must immediately look for improvement in human rights...." (p. ix) The author selected Yugoslavia and Hungary since they were the most liberal of the communist countries. The sections on each country provide the reader with general background on the countries. The author then turns to problems specific to the country, with discussions of national minorities, freedom of expression, freedom of religious belief, freedom of association and assembly.

THE SOCIETY, SOCIOLOGY

303. Brook, Stephan, **Vanished Empire: Vienna, Budapest, Prague: The Three Capital Cities of the Habsburg Empire as Seen Today**. New York: W. Morrow, 1988. vii, 336 p. ISBN: 0688092128. Includes index.

The authors looked at the three most important cities of the Habsburg Empire: Vienna, Budapest and Prague. The book was published in 1988. Thus, the author sees Prague and Hungary as "culturally diminished" lacking the grandeur of their years as part of Austro-Hungarian Empire. Each of the national areas ruled by the Habsburgs maintained its national flavor as the rulers did little to unify their Empire. The book is divided into three parts, each devoted to one of the cities. Each section is preceded by a city map. There is no bibliography.

304. Broun, Janice, and Grazyna Sikorska, **Conscience and Captivity: Religion in Eastern Europe**. Washington D.C.: University Press of America, 1988. xiii, 376 p. ISBN: 089633130 (pbk); 0896331296 (alk. paper). Includes bibliography (p.355-361) and index.

The author intends to describe the current status of religion in the Eastern European countries of Albania, Bulgaria, Czechoslovakia, the German Democratic Republic, Hungary, Poland, Romania and Yugoslavia. She begins with two chapters devoted to the historical and cultural background and then devotes a chapter to each country listed. In a concluding chapter she sums up the problems and prospects. Several appendices provide key primary source documents for Czechoslovakia, Hungary, Poland and Romania. Reviews: *Journal of Church and State* 32, no.3 (Summer 1990): 640-641. *Modern Greek Studies Yearbook* 5 (1989): 519-529.

305. Chamberlain, Lesley, **In the Communist Mirror: Journeys in Eastern Europe**. London: Faber, 1990. xii, 196 p. ISBN: 057114165X.

A personal account of one individual's reactions to life under the Communist regime in Russia, Poland, Yugoslavia, Hungary, Banat, Romania, East Germany and Hungary. The author describes the economic situation, political system, art and psychological condition which were associated with the Communist regime. The work is set in an autobiographical framework, with each chapter devoted to a different country. The essays are also chronologically arranged. They cover a three-year period.

306. **Children and the Transition to the Market Economy: Safety Nets and Social Policies in Central and Eastern Europe,** edited by Giovanni A. Cornia and Sandor Sipos. Brookfield, VT: Avebury, 1991. xxvii, 251 p. ISBN: 1856282465 (pbk); 1856282414. Includes bibliographical references (p.235-244) and indexes.

Children have faced steadily deteriorating health and welfare conditions in Eastern Europe since the 1970s. The infant mortality rate has either stagnated or worsened. Respiratory, allergic and degenerative diseases are on the rise due to the degradation of the environment. "This book is a contribution to the growing debate on how to minimize the social costs of the transition to the market economy and what social policies should be developed in the years ahead. It argues that, in view of the problems of implementation and sequencing encountered by the economic policies and in view of negative external shocks, broader safety nets and social policies which show more solidarity are required to avoid a further spread of poverty and deprivation among children and other groups." (p. xxv) The contributors are both scholars and government officials who have an interest in child welfare and the institutions that support it. This volume of essays is divided into two parts. The first includes essays that discuss the East European region as a whole. The individual essays focus on structural problems affecting children in the region, social security, welfare state models and the effect of reforms on child welfare. Part two consists of four case studies on Hungary, Poland, Bulgaria and Czechoslovakia.

307. **Superwomen and the Double Burden: Women's Experience of Change in Central and Eastern Europe and the Former Soviet Union,** edited by Chris Corrin. Toronto: Second Story press, 1992. 297 p. ISBN: 0929005341. Includes index. Includes bibliographical references (p. 264-278).

This book contains essays by various contributors, each of whom focuses on a specific Central European country. "To understand the revolutionary upheavals that swept across Europe in 1989 and their implications for women, some basis of knowledge of the social, political and economic conditions of these societies before the later 1980s—how they developed and differed from each other—is required. This book seeks to lay such a foundation." (p. 1) Each of the case studies covers three main areas in attempting to give a woman's perspective on social conditions in these countries. These areas are 1) women as producers and reproducers (workers and mothers); 2) women as decision makers; and 3) women's personal autonomy.

308. **Social Policy in the New Eastern Europe: What Future for Socialist Welfare?,** edited by Bob Deacon and Julia Szalai. Brookfield, Vt.: Avebury, 1990. xi, 234 p. *Studies in the Social Policy of Eastern Europe and the Soviet Union,* ISBN: 1856280500. Includes bibliographical references and index.

The papers in this volume were originally presented at a conference in Leeds in 1988. The papers are arranged in four sections: (1) introduction and dialogue; (2) Hungary and Poland: economic and political reform and the Space for an independent social policy; (3) Bulgaria, the German Democratic Republic and Yugoslavia: different realities; different interpretations; and (4) women, the family and East European social policy.

309. Gella, Aleksander, **Development of Class Structure in Eastern Europe: Poland and Her Southern Neighbors.** New York: State University of New York Press, 1989. xvii, 326 p. ISBN: 0887068332. Includes bibliography (p.217-307) and indexes.

In eleven chapters Gella examines the development and eventual demise of the old social structure in Romania, Hungary, Poland and Czechoslovakia. After an introductory chapter on the history of Eastern Europe, each of the next four chapters are devoted in turn to Poland, Czechoslovakia, Hungary and Romania until World War II. Chapters six through nine cover the peasantry, nobility and bourgeoisie, proletariat and working class, and the intelligentsia.

The last two chapters analyze the effects of World War II and imported revolutions on social structure. Review: *Canadian Review of Sociology and Anthropology* 27, no.2 (May 1990): 241-243.

310. Hedberg, Augustin, **Faith Under Fire & the Revolutions in Eastern Europe: An Eyewitness to the Victory of the Human Spirit**, by Augustin Hedberg; based on transcripts from the film Faith under Fire; with photography by Uli Bonnekamp. 1st ed. Princeton, N.J.: Sturges Pub., 1992. xvii, 167 p. ISBN: 0936373040.

Here are published the transcripts of the interviews used in the film "Faith under Fire." The author's purpose in conducting the interviews was to gain first hand information on what role religion played in the downfall of the communist system. The interviews were done mainly in Poland and Czechoslovakia.

311. **Revolutions for Freedom: The Mass Media in Eastern and Central Europe**, A. Hester & L. Earle Reybold, eds. Athens, GA: Center for International Mass Communications Training and Research, 1991. x, 232 p. Includes index.

This volume contains essays by different authors on various aspects of mass media in Eastern Europe generally and in specific countries, especially Poland, Czechoslovakia, Yugoslavia, Hungary, and East Germany.

312. **Professions and the State: Expertise and Autonomy in the Soviet Union and Eastern Europe,** edited by Anthony Jones. Philadelphia: Temple University Press, 1991. x, 256 p. *Labor and Social Change*, ISBN: 0877228019. Includes bibliographical references.

This book explores what happens to professionals who operate in a bureaucratic society, rather than a market society. "What happens to the way the occupation is organized, the recruitment and training, to the terms and conditions of work, to client-professional relations, to the quality of services provided, to the control of standards and practices?" (p. x) Review: *Contemporary Sociology* 20, no.5 (September 1991): 569-570.

313. **Equality and Inequality in Eastern Europe,** edited by Pierre Kende and Zdenek Strmiska, translated from the French by Francoise Read. New York: St. Martin's Press, 1987. 422 p. ISBN: 0854965025. Translation of: Egalite et inegalites en Europe de l'Est. Includes bibliographies.

This group of essays intends to answer whether in Eastern Europe "socialist ambitions have borne fruit in the fields of distribution and social equality, and how these results compare with the contemporary evolution of Western societies." (p. 1) The eleven essays are divided into two parts: part one contains specific studies in economic and social inequality. These address such issues as income distribution, division of resources, housing, and social mobility. Part two focuses on the change from old to new inequalities—social classes, political power, education and meritocracy.

314. **Urban Society of Eastern Europe in Premodern Times,** edited by Barisa Krekic. Berkeley: University of California, 1987. xii, 232 p. ISBN: 0520057880. Includes bibliographies and index.

These studies of medieval Eastern European cities not only focus on the cities' politics, history, economic development and cultural life, but also on the realities of daily life. Cities studied include Moscow, Kiev, Novgorod, Krakow, Buda and Dubrovnik.

315. Moss, Joyce, **Peoples of the World, Eastern Europe and the Post-Soviet Republics: The Culture, Geographical Setting, and Historical Background of 34 Eastern European Peoples**, Joyce Moss, George Wilson. 1st ed. Detroit: Gale Research, 1993. xix, 415 p. ISBN: 0810388677. Includes bibliographical references and index.

This volume is divided into three sections: Old Cultures, Cultures of Today, and Country Briefs. "The section on the old cultures provides a brief overview of the region's ancient peoples, which includes peoples who appeared in greatest strength as recently as the fifteenth and sixteenth centuries A.D. Organized alphabetically by culture names, Cultures of Today includes the dominant cultures of the region today.... The entries in the third section, Country Briefs, contain information about population, languages, and cities, describe the nation's topography, and relate current events and issues within each country." (p. xvi)

316. Ramet, Pedro, **Cross and Commissar: The Politics of Religion in Eastern Europe and the USSR**. Bloomington: Indiana University Press, 1987. x, 244 p. ISBN: 0822311488 (paper); 0822311291. Includes bibliography (p.235-238) and index.

This book is "the first systematic attempt at theorizing about church-state interaction in Eastern Europe and the Soviet Union, grounding these theories in extensive substantive research." (p. ix) Individual chapters concentrate on the relationship between religion and nationalism, contemporary dynamics in church-state relations, the importance of factionalism in church-state relations, and current trends.

317. **Religion and Nationalism in Soviet and East European Politics,** edited by Pedro Ramet, rev. and expanded ed. Durham: Duke University Press, 1989. vi, 516 p. *Duke Press Policy Studies, 0020-6555*, ISBN: 0822308916 (pbk); 0822308541. Includes index.

A revised edition of the original volume that appeared in 1985 and contained papers from a conference on "Religion and Nationalism in the Soviet Union and Eastern Europe" held at UCLA and UC at Santa Barbara October 29-30, 1982. The updated edition has added essays on the religious institutions in the Communist state, Jews in the USSR and Eastern Europe, religion and nationalism in Georgia and Armenia, revival of Lutheranism in Eastern Germany and Christianity in Czechoslovakia. The volume is divided into four parts, an opening section of essays giving comparative studies; two regional sections, one on the Soviet Union and the other on the Eastern Europe; and a concluding essay.

318. Ramet, Sabrina P., **Social Currents in Eastern Europe: The Sources and Meaning of the Great Transformation**. Durham: Duke University Press, 1991. xii, 434 p. ISBN: 0822311291. Includes bibliographical references (p. 411-413) and index.

A review of the social changes that have taken place in Czechoslovakia, Hungary, Bulgaria, East Germany, Poland and Yugoslavia. The author believes that social developments do not appear in isolation. Rather she shows that the trends in one area of the society can be seen in other areas. "I wanted to bring out this interrelationship and to show how changing social currents present political authorities with policy challenges, indeed with challenges that may bear on the fundamental questions of governance: system legitimacy and system stability." (p. ix) To accomplish this the author examines a variety of trends: those found among religious and ethnic groups, feminism in Yugoslavia, rock music, dissent groups such as Solidarity and independent activists in Czechoslovakia, Hungary and Romania. The final section of the book includes appendices of public opinion polls taken in Eastern Europe from 1989 on. Albania is largely omitted from this study since the author felt it did not share in the general patterns of culture change in the rest of Eastern Europe.

319. **The Reemergence of Civil Society in Eastern Europe and the Soviet Union,** edited by Zbigniew Rau. Boulder, Colo.: Westview Press, 1991. xi, 181 p. ISBN: 0813384044. Includes bibliographical references and index.

The essays appearing in this volume were originally presented at a conference at the University of Texas at Austin on April 20-21, 1990. "The purpose of this volume is to analyse the developments in the former Soviet bloc from the perspective of the ruled. The key explanatory tool in this analysis is the notion of civil society; its conceptual framework is the interaction between the civil society and the state." (p. 3) Individual essays explore this topic in Poland, Estonia, Ukraine, and in the Crimea.

320. Riordan, James, **Sport, Politics, and Communism**. New York: St. Martin's Press, 1991. vi, 169 p. *International Studies in the History of Sport*, ISBN: 0719028507. Includes bibliographical references and index.

Like other volumes in this series, this work explores "the political, cultural, social, and economic aspects of sports internationally." (p. i) Topics covered include differing perceptions of sport and politics in East and West, the philosophical roots of communist sport, the practical roots of communist sport, sport and modernizing communities, sport and state, provision for giftedness, sports medicine, and foreign policy, and trends and transformations.

321. Skilling, Harold Gordon, **Samizdat and an Independent Society in Central and Eastern Europe**. Columbus: Ohio State University Press, 1989. xi, 293 p. ISBN: 0814204872. Includes bibliographical references and index.

Skilling's purpose is to analyze the phenomenon of a 'second culture' and a 'second society' in each of the countries in Eastern Europe. Further, he hoped "to compare and contrast its scope and character in each of the countries of the region, and to estimate the degree to which it could properly be conceived of as a genuine independent society and as a precursor of a future civil society." (p. ix).

322. Tanner, Marcus, **Ticket to Latvia: A Journey from Berlin to the Baltic**. New York: Holt, 1989. 197 p. ISBN: 0805013466.

This is a narrative of a journey taken by the author from Berlin through Erfurt, Wittenberg, Quedlinburg, Weimar, Prague, Wroclaw, Krakow, Warsaw, Vilnius, Riga and Leningrad.

THE ARTS AND CULTURE

323. **Art as Activist: Revolutionary Posters from Central and Eastern Europe**. London: Thames and Hudson in association with Smithsonian Institution Traveling Exhibition Service, 1992. 160 p. ISBN: 0500276862. Includes index.

This volume presents over 100 examples of political posters from several countries of Eastern Europe that were produced in 1989 and 1990. They offer a unique perspective, that of art, on the events taking place at that time. Poems, commentary and notes on the posters complement the reproductions.

324. Aman, Anders, **Architecture and Ideology in Eastern Europe During the Stalin Era: An Aspect of Cold War History**. New York: Architectural History Foundation, 1992. viii, 285 p. ISBN: 0262011301. Includes indexes.

This history of architecture in East Germany, Poland, Czechoslovakia, Hungary, Romania, and Bulgaria was originally written in Swedish and published in 1987. The author approaches his subject, and frames his discourse, from three equally important perspectives: geographic, ideological and political, and architectural. In addition to providing background information for all these perspectives, the author highlights monumental buildings in the capital cities, the first socialist cities (Stalinstadt, Nowa Huta, Sztalinvaros, Dimitrovgrad), eight prominent socialist realist architects, and an interesting contrast with architecture in West Berlin during the same period.

325. Baranczak, Stanislaw, **Breathing under Water and Other East European Essays.** Cambridge, Mass.: Harvard University Press, 1990. 258 p. ISBN: 0674081250 (alk. paper). Includes bibliographical references (p.247-251) and index.

Baranczak is an exile from Poland who came to this country in 1982. The essays presented in this book all revolve around the theme of the perceptions of an East European exile in America and reflections on life in Eastern Europe. Since Baranczak is a literary critic, many of his pieces are related to literature and cultural criticism.

326. Barnes, Julian, **The Porcupine.** 1st American ed. New York: Knopf, 1992. 138 p. ISBN: 0679419179.

"Powerful and unsettling, *The Porcupine* is a novel about the fall of Communism and the hold it retains on its successors; about the particular uncertainties of politics in our time; and about the stubborn, disturbingly grey areas hidden in any black-and-white vision of the world." (cover)

327. Birnbaum, Marianna D., **Humanists in a Shattered World: Croatian and Hungarian Latinity in the Sixteenth Century.** Columbus, Ohio: Slavica Publishers Studies, 1986. 433 p. *UCLA Slavic Studies, v.15*, ISBN: 0893571555. Includes bibliography (p. 389-413) and index.

Birnbaum examines the Renaissance and Humanism as it developed in Hungary and Croatia. The thirteen chapters either deal with individuals, such as Stephanus Brodericus or Antonius Verantius, or with various themes relating to latinity in that area.

328. International Conference of Slavic Librarians and Information Specialists (2nd: 1985: Washington, D. C.). **Books, Libraries and Information in Slavic and East European Studies: Proceedings of the Second International Conference of Slavic Librarians and Information Specialists,** edited by Marianna Tax Choldin. New York: Russica Publishers, 1986. 530 p. *Russica Bibliography Series, no. 8.* Includes bibliographies.

This volume contains a number of papers originally presented at the Second International Conference of Slavic Librarians and Information Specialists held in Washington D.C. in 1985. A wide range of topics are covered reflecting the diversity of the field in the 1980s. The papers are divided into sections on book studies in the Soviet Union (1917-1935), book studies in contemporary Eastern Europe, historic analyses of the Slavic book trade in the West, Polish "Solidarity" publications, East European émigré publications, government's role in publishing in the USSR, Slavic and European archives, special bibliographic projects, the role of machine-readable data in the Slavic and East European fields, East-West technology transfer, national bibliographies and papers from an international book exchange conference. Almost every interest in Slavic librarianship is represented in this volume.

329. Kiel, Machiel, **Studies in the Ottoman Architecture of the Balkans.** Aldershot: Variorum, 1990. *Collected Studies*, ISBN: 086078276X. Includes index.

These collected articles have been reprinted from their original sources, with the original pagination. Kiel's articles cover a wide variety of buildings: utilitarian, religious, educational and recreational.

330. **Before the Wall Came Down: Soviet and East European Filmmakers Working in the West,** edited by Graham Petrie and Ruth Dwyer. Lanham, Md: University Press of America, 1990. 249 p. ISBN: 0819178594; 0819178586. Includes bibliographical references.

Papers from the 1989 conference on "Soviet and East European Directors Working in the West" are presented in this volume. The contributors look at how being forced to produce films in the West had affected these directors. Some examine artistic freedom in the West within the context of commercial constraints. The papers are grouped into sections by country with two sections on the Soviet Union and others on Czechoslovakia, Hungary, Poland, and Yugoslavia. Each section includes several papers and discussion and responses. There is an appendix on Makavejev. Some of the directors discussed include Forman, Skolimkowski, Kieslowski, Makavejev. There is no index in the volume.

331. Roberson Center for the Arts and Sciences, **Goddesses and Their Offspring: 19th and 20th Century Eastern European Embroideries**, Merrill Oliver editor. Binghamton, N.Y.: Roberson Center for the Arts and Sciences, 1986. 77 p.

This is a catalog of the exhibit of the same title which presents samples of embroidery from Carpatho-Russians, Slovaks, Moravians, Russians, Hungarians, Ukrainians and Poles. The authors hope to introduce the reader to the rich aesthetic heritage of these people. The volume is divided into several chapters each presenting numerous examples of a particular motif or ethnic style as well as a discussion of the abstract qualities of the designs. The chapter entitled "The Goddess" follows the development of the Goddess image over time. Mary Kelly's essay "Eastern European Embroideries" discusses various motifs in East European embroidery relating them to annual ritual cycles. A checklist of pieces from the exhibit and a bibliographic essay are included.

332. Ryback, Timothy W., **Rock Around the Bloc: A History of Rock Music in Eastern Europe and the Soviet Union**. New York: Oxford University Press, 1990. xii, 272 p. ISBN: 0195056337. Includes index.

The growth of the popularity of rock and roll music and the significance this had in the changing East European and Soviet societies are the subjects of this study. "The following account of Soviet-bloc rock should dispel the Western impression that rock music is new to Eastern Europe and the Soviet Union. Further, it should challenge assumptions about everyday life under socialism, about the relationship between the state and the individual, and ultimately, about the nature of these societies." (p. 5) The chronological arrangement begins in 1946 and traces the growth in popularity of rock music in each Eastern European country and the official attempts to stop its spread. The book contains a chronology. Reviews: *Fletcher Forum of World Affairs* 14, no.2 (Summer 1990): 458-460. *Slavic and East European Journal* 34, no.4 (Winter 1990): 521-522. *Tikkun* 5, no.4 (1990): 70-72.

333. **National Theatre in Northern and Eastern Europe, 1746-1900,** edited by Laurence Senelick; associate editors Peter Bilton et al. New York: Cambridge University Press, 1991. xxx, 480 p. *Theatre in Europe*, ISBN: 0521244463. Includes bibliographical references (p.421-439) and index.

This book is a documentary history of theatre in Denmark, Sweden, Norway, Poland, Czechoslovakia, Hungary, Romania, and Russia. Besides a general introductory essay each country section also includes an informative essay relative to that country. The bibliographical references at the end of the volume are also subdivided by country.

SCIENCE AND TECHNOLOGY

334. **Data Goods and Data Services in the Socialist Countries of Eastern Europe**. New York: United Nations, 1988. viii, 103 p. ISBN: 9211043042. Includes bibliographical references.

The United Nations Centre on Transnational Corporations has conducted research on the role of trade in data goods and data services in the world wide economy. The growth of data resources, the importance of data flow in economic development and policy options on this kind of trade have all been largely ignored in the literature. This study seeks to fill this gap by looking at the role of CMEA countries in the trade of data goods and services and the development of data goods and services in these countries. Besides a general overview and discussion of basic concepts in the field; part of this work is devoted to trade in data goods and services and policies and regulations in CMEA countries.

335. **After the Revolution: East-West Trade and Technology Transfer in the 1990s,** edited by Gary K. Bertsch Heinrich Vogel, and Jan Zielonka. Boulder, Colo.: Westview Press, 1991. viii, 227 p. ISBN: 0813382785. Includes bibliographical references.

Papers originally prepared for a Leiden conference on technology transfer were revised and expanded to take into account the dramatic changes of 1989. The beginning of the end of the cold war signaled significant changes in the policy options of East-West technology transfer. These essays suggest some of the possibilities for the future. "The book consists of three parts, dealing with the evolution of national approaches towards trade and technology transfer, economic factors behind the current change, and relationship between security and economics in the new circumstances." (p. vii) Review: *Foreign Affairs* 70, no.4 (Fall 1991): 172.

336. Monkiewicz, Jan, and Jan Maciejewicz, **Technology Export from the Socialist Countries**. Boulder, Colo.: Westview Press, 1986. x, 170 p. *Westview Special Studies in International Economics and Business*, ISBN: 0865318476.

"Only since the 1970s have the East European Socialist countries (known collectively as Comecon) participated in the international exchange of technology as exporters. In this book, Drs. Monkiewicz and Maciejewicz analyze the technology export performance of the Comecon countries. They begin by defining the nature of technology as a commodity, analyzing the structural characteristics of the international market, and outlining both the cost and benefits of technology export. Later chapters provide an overview of Comecon technological policies in the 1970s, with particular attention to the export-import factor and Comecon regional technological cooperation. In-depth analysis is presented through case studies of the experiences of Poland and Czechoslovakia. The book concludes with a discussion on the implication of technology export by socialist countries, particularly its potential impact on existing global patterns of technological dependence and domination." (p. iii)

337. Symposium on Science in Eastern Europe, **The Status of Civil Science in Eastern Europe: Proceedings of the Symposium on Science in Eastern Europe, NATO Headquarters, Brussels, Belgium, September 28-30, 1988,** edited by Craig Sinclair. USA and Canada: Kluwer Academic Publishers, 1989. xxviii, 363 p. ISBN: 0792302672. Includes bibliographical references.

"NATO's Science Committee organized a symposium to examine the state of science in Eastern Europe. The meeting brought together more than 120 participants from all the Alliance countries and several other countries, from the UN and its agencies, OECD and the Commission of the European Communities. Various areas of interest were examined—biotechnology, pharmaceuticals, materials, lasers and nuclear energy—through the presentation of case studies by bench scientists with experience of working in Bulgaria, Czechoslovakia, Hungary, the German Democratic Republic, Poland and Romania." (backcover) The essays are grouped into four sections. The first gives an overview of science in Eastern Europe focusing on scientific and technical cooperation. Part two is called "Procedures and Linkages" with general comparison of science in the East and West, and a discussion of incentives for research using Poland as an example. There is also an essay on the myth of science as the economic savior of the economy. Part three is composed of the case studies described above. The final section gives an overview of the present state of East European science and its future.

THE DOWNFALL OF COMMUNISM

338. Abel, Elie, **The Shattered Bloc: Behind the Upheaval in Eastern Europe**. Boston: Houghton Mifflin, 1990. 278 p. ISBN: 0395420199.

An analysis of the changes in Eastern Europe by scholar and former journalist Elie Abel. Each country is examined in turn, looking at the tremendous changes that have occurred as the "Soviet/East European Bloc" dissolves. The book is divided into two parts. In part one the author focuses on each country individually. In the second part, general aspects of reform and the difficulties that have arisen are considered. This is a thoughtful, impressionistic analysis.

339. **Eastern Europe in Revolution,** edited by Ivo Banac. Ithaca, N.Y.: Cornell University Press, 1992. x, 255 p. ISBN: 0801499976. Includes bibliographical references and index.

The essays in this book were the result of a conference held at Yale University, November 5, 1990. "The articles assembled in this book represent the first thoroughgoing assessments of the Eastern European revolution of 1989... whether they discuss the Hungarian 'revolution' that ended a decade of piecemeal retreat by the ruling Communists, or the strange turnabout of 1991 in Albania, where the revisionism of the Krushchev era, the move toward a free market of the early 1980s, and the pluralist upsurge of 1989 were telescoped in an odd revolution interrupta, they always seek to explain the sources, issues, and political contenders in the unheroic fall of East European communism." (p. ix) The contributors are scholars from all over the world.

340. **The New Democracies in Eastern Europe: Party Systems and Political Cleavages,** edited by Sten Berglund and Jan Ake Dellenbrant. Brookfield, Vt., USA: E. Elgar, 1991. xii, 237 p. *Studies of Communism in Transition*, ISBN: 1852785241. Includes bibliographical references and index.

The emphasis of these articles by Finnish and Polish scholars "is on the recent party system and party arena events in Eastern Europe and the Baltic republics. The focus is on the breakdown of authoritarianism in the late 1980s and the early 1990s." (p. xi) Besides several articles covering the entire regime, there are individual ones devoted to Poland, the Baltics, GDR, Czechoslovakia, Hungary and Bulgaria.

341. **Liberalization and Democratization: Change in the Soviet Union and Eastern Europe,** edited by Nancy Bermeo. Baltimore: Johns Hopkins University Press, 1992. 205 p. ISBN: 0801844185. Includes bibliographical references and index.

The essays collected here were intended for a special issue of *World Politics*. They do not share any common theoretical base but all do focus not only on why Eastern Europe and the Soviet Union changed but also why we in the West were so unprepared for that change. Each of the six essays examines a different aspect of the "disintegration of communist rule." "Timur Kuran and Giuseppe DiPalma focus on what the former calls the East European Revolution; Russell Bova and David Laitin focus on liberalization in the Soviet Union; and Andrew Janus focuses on the dynamics of political change in Eastern Europe, the Soviet Union, and China." (p. 1)

342. Bornstein, Jerry, **The Wall Came Tumbling Down: The Berlin Wall and the Fall of Communism,** introduction by Willy Brandt, photo research by Joan Levinstein, photographs courtesy of AP/ Wide World Photos. New York: Portland House, 1990. 95 p. ISBN: 0517033062.

This is a collection of photographs with accompanying text of the Berlin Wall, its history and eventual demise on November 9, 1989.

343. **Dilemmas of Transition in the Soviet Union and Eastern Europe,** edited by George W. Breslauer. Berkeley, CA: University of California at Berkeley, International and Area Studies, 1991. xi, 166 p.
These essays were originally presented at a conference at Berkeley in 1991. Five of the essays deal with general problems of transition. The other five essays focus on transition problems in specific countries: Poland, Yugoslavia, Hungary, Germany, and Romania.

344. Brown, James F., **Surge to Freedom: The End of Communist Rule in Eastern Europe.** Durham, NC: Duke University Press, 1991. x, 338 p. *Soviet and East European Studies*, ISBN: 0822311453 (pbk); 0822311267 (cloth). Includes bibliographical references (p. 323-324) and index.
Brown sees this book as both a companion to and revision and update of his 1988 work *Eastern Europe and Communist Rule.* In that earlier work he traces the history of Communism in Eastern Europe. Here he examines its downfall and the factors that caused that downfall. "An introduction giving a concise explanation of the immediate causes for the 1989 revolutions is followed by a longer chapter delving into their deeper reasons and posting the most important landmarks in the forty years of communist rule. A brief review of Gorbachev's revolution in Soviet policy toward Eastern Europe is followed by six 'country' chapters.
Finally there is a concluding chapter on the problems facing the new East European Democracies." (p. ix) An appendix containing a chronology of the events of 1989 in Eastern Europe is included. Review: *Foreign Affairs* 70, no.4 (Fall 1991): 182.

345. Cipkowski, Peter, **Revolution in Eastern Europe: Understanding the Collapse of Communism in Poland, Hungary, East Germany, Czechoslovakia, Romania, and the Soviet Union.** New York: Wiley, 1991. 184 p. *Our Changing World*, ISBN: 0471539686; 0471539678. Includes bibliographical references.
"The purpose of this book is to provide a general overview of the dramatic events that took place in Eastern Europe in 1989." (acknowledgments) Individual chapters are devoted to Poland, Hungary, East Germany, Czechoslovakia, Romania, and the Soviet Union. The volume also includes a pronunciation guide, glossary, and suggestions for further reading.

346. Drakulic, Slavenka, **How We Survived Communism and Even Laughed.** London: Hutchinson, 1992. xvii, 193 p. ISBN: 0091749255.
The author traveled on assignment for Ms. magazine to Hungary, Poland, Czechoslovakia, Bulgaria and East Germany in January and February of 1990 in order to understand at a more personal level than had been done, the reality of life in the East bloc, especially the lives and feelings of women in these countries. The result is a series of vignettes about people from those countries and the reality they face even now after the fall of communism.

347. Duignan, Peter, **Eastern Europe: The Great Transformation, 1985-1991,** Peter Duignan and L.H. Gann. Stanford, CA: Hoover Institution, 1992. 51 p. *Essays in Public Policy. no. 30*, ISBN: 0817953523. Includes bibliographical references.
This brief report issued by the Hoover Institution summarizes the events that led to the downfall of Communism in Eastern Europe. The Eastern European governments under communism were internally flawed particularly in that they were never able to gain legitimacy in the eyes of their own people. While making note of the serious problems facing these countries the authors feel that the new systems offer some hope of a better life for the people.

348. Echikson, William, **Lighting the Night: Revolution in Eastern Europe.** New York: W. Morrow, 1990. vii, 295 p. ISBN: 0688092004. Includes bibliographical references (p. 283-288) and index.

A journalist who has been reporting on Eastern Europe for many years recounts the events of the revolutions of the late 1980s. He surveys the events of the revolutions in the first section then turns to a broader portrayal of the area. The second part of the book examines the people: workers, intellectuals and students who had a direct role in the revolution. The third part focuses on issues of particular importance in motivating anti-Semitism and rising patriotism. Though most of the book is based on the author's reporting, some sources in English are listed in an annotated bibliography included at the end of the book. Review: *New York Times Book Review* (September 30,1990): 34.

349. **Crisis and Reform in Eastern Europe,** edited by Ferenc Fehrer and Andrew Arato. New Brunswick, USA: Transaction Publishers, 1991. ix, 531 p. ISBN: 0887383114. Includes bibliographical references and index.

This book grew out of a lecture series on East European societies organized by the graduate faculty of the New School for Social Research. The selection of materials for this volume was determined by the editors who wish to present a scholarly study of a region in flux. Essays on all countries are included but the topics discussed vary. The work begins with a general discussion of the transformation of socialist society. The concluding essay also discusses general themes. The intervening papers discuss economic, social, political and cultural problems of change facing Hungary, Romania, Poland, Yugoslavia and Czechoslovakia. Review: *Political Science Quarterly* 106, no.4 (Winter 1991-92): 749-751.

350. Garton Ash, Timothy, **The Magic Lantern: The Revolution of 1989 Witnessed in Warsaw, Budapest, Berlin, and Prague**. New York: Random House, 1990. 156 p. ISBN: 0394588843.

An account of the momentous changes in Poland, Hungary, East Germany and Czechoslovakia in 1989. The events described are from Garton Ash's first-hand experiences. The author is a well-known journalist who has worked many years in Eastern Europe and has connections with many of the leaders of the opposition to the Communist governments. Reviews: *Foreign Affairs* 69, no.5 (Winter 1990/91): 202. *New York Times Book Review* (July 22, 1990): 29.

351. Glenny, Misha, **The Rebirth of History: Eastern Europe in the Age of Democracy**. Harmondsworth: Penguin, 1990. 245 p. ISBN: 0140143947. Includes bibliographical references and index.

Misha Glenny was the reporter on Central Europe for the BBC's World Service in 1990. He experienced first hand the historical events that changed the political course of Eastern Europe and he has been friend to many of the major figures in the East European revolutions. In this book he describes what transpired in each of the East European countries during their break with Communism, what led up to it and suggests what the future may hold for these countries. He presents eyewitness accounts of many of the historic events of 1989 and 1990.

352. **The Collapse of Communism,** edited by Bernard Gwertzman and Michael T. Kaufman. New York: Times Book/Random House, 1990. 353 p. ISBN: 081291872X.

After a brief introductory chapter that outlines the events leading up to the fall of communism in 1989, six other chapters follow. These chapters are arranged chronologically from the winter of 1988-1989 to the winter of 1989-1990. Each chapter consists of *New York Times* articles arranged to give a semi-coherent account of events as they unfolded.

80 / Eastern Europe

353. **Restructuring Eastern Europe: Towards a New European Order,** edited by Ronald Hill and Jan Zielonka. Brookfield, Vt.: E. Elgar, 1990. viii, 226 p. *International Library of Studies in Communism*, ISBN: 185278377X. Includes bibliographical references.

This series of essays, written by a research theme group at the Netherlands Institute for Advanced Study, focused on two distinct sets of issues: "first, changes in the social, economic and political fields and their meaning for Western Europe; and second, human rights and their significance for European security." (p. l)

354. Laufer, Peter, **Iron Curtain Rising: A Personal Journey through the Changing Landscape of Eastern Europe.** San Francisco: Mercury House, 1991. 212 p. ISBN: 1562790153.

Laufer traveled for three years through Eastern Europe. "He spoke with apparatchiks and their victims, with those who were misled and those who thought ahead, with people in conflict and with bystanders. He watched them, and he was curious and inquisitive enough to get into some trouble himself." (p. xv) This narrative is, therefore, much more than your typical travel diary. He captures the taste and feeling of the East European revolution itself.

355. Lesourne, Jacques, and Bernard Lecomte, **After Communism: From the Atlantic to the Urals,** translated from the French by Chris Miller. Philadelphia: Harwood Academic Publishers, 1991. 271 p. ISBN: 3718652129; 3718652110. Translation of L'Apres Communisme. Includes bibliographical references (p. 267) and index.

Eastern Europe has changed dramatically since Gorbachev came to power. How the changes came about and what is in store for the future are the main themes of this study. The authors approach their subject through an analysis of political and economic history. "The first part of the book covers the years of Gorbachev's greatest impact on European affairs: the reunification of Germany, the end of the Cold War; Poland, Hungary and Czechoslovakia freed from Soviet domination. The second part provides different scenarios for Europe's future in a bold attempt at geopolitical and economic forecasting." (back cover) The authors are both well known French journalists. This book originally appeared in French in November, 1990.

356. Mason, David S., **Revolution in East-Central Europe: The Rise and Fall of Communism and the Cold War.** Boulder, Colo.: Westview Press, 1992. xiv, 216 p. ISBN: 0813313414. Includes bibliographical references and index.

Mason's five chapters provide an introduction to the 1989 revolution in Eastern Europe. Topics covered include the establishment and decay of communism in East-Central Europe, reform and revolution in the Soviet Union and East-Central Europe, Eastern European responses to revolution, theories of social, economic and political change, and the postcommunist era in international politics.

357. **Post-Communist Eastern Europe: Crisis and Reform,** edited by Andrew A. Michta and Ilya Prizel. New York: St. Martin's Press, 1992. x, 205 p. ISBN: 0312075642. Includes bibliographical references and index.

This collection of essays by East European specialists intends to analyze the political, social, and economic changes that resulted from the 1989 revolution.

358. **The New Political Geography of Eastern Europe,** edited by John O'Loughlin and Herman van der Wusten. London: Belhaven, 1993. x, 280 p. ISBN: 0470219335. Includes bibliographical references and index.

"This book examines the background to the events that led up to the fall of the former Communist regimes, the major problems confronting Eastern European politicians and the outcomes of the first democratic elections in over 40 years." (back cover) The chapters, each written by an expert, are divided into four sections. Part I is an introduction that emphasizes main themes and the transition to democracy. Part II discusses geopolitical shifts that have occurred as a result of the upheaval. Part III focuses on social and political transformations and Part IV analyzes new electoral geographies.

359. Rapoport, Roger, **Into the Sunlight: Life after the Iron Curtain**. Berkeley, Calif.: Heyday Books, 1990. vii, 104 p. ISBN: 0930588495 (pbk). Includes bibliographical references.

This book is "a collection of incidents, experiences and conversations with Eastern Europeans and Soviets" (p. 2) that the author gathered during January and February of 1990. It focuses primarily an everyday life and social mores.

360. **Perestroika: A Comparative Perspective,** edited by Avraham Shama. New York: Praeger, 1992. xiv, 132 p. ISBN: 0275940381. Includes bibliographical references (p. 119-124) and index.

"This book provides an overview of economic and political democratization in Eastern European countries, as well as a comparative perspective of these processes. Equally important is that the contributors to this book include several Eastern European scholars with distinctive points of view." (p. xi)

361. Staniszkis, Jadwiga, **The Dynamics of the Breakthrough in Eastern Europe: The Polish Experience,** translated by Chester A. Kisiel, foreword by Ivan Szelenyi. Berkeley: University of California Press, 1991. xiii, 303 p. *Society and Culture in East Central Europe, 6*, ISBN: 0520072189. Includes bibliography (p.249-294) and index.

This collection of essays is "an ongoing, theoretically informed commentary of revolutionary events by a 'participant observer' " (p. vii) Topics covered include the logic of privatization in Eastern Europe, the public scene during the decline of the socialist system, the collapse of the new center and its reorganization, and the role of society in the revolution from above.

362. **The Road to Disillusion: From Critical Marxism to Post-Communism in Eastern Europe**, edited by Raymond Taras et al. Armonk, N.Y.: M.E. Sharpe, 1992. x, 206 p. ISBN: 0873327918. Includes bibliographical references and index.

Each of the contributors to this volume describes and analyzes the role critical Marxism played in the events that culminated in the revolution in Eastern Europe in 1989. Individual essays are devoted to the Soviet Bloc as a whole, the Soviet Union, Hungary, the GDR, Poland, Czechoslovakia, Romania, Bulgaria, and Yugoslavia.

363. Weigel, George, **The Final Revolution: The Resistance Church and the Collapse of Communism**. New York: Oxford University Press, 1992. xvi, 255 p. ISBN: 0195071603. Includes index.

Many books have examined the role of political or economic factors in the revolution of 1989. In this work, George Weigel looks at the role of religion in the fall of communism. "...It treats more of priests than of politicians, takes the world of the spirit more seriously than the world of economics, and argues that a religious institution typically regarded as cautious and conservative was instrumental in demolishing one of the twentieth century's greatest (and most despicable) concentrations of aggressively secular power." (p. ix) The book is organized topically beginning with several chapters providing background on the political and religious institutions of Eastern Europe as they developed in the twentieth century. The later chapters of Weigel's book focus on Pope John Paul II and the role of the Catholic Church in Eastern Europe as a whole but with particular emphasis on Poland and Czechoslovakia.

364. **Handbook of Reconstruction in Eastern Europe and the Soviet Union**, edited by Stephen White. Detroit, Michigan: Gale Research Co., 1991. viii, 407 p. *Longman Current Affairs*, ISBN: 0582085020. Includes index.

"The various contributors to this volume explore in detail the changes that have come about in Eastern Europe and the USSR over these recent years and months. All the chapters follow a similar format: there are chronologies to begin with, then overviews of recent political and economic developments, and then more detailed entries on economic sectors, foreign trade, key personalities, the media, and foreign policy." (p. vi) Also included are treaties and constitutions of the period, as well as individual chapters in East-West economic relations and COMECON and the Warsaw Treaty Organization.

Chapter 2
ALBANIA

365. Biberaj, Elez, **Albania: A Socialist Maverick**. Boulder, Colo.: Westview Press, 1990. vii, 157 p. *Westview Profiles. Nations of Contemporary Eastern Europe*, ISBN: 0813305136. Includes bibliographical references and index.

This is a brief profile of Albania as it goes through the changes of the 1980s and 1990s. The chapters discuss the geographical setting, political context, governmental structure, economy, foreign policy and the problems faced by Albanians in Yugoslavia. A selected bibliography is included. Review: *Canadian Slavonic Papers* 32, no.2 (June 1990): 199-200.

366. ———, **Albania and China: A Study of an Unequal Alliance**. Boulder, Colo.: Westview Press, 1986. xi, 183 p. *Westview Special Studies in International Relations*, ISBN: 0813372305. Includes index and bibliography (p. 167-179).

This is the first study of relations between Albania and China. One of the most unusual features of their relationship is that China has not always been the dominant force in the interaction between the two countries. "This interaction, examined here from the Albanian viewpoint, was made all the more unique by a basic incongruity of interests, a great geographical distance, profound historical and cultural differences, and significant disparities in economic and military capabilities." (p. iii) Biberaj uses a cost-benefit analysis in his study. The book has a chronological arrangement tracing their relations up to 1985. An extensive bibliography of English language and Albanian sources is included.

367. **Albania, from Isolation Toward Reform,** Mario I. Blejer et al. Washington, D.C.: International Monetary Fund, 1992. vii, 84 p. ISBN: 1557752664. Includes bibliographical references (p. 58).

This report, prepared by a team of experts at the International Monetary Fund, sheds some light on the previously hidden state of the Albanian economy. Individual chapters give an overview and a historical and political background, a sketch of the pre-reform economic system, economic performance in the 1980s, political and economic developments in 1991 and a final chapter looking toward further economic reform. An especially valuable part of this publication are the statistics on various aspects of the Albanian economy.

368. Camaj, Martin, **Selected Poetry,** translated from the Albanian by Leonard Fox. New York: New York University Press, 1990. xvii, 207 p. *New York University Studies in Near Eastern Civilization, no. 14*, ISBN: 0814714447.

Martin Camaj has been called the best of the exiled Albanian writers (see *Columbia Dictionary of Modern European Literature,* p. 13). In his work can be found archaic and modern elements. This collection of poems has been translated with the assistance of the author. Works from both the author's early and more recent works are included. The Albanian and English translation of each work appear in this volume. A linguistic commentary is also included. Review: *World Literature Today* 65, no.4 (Autumn 1991): 746.

369. Elsie, Robert, **Dictionary of Albanian Literature**. Westport, Conn.: Greenwood Press, 1986. viii, 170 p. ISBN: 031325186X. Includes index and bibliography (p. 157-59).

The paucity of English-language reference sources on Albania is remarkable. This volume, the purpose of which is to provide "the Western reader with basic information on Albanian literature from its origins to the present day," is a welcome addition to this category. Elsie provides annotations on over five hundred Albanian writers and literature-related topics. Although noted scholars, journalists, and publishers are included, this is done only selectively, based on their relevance to Albanian literature. Entries are arranged according to English alphabetical order, not Albanian. Each name entry includes pseudonyms when applicable, major works and dates of publication with translated titles, a select bibliography of critical works, and other relevant biographical information such as education and current town of residence. A name and anonymous work index that includes cross-references is also provided. The entries are clearly and concisely written. Elsie admits that some source data (e.g., publication dates) are "in an extremely poor state due to the inadequate system of national bibliographic control." Review: *Choice* 452 (November 1986).

370. Hibbert, Reginald, **Albania's National Liberation Struggle: The Bitter Victory.** New York: Pinter Publishers, 1991. xiv, 269 p. ISBN: 086187109X. Includes bibliographical references (p. 255-56) and indexes.

"This book concentrates on trying to throw light in the events of 1943 and 1944 and on the circumstances of Albania's re-birth as a communist state." (p. 2) The author was a British liaison officer in Albania during World War II and this description and analysis is based partly on a diary he kept at the time.

371. Kadare, Ismail, **The General of the Dead Army,** translated from the French by Derek Coltman. New York: New Amsterdam, 1991. 251 p. ISBN: 1561310077. The French edition: Le general de l'armee morte was translated from the original Albanian, Gjenerali i ushterise se vdekur.

Ismail Kadare is recognized as one of the great writers of the twentieth century. His international reputation has been based largely on his prose. "*The General of the Dead Army* is a study of post war Albania as seen through the eyes of an Italian general accompanied by a priest on a mission to Albania to find and repatriate the remains of soldiers fallen in the war,...." (Robert Elsie, *Dictionary of Albanian Literature*, p. 72) Reviews: *World & I* 6, no.4 (April 1991): 381-389. *World Literature Today* 65, no.4 (Autumn 1991): 746-747.

372. Pipa, Arshi, **Contemporary Albanian Literature**. New York: Columbia University Press, 1991. vii, 175 p. *East European Monographs,* no. 305, ISBN: 0880332026. Includes bibliography (p. 165-175).

Pipa examines contemporary Albanian literature in this two part work. Part one looks at Albanian socialist realism, with a special focus on Ismaul Kadore. Part two focuses exclusively on Martin Camaj's poetry and poetics.

373. ———, **The Politics of Language in Socialist Albania**. New York: Colombia University Press, 1987. xvi, 283 p. *East European Monographs,* no. 271, ISBN: 0880331682. Includes bibliographical references (p.238-267).

Under the communist regime the Gheg (northern) and Tosk (southern) dialects of Albanian were brought together into unified literary Albanian. This linguistic imperialism (Gheg speakers were anti-communist) has a fascinating history. Pipa describes the process by which this transformation took place, some phonemic and morphemic aspects of both languages, and other topics relevant to linguistic politics in Albania.

374. Zymberi, Isa, **Colloquial Albanian**. New York: Routledge, 1991. x, 359 p. *Colloquial Series,* ISBN: 0415056640 (cassette); 0415056659 (book, cassette pack); 0415056632.

This textbook is designed to give its users an intermediate knowledge of Albanian. Each lesson begins with sample conversations for everyday situations. This is followed by grammatical explanations and reading passages. Exercises in each chapter provide the student with practice in responding to questions in Albanian, as well as translating. A glossary of 2,000 terms appears at the end of the volume in both Albanian-English and English-Albanian versions. A cassette to accompany the lessons is also available from the publisher.

Chapter 3
BULGARIA

GENERAL REFERENCE WORKS

375. **Bulgaria, a Country Study.** Federal Research Division, Library of Congress; edited by Glenn E. Curtis. 2nd ed Washington, D.C.: Federal Research Division, Library of Congress, 1993. 328 p. *Area Handbook Series, 1057-5294, DA pam; 550-168*, ISBN: 0844407518. Includes bibliographical references and index.

This is one of a series of handbooks on countries of the world. This specific edition was prepared by several specialists after the ouster of Todor Zhivkov in 1989. "The authors of this edition have described the changes in Bulgaria occurring in the last twenty years, with special emphasis on the last three. They have used the historical, political, and social fabric of the country as the background for these descriptions to ensure understanding of the context of the important recent events that have shaped the Bulgaria we see today. The authors' goal was to provide a compact, accessible, and objective treatment of five main topics: historical setting, society and its environment, the economy, government and politics, and the military and national security." (p. xiii)

376. McIntyre, Robert J., **Bulgaria: Politics, Economics, and Society.** New York: Pinter Publishers, 1988. vii, 201 p. *Marxist Regime Series*, ISBN: 0861873998 (pbk); 086187398X. Includes bibliography (p.177-190) and index.

His work "provides the reader with an in-depth analysis of the background, current state and prospects of success of the various experiments taking place in the country's economic, social and political life." (p. v)

377. Ward, Phillip, **Sofia: Portrait of a City.** Cambridge, England: Oleander Press, 1993. x, 211 p. ISBN: 0906672651. Includes index.

This handy volume is both a guide to the city of Sofia and a municipal travelogue by the author. Not only does he describe the many sights, monuments and attractions of Sofia, but he also enters the private lives of several of its citizens. Along the way he also manages to provide some of the history of this city. A section at the end of the book contains useful travel information.

HISTORY

378. Clarke, James Franklin, **The Pen and the Sword: Studies in Bulgarian History,** edited by Dennis P. Hupchick. New York: Columbia University Press, 1988. xxii, 537 p. *East European Monographs,* no. 252, ISBN: 0880331496. Includes bibliography (p. 491-528).

James F. Clarke was considered by many to have been the dean of Bulgarian historical scholarship in America. This volume includes thirty four studies by this eminent scholar written over a period of years from the 1940s to the 1980s. The essays are grouped under six headings: "General Studies," "Historiography and Historical Sources," "The Bulgarian National Revival, Part 1: Literature and Printing," "The Bulgarian National Revival , Part 2: Bible Translation," "Americans and Bulgarians, Part 1: Missionaries," "Americans and

Bulgarians, Part 2: The 1876 April Uprising and the Russo-Turkish War of 1877-78." The title of the volume reflects the theme of his writing. "One of the fathers of modern East European studies in the United States, Clarke was primarily interested in studying the rise and consequences of modern nationalism among the Christian subject peoples of the Ottoman-dominated Balkan Peninsula. In his perception of that historical process, the written word ..., and armed revolt ..., were the subject Christian's only recourses in battling for their respective national independence from their common Ottoman masters." (p. vi)

379. Crampton, R. J., **A Short History of Modern Bulgaria**. New York: Cambridge University Press, 1987. xiii, 221 p. ISBN: 0521273234 (pbk); 0521253403. Includes bibliography (p. 210-213) and index.

A chronological study of Bulgarian history emphasizing the events from 1878 to the mid 1980s. The book is divided into four chapters. The first gives an overview of pre-modern Bulgaria (to 1878), creating the context for the remainder of the study. Chapter two examines events from liberation in 1878 to the end of the First World War. The third chapter covers events from 1918 to 1944. The final section reviews events in Bulgaria during the years of Communist rule. The book was intended as an introductory history of the country. The emphasis throughout this study is on political events. Cultural issues have, in some cases, been treated in a cursory way and the author is well aware of the problems this creates. The work is intended for the general reader and includes a list of suggested further readings. Reviews: *Canadian-American Slavic Studies* 24, no.3 (Fall 1990): 362-363. *Problems of Communism* 39, no.5 (September-October 1990): 75-83.

380. Groueff, Stephane, **Crown of Thorns**. Lanham, MD: Madison Books, 1987. 411 p. ISBN: 0819157783. Includes bibliography (p. 399-402).

This biography of King Boris is also a narrative of the events that took place in Bulgaria during his reign. The book is arranged chronologically and relies heavily on primary source materials and published memoirs.

381. Hupchick, Dennis P., **The Bulgarians in the Seventeenth Century: Slavic Orthodox Society and Culture Under Ottoman Rule**. Jefferson, N.C.: McFarland, 1993. xxvii, 314 p. ISBN: 0899508227. Includes bibliographical references (p. 269-298) and index.

Dennis Hupchick has set out to discover how the Bulgarians as an ethnic group survived their domination by the Ottomans and maintained their cultural identity. Hupchick believes that a large part of the explanation lies with the Bulgarians' tie to the Orthodox Church. "First, it was widely recognized that the Orthodox Church played a seminal role in preserving ethnic traditions among its faithful both because it was never a monolithic entity, like the Roman Catholic Church, but rather was composed of various separate ethnic church organizations,... and because it enjoyed a position under the Ottoman empire that imparted a certain amount of autonomy to its membership. Second, in the writings of the early literary figures of the Bulgarian national revival,... Orthodox religious culture was the bridge used to link fellow Bulgarians to their medieval ancestors." (p. ix) The author has focused on this particular period because it was the low point in Bulgarian national history. The book is arranged topically beginning with an overview of Bulgarian life under the Ottomans and then turning to specific aspects of Bulgarian culture; monasticism, education, literature and art. The final section examines Orthodox cultural activity.

ECONOMICS, TRADE AND BUSINESS

382. **Bulgaria: Crisis and Transition to a Market Economy**. Washington, D.C.: World Bank, 1991. 2 v. *World Bank Country Study*, ISBN: 0821318942 (v. 1); 0821318950 (v. 2).

Just prior to Bulgaria becoming a member of the World Bank on September 25, 1990, a World Bank economic mission visited Bulgaria in June and July. These two volumes are a partial result of that visit. Volume one deals with the overall economic structure, the macroeconomic situation and details the needs for reform of the entire economic system. Individual chapters are devoted to the emerging economic crisis (balance of payments, fiscal and monetary policy, prices, wages, and benefits), macroeconomic issues, market reforms, and the pace and sequence of reforms. Volume II deals with an analysis of individual sectors, including industry, energy, agriculture, the environment, the financial system, social services, social assistance, tourism, housing, transportation, education, and health. Volume one also includes a sixty page statistical annex.

383. Lampe, John R., **The Bulgarian Economy in the Twentieth Century**. London: Croom Helm, 1986. x, 245 p. *Croom Helm Series on the Contemporary Economic History of Europe*, ISBN: 0709916442. Includes index and bibliography (p. 231-236).

Lampe's treatise on the Bulgarian economy is similar to other volumes in this series in that they all present the economic history of the country coupled with an assessment of current economic conditions and prospects for the future. The author's first six chapters are devoted to economic history including its initial growth period from 1878 to 1918, the economic recovery of the 1920s, the isolation of the 1930s, the Second World War, the communist revolution of 1944 to 1947 and the first five year plans. The remaining three chapters cover contemporary conditions focusing on industry and agriculture since 1960, foreign trade and domestic living standards and economic reform since 1960. In his conclusion Lampe speculates on the path of the economy for the remainder of this century. Review: *Journal of Economic History* 47, no.4 (December 1987): 1024-26.

384. **Bulgaria—an Economic Assessment**. Paris: Centre for Co-operation with the European Economies in Transition, 1992. 101 p. ISBN: 926413753X. Includes bibliographical references.

"This is the first OECD study of Bulgaria's economy. It analyzes the economic situation, describes the reform effort so far, and identifies priority areas from further policy action. The study argues that structural reform and macroeconomic stability are closely linked. Progress in these two areas could lead to a substantial reduction of the heavy external debt burden." (back cover)

385. Solimano, Andres, **Inflation and Growth in the Transition from Socialism: The Case of Bulgaria**. Washington D.C.: Country Economics Dept. World Bank, 1991. 51 p. *Policy, Research and External Affairs Working Papers,* WPS 659. Includes bibliographical references (p. 46).

Bulgaria is faced with an expanding foreign debt, rising domestic inflation, a devaluation of its currency, in short a general deteriorization of its situation. This study examines how a nation makes the transition from socialism to a market economy when faced with a collapsing economy. After providing some background to the situation the author looks at inflation and the fiscal deficit. Next Solimano turns to inflation from the cost side examining how two factors, devaluation of the leva and increase in the price of CMEA imports, impact the inflationary process. The determinants of growth in the 1980s, a description of the economic collapse of the 1990s and the transition to a market economy are the topics of the next section. A list of references and appendix on the equations used are provided.

LANGUAGE AND LITERATURE

386. Gribble, Charles E., **Reading Bulgarian Through Russian**. Columbus, Ohio: Slavica, 1987. 181 p. ISBN: 0893571067. Includes bibliography (p. 175-181).

The purpose of this book is to teach the user to read contemporary literary Bulgarian. It assumes that the user has a good knowledge of modern Russian, the book explains the most important features of Bulgarian in comparison with Russian; this expository material is then followed by exercises and readings.

387. **Window on the Black Sea: Bulgarian Poetry in Translation,** edited by Richard Harteis; in collaboration with William Meredith. 1st ed Pittsburgh, Pa.: Carnegie Mellon University Press, 1992. 183 p. ISBN: 0887481418.

Thirty-three of Bulgaria's contemporary poets are included in this volume. The poems have been "adapted" to English by American poets who worked with translators on the poems. "Many of the poems in this volume reflect the changes and hopes for the future that the recent political ferment has produced. Others, however, were written in that difficult period when survival as an artist meant walking a dangerous tight rope, where poetry became a kind of secret code, a way of speaking through metaphor when more direct speech might simply eliminate the poet from the scene." (pp. 15-16) A biographical list providing the author's dates of birth and the titles of their most recent publications is included at the back of the book.

388. Holloway, Ronald, **The Bulgarian Cinema**. Rutherford, N.J: Fairleigh Dickinson University Press, 1986. 216 p. ISBN: 0838631835 (alk. paper). Includes index.

Holloway presents an historical overview of Bulgarian cinema. In the three chapters of part one he offers cultural background information, covers the principal directors of the post war period, and examines trends and key films. Part two contains a filmography (1915-1985) and an index of film titles.

389. Rudin, Catherine, **Aspects of Bulgarian Syntax: Complementizers and WH Constructions**. Columbus, Ohio: Slavica Publishers, 1986. iv, 232 p. ISBN: 0893571563. Based on the author's thesis (Ph.D.), Indiana University, 1982. Includes bibliography (p.211-221).

Rudin offers a detailed study of Bulgarian syntax with special emphasis on interrogations and relative clauses.

390. **Clay and Star: Contemporary Bulgarian Poets,** translated and edited by Lisa Sapinkopf and Georgi Belev; introduction by Charles A. Moser. Minneapolis, Minn.: Milkweed Editions, 1992. 227 p. ISBN: 0915943859.

"*Clay and Star* is a vibrant English-language anthology of Bulgarian poetry. This collection includes twenty-seven of Bulgaria's most talented and original poets, revealing an array of voices—vibrant and subtle, whimsical and contemplative, wickedly satiric and hauntingly elegiac—that managed to flourish during the repressive post-war years." (back cover) Charles Moser, a distinguished scholar of Bulgarian literature, has also written a brief essay on poetry and politics in Bulgaria that is included in this volume.

391. **Young Poets of a New Bulgaria: An Anthology,** edited by Belin Tonchev, illustrated by Petur Petsin, introduced by Sebastian Barker. Boston: Forest Books, 1990. xvii, 150 p. ISBN: 094825971X.

This anthology of twenty-two contemporary Bulgarian poets presents a good selection of poets with "a renewed vision of life."

GOVERNMENT, POLITICS AND LAW

392. Bell, John D., **The Bulgarian Communist Party from Blagoev to Zhivkov**. Stanford, Calif.: Hoover Institution Press, 1986. xii, 202 p. *Histories of Ruling Communist Parties.* Hoover Press Publication 320, ISBN: 0817982027. Includes bibliography (p.181-191) and index.

This is a history of the Bulgarian Communist Party from its origins to the early 1980s. In addition to various statistical tables on party membership, elections, and trade data, the author has also included ten appendices concerning the party congresses and plenums from 1944 to 1981.

393. **Violations of the Helsinki Accords, Bulgaria: A Report Prepared for the Helsinki Review Conference, Vienna, November 1986** (by Daphne Eviatar). New York: US Helsinki Watch Committee, 1986. iv, 33 p. ISBN: 0938579789. Includes bibliography (p. 33).

This report, with others, was prepared for the Helsinki Review Conference in Vienna, Austria in 1986. Like its comparison volumes, it deals with severe human rights violations in the country in question. Separate chapters are devoted to the Turkish minority, the freedom of expression, privacy, movement, association, and religion, and the existence of political prisoners.

394. Perry, Duncan M., **Stefan Stambolov and the Emergence of Modern Bulgaria, 1870-1895.** Durham, NC: Duke University Press, 1993. xiv, 308 p. ISBN: 0822313138. Includes bibliographical references and index.

After the defeat of the Serbs in 1886, Stambolov emerged as a national savior. From then until 1894 when he departed as prime minister, he was both hated and respected. This biography of Stambolov is set in the context of those years and the national and international events that affected his tenure as prime minister.

395. Petkov, Petko M., **The United States and Bulgaria in World War I**. New York: Distributed by Columbia University Press, 1991. vi, 252 p. *East European Monographs,* no. 306, ISBN: 0880332034. Includes bibliographical references (p. 142-159).

The U.S. was the only major power at the Paris Peace Conference that supported the Bulgarian national cause. Petkov's book examines the involvement of both nations in World War I and the diplomatic history that led to U.S. support of Bulgaria. Essential elements of the Balkan Question are also investigated.

396. Zhivkova, Lyudmila, **Lyudmila Zhivkova: Her Many Worlds, New Culture and Beauty, Concepts and Action**. New York: Pergamon Press, 1986. 335 p. ISBN: 0080348556. Includes bibliography (p. 329-330) and index.

Biographical materials on and essays of Lyudmila Zhivkova are collected in this volume. Lyudmila was the daughter of Todor Zhivkov, former head of the Bulgarian Communist government. The volume includes essays about Zhivkova, a chronology of her life, and a bibliography.

397. Zang, Ted, **Destroying Ethnic Identity. The Gypsies of Bulgaria**. New York: Human Rights Watch, 1991. 73 p. *Helsinki Watch Report*, ISBN: 0300056052; 1564320324. Includes bibliographical references.

The Gypsies of Eastern Europe have always been a target of discrimination in the area. Bulgaria is no exception. In that country the Gypsies have been denied access to the university system, they are forced to live in the most densely populated areas, they are not allowed to form a political party representing their ethnic interests and they find it difficult to be promoted. This report, issued by the Helsinki Watch Committee, discusses the historical situation of Gypsies and then goes on to look at contemporary conditions, suggesting changes to improve the situation. Two appendices are translations of the actions of the Central Committee of the Bulgarian Communist Party taken against the Gypsies in the past.

THE SOCIETY, SOCIOLOGY

398. Hadjihristev, Argir Kirkov, **Life-Styles for Long Life: Longevity in Bulgaria,** translated and edited with an introduction by Gary Lesnoff-Caravaglia. Springfield, IL: Charles C. Thomas, 1988. xxviii, 96 p. ISBN: 0398054835. Includes bibliography (p. 77-86) and index.

The author's translated study contains two parts: part one on longevity in general and part two on the longevous of the Smolian Province of Bulgaria. Factors examined include economic, geographic and demographic data, life style, dietary regimen, work capacity, ancestry, lipid and protein profiles and condition of cardiovascular system. Reviews: *American Anthropologist* 92, no.2 (June 1990): 594-550. *Contemporary Sociology* 19, no.1 (January 1990): 40-42.

399. Ward, Philip, **Bulgarian Voices: Letting the People Speak**. Cambridge, England: Oleander, 1992. xiii, 330 p. ISBN: 0906672643. Includes index.

Bulgarian Voices is the collection of discussions by Bulgarians on a wide range of topics after the fall of the communist regime. The subjects under discussion range from politics and the economy to sports and fashion design. Many monologues occurred by chance but the compiler notes a bias toward the intelligentsia. Nevertheless, this compilation gives the reader a unique view of life in Bulgaria.

Chapter 4
CZECHOSLOVAKIA

GENERAL REFERENCE WORKS

400. Dubcek, Alexander, **Hope Dies Last: The Autobiography of Alexander Dubcek,** edited and translated by Jiri Hochman. New York: Kodansha International, 1993. 354 p. ISBN: 1568360002. Includes index.

This autobiography of Alexander Dubcek, who was head of state of Czechoslovakia until 1968 when the Soviets crushed the flowering of freedom known as Prague Spring, covers the author's life from childhood until 1989 and the commencement of the Velvet Revolution.

401. **Czechoslovakia, a Country Study,** edited by Ihor Y. Gawdiak. Washington, D.C.: The Division: for sale by the Supt. of Docs., U.S. G.P.O., 1989. xxix, 421 p. *DA Pam,* 550-158. Includes bibliography (p.363-391) and index.

This reference handbook, written by a team of social scientists, describes and analyzes the history, society, economy, and politics and national security of Czechoslovakia. It also contains four appendices that provide statistical tables, a chapter on the Council of Mutual Economic Assistance, the Warsaw Pact, and the Manifesto of Charter 77.

402. Ryznar, Eliska, and Murlin Croucher, **Books in Czechoslovakia: Past and Present.** Wiesbaden: Harrassowitz, 1989. vi, (i), (6) p. of plates, 107 p. *Publishing, Bibliography, Libraries, and Archives in Russia and Eastern Europe,* v.2, ISBN: 3447029307. Includes bibliographical references (p.99-101) and index.

Until the publication of this volume there were no major studies of Czech and Slovak books and libraries in the West. In Czechoslovakia such studies focused, almost exclusively, on the pre-World War I period. "The present work hopes to make a contribution towards filling this gap. The authors make an effort to summarize in brief form the crucial components of the history which shaped the development of books, libraries, and bibliography in Czechoslovakia and to indicate the forces and events which shape the future." (p.vii) The book is divided into two parts, one on Czech book culture, the other on Slovak book culture. Each contain sections on the development of book culture, libraries and archives, and bibliography. Works cited in the text are in translated form.

403. Short, David, **Czechoslovakia.** Santa Barbara, CA: ABC-Clio Press, 1986. xxv, 409 p. *World bibliographical series,* v.68, ISBN: 1851090118. Includes index.

An annotated bibliography covering a wide range of topics. It includes English, West European and Czech language sources. The compiler admits to a somewhat random selection of titles. Monographic works have been preferred over periodical titles. "The bibliography covers a broad range of subjects including history, the 'Prague Spring' and the events of 1968, literature, language, music and the arts, foreign relations, the economy, education, religion, nationalities and minorities, flora and fauna and sports and recreation. Containing 1000 critically annotated and informative entries the volume provides the English-speaking reader with a panorama of Czechoslovakia." (back cover) A map of Czechoslovakia is included. Review: *Kosmas* 6, no.2 (Winter 1987): 180-182.

HISTORY

404. Bartos, Frantisek Michalek, **The Hussite Revolution, 1424-1437,** English edition prepared by John M. Klassen. New York: Columbia University Press, 1986. xx, 204 p. *East European Monographs,* no. 203, ISBN: 088033097. Translation of: Husitska revoluce. Includes bibliographical references and index.

This study goes well beyond other extant works on the Hussite revolution, by extending the history of the revolution to 1437. This translation is an abridgment of the Czech original and polemics with other Czech authors have also been omitted in the footnotes. Review: *Canadian Slavonic Papers* 29, no.2/3 (June/ September 1987): 356-58.

405. Chnoupek, Bohus, **A Breaking of Seals: The French Resistance in Slovakia,** translated from the Slovak by Robert Pynsent, with an introduction by Karel Brusak and Robert Pynsent. New York: Pergamon Press, 1988. xi, 97 p. ISBN: 0080371299 (pbk); 0080348696.

Chnoupek is an accomplished journalist and author. The present work is a documentary one, but includes vivid narration and dialogue. "The book deals with the participation in the Slovak Uprising in 1944 of the French soldiers who escaped from prisoner-of-war camps in Hungary and Dubnica in Slovakia. They formed, under the leadership of Captain Georges de Lannurien, a Detachement francais des combattants de la Tchecoslovaquie, and fought at the side of the Slovak Army, which rose against their own state. Later, as part of the Stefanik Brigade, they fought side by side with the partisans. Their lot, both as members of the collective and as individuals, is depicted against the backcloth of the Uprising." (p.viii)

406. Crane, John O., and Sylvia E. Crane, **Czechoslovakia: Anvil of the Cold War**. New York: Praeger, 1991. xxvi, 352 p. ISBN: 0275935779. Includes bibliography (p.335-342) and index.

John Crane, former secretary to Tomas Masaryk, and his wife, journalist Sylvia Crane, have set about describing Czechoslovakia's role in the Cold War. "The title of this book is self-explanatory. It is the contemporary story of how this Slavic nation located astride the East-West watershed innocently and for no reasons of her own became involved in the Cold War on four successive occasions and emerged as its principal victim." (xvii) The authors focus on the economy of Czechoslovakia in 1918, the Munich betrayal in 1938 and the communist coup of 1948. They have deliberately stopped with the death of Jan Masaryk in 1948, omitting discussion of the events of 1968 as the archives on this topic are unavailable to them. The study is chronological in structure.

407. Kalvoda, Josef, **The Genesis of Czechoslovakia**. New York: Distributed by Columbia University Press, 1986. viii, 673 p. *East European Monographs,* no. 209, ISBN: 0880331062. Includes bibliography (p. 611-648) and index.

A history of the origins of Czechoslovakia. The author does not subscribe to the concept of "Czechoslovak nation." The study is chronologically arranged. The author has drawn on his own extensive collection of documents as well as many other sources for his material. The main purpose of this account is to present a "true" picture of the formation of the Czechoslovakian state. In so doing the author concludes that that state arose largely as the result of historical accidents domestically and internationally. Further he believes that the Czechs and Slovaks should learn to ally themselves with other Central European Nations. "When Soviet rule comes to its end—and this will happen one day—the Czechs and Slovaks should cooperate with other small nations in the area and find a federal solution to the problem common to all of them: they are too weak to stand alone between the solid masses of Germans and Russians." (p. 506) Review: *Canadian Slavonic Papers* 29, no.4 (December 1987): 461-62.

408. Kantor, Marvin, **The Origins of Christianity in Bohemia: Sources and Commentary**. Evanston, IL: Northern University Press, 1990. 299 p. ISBN: 0810108747. Includes bibliography (p. 253-299).

This volume contains translated Church Slavonic and Latin works relating to early Bohemian spirituality. The work is divided into four parts. Part one contains Church Slavonic fragments and hymns; part two consists of Church Slavonic works about Wenceslas and Ludmila. Part three has other Church Slavonic works and part four Latin works about Wenceslas and Ludmila. The book also has an introduction that describes the historical background through the twelfth century. Detailed notes accompany each translation.

409. **Reflections on Slovak History,** edited by Stanislav J. Kirschbaum and Anne C. R. Roman. Toronto: Slovak World Congress, 1987. x, 183 p. ISBN: 0921985002. Includes bibliography (p. 153-178) and index.

A collection of essays generated by a conference on Slovak history held in 1984 are presented in this volume "This volume of essays offers reflections on Slovak history by Slovaks abroad who realize the importance of approaching Slovak history on its own merits and who hope thereby to make a contribution to the history of their fathers." (p. ix) The essays cover such topics as the history of Moravia, Slovaks under Hungarian rule, the Slovak national movement, Slovakia in post-war Czechoslovakia and Slovak literature.

410. Kovtun, George J., **Masaryk & America: Testimony of a Relationship**. Washington: Library of Congress, 1987. 82 p. ISBN: 084440585X. Bibliography (p. 81-82).

This is intended as a sourcebook on Thomas Masaryk's relationship with America. A variety of documents have been selected from US archives and are presented here in translation. The author hopes to present a picture of Masaryk's views of America from such sources as speeches, magazine articles, newspaper editorials and interviews, letters and personal reminiscences. The documents are arranged in six sections. The first section deals with the period before 1914 and the materials are largely apolitical. In the second section Masaryk's political views come to the fore. In section three Masaryk is the center of attention, this covers his fourth and most important trip to America. Sections four and five emphasize the value Masaryk placed on the democratic tradition. In the final section the writings of Masaryk's book *The New Empire*, is the subject. Review: *East Central Europe* 17, no.2 (fall 1990): 216-217.

411. Krejci, Jaroslav, **Czechoslovakia at the Crossroads of European History**. New York: Tauris, 1990. xiv, 255 p. ISBN: 1850431949. Includes bibliography (p. 236-246) and index.

This study examines the "crucial points" in the development of the Czechs and the Slovaks. The author feels the Czechs have more fully participated in West European history than have the Slovaks who were "incorporated into the Hungarian kingdom" for much of their history. "The aim of this book is to give a synoptic view of the predicament of the two related nations." (p. xi) The approach is chronological and topical and the book includes a general chronology of Czechoslovak history to 1989.

412. MacDonald, C. A., **The Killing of SS Obergruppenfuhrer Reinhard Heydrich**. New York: Free Press, 1989. viii, 239 p. ISBN: 0029195616. Includes bibliographical references.

Heydrich was the head of the Nazi security police and government of occupied Bohemia-Moravia. A powerful man, he was seen by many as a likely successor of Hitler. This book is the account of his assassination by Czech military intelligence in 1942.

413. Magocsi, Paul Robert, **The Rusyns of Slovakia: An Historical Survey.** Boulder, Colo.: East European Monographs, 1993. 185 p. *East European Monographs; 381,* ISBN: 0880332786. Includes bibliographical references (p. 141-170) and index.

"Rusyn" is the name of an ethnolinguistic group that has become geographically dispersed over the centuries. Originally, the term derived from the term "Rus" and identified the people as adherents to Eastern Orthodoxy. Usually they were of Ukrainian or Russian heritage. "This volume is a translation of an introductory historical survey published in the newly codified Rusyn literary language as well as in Slovak by the Rusyn Renaissance Society in Presov. The original work was intended to inform Rusyns in Slovakia of the historical developments of their people." (p. ix) The book is chronologically arranged and covers Rusyn history in Slovakia from earliest times to the revolution of 1989. A very extensive bibliography, organized by subject, is included.

414. Neher, Andre, **Jewish Thought and the Scientific Revolution of the Sixteenth Century: David Gans (1541-1613) and His Times.** New York: Oxford University Press, 1986. x, 285 p. *The Littman Library of Jewish Civilization,* ISBN: 0197100570. Includes bibliography (p. 261-276) and index.

Gans worked with Kepler under Tycho Brahe. Neher focuses on Gans in order to describe and evaluate Jewish intellectual thought in sixteenth century Central Europe.

415. Polisensky, Josef V., **History of Czechoslovakia in Outline.** Praha: Bohemia International, 1991. 142 p. ISBN: 80851950504. Includes bibliographical references (p. 132) and index.

This reprint of the 1946 *History of Czechoslovakia* traces the history of that country from earliest times. As it is intended as an outline, it discusses its topic rather briefly. It is a helpful introduction to the history of that country. A comparative chronology of Czech and British history is included.

416. Salzmann, Zdenek, and Vladimir Scheufler, **Komarov: A Czech Farming Village.** Prospect Heights, Ill.: Waveland Press, 1986. x, 166 p. ISBN: 0881332089. Includes bibliography (p. 165-166).

This revised and updated edition of the original 1974 study seeks to begin to fill the gap of English language ethnographic studies of the Czech people. It is also a picture of a group rapidly disappearing from the European scene, the European peasant. The village of Komarov, the focus of this study, has long been an agricultural village. It has been suffering the same loss of its youth to the cities common in American farming communities. This phenomena has forced the mechanization of the farm to proceed at a rapid rate. Against this background the authors have done an ethnographic study of this village as it faces many changes. They begin with a historical description of the area. The authors then turn to the ethnographic details that define the culture of the area: economic patterns of the households, village structure, interaction between villages and outsiders, traditional observances, rituals and beliefs, arts and crafts, music, farm buildings and houses, and family relationships. The volume includes a chronology of events, pronunciation guide and glossary of Czech terms.

417. **Czechoslovakia: Crossroads and Crisis, 1918-88,** edited by Norman Stone and Eduard Strouhal. New York: St Martin's Press, 1989. xviii, 336 p. ISBN: 0312032013. Includes bibliographical references.

These essays by prominent Czech and Slovak émigrés focus on the four "8" anniversaries: "1918, when the republic was founded; 1938, when its western parts were handed over, by Great Britain and France to Hitler; 1948, when the communists took power; and 1968, when an effort to create socialism with a human face was arrested by Soviet tanks." (p. l) In general the authors concentrate on the political, economic and social factors surrounding each of these key years.

418. Unterberger, Betty Miller, **The United States, Revolutionary Russia, and the Rise of Czechoslovakia**. Chapel Hill: University Of North Caroline Press, 1989. xiv, 463 p. ISBN: 0807818534. Includes bibliographical references and index.

A study of the emergence of the Czechoslovak nation focusing of the years 1914 to 1918. "This study, then, will endeavor to present a history of the role of the United States in the dissolution of the Austro-Hungarian Empire and the rise of the Czechoslovak nation within the context of two of the most cataclysmic events of the twentieth century: the First World War and the Bolshevik Revolution." (p xiii) The volume is chronologically arranged with numerous maps and illustrations. Reviews: *Journal of American History* 77, no.3 (December 1990): 1070-1071. *International History Review* 12, no.2 (May 1990): 389-392. *Journal of Military History* 54, no.3 (July 1990): 366-367. *Fletcher Forum of World Affairs* 14, no.2 (Summer 1990): 417-419.

419. Valenta, Jiri, **Soviet Intervention in Czechoslovakia, 1968: Anatomy of a Decision,** with a New Foreword by Alexander Dubcek. Baltimore: John Hopkins University Press, 1991. xx, 264 p. ISBN: 0801841178; 0801842972. Includes bibliographical references and index.

This revised edition of Jiri Valenta's 1979 publication has drawn on sources unavailable to the author when he first published this title. At that time he was forced to examine how the Soviets decided on their actions in Czechoslovakia in 1968 without the advantage of viewing the Czech archives or discussing events with policy makers of the time. Two chapters have been added to this edition that draw on such sources, including interviews with Alexander Dubcek. "Chapter 7 examines the new evidence regarding the Soviet decision to intervene...: the role of the East European debate, the bureaucratic politics, the biased information and the Soviet reassessment of the 1968 decision all contributed to conditions conducive to the 'gentle revolution' of 1989 in the light of the new evidence." (p. xiv)

420. World Congress for Soviet and East European Studies (4th: 1990: Harrogate, England), **The Czech and Slovak Experience: Selected Papers from the Fourth World Congress for Soviet and East European Studies, Harrogate, 1990,** edited by John Morrison. New York: St. Martin's Press, 1992. xiv, 235 p.

The papers for this volume were originally presented at the 4th World Congress for Soviet and East European Studies in 1990. The papers deal with major issues in Czech and Slovak history from the 18th century to the modern day. Included are papers on linguistic separatism, Slovakia in the Czech press, Masaryk as a religious heretic, interwar Czechoslovakia, Benes and the German minority, the German Social Democratic Party of Czechoslovakia, and the Jewish Community of Prague during the interwar period.

GOVERNMENT, POLITICS AND LAW

421. **T. G. Masaryk (1850-1937)**. New York: St. Martin's Press, 1989. 3 v.

The three volumes of this work consist of essays by noted authorities on Thomas G. Masaryk, the first president of the Czechoslovak Republic. The volumes in turn explore Masaryk as thinker and politician (vol. 1), thinker and critic (vol. 2), and statesman and cultural force (vol. 3).

422. **Violations of the Helsinki Accords, Czechoslovakia: A Report Prepared for the Helsinki Review Conference, Vienna, November 1986**. New York: U.S. Helsinki Watch Committee, 1986. iv, 41 p. *A Helsinki Watch Report*, ISBN: 0938579797. Includes bibliography (p. 41).

This report chronicles human rights violations in Czechoslovakia. It is arranged topically, covering violations in the areas of recent arrest, cultural freedom, freedom of expression, Charter 77, freedom of movement, freedom of religion, the peace movement, and the Hungarian minority.

423. Bradley, John Francis Nejez, **Politics in Czechoslovakia, 1945-1990**. New York: Columbia University Press, 1991. vi, 137 p. *East European Monographs,* no. 315, ISBN: 0880332123. Includes bibliographical references (p.135-137).

Bradley traces the history of politics in Czechoslovakia from 1945 to the late 1980s. Individual chapters in part one are devoted to the immediate post-war years, democratic elections, the dissolution of democratic Czechoslovakia, communist apparat, Prague Spring 1968 and Hungary's rise and fall. Part two covers constitutions and parliaments, central governments under communism and the judicial system.

424. Dubcek, Aleksander, **Dubcek Speaks, Aleksander Dubcek with Andras Sugar**. New York: St. Martin's Press, 1990. 110 p. ISBN: 1850432082.

This volume contains the text of an interview, screened on Hungarian television in April 1989, conducted by Andras Sugar with Aleksander Dubcek. Dubcek's association with the events of 1968 in Czechoslovakia made this a highly controversial interview even though it was broadcast only in Hungary. The opinion of the Czech leader on the events of 1968 and their aftermath are presented here, as Dubcek came out of his "retirement" to tell his version of the 1968 uprising.

425. Havel, Vaclav, **Summer Meditations,** translated from the Czech by Paul Wilson. New York: Vintage Books, 1993. xviii, 149 p. ISBN: 0679414622. Translation of: Letni premitani.

This is the first book that Havel wrote as president of the Czechoslovak Republic. It is "not a collection of occasional speeches but a profound reflection on the nature and practice of politics by a man who, until November 1989, was a marginalized and banned author in his own country, and who wrote about himself and his society from a perspective that sometimes included the prison cell." (p. ix) Also included are background notes to the individual essays.

426. Husak, Gustav, **Speeches and Writings**. New York: Pergamon Press, 1986. xxiii, 267 p. *Leaders of the World,* ISBN: 0080340385. Includes index.

A collection of speeches and essays by the former President of Czechoslovakia is presented in this volume. Mr. Husak hoped to further understanding of his people and their goals as a socialist state. The volume includes an interview with Husak and some statistical data on Czechoslovakia.

427. Kaplan, Karel, **Report on the Murder of the General Secretary,** translated by Karel Kovanda. Columbus: Ohio State University Press, 1990. xvii, 323 p. ISBN: 0814204775. Includes bibliography (p. 311-312) and index.

A history of the show trial of Rudolf Slansky. The author wished to inform the reader as to how the communist show trials of post-war Czechoslovakia were fabricated. The author feels these trials are particularly important in understanding the nature of communist systems. "In as much as political trials constitute the truest picture of a communist regime's character, it is impossible to understand the system that generated them, or indeed to grasp the history of postwar Europe, without comprehending the trials themselves." (p. xiii) The author is uniquely qualified to describe the planning of this trial. He had access to the secret archive containing the communist party's records of the trial during his tenure on the commission established in the 1960s to rehabilitate the victims of the show trials. Although many of his notes were confiscated after 1968 he was able to retain enough to publish this book after his emigration to the West. It takes the reader through all stages of a show trial and includes four appendices with information on the victims. Reviews: *New Republic* 203, no.8 & 9 (August 20 & 27, 1990): 36-38. *New York Review of Books* 37, no.13 (August 16, 1990): 41-44.

428. Kovaly, Heda Margolis, **Under a Cruel Star: A Life in Prague 1941-1968,** translated from the Czech by Franci Epstein and Helen Epstein with the author. Cambridge, Mass.: Plunkett Lake Press, 1986. 192 p. ISBN: 0961469617 (pbk). Translation of: Na vlastni kuzi.

Heda Margolius Kovaly is a survivor of the ordeal so many Czechs suffered during the Stalinist period in Czechoslovakia. Josef Skvorecky has described this work as " 'Written with the sophistication of a literateur and the immediacy of a survivor, this is the story of the infamous Slansky Trial in which Heda Kovaly's young husband was one of eleven executed Jews, victims of Stalinism who were 'rehabilitated' years after they were hanged.' " (back cover) Kovaly has translated numerous works and written a novel entitled *Innocence*.

429. Leff, Carol Skalnik, **National Conflict in Czechoslovakia: The Making and Remaking of the State, 1918-1987**. Princeton, NJ: Princeton University Press, 1988. viii, 304 p. ISBN: 0691077681. Includes bibliographical references and index.

In her study of Slovak national assertion Leff defines "with greater precision the ways in which political institutions shape the expression of those unsatisfied needs that cluster under the banner of national identity." (p. 3) At the same time she recognizes that "political institutions do not influence national sentiments unilaterally. A determined nationalism can pose a fundamental threat to the basic political order." (p. 3) Her book in five parts examines the emergence of the Czechoslovak State political structure and national conflict, the failure of unification, 1918-1968, leadership interaction and national conflict, and federalization and the Czech-Slovak relationship.

430. **Reviews of National Science and Technology Policy. Czech and Slovak Federal Republic.** Paris: Centre for Co-operation with European Economies in Transition, 1992. 197 p. ISBN: 9264137963. Includes bibliographical references.

"This is the first OECD study of the Czech and Slovak Federal Republic's science and technology (S&T) system. It analyzes the present S&T system, describes reform measures carried out to date, and identifies priority areas for further policy action. The study argues that, irrespective of how the federal issue is resolved, it is crucial to take decisive measures to create a consensus on the direction of science and technology policy and to organize S&T activities to reflect both this policy and the evolving social and economic situation." (back cover)

431. **The Prague Spring: A Mixed Legacy,** edited by Jiri Pehe. New York: Freedom House, 1988. 223 p. *Perspectives on Freedom,* no. 10, ISBN: 0932088287 (pbk); 0932088279. Includes index.

A variety of authors reflect on the events of 1968 in Czechoslovakia, known as the Prague Spring. This resurgence of democracy was violently repressed by the Soviets. The writings collected for this book assume a special significance in light of the changes in the USSR. "They become reflections on the Soviet system and the Communist system in general. The essays describe not only the Czechoslovak reality but what a neo-Stalinist, anti-reform period may look like in the Soviet Union if the current attempt at change is stopped by force." (p. 6) The contributors to this volume come from a wide variety of backgrounds ranging from those directly involved in the events of 1968 to those who viewed the changes from exile. There is no unifying theme to the essays other than that they all deal in some way with the Prague Spring.

432. Rees, H. Louis, **The Czechs During World War I: The Path to Independence**. Boulder, Colo.: East European Monographs, 1992. vii, 170 p. *East European monographs;* no. 339, ISBN: 0830332360. Includes bibliographical references (p. 156-164) and index.

Rees' main emphasis is on the final two years of World War I, when the Czechoslovak Republic came into being. He concentrates on the domestic situation and describes "the actions of the political leaders inside the empire, in Prague and in Vienna, and to place them within the economic, social and political context in which they were carried out." (p. vii) Part of this description and analysis includes the effects of the October revolution in Russia on Austria-Hungary.

433. Vondrácek, Theodor Jan, **Commentary on the Czechoslovak Civil Code**. Norwell, MA: Kluwer Academic, 1988. xxix, 473 p. *Law in Eastern Europe,* no. 37, ISBN: 9024736692. Includes bibliography (p. xi-xviii) and index.

In addition to the well researched and documented commentary that occupies most of this volume, the author has also provided introductory observations in Czechoslovak legal history, the institutions, the judiciary, civil proceedings, notaries, administrative proceedings and procurators.

COMMUNISM

434. Kaplan, Karel, **The Communist Party in Power: A Profile of Party Politics in Czechoslovakia,** edited and translated by Fred Eidlin. Boulder, Colo.: Westview Press, 1987. 231 p. *Westview Special Studies on the Soviet Union & Eastern Europe,* 0163-6057, ISBN: 0865318239.

Karel Kaplan held various positions in the hierarchy of the Communist Party of Czechoslovakia for eighteen years. His years of experience and detailed knowledge form the basis of this study and analysis of the internal life and operation of the Communist Party. Kaplan believes that the Party exerts such tremendous influence in Communist societies because of the ideological, power, and social ties between its members. "These ties may vary in substance and effectiveness, but they operate at all levels and in all domains of the party organization. His insider's account of how power is brokered and maintained lends a unique perspective to our understanding of the party in Communist society today." (p. iii) The book is divided into five topical chapters covering societal institutions, power groups, the party apparat, party functionaries, and external influences. Reviews: *Foreign Affairs* 66, no.4 (Spring 1988): 885. *Canadian Slavonic Papers* 30, no. (September 1988): 411-412.

435. Kavan, Rosemary, **Freedom At a Price: An Englishwoman's Life in Czechoslovakia with an Introduction by William Shawcross and an Epilogue by Jan Kavan**. London: Verso, 1985. xi, 278 p. ISBN: 0860911187.

This is the story of an English woman's life in Czechoslovakia from 1945 to 1971. Having married a Czech communist after the war, she settled in Prague to raise her family. She describes the coming of a Stalinist system, to which her husband fell victim. It provides the reader with a Westerner's view of day to day life in Communist Eastern Europe.

436. McDermott, Kevin, **The Czech Red Unions, 1918-1929: A Study of their Relations with the Communist Party and the Moscow International**. New York: Distributed by Columbia University Press, 1988. xiii, 350 p. *East European Monographs,* no. 239, ISBN: 0880331364. Includes bibliography (p.315-344) and index.

It is generally believed the Bolshevization process that began in the mid 1920s was imposed successfully on foreign communist parties. This book attempts to prove that the Czech Red Unions "were not merely subordinate organs of the party and Moscow, but, on the contrary, were able to preserve a degree of independence and national specificity in the face of growing pressure from the Bolshevizers." (p. xi)

437. Wheaton, Bernard, **Radical Socialism in Czechoslovakia: Bohumir Smeral, the Czech Road to Socialism and the Origins of the Czechoslovak Communist Party (1917-1921)**. New York: Columbia University Press, 1986. xxvii, 204 p. *East European Monographs,* no. 213, ISBN: 0880331100. Includes bibliography (p. 191-199) and index.

This study examines the school of socialism known as Smeralism. The author traces its rise and development focusing on the years 1917-1921. Part one examines the goals and tactics of Smeralism. Part two is divided into five chapters each devoted to some aspect of the domestic situation in Czechoslovakia during the period. The rise of nationalism, the political environment, the radical socialists, the economic conditions of the time and social problems, urban and rural are each analyzed as they relate to the development of radical socialism. The final part turns to the international situation. The author feels that Smeralism was not a type of utopian socialism and is interested in studying the historical and social factors affecting its rise and popularity.

LANGUAGE AND LITERATURE

438. **Reader in Czech Sociolinguistics,** edited by Jan Chloupek, Jiri Nekvapil et al. Amsterdam: J. Benjamins Pub. Co., 1987. 344 p. *Linguistic & Literary Studies in Eastern Europe,* 0165-7712, v. 23, ISBN: 9027215286. Includes bibliographies.

Although sociolinguistics in Czechoslovakia is not institutionalized, the editors have managed to bring together eighteen essays in sociolinguistics. The papers cover such individual topics as norms, functional styles, informal vs. formal utterance, linguistic geography, slang, language planning, and others. Review: *Language* 64, no.4 (December 1988): 833.

439. **Good-bye, Samizdat: Twenty Years of Czechoslovak Underground Writing,** edited by Marketa Goetz-Stankiewicz; with a foreword by Timothy Garton Ash. Evanston, Ill.: Northwestern University Press, 1992. xxxi, 309 p. ISBN: 0810110350.

The Samizdat writings of Eastern Europe have moved into the world of the Russian press. This anthology has collected Czech samizdat publications on philosophy, culture, and politics as well as literature. The editor has selected works that may not be the most representative of an author's style. "What emerges here, in a nutshell, is a many-voiced chorus of passionate commitments to the search for a context in which to define one's own voice, a careful probing of the past, an oddly unassuming yet highly conscious use of language, and a marked urge to preserve optimism about the future." (p. xix) Some of the authors whose works are gathered in this volume include Igor Hajek, Pavel Kohout, Karel Pecka, Milan Uhde, Jan Patocka, Miroslav Kusy, Vaclav Havel, Milan Simecka, and many others. A section of brief biographies on each of the contributors is included at the end of the book.

440. **The Vanek Plays: Four Authors, One Character,** edited by Marketa Goetz-Stankiewicz. Vancouver: University of British Columbia Press, 1987. xxix, 258 p. ISBN: 0774802804. Includes bibliography (p. 255-258).

Ferdinand Vanek is a character invented by Czech play writer Vaclav Havel. Three other playwrights, Pavel Kohout, Pavel Landovsky, and Jiri Dienstbier, have also used Vanek in their plays. This book presents English translations of all the Vanek plays by their playwrights. An informative historical-critical introduction by the editor is provided. Review: *Canadian Slavonic Papers* 30, no.2 (June 1988): 298-301.

441. Hruby, Peter, **Daydreams and Nightmares: Czech Communist and Ex-Communist Literature 1917-1987**. Boulder, Colo.: East European Monographs, 1990. 362 p. *East European Monographs,* no. 290, ISBN: 0880331873. Includes bibliographical references (p. 312-356) and name index.

Hruby examines several Czech writers who enthusiastically embraced Communism in literary and political activities. The book is divided into three parts. In part one the author introduces Pan-Slav, pro-Russian and socialist antecedents in Czech literature. In part two he examines poets and their role. The third part is devoted to novelists and dramatists.

442. Misurella, Fred, **Understanding Milan Kundera: Public Events, Private Affairs**. Columbia, S.C.: University of South Carolina Press, 1993. xv, 216 p. *Understanding Modern European and Latin American Literature,* ISBN: 0872498530. Includes bibliographical references (p. 201-206) and index.

"Professor Misurella's *Understanding Milan Kundera* provides a much needed overview of the literary and critical works of Milan Kundera, one of the seminal writers and theoreticians of our time. Kundera, born in Brno, Czechoslovakia, and now living in France, has been much influenced by German and especially Austrian literature, as well as by Western European writers." (p. ix) Misurella's analysis will be of particular interest to students of comparative literature. The essays cover a wide range of titles including *The Book of Laughter and Forgetting*, *The Joke*, *The Unbearable Lightness of Being*, and *The Art of the Novel*. A bibliography of works by and about Kundera is included.

443. Rubach, Jerzy, **The Lexical Phonology of Slovak**. Oxford: Clarendon Press, 1993. xvi, 312 p. *The Phonology of the World's Languages,* ISBN: 0198240007. Includes bibliographical references (p. 306-310) and index.

This scholarly study of the lexical phonology of the Slovak language is the first to appear in English. It is also the first monograph length description of Slovak in generative terms. "Part I provides background information about the theoretical framework (Chapter 1), segmental structure (Chapter 2), and morphology viewed from the perspective of the needs of phonological analysis (Chapter 3). Part II, which forms the core of this book, is a study of cyclic rules as well as of the relations which hold inside and between various levels of phonological representation (Chapters 4-7). Part III (Chapters 8 and 9) is devoted to investigating the properties of non-cyclic (postcyclic and postlexical) rules." (p.ix) The volume is one in the series *The Phonology of the World's Languages*.

444. Sgall, Petr, **Variation in Language: Code Switching in Czech as a Challenge for Sociolinguistics.** Amsterdam: J. Benjamins Pub. Co., 1992. xii, 368 p. *Linguistic & Literary Studies in Eastern Europe;* v. 39, ISBN: 1556192649. Includes bibliographical references (p. 322-358) and indexes.

The authors discuss language varieties and code switching in modern Czech. The volume includes a "summary description of the Czech central vernacular, of the historical origin of the difference between it and the Standard, of the switching between the two codes, and short concluding remarks concerning some requirements on sociolinguistic inquiry, starting points for a theoretical description of a national language with intralingual variation and a preliminary formulation of perspectives on the stratification of Czech." (p. vi)

445. Striedter, Jurij, **Literary Structure, Evolution, and Value: Russian Formalism and Czech Structuralism Reconsidered**. Cambridge, MA: Harvard University Press, 1989. 317 p. *Harvard Studies in Comparative Literature,* 38, ISBN: 0674536533. Includes bibliography (p. 301-303) and index.

A reanalysis of Russian Formalism and Czech Structuralism. The author believes that earlier studies of these two schools have failed to see all of the facets of these two schools of literary criticism. The book contains four essays. The first is a general discussion of Russian Formalism in the context of its significance for scholars today. The second essay focuses on the relationship between Russian Formalism and Czech Structuralism. The development of Czech Structuralism as manifest in the work of Felix Vodilka is the topic of the third essay. In the final essay the author brings the study into the present by relating the elements of these two schools of literary criticism to the American context. A selected bibliography is included. Review: *Slavic Review* 49, no.1 (Spring 1990): 117-118.

446. Timrava, **That Alluring Land: Slovak Stories**, Norma L. Rudinsky editor and translator. Pittsburgh, Pa.: University of Pittsburgh Press, 1992. xvi, 324 p. *Pitt Series in Russian and East European studies;* no. 15, ISBN: 0822954737. Translation of: Ta zem vabna.

Timrava was the pseudonym of the Slovak woman author Bozena Slancikova. Slancikova's most active literary period was from 1886 to 1938, but the majority of her writings were completed by 1920. Her stories and novellas reflected the village life she experienced. Her stories provide the reader with a rich description of the life of both the village peasantry and nobility. "Whether we read Timrava's work in archetypal terms or as a historically proven text, most striking are her condemnations, her refusal to gloss over reality, her destructive irony, and her feminist inclination." (p. xv) This volume includes six works by Timrava as well as a bibliography of writings by and about Timrava.

447. Townsend, Charles Edward, **A Description of Spoken Prague Czech**. Columbus, Ohio: Slavica Publishers, 1990. 151 p. ISBN: 089357211X. Includes bibliographical references (p.147-151).

Professor Townsend attempts to define the unique aspects of Prague Czech as a spoken language. While he does not attempt an exhaustive description of the language, he does hope to include its major characteristics. Only those features will be included which all his native informants agreed were unique to spoken Czech. He is attempting primarily a distinction between literary Czech, which is described in traditional grammars, and the spoken language. The book is divided into four chapters on phonology, morphology, syntax and lexicon. A glossary is included of some terms. Unfortunately there is no index.

INDIVIDUAL AUTHORS

448. Havel, Vaclav, **Letters to Olga June 1979-September 1982,** translated from the Czech with an introduction by Paul Wilson. New York: Knopf, 1988. 397 p. ISBN: 0394547950. Translation of: Dopisy Olze. Includes index.

Vaclav Havel was sentenced to prison for 4-1/2 years on October 23, 1979. During this time he wrote 144 letters to his wife Olga, of which 125 were kept. Most of them appear in translation in this volume. Review: *New York Review of Books* 37, no.10 (June 14, 1990): 35-38.

449. **Vaclav Havel, or, Living in Truth: Twenty-two Essays Published on the Occasion of the Award of the Erasmus Prize to Vaclav Havel,** edited by Jan Vladislav. London: Faber, 1987. xix, 315 p. ISBN: 0571148743.

Of these twenty-two essays, six are by Havel himself and published here for the first time. The other sixteen are reprints of earlier published texts on Havel. The non-Havel essays are by writers such as Heinrich Boll, Samuel Beckett, Timothy Garton Ash, Milan Kundera, Arthur Miller, Josef Skvorecky and others. The volume also contains a short bio-bibliography of Havel.

450. Holan, Vladimir, **Mirroring: Selected Poems of Vladimir Holan,** translated from the Czech by C. G. Hanzlicek and Dana Habova. Middletown, Conn.: Wesleyan University Press, 1985. ix, 125 p. ISBN: 0819561193 (pbk); 0819551295 (alk. paper).

Holan, who was named National Artist and Laureate of the State, is widely considered to be the greatest of Czech poets. This collection includes poems written between 1943 and 1977. Holan died in 1980.

451. Holub, Miroslav, **Vanishing Lung Syndrome,** translated by David Young and Dana Habova. London: Faber and Faber, 1990. 68 p. ISBN: 0571143393; 0571143784.

Miroslav Holub is surely one of Czechoslovakia's most prolific writers, publishing one book a year between 1954 and 1969. At that time he became an "unperson" in the Communist dominated Czechoslovakia. Holub has published over 140 scientific papers in his other area of expertise, immunology. The poems collected in this volume were written between 1985 and 1989. Review: *World Literature Today* 65, no.2 (Spring 1991): 324.

452. Hrabal, Bohumil, **I Served the King of England,** translated from the Czech by Paul Wilson. San Diego: Harcourt Brace Jovanovich, 1989. 243 p. ISBN: 015145745X. Translation of: Jak jsem obsluhoval anglickeho krale.

A popular novel by Czech novelist Hrabal. Review: *World Literature Today* 64, no.4 (Autumn 1990): 663-664.

453. ———, **Too Loud a Solitude**, translated from the Czech by Michael Henry Heim. San Diego: Harcourt Brace Jovanovich, 1990. 98 p. ISBN: 015190491X.

A new translation of Bohumil Hrabal's 1976 novel *Prilis Hlucna Samota*. The author is best known in the West for his book *Closely Watched Trains*. Review: *New York Review of Books* 38, no.4 (February 14, 1991): 14-17.

454. Klima, Ivan, **Love and Garbage,** translated from the Czech by Ewald Osers. 1st American New York: Knopf, 1991. 223 p. ISBN: 0384589769. Translation of: *Laska a Smeti*.

In this novel a Czech artist, unable to get his manuscripts published because they are suppressed by the state, joins a street-sweeping gang. This gives him the opportunity to observe his repressive society from the underside and to remember his love affairs and the inevitable choice it forces on him. Reviews: *New York Review of Books* 37, no.6 (April 12, 1990): 14-22. *New Republic* 205, no.5 (July 29, 1991): 36-39. *New York Times Book Review* (May 12, 1991): 9. *World Literature Today* 65, no.2 (Spring 1991): 325.

455. Banerjee, Maria Nemcova, **Terminal Paradox: The Novels of Milan Kundera**. New York: Grove Weidenfeld, 1990. ix, 294 p. ISBN: 0802111270. Includes bibliographical references.

A collection of essays by Professor of Slavic languages and literature Maria Banerjee on the novels of Milan Kundera. "*Terminal Paradox* is the first full length study of his work, from his extraordinary first novel, *The Joke*, through the brilliant and varied books that followed—including *The Unbearable Lightness of Being* and Kundera's latest best-seller, *Immortality*." (back cover)

456. Kundera, Milan, **The Art of the Novel**. New York: Grove Press, 1988. 165 p. ISBN: 0802100112. Translation of: L'art du roman.

Seven essays by Czech author Milan Kundera are brought together by the author to present his views on what a novel is. His essays "The Depreciated Legacy of Cervantes" describes Kundera's views on the European novel. "Notes inspired by 'The Sleepwalkers' " is a testament to the influence this work had on Kundera's writing. "Somewhere Behind" summarizes his view on Kafka's writing. Several other essays are included. All give the reader insight into Kundera's idea of the novel. "Every novelist's work contains an implicit vision of the history of the novel that is inherent in my own novels." (p. x)

457. ———, **Immortality,** translated from the Czech by Peter Kussi. New York: Grove Weidenfeld, 1991. 345 p. ISBN: 0802111114. Translation of: Nesmrtelnost.

"Milan Kundera's sixth novel springs from a casual gesture of a woman to her swimming instructor, a gesture that creates a character in the mind of a writer named Kundera. Like Flaubert's Emma or Tolstoy's Anna, Kundera's Agnes becomes an object of fascination, of indefinable longing. From that character springs a novel, a gesture of the imagination that both embodies and articulates Milan Kundera's supreme mastery of the novel and its purpose: to thoroughly explore the great themes of existence." (jacket) Reviews: *New York Review of Books* 38, no.10 (May 30, 1991): 3-4. *New Republic* 205, no.5 (July 29, 1991): 36-39. *World & I* 6, no.6 (June 1991): 374-380. *New York Times Book Review* (April 28, 1991): 7.

458. Lustig, Arnost, **Indecent Dreams,** afterword by Josef Skvorecky. Evanston, Ill.: Northwestern University Press, 1988. 159 p. ISBN: 0810107732.

Czech writer Arnost Lustig presents three stories that are "studies of the last days of the war, psychological probings into the souls of hardened Nazis now at the end of their tether; of simple-minded Germans who without thinking, made hay of the opportunities that the liquidation of the Jews brought them and of Czechs who lived through the dusk of the war with a mixture of hope, yearning for revenge, and revulsion at the butchery that marked those last days of the man-made inferno." (p. 158)

459. ———, **Street of Lost Brothers,** with a foreword by Jonathan Brent. Evanston, Ill.: Northwestern University Press, 1990. 207 p. ISBN: 081010959X.

"The stories in *Street of Lost Brothers* depict the imagination in its attempts at grasping unimaginable reality. Each story leads to a different, subtly attended encounter with this world." (p. xi) Lustig juxtaposes the world of the Nazi totalitarian state with the liberal imagination. This collection of short stories delves into the world of the Nazi terror. Lustig is known as a prose writer, scenarist, publicist and author of plays. Review: *World Literature Today* 65, no.4 (Autumn 1991): 733.

460. Paral, Vladimir, **Catapult: A Timetable of Rail, Sea, and Air Ways to Paradise**. Highland Park, NJ: Catbird Press, 1989. 226 p. ISBN: 0945774044. Translation of: Katapult.

"*Catapult* is a parodic exposure of Eastern European socialism, of wasted economic potential, of a lazy and self-indulgent managerial class to which the novel's hero belongs, and of indifference to Marxist ideology." (cover) The story's action centers around Jalek Jost, a neurotic man reminiscent in some ways of Don Juan, in others of Faust. The novel demonstrates Paral's originality of style, as he experiment's with sentences separated by commas. *Catapult* was originally published in 1967 and was greeted as a masterpiece, Paral's finest novel. Review: *Slavic and East European Journal* 34, no3 (Fall 1990): 398-399.

461. Pavel, Ota, **How I Came to Know Fish**. New York: New Directions Pub. Corp., 1991. 150 p. ISBN: 0811211657.

"Unassuming and unforgettable, the stories of *How I Came to Know Fish* memorialize Ota Pavel's childhood in Czechoslovakia—his beloved family, the flash of fish in clear streams, and the annihilation of this world by the Nazis. His father (a wildly canny fisherman) first has his fish pond confiscated ("How can a Jew breed carp?") and then, with his two older sons, is sent to a concentration camp. Too young to work in the camps, Ota remains with his gentile mother. Fish saves them from starving, as he takes to poaching carp reserved for the Wehrmacht. These stories, some of which originally appeared in a Czech version of *Field and Stream*, are profoundly poignant and have long been treasured by the Czechoslovakians." (cover) Review: *World Literature Today* 65, no.4 (Autumn 1991): 733.

462. Pekarova, Iva, **Truck Stop Rainbows,** translated by David Powelstock. 1st ed. New York: Farrar, Straus and Giroux, 1992. 279 p. ISBN: 0037420655. Translation of: Pera a perute.

"*Truck Stop Rainbows* offers a startling portrait of a country in which both nature and human life have been reduced to a poor, passive imitation of what they once were." (book jacket)

463. Simecka, Martin M., **The Year of the Frog: A Novel,** translated by Peter Petro; foreword by Vaclav Havel. Baton Rouge: Louisiana State University Press, 1993. viii, 247 p. ISBN: 0807118699.

"*The Year of the Frog* narrates the coming of age of Milan, a young former track star prevented by the communist authorities from university enrollment because of the dissident activities of his father. But while political oppression is indeed an important element in the book, it serves as a backdrop to Milan's maturation. These experiences—operating room tedium, medical tragedy, pushing one's body to the limit on solitary runs, the bliss and sorrow of love, and the sometimes horrible cycle of birth, fertility, and death—serve as fuel for Milan's ever-reflective mind, which always tries to extract philosophical truth from the confusion of events around him." (pp. vii-viii) Martin Simecka is a Czech-born writer who publishes in Slovak.

464. Skvorecky, Josef, **Dvorak in Love: A Light-Hearted Dream,** translated from the Czech by Paul Wilson. Canada: Lester & Orpen Dennys, 1986. 325 p. ISBN: 088619122X (pbk); 0886190592. Translation of: Scherzo capriccioso.

This historical and biographical novel focuses in Antonin Dvorak. Reviews: *Book World*, 29 (March 1987): 6. *New York Times Book Review*, 22 (February 1987): 11.

465. ———, **The End of Lieutenant Boruvka,** translated by Paul Wilson. New York: W. W. Norton, 1990. 185 p. ISBN: 0393027856. Translation of: Konec porucika Boruvky.

These five stories are based loosely on actual events that occurred after the repression by Soviet forces in 1968.

466. ———, **Sins for Father Knox,** translated from the Czech by Kaca Polockova Henley. London: W. W. Norton & Co. Inc., 1988. 268 p. ISBN: 0393025128. Translation of: Hrichy pro patera Knoxe.

In these tales "the reader is called upon to determine the culprit, the motive, the method, or all three. But unlike other detective stories, these tales also pose a further question: which of Father Knox's ten commandments has been violated?" (p. 10)

467. ———, **Talkin' Moscow Blues,** edited by Sam Solecki. New York: Ecco Press, 1990. 367 p. ISBN: 0880012315. Includes bibliographical references.

The essays of Czech writer Josef Skvorecky, now living in Canada, are collected in this volume. All were written since he left Czechoslovakia and they mark his entry into American journalism. The essays cover a broad range of topics including jazz, literature, politics, and film. The volume includes an interview with Skvorecky. "Here are deeply personal stories about the friends and events that have shaped his beliefs and his writing; thoughtful examinations of the nature of art, politics, and freedom; reviews of writers such as Faulkner and Kafka, and filmmakers Jiri Menzel and Francis Coppola.

468. Urbanek, Zdenek, **On the Sky's Clayey Bottom: Sketches and Happenings From the Years of Silence,** Zdenek Urbanek; translated from the Czech by William Harkins. New York: Four Walls Eight Windows, 1992. vii, 232 p. ISBN: 094142376X.

Many of the short works of Czech author Zdenek Urbanek are collected in this volume. Of his influence on Czech literature Vaclav Havel says, "Without him, I can hardly form an adequate conception of what Czech fiction, Czech essay writing, or Czech translation today have to tell us." (p. vii)

NATIONAL MINORITIES

469. Kieval, Hillel J., **The Making of Czech Jewry: National Conflict and Jewish Society in Bohemia, 1870-1918**. New York: Oxford University Press, 1988. viii, 279 p. *Studies in Jewish History*, ISBN: 0195040570. Includes bibliography (p. 245-272) and index.

During the last third of the 19th century and the first two decades of the 20th century, Bohemian Jewry changed in several aspects: demographically, occupationally, politically and linguistically. Kieval's purpose is to explain and interpret these changes. His study begins with population movements and cultural discontinuity in Prague and covers communal politics and the national struggle between 1883 and 1900, anti-Semitism and the reorientation of Czech Jewry, Zionism in Prague (Bar Kocha), Martin Buber and the Prague Zionists, the test of World War I, and the politics of integration in the new state from 1918-1920. Review: *American Historical Review* 95, no.2 (April 1990): 543-544.

470. **The Jews of Bohemia and Moravia: A Historical Reader,** edited by Wilma Abeles Iggers; translations by Wilma Abeles Iggers, Kaca Polackova-Henley, Kathrine Talbot. Detroit: Wayne State University Press, 1992. 412 p. ISBN: 081432228X. Includes bibliographical references (p. 385-389) and index.

This book "portrays the Jews of Bohemia and Moravia in their own words beginning with the age of Enlightenment" (p. 11) through the death of Stalin in 1952. The sources are varied: some are newspaper and magazine articles and others from family histories, descriptions of trips, wills and letters. The selections are arranged in five sections: 1) From the Expulsion of the Jews by Maria Theresa to the Dissolution of the Ghettos (1744-1848); 2) The Age of Liberal Optimism and Religious Indifference (1849-1873); 3) Diversity and Disquiet in the Modern World (1874-1918); 4) The Jews in the First Czechoslovak Republic (1918-1938); and 5) From Hitler to Stalin (1938-1952). Each section begins with an introduction by the editor. Brief biographies of the contributors are also included.

471. Tritt, Rachel, **Struggling for Ethnic Identity: Czechoslovakia's Endangered Gypsies**. New York: Human Rights Watch, 1992. xi, 152 p. *Helsinki Watch Report*, ISBN: 1564320782. Includes bibliographical references.

This Helsinki Watch Report is based on information gleaned from interviews collected from 1991 to 1992. As in many other East European nations there is a great deal of prejudice against this ethnic group which manifests itself in a number of ways. "This report begins with a brief overview of the history of the Romanies since their arrival in what is now Czechoslovakia. In the following chapters, past (when relevant) and current conditions of Romanies in the areas of education, housing, employment, relations with the police, cultural and linguistic rights, health care, access to services and media portrayal are discussed. The chapter on International Law describes the obligations of the Czech and Slovak Federal Government under international law. The final chapter summarizes our recommendation to the government of the Czech and Slovak Federal Republic." (p. xi)

ARTS AND CULTURE

472. North, Jacqueline Y. Jones, **Czechoslovakian Perfume Bottles and Boudoir Accessories**. Ohio: Antique Publications, 1990. 126 p. ISBN: 0915410699 (pbk); 0915410656. Includes bibliography.

This book was meant as a guide to the value and rarity of 842 Czechoslovak perfume bottles and boudoir accessories. It also illustrates one of Czechoslovakia's most highly developed art forms, glassmaking, in one of its less public manifestations. The values for each object are listed in a separate pamphlet accompanying the book.

473. Simek, Milan, and Jaroslav Dewetter, **Cultural Policy in Czechoslovakia**. Paris: UNESCO, 1986. 85 p. *Studies and Documents on Cultural Policies*, ISBN: 9231023608.

UNESCO has issued a series on cultural policy for its Member States to show differences and similarities in the planning and implementation of cultural policy. This volume in the series was first published in 1970 and is here updated to account for changes in population. The basic discussion has not been significantly altered. The chapters cover a variety of topics including art, the relationship between culture and science, Czechoslovakia's cultural heritage, the life of the artist in Czechoslovakia, the cultural life of the population, mass media and international cooperation.

474. **Czech Cubism: Architecture, Furniture, and Decorative Arts, 1910-1925,** edited by Alexander von Vegesack, with texts by Milena B. Lamarova et al. New York: Princeton Architectural Press, 1992. 337 p. ISBN: 1873271660. Includes bibliographical references (p. 331-333) and index.

This catalog describes the first "conceptually thorough presentation of Czech cubist architecture and design." (p. 8) The exhibition was prepared by and held in the Museum of Decorative Arts in Prague. The catalog not only presents a rich illustrative guide to Czech cubist works, but also includes extensive discussion of the development of Czech cubism. The volume also has biographical entries on the artists with photographs of the artists, a chronology of Czech cubism, a listing of exhibitions held between 1912 and 1990 and a lengthy bibliography.

DISSIDENT MOVEMENT

475. Bugajski, Janusz, **Czechoslovakia, Charter 77's Decade of Dissent,** foreword by Walter Laquer. New York: Praeger, 1987. xii, 118 p. *Washington Papers,* 125, 0278-937x, ISBN: 0275927709; 0275927695. Includes bibliography (p. 97-103) and index.

Bugajski presents a history of dissent in Czechoslovakia, focusing on the Charter 77 groups. He examines its origins and aims, its primary activists and supporters, its achievements and setbacks, the various issues and developments with which it grappled, and the repression that it suffered.

476. Havel, Vaclav, **Open Letters: Selected Writings, 1965-1990,** selected and edited by Paul Wilson. New York: Knopf, Distributed by Random House, 1991. xiv, 415 p.

"Here, brought together for the first time in authorized translations, are his most important writings—spanning twenty-five years of political activism—from the early sixties when he was a relatively unknown dissident playwright to the remarkable New Year's address, his first as president." (jacket) The volume also contains pieces previously untranslated, as well as interviews with Havel. Review: *Foreign Affairs* 70, no.4 (Fall 1991): 184.

477. **Civic Freedom in Central Europe: Voices from Czechoslovakia,** edited by H. Gordon Skilling and Paul Wilson. New York: St. Martin's Press, 1991. xiv, 152 p. ISBN: 0312058039. Includes bibliographical references and index.

This book consists of a special collection of essays, divided into five parts. Part one contains an introductory essay by H. Gordon Skilling, a set of mini-essays by Czech dissidents on the concept of the parallel polis, an idea originally expressed by Vaclav Berda to refer to the concept of an independent society. Part three and four have essays by Martin Palous and Vaclav Havel on this concept and the rebirth of politics. Two appendices contain the manifesto of the movement for Civic Freedom and a list of independent civic initiatives in Czechoslovakia.

VELVET REVOLUTION

478. Bradley, J. F. N., **Czechoslovakia's Velvet Revolution: A Political Analysis.** Boulder, Colo.: East European Monographs, 1992. xxiii, 140, 8 p. *East European Monographs;* no. 345. Includes bibliographical references (p. 138-139.).

This brief study is intended as "a political crisis analysis." (p. vi) Drawing on interviews, journalists' reports and radio and television broadcasts, Bradley attempts to analyze and explain the events that led to the fall of communism in Czechoslovakia. The author provides extensive historical background and reproduces in the appendixes numerous documents to the Velvet Revolution.

479. Havel, Vaclav, **Disturbing the Peace: A Conversation with Karel Hvizdala,** translated from the Czech with an introduction by Paul Wilson. New York: Knopf, 1990. xvii, 228 p. ISBN: 0394584414. Includes index.

This was the first samizdat book to come out legally in Czechoslovakia. It consists of an interview of Havel conducted by Karel Hvizdala in 1986 while Hvizdala was living in West Germany and Havel in Prague. The interview is divided into chapters, reflecting the different topics covered. The topics range the gamut from politics and theater to personal assessment. A glossary at the back of the book helps the reader understand the context out of which Havel speaks. Reviews: *New Republic* 203, no.4 (July 23, 1990): 27-32. *New York Times Book Review* (June 17, 1990): 1ff. *Foreign Affairs* 69, no.4 (Fall 1990): 193.

480. Leviatin, David, **Prague Sprung: Notes and Voices From the New World.** Westport, Conn.: Praeger, 1993. 142 p. ISBN: 0275945367. Includes bibliographical references (p. 135-137) and index.

In this volume David Leviatin sets out to produce a new sort of social history. It is oral history in a sense but Leviatin feels it can be more aptly described as oral shock, as the predominant attitude of those people he spoke with in 1990 were shocked by the fall of Communism and somewhat perplexed as to what to expect and by their own reactions. The lengthy interviews were carried on mainly with scholars from Charles University in Prague. They are of interest to anyone who wishes to understand the changes in Eastern Europe and their effects on the population.

481. Wheaton, Bernard, **The Velvet Revolution: Czechoslovakia,** 1988-1991, Bernard Wheaton and Zdenek Kavan. Boulder, Colo.: Westview Press, 1992. xvi, 255 p. ISBN: 0813312043. Includes bibliographical references and index.

The nine chapters of Wheaton's book are divided into three parts. Part one (ch. 1-2) deals with the long decay of the Communist system in Czechoslovakia through October 1989. Part two focuses on the November 1989 revolution (ch. 3-6) and the collapse of the old regime. Part three (ch. 7-9) describes the foundations of the post-Communist state through January 1992. In addition there are four appendices containing slogans of the revolution, documents of the revolution, public opinion during the revolution and a biographical cameo of Vaclav Havel.

482. Wolchik, Sharon L., **Czechoslovakia in Transition: Politics, Economics and Society**. New York: Pinter, 1991. ix, 390 p. ISBN: 0861874080. Includes bibliography (p.322-381) and index.

"This book begins with a look at the history of Czechoslovakia prior to the institution of a communist system. It then discusses the main developments in the country's politics, economics, society, and a number of important aspects of public policy during communist rule and the changes that have occurred in each area in the early post-communist period as the transition to democratic rule and a market economy continues." (p. vi-vii)

ECONOMICS, BUSINESS AND TRADE

483. **Czechoslovakia: Transition to a Market Economy**. Washington, DC: World Bank, 1991. xxviii, 192 p. *World Bank Country Study*, ISBN: 0821318276.

"The report provides an overview of the economy and discusses policy reforms and institutional changes deemed necessary for achieving a quick transition from a centrally planned to a market economy. It stresses the need to pursue policy and institutional reforms in parallel, and puts particular emphasis on creating a stable macroeconomic framework within which the fundamental structural changes will take place. The report focuses on systematic reforms in ownership and management of enterprises, price and trade liberalization on goods and factor markets, including active enhancement of competition, and provision of a social safety net for those population groups most adversely affected during the transformation process." (p. iii)

484. **Doing Business in Czechoslovakia**. New York: Price Waterhouse, 1991. *Information Guide/Price Waterhouse*.

A guide to business conditions in Czechoslovakia by Price Waterhouse. It is one in a series providing business people with information on the investment climate, auditing and accounting rules, taxation laws, industrial climate, regulations on business, banking and finance information, labor laws. The book includes numerous appendixes with statistical information, checklists for establishing a business in Czechoslovakia and much more.

485. Myant, Martin R., **The Czechoslovak Economy, 1948-1988: The Battle for Economic Reform**. New York: Cambridge University Press, 1989. xii, 316 p. *Soviet and East European Studies*, ISBN: 0521353149. Includes bibliography (p. 295-311) and index.

Inspired by the "fresh wave of interest in economic reform," the book explores "the widely held belief that a serious programme for the renewal of socialism is possible only on the basis of a thorough assessment of past experience." (p. l) But this is not a conventional economic history of Czechoslovakia. "It explores consistently the three interrelated themes of the development of the system, its relationship to the wider political and international climate and the performance of that system" (p. 1) Review: *American Political Science Review* 84, no.4 (December 1990): 1426-1428.

486. **Czechoslovakia's Agriculture: Situation, Trends, and Prospects.** Lanham, MD: UNIPUB, 1991. 189 p. ISBN: 9282629244. Includes bibliography (p.127-133).

This report on Czechoslovakia's agricultural development and prospects was prepared for the Commission of European Community. It is a fairly detailed, general study of the status of Czechoslovak agriculture, and the difficulty of reform in that sector of the Czechoslovak economy. One final chapter presents various approaches to reform, analyzing the probability for success of each approach. The conclusion is that free trade, while most labor intensive, would be the best environment for Czech agricultural development. A statistical analysis of the status, trends and future of agriculture in Czechoslovakia is also included.

487. **The Czech and Slovak Federal Republic: An Economy in Transition** by Jim Prust (et al). Washington D.C.: International Monetary Fund., 1990. vii, 70 p. *Occasional Paper,* no.72.

This report was prepared in connection with an application of the Czech and Slovak Federal Republic for membership in the IMF. It covers the evolution of the economic system and the economy, the economy in the late 1980s, and reform efforts to 1990.

488. Teichova, Alice, **The Czechoslovak Economy, 1918-1980**. New York: Routledge, 1988. xxiii, 178 p. *Contemporary Economic History of Europe Series*, ISBN: 0415003768. Includes bibliography (p.164-165) and index.

This volume in the series *Contemporary Economic History of Europe* looks at Czechoslovakia's economic development in the twentieth century. Its high level of industrialization set it apart from other Eastern European nations early in its history. "This together with its tradition of democracy has had a profound effect on its economic, social and cultural development. In this context the book outlines the history of the Czechoslovak economy which began to exist in 1918, was destroyed between 1938 and 1945, and restored after 1945. It assesses social and economic change against the background of the international economy and the dramatic political events of the twentieth century...." (p. 1) Dr. Teichova has arranged the work in two parts, the first covering the years 1918-1945 and the second examining the changes since World War II. Each part covers population, society, the economy and state and then turns to significant problems of the period. This work attempts to provide information to the Western reader unfamiliar with Czechoslovak history.

489. **Czechoslovakia: Integrating into the Global Economy: A Transition Strategy**. Washington, D.C.: World Bank, 1992. vii, 108 p. *UNDP-World Bank Trade Expansion Program Country Report;* 8. Includes bibliographical references (p. 107-108).

This brief study of Czechoslovakia's trade policies contains a wealth of statistical data. The report was provided by the World Bank and discusses Czechoslovakia's transition to the free market in terms of its trade policies. The study team notes that the Czechoslovak government was quick to liberalize its trade policies after the fall of the communist regime. Its previous dependence on Soviet imports was quickly corrected. But other problems such as diversifying exports, integration into the European community as well as domestic problems remain. The study group presents a variety of possible solutions. The book includes a suggested stabilization program and trade performance and numerous statistical data outlining Czechoslovakia's economic performance in the appendix tables.

Chapter 5
GERMAN DEMOCRATIC REPUBLIC

GENERAL REFERENCE WORKS

490. **East Germany: A Country Study,** edited by Stephen R. Burant. Washington, D.C.: Headquarters, Dept. of the Army: For sale by the Supt. of Docs., U.S. G.P. O., 1988. xxxiii, 433 p. *Area Handbook Series, DA Pam,* 550-155. Includes index.

This reference handbook, written by a team of social scientists, describes and analyzes the history, society, economy, politics, and national security of former East Germany. Three appendices contain statistical information, a chapter on the Warsaw Pact and a chapter on the Council for Mutual Economic Assistance.

491. Fermor, Patrick Leigh, **Between the Woods and the Water: On Foot to Constantinople from the Hook of Holland: The Middle Danube to the Iron Gates**. 1st American ed. New York: Viking, 1986. 248 p. *"Elisabeth Sifton Books,"* ISBN: 0670811491. Includes index. Continues: A time of gifts.

In 1933 Patrick Fermor set off from Amsterdam with a borrowed rucksack and one pound sterling per week, intending to walk to Constantinople. He reached it a year and a half later. As the book jacket says, "It was a double exploration across a continent which was already showing signs of the holocaust to come, and it provides a coherent understanding of the dramatic events that were to transform middle Europe."

492. McKenna, David, **East Germany**. New York: Chelsea House, 1988. 96 p. ISBN: 1555461972. Includes index.

A popular handbook that gives general information about East Germany's history, politics, economy and social conditions.

HISTORY

493. Elkins, Thomas H., **Berlin: The Spatial Structure of a Divided City**. London: Methuen, 1988. vii, 274 p. Includes index and bibliography (p.253-264).

This work is a history of Berlin, but also goes beyond traditional history. Its nine chapters also cover such topics as the Berlin countryside, its water, climate and environment, transportation, economy, urban development and post-war redevelopment, and population. A concluding chapter speculates on the future of Berlin after the wall. Reviews: *Geographical Review* 79, no.3 (July 1989): 361-62. *Association of American Geographers Annals* 79, no.4 (December 1989): 616-620.

494. Keithly, David M., **Breakthrough in the Ostpolitik: The 1971 Quadripartite Agreement**. Boulder, Colo.: Westview Press, 1986. xi, 247 p. *Westview Special Studies in International Relations*, ISBN: 0813371783. Includes index and bibliography (p.231-240).

In this study of the 1971 Quadrapartite Agreement the author sees Berlin as a part of Central Europe. The settlement reached on Berlin affected other Central European nations. "This book examines how the Quadrapartite Agreement dealt with the salient problems of Berlin and what role this treaty assumed within a broader political framework. The agreement, in addition to improving daily life in and around the city, provided an important impetus for the Bonn-Moscow Treaty, the FRG treaties with Poland and Czechoslovakia, and above all the basic treaty between the German states." (p. iii) The book is arranged chronologically and includes appendices containing the text of the treaty.

495. McElvoy, Anne, **The Saddled Cow: East Germany's Life and Legacy**. Boston: Faber and Faber, 1992. xiii, 258 p. ISBN: 0571165915. Includes bibliographical references (p. 251) and index.

Anne McElvoy was the Berlin correspondent for *The Times* during Germany's most recent upheavals from 1989-1990. "*The Saddled Cow* makes no pretense to the exhaustiveness of academic history, but attempts to cover the key periods in the country's developments and those aspects of life behind the Wall which have absorbed me over many years, be they major political chapters or individual fates. It is shamelessly subjective and selective, but aims to provide as wide a picture as possible of what this strange, unloved country was like, from its beginnings, in the chaos of the defeat of fascism, to its end in the unification of Germany and beyond, as its people come to terms with life in the West." (p. xiii)

496. Pike, David, **The Politics of Culture in Soviet-Occupied Germany, 1945-1949**. Stanford, Calif.: Stanford University Press, 1992. xii, 691 p. ISBN: 0804720932. Includes bibliographical references (p. 661-672) and index.

Pike's book about the politics of culture is in four parts. Part one deals with doctrinal adjustments and cultural corollaries (1945-1946); part two with two ideological camps in 1947; part three focuses on ideological reversion and cultural conformity in 1948, and part four concludes with Stalin and the fate of the nation (1949).

497. Steininger, Rolf, **The German Question: The Stalin Note of 1952 and the Problem of Reunification,** translated by Jane T. Hedges, edited by Mark Cioc. New York: Columbia University Press, 1990. xvii, 186 p. ISBN: 0231072163. Translation of: Eine vertane Chance. Includes bibliographical references (p. 159-182) and index.

This translation makes accessible to Western readers a publication that caused some controversy. The question of the sincerity of Stalin's offer to reunify Germany in 1952 and why it was seemingly not supported in the West has been a vexing one. In this volume Steininger uses documents from American and British archives to show that the opposition came from Konrad Adenauer primarily and why. Besides the text of the note numerous documents have been included.

498. Turner, Henry Ashby, **The Two Germanies Since 1945**. New Haven: Yale University Press, 1987. 228 p. ISBN: 0300038658. Includes index.

Unwilling to write about the post-war Germanies in isolation from one another, the author points out that "neither can be viewed in isolation without omitting essential influences in their development." (p. vii) Topics covered include: defeat, cold war and division; the birth of two new governments; two decades of Christian Democratic leadership in the Federal Republic 1949-1969; the Ulbricht era in the GDR, 1949-1971; the social-liberal era in the Federal Republic 1969-1982; and the two Germanies in an era of mutual accommodation.

499. Tusa, Ann, and John Tusa, **The Berlin Airlift**. New York: Atheneum, 1988. 445 p. ISBN: 068911513X. Includes index.

This is the story of how Berliners, aided by the West, survived the blockade that was in force from the Spring of 1948 to mid summer 1949. "How the time was used, how Berlin endured the siege is the story of most of this book. To understand why the time was needed it is necessary to go back—to see why the four powers were in Berlin and why the city was so vital to them all; why the Western allies were so vulnerable to Soviet pressure; why some would countenance another world war to retain Berlin; ..." (p. xiv) The authors spent four years researching their subject. Review: *Journal of American History* 76, no.4 (March 1990): 1320-1321.

500. **World Views and Scientific Discipline Formation: Science Studies in the German Democratic Republic,** edited by William R. Woodward and Robert S. Cohen. Boston: Kluwer Academic Publishers, 1991. xvi, 462 p. *Boston Studies in the Philosophy of Science,* v. 134, ISBN: 0792312864. Includes bibliographical references and index.

This group of essays on various aspects of science studies is divided into twelve parts: introduction, ideas and institutions, mathematics in a socio-political context, psychology constructs its subject matter, physics in the context of philosophy and theory of science, theory as a method, discipline formations of philosophy, biological evolution in the minor theories of evolution, chemistry laboratories and dissertations, natural science and nature philosophies, science and society, and the social construction of scientific knowledge.

501. Wyden, Peter, **Wall: The Inside Story of Divided Berlin**. New York: Simon and Schuster, 1989. 762, xvi p. ISBN: 0671555103. Includes bibliographical references (p. 707-732).

Wyden's history of the Berlin wall begins with Kennedy's confrontation with Khrushchev in 1958, and continues with the building of the wall, various escape attempts and ends with Erich Honecker's visit to West Germany in September of 1987 when he predicts the day "when borders will no longer divide us but unite us." The narrative is made especially poignant by focusing an Bärbel and Ota Grubel, who escaped, but whose two children were taken from them in 1973. Review: *Foreign Affairs* 69, no.2 (Spring 1990): 170.

GOVERNMENT, POLITICS AND LAW

502. Allen, Bruce, **Germany East: Dissident and Opposition**, rev.ed. New York: Black Rose Books, 1991. 226 p. ISBN: 0921689977; 0895431969; 0895431977; 0921689969. Includes bibliographical references (p. 218-226).

Allen's purpose is to formulate "an in-depth, chronological study of the phenomena of dissent and critical thought in the German Democratic Republic which is designed, ultimately, to demonstrate their significance for the DDR and, by implication, for Europe as well as for the global place movement." (p. 13) Topics covered include the impact of the 1956 East bloc crisis, the significance of the Church and the Berlin wall, intellectual dissent, the impact of the Polish crisis and Solidarity, the autonomous peace movement, and human rights and ecology.

503. **East Germany in Comparative Perspective,** edited by David Childs, Thomas A. Baylis and Marilyn Ruschemeyer. London: Routledge, 1989. xvi, 238 p. ISBN: 0415004969. Includes index.

The papers presented in this volume were originally presented at a conference in 1986. The intention of the conference was "to compare the institutions, policies and practices of the GDR with those of its neighbors and to examine the role played by the GDR in bloc-wide policy." (p. xiii)

504. Darnton, Robert, **Berlin Journal: 1989-1990**. New York: Norton, 1991. 352p. ISBN: 0393029700. Includes index.

In this journal of events witnessed by the author, Darnton fuses two genres: "event history" and "the history of mentalities" to provide a description and analysis of the fall of communism in East Germany in 1989.

505. Gedmin, Jeffrey, **The Hidden Hand: Gorbachev and the Collapse of East Germany**. Washington, D.C.: AEI Press, 1992. ix, 169 p. ISBN: 0844738158.

Gedmin describes the role of Gorbachev's reforms in the Soviet Union in hastening the collapse of communism in East Germany. After an introduction in which the author sets perestroika, Eastern Europe and the German question in its historical and political context, subsequent chapters cover the new world view and the new Europe, East Germany and the dilemma of legitimacy, the prelude to upheaval with East German dissent and the Kremlin allies for reform, the revolution of 1989 and the aftermath of an inadvertent revolution.

506. Gleye, Paul, **Behind the Wall: An American in East Germany, 1988-89**. Carbondale: Southern Illinois Press, 1991. xii, 207 p. ISBN: 0809317435.

Gleye was a visiting Fulbright professor in the East German provinces for ten months during the academic year 1988-89. This book is the result of his observations of what life was like there just prior to the fall of communism in the fall of 1989.

507. Keithly, David M., **The Collapse of East German Communism: The Year the Wall Came Down, 1989**. Westport, Conn.: Praeger, 1992. x, 241 p. ISBN: 0275942619. Includes bibliographical references (p. 231-237) and index.

"This book is intended to be in part an account of history in the making, and my hope is that it will have some appeal beyond specialist circles. I have attempted to combine scholarly analysis with eyewitness record, endeavoring thereby to stake out the middle ground between scholarship and journalism." (p. 3) Keithly argues that the division of Germany was a source of instability in Europe. The book is divided into three parts. The first describes the East German state before the revolution: East German communism, economic problems and the failure of the East German government to gain legitimacy in the eyes of the people. Part two looks at the causes of the revolution. The final section focuses on why events came to a head in 1989.

508. Lasky, Melvin J., **Voices in a Revolution: The Collapse of East German Communism**. New Brunswick, N.J.: Transaction Publishers, 1992. 116 p. ISBN: 1560000309. Includes bibliographical references.

Melvin Lasky looks at the events that led to the breakdown of East German Communism. It is an impressionistic account. It is supplemented with largely journalistic discussion of the relations between East and West Germany.

509. MacGregor, Douglas A., **The Soviet-East German Military Alliance**. Cambridge (England): Cambridge University Press, 1989. xi, 178 p. ISBN: 0521365627. Includes bibliographical references (p. 138-161).

"This book is about the nature and political consequences of institutionalized military cooperation between the East German and Soviet states in Central-East Europe." (p. ix) He examines the origins of cooperation prior to World War I, Nazi-Soviet collaboration, the East German rise to military prominence from 1956-1969, their collaboration in the post 1968 pact, and the military alliance and Poland. An appendix includes nine data tables dealing with events, military capabilities, trade, defense expenditures, GNP, and manpower. Reviews: *Soviet Union/Union Sovietique* 17, no.1-2 (1990): 179-181. *German Studies Review* 13, no.3 (October 1990): 587-588.

510. Marcuse, Peter, **Missing Marx: A Personal and Political Journal of a Year in East Germany, 1989-1990**. New York: Monthly Review Press, 1991. 302 p. ISBN: 0853458278; 0853458286. Includes bibliographical references.

If one were to chose the most eventful year in German history in the second half of this century, 1989-1990 could very easily be the choice. The Communist government that has been in place since the end of the war falls and Germany begins the slow process of reunification. Peter Marcuse was born in Berlin but emigrated in 1933 to the United States. He was a well known Marxist philosopher. Peter Marcuse, after practicing law for some years, got a Ph.D. in City Planning. In this journal he describes the political and economic changes he witnessed during his stay in East Germany. The book is divided into two sections each with an introduction providing background in German history and economics. The remainder of each part is comprised of the author's personal experiences while in Germany. The book also contains a glossary and chronology of events from 1985-1990. It provides the reader with a fascinating first-hand account of a political system in transition.

511. Meador, Daniel John, **Impressions of Law in East Germany: Legal Education and Legal Systems in the German Democratic Republic**. Charlottesville: University Press of Virginia, 1986. 320 p. ISBN: 0813911109. Includes bibliography (p. 310-311) and index.

The system of law and legal education in East Germany has not been studied in depth in the West. This has been due largely to the difficulty of obtaining meaningful information on East Germany. Daniel Meador was determined to fill this gap and approaches the problem from two directions. He used the published sources available and where there were gaps he relied on interviews which took place with East German law faculty in 1983. He was interested in describing the organization and administration of the law departments in the GDR, their curriculum, discovering who the law faculty and students were, what books and library resources were available to them, what careers were open to the student upon graduation and how the legal system is organized and staffed. He begins with a chapter on the historical background of Germany in the 20th century, outlining the tremendous changes the area has undergone. He then presents and discusses translations of documents on GDR legal education.

512. Phillips, Ann L., **Soviet Policy Toward East Germany Reconsidered: The Postwar Decade**. Westport, Conn.: Greenwood Press, 1986. xii, 262 p. *Contributions in Political Science,* 0147-1066, no. 142, ISBN: 0313246718. Includes bibliography (p. 233-256) and index.

"This study analyzes Soviet political and economic policies toward East Germany from 1945 to 1955, focusing on the transition in Soviet policy from ambivalence to support." (p. 3) Phillips believes that the Soviet Union pursued an ambivalent policy towards East Germany during 1945 to 1955. This was evident in a mix of political and economic goals that were often incompatible with one another.

513. **Germany and Europe in Transition,** edited by Adam D. Rotfeld and Walter Stutzle. New York: Clarendon Press, 1991. x, 237 p. ISBN: 0198291469. Includes bibliographical references and index.

In February, 1990 a conference was held on "A European Peace Order and the Responsibility of the Two German States." The purpose of the conference was to give students of international affairs a better understanding of German affairs and to give Germans a better understanding of the international situation. This volume, which is a product of that conference, is divided into two parts. The first consists of seven brief papers on various topics: German responsibility for European peace, elections in the GDR, German unity and security in Europe, and the future of Europe and Germany. Part two is a collection of some 60 documents on the external aspects of German unification. "This document is part of a larger effort at the Stockholm International Peace Research Institute devoted to examining the new dimensions of European security: to research both the traditional military aspects of security and in a broader perspective, the political, economic and structural elements of preserving stability in the New Europe." (p. 6)

514. Winrow, Gareth M., **The Foreign Policy of the GDR in Africa**. New York: Cambridge University Press, 1990. xvii, 291 p. *Soviet and East European Studies*, 78, ISBN: 0521380383. Includes index and bibliographical references (p. 228-275).

The first comprehensive English language account of East German foreign relations with Africa is contained in this volume. The author contends that East German foreign policy in Africa is not just a reflection of the Soviet Union's policies. He believes that GDR policy there is used to strengthen relations with the USSR. The author analyzed military involvement in the continent, trade and GDR assistance in Africa. "It will be of interest to specialists and students of Soviet and East European studies, with special reference to the GDR, North-South relationships, superpower competition and the politics of development." (p. i)

515. Woods, Roger, **Opposition in the GDR under Honecker, 1971-1985: An Introduction and Documentation,** with translations by Christopher Upward. Basingstoke: Macmillan, 1986. x, 257 p. ISBN: 0333393252. Includes bibliography and index.

A discussion of the extent and nature of opposition in the GDR. The first section of the book is an introduction to the topic. It traces the history of the opposition in the GDR and gives a detailed description of the groups opposing the government. The second part of the book is made up of documents, most of which have not appeared in English before. They were selected as "representative" of the views of the individuals or groups from which they came. "The documents are grouped under various headings: the official view, the western connection, dissident views, rejection of the GDR, the peace movement, the importance of the opposition." A chronology of events and postscripts are also provided.

ECONOMICS, BUSINESS AND TRADE

516. Bryson, Phillip J., and Manfred Melzer, **The End of the East German Economy: From Honecker to Reunification**. New York: St. Martin's Press, 1991. 148 p. ISBN: 0312055560.

This brief study surveys the economic conditions in East Germany before the fall of the socialist regime. In five chapters the authors discuss the ailing East German economy under Honecker, its final attempts to survive the changes from 1987 through 1989, pressures from the international market reform, domestic shortages and the impetus they gave to reform and finally, looking to the West and reunification. The focus in this work is on the problems associated with accomplishing reform in a centrally planned economy.

517. **The East German Economy,** edited by Ian Jeffries and Manfred Melzer. New York: Croom Helm, 1987. 328 p. ISBN: 0709914695. Includes bibliography (p. 314-322) and index.

The fourteen essays in this book are intended to explain how the economy of the GDR actually operates. It includes all major aspects of the economy, including the command planning and production unit, economic policies in historical perspective, the role of the Kombinat, the five year plans, pricing system, financial system, agriculture, foreign trade, the GDR's role in COMECON and economic reform. Reviews: *Problems of Communism* 39, no.2 (March-April 1990): 85-90. Review: *Slavic Review* 48, no.2 (Summer 1989): 322-23.

518. Pickel, Andreas, **Radical Transitions: The Survival and Revival of Entrepreneurship in the GDR**. Boulder, Colo.: Westview Press, 1992. xii, 242 p. ISBN: 0813383544. Includes bibliographical references (p. 217-238) and index.

"A surprisingly large private economy has survived in the GDR, and Andreas Pickel presents here a comprehensive study of entrepreneurship under communist rule. He shows how the private sector made the initial transition from a capitalist to a socialist society after World War II, was integrated into the socialist system that prevailed until 1989 and then developed in the rapid transition to a market economy." (back cover)

LANGUAGE AND LITERATURE

519. Eckart, Gabriele, **Hitchhiking: Twelve German Tales,** translated and with and afterword and notes by Wayne Kvam. Lincoln: University of Nebraska Press, 1992. xi, 142 p. *European Women Writers Series*, ISBN: 0803267223. Translation of: Per Anhalter. Includes bibliographical references (p. 143).

This is a collection of journalistic fiction by this noted East German writer. After working as a cement worker in a construction plant and then as a street sweeper in Berlin, she turned these experiences into the present collection. She has also written poetry.

520. **Neue Ansichten: The Reception of Romanticism in the Literature of the GDR,** edited by Howard Gaskill, Karin McPherson and Andrew Barker. Atlanta, GA: Rodopi, 1990. 236 p. *GDR Monitor Special Series,* no. 6, ISBN: 9051832397. Includes bibliographical references and index.

These papers were presented at a conference in Edinburgh in August of 1989. Six of them are in English. The reception of Romanticism in the GDR is viewed both through social groups (literacy salons) and the general intellectual climate, as well as through individual authors (Schwedenow, Damm, Moog, Struzyk, Wolf, Fuhmann, Bobrowski, Kuchel, Kirsten, and Braun).

521. **German Writers and the Cold War 1945-61,** edited by Rhys W. Williams, Stephen Parker and Colin Riordan; with the collaboration of Helmut Peitsch. Manchester, UK: Manchester University Press, 1992. vi, 250 p.

The essays collected here examine the development of German literary relations at the beginning of the Cold War. The contributors discuss such topics as the Western reception of East German literature, Hans Werner Richter's role in German literary relations, the role of the German Academy of the Arts and West German literature in East Germany.

522. **Socialism and the Literary Imagination: Essays on East German Writers,** edited by Martin Kane. New York: St. Martin's Press, 1991. xi, 256 p. ISBN: 0854966439. Includes bibliographical references and index.

The papers collected in this volume were originally presented at a conference at the University of Kent in April 1989. "The contributors to this volume—distinguished scholars from Britain, the United States and Germany—are all enthusiasts of East German literature who feel that the literary and artistic qualities of East German writing are all too often lost sight of in the debate about censorship, cultural control, dissident writers and related issues. Each contributor selects a particular East German writer and explains why the work of their chosen author deserves to be considered along side the best in contemporary European and world literature." (p. i) Some of the authors included are Johannes R. Becher, Anna Seghers, Erwin Strittmatter, Stefan Heym, Franz Fuhmann, Christa Wolf, Heiner Müller, Jurek Becker, Volker Braun and Christoph Hein.

INDIVIDUAL AUTHORS

523. Benjamin, Walter, **Moscow Diary,** edited by Gary Smith; translated by Richard Sieburth. Cambridge, Mass.: Harvard University Press, 1986. 150 p. ISBN: 067458743X; 0674587448 (pbk). Includes bibliographical references and index.

German author Walter Benjamin stayed in Moscow from early December 1926 to the end of January 1927. He financed his trip by advances he had received to complete some writing assignments upon his return to Germany. Although he did complete four pieces relating to his trip, his diary was not part of that corpus. The time and honesty of the diary is noteworthy, as well as his description and ruminations about the conditions prevailing in Moscow at that time and about the people, mostly Jewish intellectuals of the opposition, that he met there.

524. Fuegi, John, **Bertolt Brecht: Chaos, According to Plan**. New York: Cambridge University Press, 1987. xiv, 223 p. *Directors in perspective*, ISBN: 0521282454 (pbk); 0521238285. Includes index and bibliography (p.211-217).

Rather than deal with Brecht and his stage production theoretically, Fuegi has described how Brecht really worked with authors and the day-to-day problems of staging. He covers Brecht's staging techniques in Augsburg, Munich, Berlin, Paris, London and New York. Reviews: *Modern Drama*, 31 no.3 (September 1988): 459-462. *German Quarterly* 61, no.3 (Summer 1988):480-481.

525. **Critical Essays on Bertolt Brecht,** compiled by Siegfried Mews. Boston: G. K. Hall, 1989. vi, 287 p. *Critical Essays on World Literature*, ISBN: 0816188440. Includes bibliography (p.277-278) and index.

Brecht is perhaps the most well-known of East German writers, returning there from the United States in 1947 after having been questioned by the House Committee on Un-American Activities. This collection of essays focuses primarily on his plays, but considerable attention is also given to his poetry, epic theater and his politics. An introductory essay by the editor provides relevant biographical information.

526. Wright, Elizabeth, **Postmodern Brecht: A Representation**. New York: Routledge, 1988. ix, 154 p. *Critics of the Twentieth Century,* v. 7, ISBN: 0415023300 (pbk); 0415023297. Includes bibliographical references and index.

Wright sees Brecht in the camp of post structuralists who claim "that the author is not the creator of an original work, but someone who produces from the materials of history." (p. 1) In this volume the author examines critical responses to Brecht, his deconstructing of the comedy/tragedy dichotomy and his critical post modernist theories. Review: *German Studies Review* 13, no.1 (February 1990): 176-177.

527. Celan, Paul, **Collected Prose,** translated from the German by Rosemarie Waldrop. New York: Sheep Meadow Press, 1986. x, 67 p. ISBN: 0935296921.

Celan is the pseudonym of Paul Antschel, who was born in Cernauti Romania in 1920. After the war he moved to Paris and wrote in German. His works, especially his poetry, is influenced by both French socialism and his Jewish heritage.

528. Chalfen, Israel, **Paul Celan: A Biography of his Youth,** translated by Maximilian Bleyleben, introduction by John Felstiner. New York: Persea Books, 1991. xxviii, 214 p. ISBN: 0892551623. Includes bibliographical references (p.193-207) and index.

Celan was born in Romanian Bukovna in 1920. This translated biography of his youth (1920-1949) is based on correspondence and interviews with Celan's friends and relatives.

529. Hein, Christoph, **The Tango Player,** translated by Philip Boehm. 1st ed. New York: Farrar, Straus and Giroux, 1992. 219 p. ISBN: 0374272522. Translation of: Der Tangospieler.

This is the story of Dallow, a man who had been sentenced to 21 months in prison for playing a tango that had subversive lyrics. "As he chronicles Dallow's return, he constructs a telling portrait of life in Leipzig—loveless sexual encounters, secret police harassments, professional intrigues, and daily brutalities. He shows how a corrupt system perverts the most ordinary human interaction, and how lives are ruined by malicious caprice." (book jacket)

530. Fickert, Kurt J., **Neither Left nor Right: The Politics of Individualism in Uwe Johnson's Work.** New York: P. Lang, 1987. 182 p. *American University Studies, Series I, Germanic Languages and Literatures, vol.59*, ISBN: 0820404942. Includes bibliography (163-169) and index.

"Johnson is an author who explores the theme of the connection between personal conflicts and universal moral problems, as worked out largely on an exactly defined plane of political existence." (p.7) Fickert attempts to explicate the author's oeuvre from this perspective.

531. Giron, Arthur, **Edith Stein.** New York: S. French, 1991. 98 p. ISBN: 0573692483.

"This play was inspired by Edith Stein. It is not a documentary depiction of her life, but an attempt to dramatize the conflicts she faced." (p. 6)

532. **Responses to Christa Wolf: Critical Essays,** edited by Marilyn Sibley Fries. Detroit: Wayne State University Press, 1989. 418 p. ISBN: 0814321305. Includes bibliographical references.

The essays on this volume received their inspiration in part from a special session on Christa Wolf at the Modern Language Association of America's 1981 convention. The contributions cover a broad range of topics including feminism, essays on specific novels, poets, prose, comparative studies, and others.

533. Kuhn, Anna Katharina, **Christa Wolf's Utopian Vision: From Marxism to Feminism.** New York: Cambridge University Press, 1988. xiii, 281 p. *Cambridge Studies in German*, ISBN: 0521322332. Includes bibliography (p.265-276) and index.

Kuhn examines Wolf's writing and worldview by devoting chapter-length attention to her works *Moscow Novela, Divided Heaven, Christa T., Patterns of Childhood, No Place on Earth, Cassandra*, and *Starfall*. Review: *Modern Fiction Studies* 35, no.2 (Summer 1989): 354-356.

534. Love, Myra Norma, **Christa Wolf: Literature and the Conscience of History.** New York: P. Lang, 1991. 202 p. *DDR-Studien-East German Studies, v.6*, ISBN: 0820416517. Includes bibliographical references (p.193-202).

Love focuses on the role of literature as a moral force in society. The author is seen as a moralist and literature as a moral institution. An appendix includes an essay on Wolf's reception by the critics.

THE SOCIETY, SOCIOLOGY

535. Fishman, Sterling, and Lothar Martin, **Estranged Twins: Education and Society in the Two Germanys.** New York: Praeger, 1987. ix, 218 p. *Praeger Special Studies Series in Comparative Education*, ISBN: 0275924602. Includes bibliography (p. 199-211) and index.

The purpose of this study is "to generate an understanding of the interrelationship between political and economic systems on one hand and the aims, and achievements of schools on the other." (p. 3) After a chapter on the socio-political situation in both Germanys the author covers such topics as public and private values, the law, goals of education, who runs the schools, the curriculum and teaching and learning. Review: *Education Studies* 19, no.3/4 (Fall/Winter 1988): 430-32.

536. **Gay Voices from East Germany,** interviews by Jurgen Lemke and John Borneman. Bloomington: Indiana University Press, 1991. vi, 197 p. ISBN: 0253333199; 0253206308. Translation of: Ganz normal anders. Includes bibliographical references (p. 193-197).

This collection documents the lives of fourteen homosexual men in East Germany. Each interview set is introduced by an introductory essay written by the translator of the subsequent essays. The autobiographical narratives are candid and portray what life was like for gay men in a state that tried to deny their existence.

537. Liang, Hsi-Huey, **Berlin Before the Wall: A Foreign Student's Diary with Sketches**. New York: Routledge, 1990. 257 p. ISBN: 0415901685.

This book is the diary of a young Chinese graduate student in history who spent 1953-1954 in Berlin. It provides insight into the divided city before the erection of the Berlin wall.

538. Proctor, Robert, **Racial Hygiene: Medicine under the Nazis**. Cambridge, Mass.: Harvard University Press., 1988. viii, 414 p. ISBN: 0674745809. Includes bibliography (p. 330-337) and index.

In this well-researched study Proctor explores "the place of science, especially biomedical science, under the Nazis, with particular reference to the junctions of apology and social control.... [His] focus here, however, is not primarily on how the Nazis corrupted or abused science, but rather on how scientists themselves participated in the construction of Nazi racial policy." (p. 3) There are also two appendices, one a list of German medical journals under the Nazis and the other a list of university and research institutes devoted to racial hygiene. Reviews: *American Historical Review* 95, no.2 (April 1990): 530-531. *Bulletin of the History of Medicine* 64, no.2 (Summer 1990): 336-337.

539. Reid, J. H., **Writing without Taboos: The New East German Literature**. U.S.A. and Canada: St. Martin's Press, 1990. x, 258 p. ISBN: 0854960201. Includes bibliographical references (p. 227-245) and index.

This study examines German literacy trends over the last two decades. The author focuses on the cultural context that has produced these trends and tries to determine the degree to which it differs from literature produced in West Germany and Austria. Each chapter is an independent study as each looks at German literacy development from a different point of view. Chapter one examines differences in the literary identities of East and West Germany. Chapter two focuses on the questions of cultural politics in literature. The third chapter analyzes literary forms that have developed in East Germany. The fourth chapter looks at contemporary topics and is followed by three chapters on the stages of history treated by GDR's authors. The final chapter examines prospects for the future.

540. **Quality of Life in the German Democratic Republic: Changes and Developments in a State Socialist Society,** edited by Marilyn Rueschemeyer and Christiane Lemke. Armonk, NY: M.E. Sharpe, 1989. xiii, 242 p. ISBN: 0873324846. Includes bibliography (p.237-239).

A collection of essays that examines social structures and institutions affecting the day to day lives of the people of the German Democratic Republic (GDR). The contributors are from numerous countries including three who give the perspective of the GDR. The essays are grouped into sections such as "The Social Politics and Social Conditions"; "Family, Sex Rules and Socialization"; "The Role of Woman in Society" is of particular interest in these studies. The contributors felt their approach complemented existing studies on the analysis of the state. Reviews: *German Studies Review* 13, no.1 (February 1990): 186-187. *Problems of Communism* 39, no.2 (March-April 1990): 85-90. *Contemporary Sociology* 19, no.3 (May 1990): 366-367.

541. **Violations of the Helsinki Accords, East Germany: A Report Prepared for the Helsinki Review Conference, Vienna, November 1986,** by Daphne Eviatar. New York: U.S. Helsinki Watch Committee, 1986. iv, 43 p. *A Helsinki Watch Report*, ISBN: 0938579800. Includes bibliography (p. 43).

This report chronicles human rights violations in East Germany. It is arranged topically, covering violations in the areas of expression, association, movement, and religion, political prisoners, the peace movement and the human rights movement.

REUNIFICATION

542. **The Domestic Politics of German Unification,** edited by Christopher Anderson, Karl Kaltenthaler, Wolfgang Luthardt. Boulder, Colo.: Lynne Rienner, 1993. x, 253 p. ISBN: 1553874096. Includes bibliographical references and index.

"Prominent German and U.S. scholars examine the domestic political events that led to the unification of the two German states. The authors analyze the breakdown of the East German regime, the electoral politics of the unification year, political parties and their strategies, political elites and the rise of right-wing extremism." (p. 254) The essays are divided into two sections. The first part includes those that deal with the processes and political aspects of unification. In the second part papers discussing new challenges and problems arising from unification are presented.

543. Freney, Michael A., and Rebecca S. Hartley, **United Germany and the United States**. Washington, DC: National Planning Association, 1991. xvii, 178 p. *CIR Report, 21, NPA Report, 250*, ISBN: 0890681074. Includes bibliographical references and index.

The authors examine the future of the relationship of the United States and united Germany. "An important goal of the analysis is to consolidate information for public and private sector leaders dealing with the transition taking place in Europe. A broad range of issues is covered, with emphasis on developments within Germany, the rapidly shifting European economic landscape, and dramatic changes in security arrangements on that continent." (p.xvii)

544. Fulbrook, Mary, **The Two Germanies, 1945-1990: Problems of Interpretation**. Atlantic Highlands, NJ: Humanities Press International, 1992. 114 p. ISBN: 0391037498. Includes bibliographical references (p. 97-109) and index.

"The two Germanies—uniquely related, uniquely divided—have been the object of a heated controversy and political debate. Academic interpretations of the two Germanies have often both informed and been colored by wider controversies. In *The Two Germanies*, Mary Fulbrook charts a clear and informative path through the major topics and areas of debate and provides a useful guide to further reading." (back cover) The book is organized topically with discussions of Germany's historical development, politics, society, economy, culture and the reunification of the two Germanies.

545. Glaessner, Gert-Joachim, **The Unification Process in Germany: From Dictatorship to Democracy, Gert-Joachim Glaessner;** translated from the German by Colin B. Grant. New York: St. Martin's Press, 1992. viii, 248 p. ISBN: 0312085702. Includes bibliographical references (p. 126-134) and index.

This is the first volume in the series The New Germany. The series is aimed at a wide readership and intends to explore a variety of issues affecting Germany's recent history. "Professor Glaessner analyzes major aspects of the unification process, focusing on the events leading to and resulting from the revolution of 1989-90. German-German relations during the 1980s are examined using previously inaccessible archival material from the former GDR as well as in-depth interviews with top politicians, including Krenz and Schabowski. The unification process itself is discussed with particular emphasis on analysis of the election, the unification treaty and the transition from dictatorship to democracy." (back cover) The appendix contains a number of documents on specific aspects of unification in translation.

546. **The Two German States and European Security,** edited by F. Stephen Larrabee, foreword by Berthold Beitz. New York: St. Martin's Press, 1989. xviii, 330 p. ISBN: 0312026838.

The papers presented here were originally presented at the seventh annual conference of the Institute for East-West Security Studies. The authors "analyze the German-German dialogue and explore the relationship of German-German affairs to East-West relations as a whole." (p. xvi)

547. Neckerman, Peter Josef, **The Unification of Germany; or, the Anatomy of a Peaceful Revolution**. Boulder, Colo.: East European Monographs, 1991. x, 113 p. *East European Monographs; no. 303*, ISBN: 0880332301. Includes bibliographical references (p. 87-113).

Peter Neckerman believes that three preconditions were necessary for the unification of Germany. In particular he saw a change in the international situation, a strong stance for unification on the part of the East Germans and a strong German leader who would speak for the people on the international scene as crucial to change. In this brief study Neckerman attempts to demonstrate the role these factors played in unification. Numerous references are included in a separate section.

548. **German Reunification: A Reference Guide and Commentary,** edited by Jonathan Osmond, with contributions by Rachel Alsop et al. Harlow, Essex, U.K.: Longman Current Affairs, 1992. xiii, 311 p. ISBN: 0582096502. Includes bibliographical references (p. 297-302) and index.

This handbook on the German reunification was prepared by several specialists in the field. It is divided into three parts. Part one is a brief historical essay on the German revolution and reunification and covers the years 1989-1992. Part two contains contributions by specialists on various aspects of politics, the economy and society. Part three, the reference section, contains texts of relevant documents, tables of governments, election results, economic indicators, institutions, places and terms that were important during the years 1989-1992.

549. Verheyen, Dirk, **The German Question: A Cultural, Historical, and Geopolitical Exploration**. Boulder, Colo.: Westview Press, 1991. xii, 228 p. ISBN: 0813383595. Includes bibliographical references (p. 209-219) and index.

"This study presents an analysis of the German Question from four different angles: German identity, German national unity, German power, and Germany's role in European and world affairs. Special emphasis is placed on a variety of cultural, ideological, and psychological, as well as geopolitical factors. The December 2, 1990, all-German elections constitute the closing-date for the period covered by the manuscript." (p. xi)

550. Waldenburg, Hermann, **The Berlin Wall Book**, photographs and introduction, Hermann Waldenburg. London: Thames and Hudson, 1990. 119 p. ISBN: 0500973857.

This is a book of reproductions of the mural art that appeared on the Berlin wall. As the compiler has stated: "This is a 'picture book' dedicated to the artists." (p. 14)

Chapter 6
HUNGARY

GENERAL REFERENCE WORKS

551. **Hungary, a Country Study,** edited by Stephen R. Burant. Washington D.C.: The Division, 1990. 320 p. *Area Handbook Series, DA pam 550-165. Includes bibliographies.*

This new edition of *Hungary, a Country Study* updates the 1973 volume issued by the federal research division of the Library of Congress. "Like the earlier edition, this study attempts to present the dominant historical, social, economic, political and national security aspects of Hungary. Sources of information included books and scholarly journals, official reports of governments and international organizations, foreign and domestic newspapers, and numerous periodicals. A brief annotated bibliographic note on sources recommended for further reading appears at the end of each chapter, and more detailed chapter bibliographies appear at the end of the book." (p. xiii) There are numerous tables and figures supplying the general reader with basic information such as governmental structure, administrative divisions of Hungary in 1989, military ranks and insignia, etc. An extremely useful general source.

552. Heinrich, Hans-Georg, **Hungary: Politics, Economics, and Society**. Boulder, Colo.: L. Rienner Publishers, 1986. xx, 198 p. *Marxist Regime Series*, ISBN: 0931477670 (pbk); 0931477662. Includes bibliography (p. 181-185) and index.

This book, in a series devoted to Marxist regimes, focuses on several aspects of contemporary Hungary. Chapters cover history and political traditions, the political system, society, economy and economic reforms and other current policies. Several preliminary pages give basic socio-economic data about Hungary. Reviews: *Canadian Slavonic Papers* 29, no.2/3 (June/September 1987): 358-59. *Slavic Review* 46, no.2 (Summer 1987): 345-46.

553. **Guide to Research and Scholarship in Hungary,** edited by Marton Tolnai and Peter Vas-Zoltan. Bloomington: Indiana University Press, 1989. p. ISBN: 0253327180. Includes index.

The Hungarian Academy of Sciences in conjunction with the International Research and Exchanges Board (IREX) have produced these two volumes to acquaint the Western students with the history and present state of Hungarian scholarship. "Part one contains ten analytical papers, each by an eminent Hungarian scholar. The studies discussed in each paper are grouped according to the organizational order established within the Hungarian Academy of Sciences: philosophy and literary studies, oriental studies and musicology; philosophy, history, art history, psychology and pedagogy; mathematics, computing sciences, physics, astronomy; agricultural sciences; medical sciences; technical sciences; chemical sciences; biological sciences; economics; legal and social sciences, earth sciences. Part two is a systematic review of the units, giving details of research" (p. xiii). For anyone seeking information on the structure and history of the Hungarian academic world this guide is invaluable. Bibliographic information is, by and large, limited to publications issued since 1980 although some earlier periodical titles are included.

HISTORY

554. **The Hungarians: A Divided Nation,** edited by Stephen Borsody. Columbus, Ohio: Slavica Publishers, 1989. xxviii, 405 p. *Yale Russian and East European Publications, no. 7*, ISBN: 0936586079. Includes bibliography (p. 382-393) and index.

This is a collection of essays that analyzes the consequences resulting from the fact that so many Hungarians live outside the borders of Hungary. The history of this situation and solution to this problem are also discussed in this volume. The problem for Hungarians is considered a classic example of the kind of problems existing for many of the other East European peoples. The area has had its borders drawn and redrawn by outside powers creating ethnic minorities of groups who had been living within their country's borders. The book is divided into three parts: historical background essay, the Hungarians of Hungary's neighbors and problems and solutions. There are also several appendices providing statistics, maps, a chronology and a bibliography.

555. Calhoun, Daniel Fairchild, **Hungary and Suez, 1956: An Exploration of Who Makes History.** Lanham: University Press America, 1991. 591 p. ISBN: 0819181862. Includes bibliographical references and index.

Calhoun examines two major geopolitical events of 1956, the Suez crisis and the Hungarian uprising. Suez was history from the top down, Hungary history from the bottom up. "In the end, the powerful seemed impotent, the national demented, and the virtuous corrupted." (p. 5) 1956 marked the end of the post-war world.

556. Fenyes, S., **Revisionist Hungary Part II: Hungarian People Accuses.** Miami Beach, Fla., USA: Romanian Historical Press, 1988. 310 p. *Romanian Historical Studies, 27*, ISBN: 0937019119 (alk); 0937019100.

"Dr. S. Fenyes, formerly a member of the Hungarian Parliament, and a fearless champion of democracy, wrote this book in 1935, at a time when Hungarian revision, i.e. the drive to revise Hungary's borders and expand them so as to comprise former possession of the Austro-Hungarian Empire, has become a driving political force in Hungary." (p. 1) This work appeared in translation in 1988 in the hope that it would call attention to the current use of revisionist arguments by the communist leaders in Hungary. The argument was being used to divert attention from real problems and defend the privileges of the communist "aristocracy."

557. Fugedi, Erik, **Castle and Society in Medieval Hungary: (1000-1437).** Budapest: Akademia Kiado, 1986. 162 p. *Studia Historica Academiae Scientarium Hungaricae, no. 187*, ISBN: 9630538024. Includes bibliographical references and index.

Fugedi's intention is "to discuss the functions of castles in medieval Hungary's social, economic and political development." (p. 12) The approach is chronological and separate chapters cover the beginning of the kingdom, the Mongol invasion, King Bela IV, castles of the oligarchs, Castellan of Anjevin kings, and the reign of King Sigismund.

558. ———, **Kings, Bishops, Nobles, and Burghers in Medieval Hungary.** London: Variorum Reprint, 1986. 346 p. *Variorum Reprints, CS229*, ISBN: 0860781771. Includes index.

The social historical works by Dr. Erik Fugedi which are available in Western languages are compiled in this volume. Of the thirteen sections five are in English: "Condition of Medieval Hungary," "Hungarian Bishops in the Fifteenth Century," "The Aristocracy in Medieval Hungary," "The 'Avus' in the Medieval Conceptual Framework of Kinship in Hungary," and " 'Verba Volant...': Oral Culture and Literacy Among the Medieval Hungarian Nobility." All of them demonstrate his psychological and sociological approach to history. The book is arranged topically. A bibliography of the author's works is included.

559. **Towns in Medieval Hungary,** edited by Laszlo Gerevich, translated by T. Szendrei, English text revised by P. C. McCulloch. New York: Columbia University Press, 1990. 151 p. *Atlantic Studies on Society in Change, no. 65, East European Monographs, no. 297*, ISBN: 0880331941. Includes bibliographical references.

"The present volume contains five studies by renowned specialists devoted to the problems of urbanization and urban development in medieval Hungary. These studies offer a fresh approach to urban studies in Hungary for the authors have based their arguments not only on the written source material, but also on the archaeological evidence. Three of these studies cover the early history of specific towns—Gyor, Sopron, Szeresfehervar, Veszprem—and touch upon such exciting issues as the possible survival and continuity of Roman towns, the emergence of urban centres as well as the development of Burgher culture. Two studies are devoted to regional case studies: the role of the Danube in the emergence of towns in Western Hungary and the development of market towns on the Great Hungarian Plain." (back cover)

560. Hoensch, Jorg Konrad, **A History of Modern Hungary, 1867-1983,** translated by Kim Traynor. New York: Longman, 1988. xiii, 320 p. ISBN: 0582251095. Includes indexes.

This updated and expanded edition is based on Professor Hoensch's 1984 publication *Geschichte Ungarns 1867-1983*. Hoensch intends to provide the Western reader with a more detailed description of Hungary's political, social and economic history than has previously been available. The book is chronologically arranged, covering Hungarian history from the 5th century through 1987. An extensive bibliography is included.

561. Kopacsi, Sandor, **In the Name of the Working Class: The Inside Story of the Hungarian Revolution,** translated by Daniel and Judy Stoffman, with a foreword by George Jonas. New York: Grove Press, 1987. xi, 304 p. ISBN: 0802100104. Translation of: Au nom de la classe ouvriere.

Colonel Sandor Kopacsi, police chief of Budapest until 1956, recounts the events leading up to and following the Hungarian Revolution of 1956. The Hungarians were seeking to reform communism, not abolish it. The Soviets felt the system would not survive the reforms and were compelled to put down the reform movement. The author believes that Khrushchev's reforms at home were misinterpreted in Eastern Europe as a sign of impending, broad-based reform. In fact the author feels they were intended to preserve the Gulag system Stalin had established. The account is factual, based on the author's observations of events at the time.

562. **Hungarian Worker's Councils in 1956,** edited by Bill Lomax, translated from the Hungarian by Bill Lomax and Julian Schopflin. New York: Columbia University Press, 1990. 666 p. *East European Monographs, no.294, Atlantic Studies on Society in Change, no. 61*, ISBN: 0880331917. Includes bibliographical references (p. 655-659).

The question of the role of the workers' councils in the 1956 Hungarian Revolution is the focus of this study. The compiler has assembled documents, journalists accounts, personal accounts, proposals and programs of the councils and documents relating to the trials of the worker's council leaders in the hope that an objective picture of the worker's council can be created. The compiler believes that the negative attitudes toward socialism have led to a general tendency to discount any positive contribution from a socialist group. He believes that the documents collected in this volume will present the reader with a balanced view. A chronology and bibliography are included.

563. Lukacs, John, **Budapest 1900: A Historical Portrait of a City and Its Culture.** New York: Weindenfeld and Nicolson, 1988. xiv, 255 p. ISBN: 1555840604. Includes bibliography (p.232-236) and index.

The pivotal year 1900 is used as the backdrop for the description of Budapest, the "other" capital of the Austro-Hungarian Empire. The author has limited his description from 1896 to 1906. He analyzes first the physical layout of the city and then goes on to examine the people, their politics, intellectual lives and spiritual inclinations. The author sees Budapest as a city of duality, manifesting "an urban sensitivity" on the one hand and a coarse provinciality on the other. The author was born in Hungary and has written a number of historical works. Review: *NewYork Times Book Review*, 22 (January 1989): 13-14.

564. **Revolutions and Interventions in Hungary and Its Neighbor States, 1918-1919**, Peter Pastor, editor. New York: Columbia University Press, 1988. x, 530 p. *Atlantic Studies on Society in Change, no. 39, East European Monographs, no. 240, War and Society in East Central Europe, vol. 20*, ISBN: 0880331372. Includes bibliographical references and index.

This collection of essays discusses the turbulent years after World War I. The essays are grouped into six parts that discuss Hungary's military, the effect of revolution on Hungarian society, Hungary's instability and its foreign relations during 1918-19, interventionary efforts, revolutions in neighboring states, and the historiography of the period. No one theme relates the essays to one another. A bibliographical index and list of maps is included.

565. Patai, Raphael, **Apprentice in Budapest: Memories of a World That Is No More**. Salt Lake City: University of Utah Press, 1988. xi, 526 p. ISBN: 0874802873. Includes index and bibliography (p. 505-508).

A biography of the early life and education of Raphael Patai. His work is drawn from personal memoirs. They create a picture of life for a Jewish family in Budapest before the war. Review: *Congress Monthly* 57, no.6 (September-October 1990): 20-21.

566. Perjes, Geza, **The Fall of the Medieval Kingdom of Hungary: Mohacs 1526-Buda 1541**, translated by Mario D. Fenyo with a Foreword by Janos M. Bak. New York: Distributed by Columbia University Press, 1989. xxii, 307 p. *East European Monographs, no. 255, War and Society in East Central Europe, v.26, Atlantic Studies on Society in Change, no. 56*, ISBN: 0880331526. Includes bibliography (p. 285-301).

This title in the series War and Society in East Central Europe is the translation of a work that was first published in Hungarian. "*The Decline of the Medieval Kingdom of Hungary,*" originally entitled *Mohacs*, is a meticulous reconstruction of events of some four-and-a-half centuries ago by a practical and theoretical expert of military science. It is also a cardinal piece in a historico-political debate that pushed history writing into the forefront of public interest in the Hungary of the 1970s, and because of these first two functions, it is a major statement about historical and not-so-historical choices and alternatives of an endangered country in the middle of central Europe." (p. xi) This is a military history and it focuses on the Hungarian-Turkish Wars and all the complexities of warfare in that time. The second part of the book examines the battle of Mohacs. In each section, strategy, objectives, battle plans, supplies and campaigns themselves are described in great detail. Numerous maps and a glossary are included.

567. Pinter, Istvan, **Hungarian Anti-Fascism and Resistance, 1941-1945**. Budapest: Akademiai Kiado, 1986. 234 p. ISBN: 9630540258. Translation of: Magyar antifasizmus es ellenallas. Includes index.

"This book is the first to provide the foreign reader with a concise scholarly history of united anti-fascist action and resistance in Hungary during World War II. Based on thorough research and a complete analysis of all available sources. It analyzes its topic against the background of a continuously shifting government policy culminating in the abortive attempt to break with Nazi Germany on 15 October, 1944.

The survey shows how there emerged a 'second' Hungary which, by shedding so much blood to free the country, secured itself a right to shape its fate at the time of a historic turning point of world-wide importance." (back cover) This topically arranged study is somewhat flawed by its lack of a bibliography. It was issued by the Hungarian Academy before the fall of the socialist government.

568. Reviczky, Adam, **Wars Lost, Battles Won,** translated by Jerry Payne. Boulder, Colo.: East European Monographs, 1992. 481 p. *East European Monographs; no. 349*, ISBN: 0880332468. Translated from: Vesztes haboruk-megnyert csatak. Budapest, Magveto, 1985. Includes bibliographical references (p. 457-481).

This is both a history of the persecution of Hungary's Jewish population by the Nazis and of one man, Imre Reviczky, who like others struggled against the Nazis. The author is the son of Imre Reviczky and draws on his own knowledge but also relied on newspapers, books and memoirs of the period.

569. **A History of Hungary, Peter F. Sugar, general editor**, Peter Hanak, associate editor, Tibor Frank, editorial assistant. New York: Tauris, 1990. xiv, 432 p. ISBN: 1850432864. Includes bibliographical references (p. 405-415) and index.

A general history of Hungary intended for the serious student, general reader, and non-specialist historian is provided in this book. While the chapters have different authors, all wrote within specific guidelines to lend consistency to the work. The major essays did not originally cover the events that pulled Hungary out of the Soviet sphere. An epilogue was added to discuss those changes and Hungary's future, making this a thorough study of Hungary's history from earliest times to the present. The essays are arranged chronologically and numerous maps are provided. A listing of additional readings arranged by chapter is also included.

570. Thuroczy, Janos, **Chronicle of the Hungarians,** translated by Frank Mantello, foreword and commentary by Pal Engel. Bloomington: Indiana University, Research Institute for Inner Asian Studies, 1991. iv, 225 p. *Medievalia Hungarica Series, v. 2; Indiana University Uralic and Altaic Series, v.155*, ISBN: 0933070276. Translation of: Chronica Hungarorum. Includes bibliographical references (p.19-20).

This chronicle, originally written in Latin, is considered a medieval chronicle, as yet untouched by the new type of humoristic historical writing that was to appear several decades after its composition. The translation here covers only the fourth part, which includes the years 1382-1474.

571. Vali, Ferenc A., **A Scholar's Odyssey,** edited by Karl W. Ryavec. Ames, Iowa: Iowa State University Press, 1990. xii, 324 p. ISBN: 08138115339. Includes bibliographical references and index.

Vali, who was born in Hungary, has left his memoirs about his experiences in World War II particularly in East Central Europe. They help explain the events there during the war and under early communist rule.

572. Vardy, Steven Bela, **The Hungarian-Americans**. Boston: Twayne Publishers, 1985. 215 p. *Immigrant Heritage of America Series*, ISBN: 080578425X. Includes bibliography (p. 183-195) and index.

This work traces the history of Americans of Hungarian origin, focusing on causes for their migration and cultural problems, encounters and contributions made to their new society. The study is arranged chronologically beginning with an overview on Hungary and its inhabitants and then turning to the earlier Hungarian travelers to North America in the sixteenth century. In the following chapters Professor Vardy looks at the mass migrations of the late nineteenth and early twentieth century and its causes and results. He then turns to the post World War I immigration noting the significant differences in the causes of the immigrations and the effects of those differences on the lives of the immigrants and the Hungarian-American community.

573. **Triumph in Adversity: Studies in Hungarian Civilization in Honor of Professor Ferenc Somogyi on the Occasion of his Eightieth Birthday,** edited by Steven Bela Verdy and Agnes Huszar Vardy. New York: Columbia University Press, 1988. xii, 616 p. *East European Monographs, no. CCLIII*, ISBN: 088033150X. Includes bibliographical references.

"This book is the result of the joint effort of twenty-five scholars from twelve disciplines and three continents. Although a large number of them are historians from the United States, the majority represents such diverse fields as cultural anthropology, economics, law, library science, linguistics, literature, military science, political science, social work and theology...." (p. xi) The scholars are not unified in their point of view but are all bound by their desire to pay tribute to Professor Ferenc Somogyi. The essays are grouped into seven sections. Section one discusses the work of Professor Somogyi and its impact on scholarship. It includes a bibliography of his publications. Sections II through IV cover historical topics from Hungary's development in the middle ages to World War II. Sections V through VII include essays on Hungary's national minorities, socio-economic development and Hungarian-American life.

574. Vardy, Steven Bela, and Agnes Huzak Vardy, **The Austro-Hungarian Mind: At Home and Abroad**. Boulder, Colo.: East European Monographs, 1989. viii, 374 p. *East European Monographs, no. 254*, ISBN: 0880331518. Includes bibliography (p.360-367).

This collection of essays was a joint undertaking. Both scholars have spent their careers studying Hungarian history, literature and culture and particular aspects of Austrian culture. This work is primarily devoted to the Hungarian experience in Hungary and abroad. The volume is divided into five parts the first dealing Austro-Germany in Hungarian Romanticism. The second section discusses the life of one individual, Baron Joseph Eotvos and his role in the liberal and nationalist movements in Austria. Part three examines the Hungarian minority question. Part four focuses on the Hungarian-American experience. The final section gives publication data on the original publication of the essays included here and provides information on the authors.

575. Zimanyi, Vera, **Economy and Society in Sixteenth and Seventeenth Century Hungary (1526-1650)**. Budapest: Akademia Kiado, 1987. 119 p. *Studia Historica Academiae Scientiarum Hungaricae, 188*, ISBN: 9630544040. Includes bibliography (p. 106-119).

This study focuses on the economic and social history of Hungary in the 16th and 17th centuries. Subtopics included are: the agrarian boom, foreign trade, urban decline, manufacturing and mining, as well as trends in social development.

GOVERNMENT, POLITICS AND LAW

576. Bird, Richard Miller, **Financing Local Government in Hungary**, Richard Bird and Christine Wallich. Washington, D.C.: Country Economics Dept., World Bank, 1992. 87 p. *Policy Research Working Papers; WPS 869*. Includes bibliographical references (p. 87).

This World Bank-sponsored study outlines "changes made in the system of local finance, assess[es] their implications, and identif[ies] areas that need further reform. [The authors] describe the so-called normative grant from the central to local governments, for example, as being largely discretionary, completely unconditional, and calculated according to a distribution formula geared to both 'equalization' and 'need'. [The authors] argue that local governments can budget with more certainty if the grant is fixed to some national tax source and distributed in accord with a known formula so they are not totally at the mercy of a discretionary central policy." (inside front cover)

577. **Post-Communist Transition: Emerging Pluralism in Hungary,** edited by Andras Bozoki, Andras Koroseny, and George Schopflin. London: Pinter Publishers, 1992. x, 196 p. ISBN: 1855670143. Includes bibliographical references and index.

"This volume focuses on the Hungarian experience, analysing in detail the process of transition from dictatorship to pluralist democracy. Some of Hungary's best political scientists examine issues such as the legitimation crisis of communist rule, resulting struggles within the ruling elite and the forces behind transition. Constitutional reform, party formation and voting behaviour at the first free elections are also taken into account. The concluding section places the Hungarian experience in comparative perspective, within the context of other Central European and Western European states." (back cover)

578. Felkay, Andrew, **Hungary and the USSR, 1956-1988: Kadar's Political Leadership**. New York: Greenwood Press, 1989. *Contributions in Political Science 0147-1066, no. 227*, ISBN: 0313259828. Includes bibliographical references and index.

Felkay analyzes Soviet-Hungarian relations over the period from 1956-1988. In addition it also is a study of Kadar's political leadership. Felkay believes that "Hungary's rapid recovery from the ruins of 1956 is the direct result of Kadar's ability to overcome the alienation of his compatriots without incurring the displeasure of the Soviet Union." (p. 2) Review: *Journal of Baltic Studies* 21, no.2 (Summer 1990): 162-164.

579. Hankiss, Elemer, **East European Alternatives**. New York: Oxford University Press, 1990. xiv, 319 p. ISBN: 0198277504. Includes bibliographical references (p. 297-303) and index.

The author analyzes "how the scope of action of various socio-economic actors has changed, widened, or been narrowed down in Hungary since 1948, when the communists came into power; of how various actors have tried to expand their own freedom and/or tried to deprive some other actors of theirs; of how they have lost their freedom and tried to regain or regenerate it; and of how, as a result of these endeavors and struggles, the country as a whole has lost, or increased, its freedom to act, to choose between meaningful alternatives, and to shape its own course." (p. 1)

580. Horvath, Agnes, **The Dissolution of Communist Power: The Case of Hungary**. English ed. London: Routledge, 1992. xviii, 254 p. ISBN: 041506709X. Includes bibliographical references (p. 238-249) and index.

The authors study the inner life of the communist party in Hungary. They conducted a sociological analysis in order to understand both the workings of the party and the effects the party had on the society as a whole. "We were interested in the routine daily activity: how the system was governed in daily life, how it was possible at all and what its lasting and hidden impacts were. We were motivated and increasingly reinforced by a feeling that the party was in no way simply a repressive institution, that the dangers it represented were more extensive than those of a simple dictatorship, and that the power of the party could locate neither in other repressive state organisations, nor in the top leadership. We had to realise that the very concept of the 'party-state' was misleading, and therefore we substituted for it the idea of the 'state-party.' (p. 15) Their study took place just at the time when communism was disintegrating in Hungary and the rest of Eastern Europe.

581. Kis, Janos, **Politics in Hungary: For a Democratic Alternative,** translated from the Hungarian original by Gabor J. Follinus with an introduction by Timothy Garton Ash. Boulder, Colo.: Columbia University Press, 1989. 275 p. *Atlantic Studies on Society in Change, no. 60,* ISBN: 0880339632. Includes bibliographical references.

Janos Kis is one of the foremost political essayists writing on Eastern Europe. In this volume a number of his essays, originally published in the underground press in Hungary are translated for the Western reader. "The essays collected in this volume treat what we can now see as a distinct, closed era in Hungarian history: the Kadar era. Although in day-to-day politics that era may be said to have closed already when Kadar was ousted from the post of Party leader in May 1988, the events of June-July 1989 furnished an essential, and fitting, historical epilogue." The author discusses many aspects of the Hungarian political landscape from efforts at reform to Hungarian minorities abroad. There is no discussion of Hungary's political situation after Kadar's downfall.

582. Molnar, Miklos, **From Bela Kun to Janos Kadar: Seventy Years of Hungarian Communism,** translated by Arnold J. Pomerans. New York: St. Martin's Press, 1990. xxiv, 281 p. ISBN: 0854965998. Translation of: De Bela Kun a Janos Kadar. Includes bibliographical references (p. 260-275) and index.

This is a history of the Hungarian Communist party from its beginnings to the 1980s. The author sees the Party as having a dual nature, pragmatic and utopian, revolutionary but threatened by revolution and as likely to produce reforms as tortures. The author feels the Hungarian Communist Party has been most heavily influenced by Bela Kun, Rakoci, Imre Nagy, Janos Kadar and, of course, the Kremlin. He will focus on these individuals and institutions in his study of the Party's development. His analysis is structured chronologically and includes some views on what the future may hold.

583. Spira, Thomas, **The German-Hungarian-Swabian Triangle, 1936-1939: The Road to Discord**. New York: Columbia University Press, 1990. vii, 275 p. *East European Monographs, no. 285,* ISBN: 0880331828. Includes bibliographical references (p. 253-269) and index.

A continuation of the author's earlier study of German-Hungarian relations which covered the years 1919-1936, this volume brings the analysis to the beginning of the war. The tension between German and Hungary's German minority, the Swabians and between Germans and Magyar's of Hungary had reached a crisis by 1939. "This book analyzes the triangle comprising German-Hungarian economic relations, German-Hungarian diplomatic affairs, and the Hungarian government's Swabian educational and linguistic policies and practices. This book documents the interaction of Hungary's minority practices with the country's economic and foreign policies." (p. iii) These topics are discussed for 1936-37, 1938, and 1939 separately.

584. Swain, Nigel, **Hungary: The Rise and Fall of Feasible Socialism**. New York: Verso, 1992. vii, 264 p. ISBN: 0860915697. Includes bibliographical references and index.

Nigel Swain believes that market socialism was fairly successful but was flawed. He feels that the economic system did not have the freedom to produce goods that would be marketable in the West. In the first chapter he describes the decline of Hungary's old regime. In chapters two and three he examines policies established in the 40's and 50's, to determine to what extent socialism had become part of the Hungarian system. Chapters four and five discuss failings in the socialist economic system. Chapters six and seven consider specific problems in Hungary's system, production relations and socialist inequality. Swain defends the notion of "soft budget constraints" as presented in the works of Janos Kornai but interprets the concept more broadly. "Rather than consider abstractions, this book has followed through four and a half decades of a socialist economy in action, and has documented how and why it did not work as intended, how it was subjected to constant revision, and why so many of those who experienced it were willing to reject altogether the idea of an economic system based on socialist ownership." (p. 230)

585. Toma, Peter A., **Socialist Authority: The Hungarian Experience**. New York: Praeger, 1988. xxvii, 288 p. ISBN: 0275926028. Bibliography (p. 267-273).

Toma examines the role of authority in Hungarian society. He is not only interested in the authority assumed by the self-elected communist government, but also that acknowledged by the populace. It is not his purpose "to try to settle the dispute between the advocates of participatory socialist democracy and pluralism on the one hand and the advocates of central authority as the only qualified members of society able to express the interests of the entire nation, on the other. Instead, it is to consider the actual changes that have taken place in the economic, social, and political structures of Hungarian society, and then to analyse the implications of these changes for individual autonomy and citizenship." (p. xiii) Reviews: *Slavic Review* 48, no.3 (Fall 1989): 525. *American Political Science Review* 83, no.3 (September 1989): 1068-69.

FOREIGN RELATIONS

586. Gati, Charles, **Hungary and the Soviet Bloc**. Durham N.C.: Duke University Press, 1986. 244 p. ISBN: 0822307472 (pbk); 0822306840. Includes bibliography (p. 233-237) and index.

Professor Gati uses Hungary's relations with Moscow since World War II to illustrate the more general problems the Soviets face in Eastern Europe. The author covers a variety of topics: bloc politics, East-West relations, and Soviet foreign policy among them. The work is not intended as a comprehensive discussion and does not even attempt a strictly chronological framework. "The connecting tissue is my attempt to come to grips with the reasons why, even in the best of times, the mighty Soviet Union experienced difficulties in taming its small communist neighbors." (p. 3) The author believes this is due to the anti-Soviet environment in Eastern Europe that motivates the rulers of the individual Eastern bloc nations to pursue their nation's interests. The first part of the book deals with the coalitionary period following World War II and provides a reinterpretation of the events of that time. The remaining two parts examine the extent to which Soviet policy in Eastern Europe, particularly Hungary, was conditioned by domestic events.

587. Vago, Raphael, **The Grandchildren of Trianon: Hungary and Hungarian Minority in the Communist States**. New York: Columbia University Press, 1989. 297 p. *East European Monographs, no. 258*, ISBN: 0880331550. Includes bibliographical references.

Vago's study analyzes the effect of Hungarian minorities on interstate relations in Eastern Europe. The primary focus is on the Hungarian minorities in Czechoslovakia, Romania and Yugoslavia since 1968. The author also provides some background information regarding immediate post World War II and the Treaty of Trianon.

ECONOMICS, BUSINESS AND TRADE

588. **Economy and Society in Hungary,** edited by Rudolf Andorka and Laszlo Bertalan, translations by Jozsef Borocz. Budapest: Karl Marx University of Economic Sciences, Dept. of Sociology, 1986. 331 p. *Hungarian Sociological Studies, 3 0236-6479.* Includes bibliographies.

The relation of the economy and society was a major focus of sociological research in Hungary. These papers by younger Hungarian scholars cover a variety of sociological research that concentrates on this general overall theme.

589. Becskehazi, Attila, **Business Information Hungary,** by Attila Becskehazi and Jason McDonald. Berkeley: Central European Research Associates, 1992. 211 p. ISBN: 188248200X. Includes bibliographical references and index.

The commercial opportunities in Eastern Europe have created the need for information for the business community. This guide sets out to meet that need for information on Hungary by providing data on opportunities in the country, its economic background, and business regulations. It also includes a directory of contacts in the Hungarian and foreign governments, private organizations, services, sources of financial and other information. Appendixes contain a calendar of expected events, a short Hungarian-English dictionary and a bibliography of recommended readings with a list of laws and decrees important to foreign businessmen.

590. Berend, Ivan T., **The Hungarian Economic Reforms, 1953-1988**. New York: Cambridge University Press, 1990. 347 p. *Soviet and East European Studies, 70*, ISBN: 0521380375.

After the disastrous five year plan, Hungarian leaders realized change was necessary and undertook economic reforms. This book describes the reform process, which the author sees as occurring in three phases. The twenty-nine chapters of his book are therefore arranged in three parts, each part focusing on one of three phases. Phase one is the intellectual antecedents and the first corrective steps, 1953-1964; phase two is the 1966 decision on comprehensive reform, and phase three is 1979 onwards.

591. **The Hungarian Economy in the 1980s: Reforming the System and Adjusting to External Shocks,** edited by Josef C. Brada and Istvan Dobozi. Greenwich, Conn.: JAI press, 1988. xv, 277 p. *Industrial Development and the Social Fabric, v.9*, ISBN: 089232936X. Includes bibliographies and indexes.

A collection of essays originally presented at the Ninth Hungarian-American Economists' Roundtable in 1985 is published in this volume. They are grouped into three sections: "Macroeconomic Policy and economic reform," "Economic Reform and Enterprise Behaviour," and "Hungary and the World Economy." The essays in the first section examine the development of economic policy in Hungary while those in the second section are case studies. The final section places Hungary's economic reform in a global context "These papers then serve as a synthesis of Hungarian and Western views of economic and reform developments in Hungary." (p. xv)

592. **Money, Incentives, and Efficiency in the Hungarian Economic Reform,** edited by Josef C. Brada and Istvan Dobozi. Armonk, NY: M.E. Sharpe, 1990. xii, 187 p. ISBN: 0873325664. Includes bibliographical references.

In 1968 Hungary began an economic reform known as the New Economic Mechanism (NEM). Essentially it was "the abandonment of central planning in favor of an organic combination of the self-regulating market mechanisms and central control exercised through indirect, market-compatible fiscal and monetary instruments." (p. 3) The essays contained in this volume assess the achievements and failures of NEM.

593. Brown, Douglas M., **Towards a Radical Democracy: The Political Economy of the Budapest School**. Boston: Allen & Unwin, 1988. xi, 226 p. *Studies in International Political Economy*, ISBN: 0043304087. Includes bibliography (p. 211-216) and index.

The Budapest School is a group of Hungarian dissidents and scholars that were followers of Marxian philosopher George Lukacs. In examining their writings Brown's purpose "is to demonstrate that in the thought of the Budapest School there exists a novel and unique defence of the mixed economy providing the basis for a realizable society that transcends the undemocratic character of both capitalism and existing socialism." (p. 2) Review: *Orbis* 33, no.3 (Summer 1989): 458-59.

594. Burawoy, Michael, **The Radiant Past: Ideology and Reality in Hungary's Road to Capitalism**, Michael Burawoy and Janos Lukacs. Chicago: University of Chicago Press, 1992. xvi, 215 p. ISBN: 0226080412. Includes bibliographical references and index.

After an introductory chapter that is a "sociological diary of research written in a time of transition," (p. ix) the author looks at the Hungarian machine factory *(Banki)* and compares the efficiencies found there with an American factory in South Chicago. The focus here is on the forces that cause factories operating in both countries to be efficient and inefficient. He then turns to examine the Lenin Steel Works and shows how "ideology becomes embodied in rituals of socialist affirmation. These rituals draw attention to the discrepancy between ideology and reality, leading workers to criticize state socialism failing to live up to its promise." (p. x-xi). His final chapter brings together what has been learned and what light it casts on the transition from state socialism to capitalism.

595. Deak, George, **The Economy and Polity in Early Twentieth Century Hungary: The Role of the National Association of Industrialists**. New York: Columbia University Press, 1990. ix, 209 p. *East European Monographs, no. 288*, ISBN: 0880331852. Includes bibliographical references (p. 170-201) and index.

"This study is primarily concerned with the attempts of the National Association of Hungarian Industrialists to sustain and extend in this period the politics and climate of opinion that had earlier served the development of industry." (p. viii) The first part of the book covers the origins, structure and aims of the Association. The second part examines the Association's political orientation.

596. Hare, P. G., **The Diffusion of New Process Technologies in Hungary: Eastern European Innovation in Perspective**, Paul Hare and Ray Oakley. London: Pinter Publishers, 1993. xii, 185 p. ISBN: 086187062X. Includes bibliographical references (p. 177-181) and index.

Technological changes in Hungary are the subject of this study. The authors believe that Hungary's experience is similar to that of other East European countries and it can be seen as a case study. The authors demonstrate that advances in other areas of the Hungarian economy have not affected technological developments as it was assumed they would. For purposes of this study Hare and Oakley focused on mechanical engineering, more specifically on the use of ENC machine tools. These tools are necessary for the production of high precision engineering products. The authors used a questionnaire, and carried out 161 interviews in developing their picture of Hungarian technology. The nine chapters provide the reader with a context for the discussion, outline economic reforms in Hungary, discuss technological changes, describe the methodology of the study, and the extent to which ENC machinery has penetrated the Hungarian market, look at the methods of introducing these products, employment issues, purchasing practices and make suggestions for the future development of this industry. The final chapter also discusses broader issues of technological advances in Eastern Europe in general.

597. Hegedus, Jozsef, Raymond J. Struyk, and Ivan Tosics, **Integrating State Rental Housing with the Private Market: Designing Housing Allowances for Hungary**. Washington D.C.: University Press of America, 1991. xiii, 177 p. *Urban Institute*

Report, 0897-7399, 91-7, ISBN: 0877665125; 0877665133. Includes bibliographical references (p. 175-177).

In this study, the Urban Institute in Washington, D.C., presents one possible option for reforming rental housing in Hungary along market lines while protecting lower income families from the high rent payments associated with other methods of reform. "The research is based on a dataset developed especially for this study by the Hungarian government.... The overall conclusion is that housing allowances are a major element in the solution to the problem of reforming the state rental sector so that it operates more efficiently and so that subsides are reduced and provided only to lower income households." (p. xv) The book's five sections describe Hungary's housing policy up to 1990, the state rental sector, how a housing allowance system would affect other sectors of the economy, a simulation of results following their suggested model after one year and general conclusions.

598. Hieronymi, Otto, **Economic Policies for the New Hungary: Proposals for a Coherent Approach**, with the participation of an International Group of Experts. Columbus: Battelle Press, 1990. xiii, 121 p. ISBN: 0935470603. Includes bibliography and index.

This study was prepared with the advice of an international group of experts. "Its main objective is to present a series of policy recommendations in view of creating the basis for sustained growth and the integration of Hungary into the European and world economies in the 1990s." (p. vii) It consists of three chapters: Challenges, Risks and Opportunities; an agenda for action and the last, the transformation of the Hungarian economy.

599. Kornai, Janos, **The Road to a Free Economy: Shifting from a Socialist System: The Example of Hungary**. New York: Norton, 1990. 224 p. ISBN: 0393306917 (pbk); 0393028879. Revised translation of: Indulatos ropirat a gazdasigi atmenet. Includes bibliographical references and index.

This book, originally intended for a Hungarian readership, "is written to convince the reader that the shift in property relations towards privatization, the package of measures needed for stabilization, liberalization, and macro adjustment, and the strengthening of political support for these changes, are inseparably intertwined." (p. 18) Reviews: *Foreign Affairs* 69, no.4 (Fall 1990): 193. *World & I* (November 1990): 413. *Bulletin of the Atomic Scientists* 46, no.9 (November 1990): 42-43.

600. ———, **Vision and Reality, Market and State: Contradictions and Dilemmas Revisited**. New York: Routledge, 1990. xi, 260 p. ISBN: 0415902851. Includes bibliographical references and index.

This book continues an earlier publication by Janos Kornai, *Contradictions and Dilemmas*. As with those earlier essays, these papers discuss the problems of reform in a socialist country with a blend of state centralized and market economy. The eight essays were written between 1983 and 1988. Most essays deal with Hungary. Those that do not, deal with issues relevant to the study of other socialist countries. The author sees Hungary as the laboratory "in which experiments on the transformation of a Stalinist regime into something else are conducted." (p. x) Topics discussed include bureaucratic and market coordination, soft budget constraints, prices and inflation, and individual freedom and reform.

601. Revesz, Gabor, **Perestroika in Eastern Europe: Hungary's Economic Transformation, 1945-1988,** with a foreword by Paul Marer. Boulder, Colorado: Westview Press, 1990. xv, 182 p. *Westview Special Studies on the Soviet Union and Eastern Europe, 0163-6017*, ISBN: 0813377528. Includes bibliographical references (p. 165-171).

"In this analytical history of the reforms in Hungary, Gabor Revesz traces government effort to transform a planned economy into a system of market socialism.... Beginning with the country's postwar economic consolidation, the author assesses the introduction of strict central planning, forced mobilization and industrialization, the economic causes and consequences of the 1956 Hungarian Revolution; and the reconsolidation of economic and political power." (back cover) The author feels that Hungary's economic experience will serve as a model for the rest of Eastern Europe. The author uses a chronological structure in his study. The book includes a list of "additional readings"—Western language sources on Hungary. Review: *Canadian Slavonic Papers* 32, no.4 (December 1990): 518-519.

602. Richet, Xavier, **The Hungarian Model: Markets and Planning in a Socialist Economy,** translated by J. C. Whitehouse. New York: Cambridge University Press, 1989. xi, 209 p. *Soviet and East European Studies*, ISBN: 0521343143. Translation of: Le modele hongrois. Includes bibliographical references.

Richet examines the economic reforms introduced into Hungary since 1968. Primarily he is interested in "decentralization procedures and the effects of decentralization on the Hungarian economy and the behaviour of the agents." (p. vii) Besides individual chapters on centralization and decentralization in general, he also examines the price system, macroeconomic planning, and investment choices. Review: *American Political Science Review* 84, no.4 (December 1990): 1426-1428.

603. Siklos, Pierre L., **War Finance, Reconstruction, Hyperinflation, and Stabilization in Hungary**. New York: St. Martin's Press, 1991. xx, 281 p. ISBN: 0312057083. Includes bibliographical references (p. 260-275) and index.

Siklos studies hyperinflation in Hungary at the end of War World II and the successful attempt to control it in the period 1946-1948. The book is essentially a history of finance in Hungary from 1938 to 1948. After a general introduction to the problem and the state of the Hungarian economy just prior to the war, the author analyzes the Gyori program and its macroeconomic consequences. In his analysis the author blends both economic and social and political factors to explain the causes of hyperinflation and its termination. Two appendices provide additional statistical data.

604. **Financial Programming and Policy: The Case of Hungary,** edited by Karen Swiderski. Washington, D.C.: IMF Institute, International Monetary Fund, 1992. v, 205 p. ISBN: 1557753040. Includes bibliographical references.

The International Monetary Fund Institute has issued this study as part of its financial programming course. It covers the period through 1990. "The various chapters of the study are designed to provide the basic materials needed to develop consistent projections of macroeconomic development in Hungary for 1990 and their implications for the medium-term." (p. v) The study includes sections on macroeconomic developments in Hungary, financial programming, prices and output, balance of payments, fiscal sector, and the monetary sector. The data used has been drawn from official sources. A large amount of statistical data is included. Unfortunately, no index is included making identification of specific information somewhat difficult.

605. **Hungary: An Economy in Transition,** edited by Istvan P. Szekely and David M.G. Newbery. New York: Cambridge University Press, 1993. xxvii, 360 p. ISBN: 0521440181. Includes bibliographical references and index.

These papers, containing the proceedings of a conference held in London in February of 1992, cover several topics concerned with economic transition in Hungary. The essays are divided into seven parts. Each part is followed by a discussion paper. The topics covered are foreign trade, privatization and competition policy, the financial system and private savings, foreign debt and monetary policy, legislative and tax reform, labor markets, unemployment and social security and state desertion and convertibility.

606. **Market Reforms in Socialist Societies: Comparing China and Hungary,** edited by Peter Van Ness with contributions by George Barany (et al). Boulder, Colo.: L. Rienner, 1989. ix, 323 p. ISBN: 1555870961. Includes bibliographies and index.

"This book is a comparative study of the process of dismantling the Soviet Type command economy in China and Hungary, and the problems of implementing a market mechanism in its place." (p. l) The volume's fourteen chapters are divided into three parts, plus an introduction and a conclusion. Part one is devoted to Hungary, part two to China, and part three to socialist reforms and the world market economy.

LANGUAGE AND LITERATURE

607. Abondolo, Daniel Mario, **Hungarian Inflectional Morphology**. Budapest: Akademiai Kiado, 1988. 291 p. *Bibliotheca Uralica,9*, ISBN: 9630546302. Includes bibliography (p. 272-275) and index.

Abondolo provides a "complete account of Hungarian nominal and verb inflection." (p. 15) It is based on *A magyar nyelv ertelmezo szotara* and other sources.

608. Bisztray, George, **Hungarian-Canadian Literature**. Toronto: University of Toronto Press, 1987. viii, 116 p. ISBN: 0802057152. Includes bibliography (p. 95-113) and index.

Bisztray provides a survey of Hungarian literature produced in Canada. After a brief introduction, he gives statistics, resources and definitions of the literature of Hungarian Canadians. He then continues in subsequent chapters to analyze the stages of this literature and the sociopsychological profile of the Hungarian-Canadian writer. In the final chapter he speculates on future developments. This volume also contains a bibliography of Hungarian-Canadian authors since World War II.

609. Groot, Casper de, **Predicate Structure in a Functional Grammar of Hungarian**. Providence, RI: Foris Publications, 1989. x, 234 p. *Functional Grammar Series, 11*, ISBN: 9067654353.

The author applies the linguistic theory of functional grammar to Hungarian with an emphasis on the predicate.

610. **A Mirror to the Cage: Three Contemporary Hungarian Plays,** edited and translated by Clara Gyorgyey; introduction by Ervin C. Brody. Fayetteville: University of Arkansas Press, 1993. ix, 245 p. ISBN: 1557282676. Translated from the Hungarian.

Plays by three of Hungary's finest writers have been translated for this volume. "The selection in this volume has been designated to present variegated approaches, metaphors, voices, and dramatic techniques, including tenses of realistic and allegorical theater (*The Imposter*), the special East European absurd and grotesque (*Stevie in the Bloodbath*), and the most modern, experimental, mythical dream rituals (*Kozma*). Each play is prefaced by a brief historical background, an overview of the play, and an introduction of the playwright." (p. ix) The introduction to the volume provides the reader with the historical literary context for the plays.

611. **Present Continuous: Contemporary Hungarian Writing,** edited by Bart Istvan, translation from the Hungarian by Richard L. Aczel (et al.), translation revised by Bertha Gaster. Budapest: Corvina, 1985. 400 p. ISBN: 9631321460.

The present anthology is unusual in that its primary aim is to present, through a sample of recent Hungarian prose writing, the contemporary Hungarian scene from a historical angle. A piece each by 25 Hungarian writers, including short studies, literary reportage and "sociographical" writings, gives the reader insight into the life of the country and its people, and by evoking historical turning points, mirrors what has taken place in reality and, as a consequence, in the human soul of Hungary during the last fifty years. Among the criteria of the selection, then, the informative content of the writing figures as prominently as artistic value." (backcover). The volume is not intended as a representative anthology of Hungarian literature. However, the compiler does hope to show the importance of writers as "chroniclers of their age." No bibliography is included.

612. **Face of Creation: Contemporary Hungarian Poetry,** translated by Jascha Kessler. Minneapolis: Coffee House Press, 1988. ISBN: 091827320X.

"Jascha Kessler has given America a tremendous gift: the musical poetry of Magyar, the language of Hungary. The twenty-three men and women whose works and photographs glow in these pages reflect an ancient, sophisticated culture, and they use the marvelous instrument of their language with breathtaking diversity." (back cover) Biographical information is provided on each of the twenty-three modern authors whose works are included in this anthology.

613. Kiss, Katalin E., **Configurationality in Hungarian**. Bingham, MA: Kluwer Academic Publishers, 1987. 268 p. *Studies in Natural Language and Linguistic Theory*, ISBN: 9027724563 (pbk); 9027719071. Includes bibliography (p. 253-259) and indexes.

"In analyzing Hungarian sentence structure in the Government and Binding version of generative theory, the author claims that the Hungarian sentence contains a flat, non-configurational propositional component, preceded by configurationally determined left peripheral operators. It is demonstrated that while in the Indo-European languages phrase structure configurations express grammatical relations such as subject, object, in Hungarian phrase structure configurations encode the logical structure of the sentence. In arguing for this claim, various descriptive issues of Hungarian syntax are analyzed, among them the word order of the Hungarian sentence, long wh-movement or the traditional problem of 'sentence-intertwining', questions of anaphoric and pronominal coreference, and the major infinitival constructions of the language." (back cover)

614. Orszagh, Laszlo, **A Concise English-Hungarian Dictionary**, editor in chief L. Orszagh. New York: Oxford University Press, 1990. 1052 p. ISBN: 0198641702.

This dictionary, aimed at the Hungarian speaker, includes an introduction in Hungarian followed by the dictionary. Abbreviations within the entries are given in English and in Hungarian, as appropriate.

615. Payne, Jerry, **Colloquial Hungarian**. New York: Routledge & K. Paul, 1987. 360 p. *Colloquial Series*, ISBN: 0710209843; 0710206364.

This book, with accompanying cassette, is intended for the self-learner. It consists of sixteen lessons, a Hungarian-English and English-Hungarian glossary, and a key to the exercises. Each unit contains three parts: test with word list and notes, grammar, and functions (everyday uses of the language).

INDIVIDUAL AUTHORS

616. Zsuffa, Joseph, **Bela Balazs: The Man and the Artist**. Berkeley: University of California Press, 1987. xiii, 550 p. ISBN: 0520055454. Includes index, bibliography (p.515-527) and filmography (p.529-533).

This is the first "authentic" biography of the Hungarian author. "It aims to be a mirror of the artist's life and achievements, an amusing, poetic, passionate reflection. Yet strictly speaking, *Bela Balazs: The Man and Artist* is not a critical biography but a factual, historical one, in which the chronological events dictate the flow of the narrative." (p. x) Several appendices on the author are included, an essay on Balazs' film theory, his early film criticism and the controversy on the "Three Penny Opera," Reviews: *Slavic Review* 49, no.4 (Winter 1990): 688-690. *Slavic and East European Journal* 33, no.2 (Summer 1989): 314-16.

617. Fust, Milan, **The Story of My Wife: The Reminiscences of Captain Storr: A Novel,** preface by George Konrad, translated from the Hungarian by Ivan Sanders. New York: PAJ Publications, 1987. xiii, 336 p. ISBN: 155554018X.

This novel by reclusive Hungarian author Milan Fust is "A novel of jealousy." The story centers around the relationship between a Dutch sea captain and his wife. The sea captain, Sturr, is obsessed with his fears that his wife is having an affair. "Captain Jacob Sturr is a man without illusions, but his one passion: his undying wish to know what makes his wife tick makes him so alert, so eager, so tormented, we cannot help liking him." (p. xiii) The action takes place in London and Paris but the center of the action is in the relationship between husband and wife.

618. Goncz, Arpad, **Voices of Dissent: Two Plays,** translated by Katharina M. Wilson and Christopher C. Wilson. Lewisburg: Bucknell University Press, 1989. 114 p. ISBN: 0838751423. Translations of: Magyar Medeia and Racsok.

Two plays by one of Hungary's foremost playwrights are contained in this volume. Both were originally published in Hungary in 1979. The Hungarian Medea is based on the ancient theme of the Euripides play. Goncz maintains much of the original, emphasizing his vision of the simultaneity of past and present. "Unlike Euripides, who emphasizes Medea's cultic, racial, and geo-political otherness, Goncz stresses her suffering from a sociopolitical otherness; she is the child of a society and a culture of the past, which she rejects in order to embrace Jason's post-World War II socialist order." The second play included here, *Iron Bars,* is the author's only black comedy. The setting and time are deliberately left unclear. "It is the story of the poetaster Emmanuel who has become politically expendable in the society for which he authored a national anthem. It raises many politically difficult questions particularly for a Communist country. Both plays demonstrate the author's basic view of man. Probing, tense, fascinated with human psychology and social, emotional interaction, he has created characters that are not only essentially Hungarian and of the twentieth century but also universal; their very specificity and invariably political/ ideological casting becomes the successful vehicle for the plays' universal themes." (p. 9) Reviews: *Slavic and East European Journal* 34, no.2 (Summer 1990): 273-274. *World Literature Today* 64, no.2 (Spring 1990): 337.

619. Konrad, George, **A Feast in the Garden,** translated from the Hungarian by Imre Goldstein. 1st ed. New York: Harcourt Brace Jovanovich, 1992. 394 p. ISBN: 015130548X. Translation of: Kerti mulatsag.

George Konrad's writings were officially ignored for many years in Hungary though he was well known in the West. This story focuses on Jewish life in Budapest. Much of the work is autobiographical although it is largely told in the voice of David Kobra, Konrad's alter-ego.

THE SOCIETY, SOCIOLOGY

620. **On the Development of Socialism in Hungary, Ideological Conference, 19-21 February 1987, Szeged, Hungary.** Budapest: Corvina, 1987. 189 p. ISBN: 9631326675 (pbk). Translation of: A szocializmus fejlodesenek idoszeru kerdesei

hazankban. Orszagos elmeleti konferencia. Szeged, 1987. February 19-21, Kossuth Konyvkiado 1987.
This volume contains papers presented at a conference organized by the Hungarian Socialist Workers Party in 1987. It was intended to enrich the existing "knowledge about socialism, its reality and development in Hungary through summing up sound practice as well as the experiences of research and ideological work." (p. 7) The papers covered socialism and its relationship to the economy, politics, and social conditions.

621. **Liberty and Socialism: Writings of Libertarian Socialists in Hungary, 1884-1919,** edited and translated by Janos M. Bak, in collaboration with Andras Bozoki and Miklos Sukosd with an afterword by Wayne Thorpe. Savage, Md.: Rowman & Littlefield Publishers, 1991. xxxv, 276 p. *States and Societies in East Central Europe. Contributions to Modern Political Thought, vol. 2*, ISBN: 0847676803. Includes index.

"The texts included in this volume are intended to present different trends in socialist thought in late-nineteenth and early twentieth-century Hungary: various prophets of anarchism, a theorist of revolutionary syndicalism, a learned critic of orthodox Marxism, and an enlightened, liberal socialist opponent of bolshevism." (p. ix) Two prominent figures covered are Ervin Szabo and Oscar Jaszi.

622. Bibo, Istvan, **Democracy, Revolution, Self-Determination: Selected Writings,** edited by Karoly Nagy, translation by Andras Boros-Kazai. New York: Columbia University Press, 1991. 578 p. *East European Monographs, no.317; Atlantic Studies on Society in Change, no.69*, ISBN: 088033214X. Includes bibliographical references (p.xii-xiii) and index.

Bibo, a Hungarian professor of political science, "was one of the most profound social-political thinkers of Central Europe's recent history." (p. xi) This posthumous collection of writings was originally published in a variety of sources and focus on politics, social conditions, and political philosophy.

623. Congdon, Lee, **Exile and Social Thought: Hungarian Intellectuals in Germany and Austria, 1919-1933**. Princeton, NJ: Princeton University Press, 1991. xvi, 376 p. ISBN: 0691031592. Includes bibliographical references (p. 339-365) and index.

Several major social theorists emigrated from Hungary to Germany and Austria. This study examines six of them in detail. These theorists, who are spread across the political spectrum, were: Georg Lukacs, Bela Balazs, Lajos Kassak, Laszlo Moholy-Nagy, Aurel Kolnai, and Karl Mannheim. Congdon has "directed attention to the interrelationship between the ideas these Hungarians entertained, the world in which they lived, and the conditions of their personal existence." (p. xi)

624. Dennis, Mike, **German Democratic Republic: Politics, Economics, and Society**. London: Pinter Publishers, 1988. xxi, 223 p. *Marxist Regime Series*, ISBN: 0861874137 (pbk); 0861874129. Includes bibliography (p. 201-217) and index.

This book, one of a series on communist regimes around the world, "has the modest aim of providing a survey of the history of the GDR followed by a picture of the contemporary social, economic and political system." (p. xiii-xiv) In addition to individual chapters on history, society, politics and economics, it includes several pages of basic data useful for quick reference purposes. Reviews: *German Study Reviews* 12, no.3 (October 1989): 550-551. *Canadian Journal of Political Science* 22, no.3 (September 1989): 667-68.

625. Enyedi, Gyorgy, **Budapest: A Central European Capital,** Gyorgy Enyedi and Viktoria Szirmai; English translation by Vera Gathy; English translation revised by

Charles Hebbert. London: Belhaven Press, 1992. xi, 183 p. *World Cities Series*, ISBN: 0470219483. Includes bibliographical references (p. 171-177) and index.
Influenced by systems theory, the authors consider Budapest as a macro-system consisting of three systems: the natural environment, the built environment, and the society. The twelve chapters of the volume are arranged in four parts. Part one focuses on the urban environment, physical geography, and urban landscapes. Part two concerns itself with the city dwellers, the people of Budapest, the urban society, and human ecology and the problems of housing. Part three has a more complex perspective and looks at functional spaces, urban functions and the "Budapest agglomeration." The final part gives a history of urban planning and the administration of the city.

626. **Violations of the Helsinki Accords, Hungary: A Report Prepared for the Helsinki Review Conference, Vienna, November 1986,** by Janet Fleischman. New York: U.S. Helsinki Watch Committee, 1986. iv, 40 p. *A Helsinki Watch Report*, ISBN: 0938579819. Includes bibliography (p. 40).

This report chronicles human rights violations in Hungary. It is arranged topically, covering violations in the area of new legislation, Cultural Forum, the samizdat press, freedom to publish, freedom of assembly and association, freedom of movement, the elections, freedom of religion, the peace movement, the ecological movement, and the Gypsy minority.

627. Gabel, Joseph, **Mannheim and Hungarian Marxism,** translated by William M. Stein and James McCrate. New Brunswick, N.J.: Transaction Publishers, 1991. xii, 122 p. ISBN: 0887383777. Translation of: Mannheim et le marxisme hongrois. Includes bibliographical references (p. 119-122).

The author traces the influence that Karl Mannheim had on Hungarian Marxism. The ten chapters are divided into two sections: part one explores the socio-historical context of Hungarian Marxism, looks at three representative figures: Szabo, Szende, and Fogarasi, and describes Hungarian Marxism after 1920. In part two the author focuses on the intellectual development of Karl Mannheim, including a critique of his sociology of knowledge.

628. Haraszti, Eva, **Kossuth as an English Journalist,** translated by Brian McLean, translation revised by Christine Molinari. New York: Columbia University Press, 1990. 404 p. *East European Monographs, 295, Atlantic Studies on Society in Change, no. 63*, ISBN: 0880331925. Includes bibliographical references and index.

This volume in the series *East European Monographs* deals with the international journalistic career of the Hungarian political leader Louis Kossuth. His reporting often sparked a great deal of controversy. This volume discusses his career as an journalist in England and England's role during the Crimean War. The majority of the volume is taken up with documents, primarily Kossuth's published writings in England during the period. As with other volumes in this series, this work focuses on East Central European society.

629. **Hungary and European Civilization**, Gyorgyi Ranki editor. Budapest: Akademia Kiado, 1989. *Indiana University Studies on Hungary, vol. 3*, ISBN: 9630555026.

This series of essays explores various aspects of Hungary's role in European civilization. Individual topics touch on economics, religion, philosophy, social structure, Jewish influence, education, assimilation, literature, and music.

630. Szelenyi, Ivan, and Robert Manchin, **Socialist Entrepreneurs: Embourgeoisement in Rural Hungary,** in collaboration with Robert Manchin (et al.) Madison: University of Wisconsin Press, 1988. 255 p. ISBN: 029911347 (pbk); 0299113604. Includes bibliographical references (p. 235-247) and index.

"The purpose of this book is to explore the transformation of rural social structure during the epoch of industrialization and collectivization of agriculture in a state socialist society, Hungary. [The authors] are particularly interested in understanding the logic of and limits to 'socialist proletarianization': how, under the dual pressure of industrialization and collectivization, former peasants and small agricultural entrepreneurs were pushed toward a wage-laborer existence." (p. 3)

631. Vasary, Ildiko, **Beyond the Plan: Social Change in a Hungarian Village**. Boulder: Westview Press, 1987. xvii, 308 p. *Westview Special Studies on the Soviet Union & Eastern Europe, 0163-6057*, ISBN: 081337412X. Includes index and bibliography (p.297-303).

Based on extensive fieldwork, this study examines social change in the village of Pecsely from 1945 to the late 1970s. The work is divided into four parts. Part one describes the village and the land reform of 1945. Part two examines agricultural collectivization; part three turns to plot farming and the second economy. Part four analyzes community institutions, social stratification and family and system of value.

NATIONAL MINORITIES

632. Cohen, Asher, **The Halutz Resistance in Hungary, 1942-1944.** New York: Columbia University Press, 1986. vii, 277 p. *East European Monographs, no. 206, Holocaust Studies Series*, ISBN: 0880331038. Includes bibliography (p. 249-277) and index.

The Halutz resistance movement developed out of Zionist Halutz youth movements related to various Kibbutz organizations in Palestine. Cohen chronicles the movement in Hungary, particularly in Budapest between 1942 and 1944. The book is based on memoirs and other primary and secondary source material.

633. Fenyvesi, Charles, **When the World Was Whole: Three Centuries of Memories**. New York: Viking, 1990. xvii, 266 p. ISBN: 0670831808.

The history of one Hungarian Jewish family, as it was passed down through generations, is contained in this book. While legend has no doubt played some role in the compilation of this work it still provides a picture of daily Jewish life over three centuries in Hungary. The author is a writer from *US News and World Report*. Review: *New York Times Book Review* (October 14, 1990): 9.

634. Isaacson, Judith Magyar, **Seed of Sarah: Memoirs of a Survivor**. Urbana, IL: University of Illinois Press, 1991. xi, 193 p. ISBN: 0252062191. Includes bibliographical references and index.

Isaacson's memoir covers her war-time experiences in her native Hungary and in German concentration camps.

635. Perlman, Robert, **Bridging Three Worlds: Hungarian-Jewish Americans, 1848-1914**. Amherst: University of Massachusetts Press, 1991. xii, 302 p. ISBN: 0870234684. Includes bibliographical references and index.

Perlman's book about Hungarian Jews is intended to answer several questions: "In what ways did the Jews of Hungary differ from other Jews? What were the distinctive characteristics of their history, their practice of Judaism, their language, and their community life? What was the nature of their relationships with the Gentiles around them?" (p. 3-4) The middle part of the book deals with emigration and immigration. A final section assesses how they made the adjustment from the old world to the new. Several appendices provide additional statistical information.

THE ARTS AND CULTURE

636. Eri, Gyongyi, and Zsuzsa Jobbagyi, **A Golden Age: Art and Society in Hungary, 1896-1914,** With essays by Ivan T. Berend, Lajos Nemeth, Ilona Sarmany-Parsons. Miami: Center for the Fine Arts, 1989. 197 p. ISBN: 0946372152; 9631329259.

Many forms of art flowered in late nineteenth century Europe. The art of Budapest was no exception although it has been little studied in the West. An art exhibit was held in Budapest in 1986 to explore Hungarian art in this period. This exhibit is being shown in Miami and San Diego. The exhibition is intended to show the parallel development in art in Budapest and Vienna. This volume is meant as a companion to the exhibit. It not only reproduces a large number of works of art shown in the exhibit, but also supplies background essays on the Hungarian culture that produced these works of art. Essays cover topics on Hungary's role in international society, the towns and architects of Hungary, biographies of major artists, the role of women in art and the element of Hungarian style. An index of artists is included.

637. Haraszti, Miklos, **The Velvet Prison: Artists Under State Socialism,** foreword by George Konrad, translated from the Hungarian by Katalin and Stephen Landesmann with the help of Steve Wasserman. New York: Basic Books, 1987. xvi, 165 p. ISBN: 0465098002.

Hungarian Socialist dissident Miklos Haraszti writes on censorship and the state in this essay. Written in a paradoxical style, parodying the state artist, he describes the severe intellectual depression of the modern communist state. The author is a well known dissident in Hungary who is best known perhaps for his exposé of shop-floor conditions in his book *A Worker in a Worker's State.* Reviews: *Problems of Communism* 39, no.3 (May-June 1990): 95-98. *World Literature Today* 64, no.1 (Winter 1990): 163. *Salmagundi,* no.78/79 (Spring/Summer 1988): 29-35. *Foreign Affairs* 66, no.5 (Fall 1988): 1133-1134. *Commentary* 85, no.1 (January, 1988): 84-85. *Orbis* 32, no.1 (Winter 1988): 156; *Society* 25, no.6 (September/October 1988): 92-93.

638. Kodaly, Zoltan, **Folk Music of Hungary,** rev. and enl. New York: Da Capo Press, 1987. 195 p. *Da Capo Press Music Series,* ISBN: 0306794667. Translation of: Magyar nepzene.

The first edition of this book was written in Hungarian in 1960. This expanded edition and translation into English consists of nine chapters: the folk music tradition, the primitive stratum of Hungarian folk music, the new style of folksong, children's songs and "regos" songs, laments, interrelations in folk music, the traces of art music, instrumental music, and folk tradition and musical culture.

639. Lajtha, Laszlo, **Instrumental Music from Western Hungary: From the Repertoire of an Urban Gypsy Band,** edited by Balint Sarosi, translated by Katalin Halacsy. Stuyvesant, NY: Pendragon Press, 1988. 244 p. *Studies in Central and Eastern European Music, 3,* ISBN: 9630546590.

"This volume contains instrumental music collected from the band leader Istvan Csejtei and his gypsy band, who were active in Szombathely, a town located on the Western fringe of Transdanubia, i.e. the western most part of the Hungarian-speaking territory." (p. 7) The pieces selected for inclusion in this volume are important in terms of the history of folk music but not necessarily representative of the composer's works. Professor Lajtha made recordings of Csejtei's work which were issued in 1958, 1959, 1962 and 1963.

640. Mansbach, Steven A., **Standing in the Tempest: Painters of the Hungarian Avant-Garde, 1908-1930,** with contributions by Richard V. West et al. Santa

Barbara, Calif.: MIT Press and the Santa Barbara Museum of Art, 1991. 240 p. ISBN: 0899510795. Includes bibliographical references (p. 213-227) and index.

Hungarian avant-garde artists made significant contributions to modern art. This collection of essays has as its goal familiarizing the Western reader with the importance of Hungarian artists working from 1908 to 1930. The opening essay provides some background to Hungarian social history. Other essays assess the achievement of the Hungarian avant-gardists, examine trends in techniques in Hungarian painting at the turn of the century and investigate the connection and interaction in Hungarian and Russian art and other progressive-movements in East-Central Europe. The volume also contains a chronology of the significant events of the avant-garde, an extensive bibliography and many reproductions.

641. Radke, Linda F., **That Hungarian's in My Kitchen: 125 Hungarian-American Recipes**. Scottsdale, Ariz.: Five Star Publications, 1990. 179 p. ISBN: 187774901X. Includes index.

A collection of Hungarian recipes. "Many of these Hungarian recipes originated in Hungary. Others started out Hungarian and became Americanized. Others started out American and were then touched by Hungarian hands. Still others have their Hungarian background with religious customs and food for religious holidays. Woven together these strands produce eminently do-able, distinctive dishes for family enjoyment." (p. viii) The recipes all come from the Weiss family. The cookbook included recipes for all the basics and a section on candy, miscellaneous and some "helpful hints" for the kitchen.

642. Sarosi, Balint, **Folk Music: Hungarian Musical Idiom**. Budapest: Corvina, 1986. 188 p. ISBN: 9631322203. Includes bibliography (p. 180) and indexes.

This volume is based on a Hungarian radio show that began broadcasting in 1969. It was inspired by "the desire to get to know, or rather not to forget the country's musical culture that preceded the general use of notation." (p. 5) The formerly broadcast ten-minute segments are arranged in three groups: discovering folk music, why the need for folk music, and instruments and their music.

Chapter 7
POLAND

GENERAL REFERENCE WORKS

643. Jordan, Alexander, **Hippocrene Insider's Guide to Poland.** New York: Hippocrene Books, 1989. xiv, 216 p. ISBN: 087052741. Includes index.

This is not a conventional guidebook. "Its goal is to help the visitor get to know the people of Poland by sharing with them enjoyable activities such as horseback riding, flying, kayaking, and many other sports or for those less athletically inclined, bridge, chess and cultural activities. The emphasis is not on what to see but on what to do, although the most interesting features of Poland are briefly described." (p. xiii)

644. Kanka, August Gerald, **Poland: An Annotated Bibliography of Books in English.** New York: Garland, 1988. xxii, 395 p. *Garland Reference Library of the Humanities, v. 743*, ISBN: 0824084926. Includes index.

Works on Poland and the Poles abroad have been compiled for this book beginning with the earliest English language publications in the early nineteenth century. Each entry includes a brief annotation and location information as well as the Library of Congress call number. The compiler excluded incunabula, translations of classical and contemporary literature, government publications, institutional publications, collections, ephemera, scholarly journals, dissertations. The Library of Congress subject headings were used. An author and title index are included. Review: *Polish Heritage* 40, no.1 (Spring 1989): 11.

645. **The Independent Press in Poland 1976-1990: Holdings in the European and Prints and Photographs Divisions, Library of Congress,** compiled by Zbigniew Kantorosinski. Washington: The Library, 1991. 66 p.

Between 1976 and 1990 the "independent" press flourished in Poland. These publications were not sponsored by the government and were distributed illegally, without being censored before distribution. This bibliography lists the independent publications of Poland collected by the Library of Congress. The materials fall into three broad categories which form the three sections of the book: serials, monographs, and miscellaneous. Around 345 serial titles have been listed alphabetically by title, each entry includes the place of publication, initial year of publication, frequency (when known) and holdings at the Library of Congress. A geographical index lists the places where the serials were published. The monograph section includes 120 titles arranged alphabetically by author or title. The approximately fifty items in the miscellaneous section include declarations, open letters, bulletins, telegraphs, posters, leaflets and cartoons. Entries are listed by author, title, issuing body or genre as appropriate. An appendix lists items in the Prints and Photograph Division. A name index is also included. The book will be of use to scholars studying the period.

646. Lerski, George J., and Halina T. Lerski, **Jewish-Polish Coexistance, 1772-1939: A Topical Bibliography,** foreword by Lucjan Dobroszycki. New York: Greenwood Press, 1986. 230 p. *Bibliographies and Indexes on World History, 0742-6852, no.5*, ISBN: 0313247587. Includes index.

The history of Jews in Poland goes back some two hundred years or more. Each culture has influenced the other. This bibliography is testimony to the depth of interaction between the two peoples. The compilers have included almost 3,000 sources arranged by subject of works published between 1771 and 1939. Works with at least one half of their material devoted to this topic have been included. Books, pamphlets, brochures and articles from journals are included. Entries from newspaper, encyclopedias, book reviews press obituaries and unpublished dissertations are omitted. The entries include full bibliographic data. All titles have been translated into English which may create some difficulty for the researcher. The actual language of the publication is indicated in an abbreviation at the end of the citation. An author index is included. The compilers have provided scholarly access to materials on an important topic. "From now on any scholar or layperson seeking to portray Jewish life in Poland from the time of partition until the eve of the Nazi invasion cannot afford to overlook the Lerski's work." (p. vii).

647. Pogonowski, Iwo, **Poland, a Historical Atlas**. New York, NY: Hippocrene Books, 1987. 321 p. ISBN: 0870522825. Includes bibliography (p.261-262) and index.

Pogonowski's historical atlas includes 180 maps and 14 diagrams preceded by a comprehensive essay entitled "Poland the Middle Ground," which is followed by a 1000-year "Chronology of Polish Constitutional and Political Development"—a unique compilation in the English language. The chronology also includes details of 19th and 20th century Polish history. Next the text on "Poland's Indigenous Democratic Process" documents the uniqueness of the early modern Polish civilization. A short summary of the evolution of Polish identity concludes the introductory texts." (p.9) An appendix also has many valuable features including texts, map and charts of prehistory and language evolution, a list of coats of arms of Polish towns, and a multilingual glossary of place names. Review: *Polish Review* 33, no.1 (1988): 94-99.

648. Walesa, Lech, **The Struggle and the Triumph: An Autobiography,** Lech Walesa with the collaboration of Arkadiuz Rybicki; translated by Franklin Philip in collaboration with Helen Mahut. New York: Arcade Pub., 1992. vi, 330 p. ISBN: 1559701498. Translation of: Les chemins de la democratie.

An autobiography of Solidarity leader and Nobel Prize winner Lech Walesa. Walesa focuses most of his attention on politics both before and after his imprisonment in the early 1980s. The story continues through 1990.

649. Wielewinski, Bernard, **Doctoral Dissertations and Master's Theses Regarding Polish Subjects, 1900-1985: An Annotated Bibliography**. New York: Columbia University Press, 1988. 200 p. *East European Monographs, no. 235*, ISBN: 0880331321. Includes indexes.

A thorough listing of all doctoral and master's theses in English on subjects relating to Poland. The compiler has drawn together work completed at 170 colleges and universities. There are omissions, according to the compiler, but no more complete listing has been published. 1108 references, and references to abstracts are included. There is access to each work by author, title, subject, discipline and school. Main entry is by author. Review: *Slavic Review* 48, no.1 (Spring 1989): 128-29.

HISTORY

650. Ascherson, Neal, **The Struggles for Poland**. New York: Random House, 1987. xiv, 242 p. ISBN: 0394559975. Includes bibliography (p. 230-231) and index.

This popular history of Poland was "written to accompany *The Struggles for Poland*, the television series in Polish history in the twentieth century." (p. xiii)

651. **Polish Democratic Thought from the Renaissance to the Great Emigration: Essays and Documents,** edited with an introduction by M. B. Biskupski and James S. Pula. New York: Columbia University Press, 1990. x, 252 p. *East European Monographs, no. 289*, ISBN: 0880331866. Includes bibliographical references (p.221-245) and index.

This volume presents students of Polish history with a collection of documents, formerly inaccessible to the English speaker. The editors are tracing the development of democratic thought in Poland from the Renaissance to the mid-nineteenth century. Their study is divided into two parts. The first is a set of five interpretive essays. The second is made up of the major documents on the topic. The volume is intended as the first in a two-volume set that will follow democratic thought in Poland as it evolved to the present time.

652. Blanke, Richard, **Orphans of Versailles: The Germans in Western Poland, 1918-1939**. Lexington, Ky.: University Press of Kentucky, 1993. xii, 316 p. ISBN: 0813118034. Includes bibliographical references (p. 246-268) and index.

Blanke has directed this work on Germans living in the territory ceded to Poland after World War I largely to German historians. However, it should be of interest to historians of Poland as well, particularly now when historical opinion is emerging there. "This book seeks to describe and analyze the dilemma of the German minority in Western Poland in all its considerable complexity.... This work focuses on those who were politically as well as ethnically German: that is, citizens of Germany until 1918." (pp. 1-3) The book has both a chronological and topical arrangement beginning with the establishment of the German minority between 1918 and 1922 and then discusses the economic and political situation of the Germans in Poland, international attitudes toward them, the rise of national socialism and their position in 1939. Two appendices are included: one on Polish place names and another on population statistics from 1910 to 1931.

653. Bromke, Adam, **The Meaning and Uses of Polish History**. Boulder, Colo.: East European Monographs, 1987. viii, 244 p. *East European Monographs, no. 212*, ISBN: 0880331097. Includes bibliographies and index.

This two-part study examines the history of Poland as a guiding force in politics. In the first part the author argues his two contentions: 1) Polish history is a strong influence on Polish contemporary politics and 2) Polish history requires more systematic study than it has so far received. The author hopes to stimulate debate on the relationship between history and politics. The second part of the book consists of excerpts from the writings of Polish political thinkers of the 20th century. The excerpts' selection concentrates on the three themes "the dichotomy between idealism and realism in Polish politics, the nature of modern Polish nationalism, and the role of Catholicism in Poland." (p. viii) None of the excerpts have previously appeared in English. Reviews: *Canadian-American Slavic Studies* 22, no.1 (Spring 1989): 90-92. *Slavic Review* 48, no.4 (Winter 1989): 680-81.

654. Burleigh, Michael, **Germany Turns Eastwards: A Study of Ostforschung in the Third Reich**. New York: Cambridge University Press, 1988. xi, 351 p. ISBN: 0521351200. Includes bibliography (p. 322-342) and index.

"This is a history of the internal and external pressures which kept an academic discipline on a fundamentally false course leading to total instrumentalisation under the Nazi regime. This work tries to show why a school which was incapable of construing its subject autonomously, heterogeneously or beyond a German central perspective, gained the ascendancy over genuine attempts to work in another direction." (pp. 8-9) The author traces academic studies in Germany from 1902 through 1945. His focus is on the use of these studies to dominate the East, particularly Poland. The book is chronologically arranged. Reviews: *International History Review* 12, no.1 (February 1990): 180-182. *American Historical Review* 95, no.4 (October 1990): 1231.

655. Fiddick, Thomas C., **Russia's Retreat From Poland, 1920: From Permanent Revolution to Peaceful Coexistence**. New York: St. Martin's Press, 1990. xiv, 348 p. ISBN: 0312039980. Includes bibliographical references (p. 328-336) and index. A history of the causes and results of Soviet-Polish War of 1920. The author investigates the internal politics of both countries before and during the war. He also examines the ideological basis for the war and West-European involvement. A note on historiography and a chronology of events are provided along with nine appendices containing various documents pertinent to the analysis. The volume is structured in such a way that each chapter focuses on a central figure related to some specific aspect of the war. Included are Leonid Krasin, Karl Radek, Leon Trotsky, George Chicherin, Lenin, M. N. Tukhachevsky, Leo Kamenev, Lloyd George, Felix Dzerzhinsky, and Sergei Kamenev. Review: *Soviet Union/Union Sovietique* 17, no.1-2 (1990): 142-143.

656. Garlinski, Jozef, **The Survival of Love: Memoirs of a Resistance Fighter**. Cambridge, Mass.: B. Blackwell, 1991. x, 231 p. ISBN: 0631176594.
Garlinski, an eminent historian of World War II, was also a member of the Polish underground. This book is a memoir of that activity and the two years he spent in Nazi concentration camps. Review: *New York Times Book Review* (August 4, 1991): 19.

657. Gorecki, Piotr, **Economy, Society, and Lordship in Medieval Poland**. New York: Holmes & Meier, 1992. 323 p. ISBN: 0841913188. Includes bibliographical references (p. 293-311) and index.
Piotr Gorecki challenges conventional historiography in his study of medieval Poland. Rather than assuming that Poland was at some backward state of development and seek out the agents of change, Gorecki uses "historical reassessments" of several areas for this study of the economic, social and institutional history of Poland. The book begins with a review of the economy of ecclesiastical estates as it affected peasants and craftsmen. Gorecki then turns to lordship in Polish society. The other major focus of the book is German immigration into the Polish duchies. "These three themes—economy, lordship, German immigration—are interrelated, but no one of them can be analytically reduced to any other. Structures of the economy, techniques of cultivation, demographic change, patterns of lordship and power, statuses of the peasantry and the elite, and ethnicity all mutually reinforce one another, and all become intelligible in their mutual context." (p. 11)

658. Gross, Jan Tomasz, **Revolution from Abroad: The Soviet Conquest of Poland's Western Ukraine and Western Belorussia**. Princeton, NJ: Princeton University Press, 1988. xxii, 334 p. ISBN: 0691094330. Includes bibliography (p. 313-319) and index.
This history chronicles the Soviet takeover of parts of Poland as it was viewed by those most affected by it—the occupants of the subjugated territories. The author has drawn on the personal accounts of Polish army personnel and their families who witnessed the Red Army takeover. The information he found has two main characteristics: it came from Poles and focuses on the early period of Soviet rule as well as on prison conditions. These determined the topics covered in this work. "The book concentrates on five broad topics—conquest, elections, socialization, prisons and deportation—treated in separate chapters and grouped in two parts: seizure and confinements." (p. xxi) The author is aware of the biases of his sources. Reviews: *Problems of Communism* 39, no.6 (November-December 1990): 106-111. *American Historical Review* 95, no.1 (February 1990): 206-207. *Freedom At Issue*, no.115 (June-August 1990): 33-35.

659. Halecki, Oscar, **Jadwiga of Anjou and the Rise of East Central Europe,** edited with a foreword by Thaddeus V. Gromada. New York: Columbia University Press, 1991. xvi, 400 p. *East European Monographs, no.328, Atlantic Studies on Society*

in Change, no.73, ISBN: 0880332069. Includes bibliographical references and indexes.

Halecki completed this manuscript in 1973, shortly before his death. Jadwiga appealed to Halecki because "as a ruling European monarch she was faithful to Christian ethics and principles in her domestic and foreign policies." (p. xiv) The study is in nine chapters, divided into three parts: Jadwiga's background, Jadwiga's reign, and Jadwiga's tradition. Genealogical tables accompany the text.

660. Harper, John Lamberton, and Andrew Parlin, **The Polish Question During World War II.** Lanham, Md.: UPA, Inc., 1989. xii, 45 p. *FPI Case Studies, no. 15,* ISBN: 0941700569; 0941700550. Includes bibliographical references.

This volume is part of the Foreign Policy Institute Case Studies Series. The study analyzes the negotiations over Poland's future in World War II for both its borders and its political rulers. "The account focuses on the roles of three main parties to the dispute, the United States, Great Britain and Soviet Union, and to a lesser extent, on the roles of the competing local factions, the so-called London and Lublin Poles. The discussion traces the controversy's development beginning with the collapse and exile of the Polish government in 1939, through the important preliminary negotiations of Tehran (1943) and Moscow (1944)." (back cover) A bibliography of English language sources is included.

661. Hoskins, Janina W., **Polish Genealogy and Heraldry: An Introduction to Research.** Washington, DC: Library of Congress, 1987. p.

This guide to research on genealogy and heraldry is intended for both Polish scholars and those individuals carrying out studies into their family histories. "Part I includes compendiums on armorials and studies in heraldry, followed by a section on genealogy where familial and clan names, codified at any early period are recorded. Part II sets forth the tools for genealogical research on both early and modern periods. The references present the basic works on Polish history, ranging from encyclopedias, biographies, and geographical dictionaries that record the changing nomenclature, to the ultimate, or archival sources." (p.v) The location of books cited is also indicated either with the Library of Congress call number indicating its presence at the library, or with a library abbreviation. Supplementary information provides useful addresses, archival sources and a chronology.

662. Kaminski, Andrzej Sulima, **Republic vs. Autocracy: Poland-Lithuania and Russia, 1686-1697.** Cambridge, Mass.: Harvard University Press, 1993. 312 p. *Harvard Series in Ukrainian Studies,* ISBN: 0916458490. Includes bibliographical references (p. 281-299) and index.

This book is a comparative study of Poland-Lithuania and Russia in the seventeenth century based on the structure and behavior of their respective diplomatic services. The two nations were rivals in the late seventeenth century not only for Ukraine which was the object of their rivalry in this study but also for dominance in Eastern Europe. Andrzej Kaminski is a Polish historian who has treated this subject in detail in this study. He believes that the crucial difference between the two nations was Russia's absolutist governmental structure. This scholarly study is arranged topically and will be of interest to the historian of Russia, Poland, Lithuania or Eastern Europe.

663. Klukowski, Zygmunt, **Diary from the Years of Occupation, 1939-44,** translated from Polish by George Klukowski; edited by Andrew Klukowski and Helen Klukowski May; foreword by Monty Noam Penkower. Urbana: University of Illinois Press, 1993. xx, 371 p. ISBN: 0252019601. Includes index.

Klukowski was in the Armia Krajowa. "His secret tasks included writing down for its information service all that occurred in a 75-100 mile radius and passing along reports from partisan unit to unit." (p. x) Another book by Klukowski, about the German occupation, won a prize in Poland for the best World War II memoir in the late 1950s. Klukowski died in 1959 and this diary was published and translated by his son George.

664. Korbonski, Stefan, **The Jews and Poles in World War II**. New York: Hippocrene Books, 1989. viii, 136 p. ISBN: 0870525913. Includes index.

Stefan Korbonski is the last surviving leader of the Polish Underground State that existed during the German occupation of Poland during World War II. As such he felt it necessary to write this work defending the Poles against the charges leveled at them by some in the Jewish community. "An individual or a nation can be blamed for denying help which could be given, but not for failing to do the impossible." (p. vii) The book is divided into six sections following a chronological arrangement. The author begins by placing the situation of the Jews in Poland before the war in historical context. He continues through the tragic events of the German occupation, the Jews in postwar Poland, and the emigration of the Jews. Two appendixes provide a biography on Stephan Korbonski and translations of two articles of special interest.

665. **The Reconstruction of Poland, 1914-23,** edited by Paul Lawtawski. New York: St. Martin's Press, 1992. xxi, 217 p. ISBN: 0312065361. Includes bibliographical references and index.

The papers in this volume were originally presented at a conference in London in 1988 on the occasion of the seventieth anniversary of the reconstruction of Poland. Each contributor focuses on a specific aspect of the problem of Polish reconstruction, including Western opinion, minorities, Polish-Ukrainian relations, the Battle of Danzig and the Paris Peace Conference, aspects of American policy towards Poland, economic integration and the origins of the Polish foreign ministry. An appendix includes documents relating to the reconstruction of Poland during this period.

666. Lukas, Richard C., **The Forgotten Holocaust: The Poles under German Occupation, 1939-1944**. Lexington, KY: University Press of Kentucky, 1986. x, 300 p. ISBN: 0813115663. Includes bibliography (p. 273-286) and index.

"It is ironic that Poland, the nation that suffered the cruelest occupation policies of the Germans during World War II, has had so little written about its war time experiences. This book is an attempt to fill that void, focusing on how the Poles responded to the German occupation and how they, as co-victims of the Holocaust, got along with the Jews during this tragic era." (p. ix) Reviews: *Slavic Review* 46, no.3/4 (Fall/Winter 1987): 568-80. *American Historical Review* 92, no.1 (February 1987): 172-173.

667. Milisauskas, Sarunas, **Early Neolithic Settlement and Society at Olszanica**. University Of Michigan: Available from Publications Office, Museum of Anthropology, 1986. xx, 319 p. *Memoirs of the Museum of Anthropology, University of Michigan, no. 19*, ISBN: 0915703033. Includes bibliography (p.225-232).

This site report discusses the archaeological findings at an early Neolithic, linear pottery culture settlement at Olszanica. Some of the objectives of the project were to establish the local chronology, determine the variability of artifact types, study the prehistorical environment of the area, determine the population's size of the area, discern status differentiation in the community and discover the social and political organization of the community. The author was also interested in establishing trading patterns of linear pottery communities. The report contains numerous diagrams and tables providing the results of the excavation.

668. Nir, Yehuda, **The Lost Childhood: A Memoir**. San Diego: Harcourt Brace Jovanovich, 1989. x, 256 p. ISBN: 0151588627.

The events of World War II as seen through the eyes of a young Jewish boy are recounted in this memoir. The atrocities the Jews suffered at the hands of the German are vividly recalled.

669. Opalski, Magdalena, **Poles and Jews: A Failed Brotherhood**, Magdalena Opalski, Israel Bartal. Hanover: Brandeis University Press, 1992. xi, 191 p. *Tauber Institute for the Study of European Jewry Series; 13*, ISBN: 0874516021. Includes bibliographical references (p. 171-185) and index.

In this study Opalski and Bartal compare the literary perceptions of the Poles and the Jews with the main focus being the years of the insurrection. "This inquiry is an attempt to reconstruct the social and ideological history of a particular literary motif. Based on fictional sources, it is primarily a comparative study of certain aspects of nineteenth century Polish and Jewish literatures." (p. 10) The authors use the analysis of literary motifs to examine larger social issues facing the two groups. They are particularly interested in the rapprochement between the two groups in the 1860s and why it failed. The book has a chronological structure and includes a general analysis of Polish and Jewish literatures before the revolt.

670. Pachonski, Jan, and Reuel K. Wilson, **Poland's Caribbean Tragedy: A Study of Polish Legions in the Haitian War of Independence 1802-1803**. New York: Columbia University Press, 1986. xii, 378 p. *East European Monographs, no. 199*, ISBN: 0880330937. Includes selected bibliography (p.364-373) and index.

This is the history of Poland's involvement in Napoleon's attempt to subjugate the rebellion of former slaves of Haiti. The story of Polish troops who died in this struggle has not been presented in English until now. Only one scholarly work in Polish exists on the topic. This study presents a unique view of Haiti's history as well as an unusual one of Polish involvement in North America at the end of the eighteenth century.

671. Peleg, Miryam, and Mordecai Ben-Tzvi, **Witnesses: Life in Occupied Krakow**, with an introduction by Antony Polonsky. New York: Routledge, 1991. xix, 187 p. ISBN: 0415065232. Translation of: Mi-huts le-homot ha-geto. Includes index.

"What makes *Witnesses* unique is that it is an account of the work of the Council for Aid to the Jews by two of its members who happened to be Jews. They were a young Jewish couple, with impeccably 'Aryan' looks, living on the 'Aryan' side, on false papers and actively involved in the work of the socialist underground in Krakow. The picture which they paint of the problems they faced in aiding those Jews who sought refuge outside the Nazi-created ghettos is complex and convincing." (p. xi) An appendix containing letters written during the war is included.

672. Pienkos, Angela T., **The Imperfect Autocrat: Grand Duke Constantine Pavlovich and the Polish Congress Kingdom**. New York: Columbia University Press, 1987. xiii, 186 p. *East European Monographs, no. 217*, ISBN: 0880331135. Includes bibliography (p. 149-156) and index.

The fifteen-year period from 1815 to 1830 during which Polish-Russian relations deteriorated to a state of war is the subject of this study. Grand Duke Constantine Pavlovich was the ruler of the "Congress Kingdom" of Poland established after the Napoleonic Wars. Constantine's role in the deterioration of Russian-Polish relations has been much debated, but has never been the subject of an in depth analysis. Here the author examines Constantine's role in establishing the "Congress Kingdom," his part in the formation of its army, his relationship with Alexander I, his behavior as ruler of Poland and his relationship with Nicholas I. The complex role Constantine played in the events of the period is reevaluated. An appendix with the Polish Constitution and Organic Statute of 1832 is included.

673. Pienkos, Donald E., **For Your Freedom through Ours: Polish American Efforts on Poland's Behalf, 1863-1991**. New York: Columbia University Press, 1991. ii, 620 p. *East European Monographs, no. 311*, ISBN: 0880332085. Includes bibliographical references (p. 571-596) and indexes.

The author describes and analyzes "the efforts of Americans of Polish origin and ancestral heritage to work in an organized fashion on behalf of the Polish nation." (p. 1) His study begins in 1863 when a committee was established in New York City to support an uprising that had occurred in partitioned Poland under Russian rule. The story ends with efforts in the 1980s with the work of the Polish American Congress. Several appendices provide documents on Polish American relations, a chronology of major dates in Polish American history, and biographies of leaders of the Polish American community.

674. Pula, James S., and Eugene E. Dziedzic, **United We Stand: The Role of Polish Workers in the New York Mills Textile Strikes, 1912 and 1916**. New York: distributed by Columbia University Press, 1990. x, 296 p. *East European Monographs, no. 286*, ISBN: 0880331836. Includes bibliographical references (p. 276-284) and index.

A recounting of the strikes in the New York textile mills in 1912 and 1916. This work is also the story of the life in this country for Polish immigrants at the turn of the century. The authors intend the work as a narrative history as opposed to one of historical theory. It is chronologically arranged. While it is primarily a work about a unique period in New York state history it is also an excellent source of information on the Polish émigré life in the U.S. at the turn of the century.

675. Roland, Charles G., **Courage Under Siege: Starvation, Disease, and Death in the Warsaw Ghetto**. New York: Oxford University Press, 1992. viii, 310 p. ISBN: 019506285X. Includes bibliographical references (p. 289-298) and index.

This work chronicles the brutal destruction of Warsaw's Jewish population at the hands of the Nazis. Roland is particularly interested in the medical community of the Warsaw ghetto as they dealt with the famine and disease of those years. "This book is an effort to tell the story of the unceasing pressure on the inhabitants of the Warsaw ghetto that resulted from constant hunger and the threat or the reality of catastrophic disease. I shall use, wherever possible, eyewitness testimony generously provided by a small group of survivors, most of them doctors, nurses or medical students in the ghetto." (p. 3) The book includes statistical data on mortality in the ghetto and a lengthy bibliography.

676. Rosman, Murray Jay, **The Lords' Jews: Magnate-Jewish Relations in the Polish-Lithuanian Commonwealth during the Eighteenth Century**. Cambridge, Mass.: Harvard University and the Harvard Ukrainian Research Institute, 1990. xv, 256 p. *Center for Jewish Studies, Harvard Judaic Texts and Studies, 7, Harvard Ukrainian Research Institute, Monograph Series*, ISBN: 0916458180. Includes bibliographical references (p. 225-248).

A study of the interaction between the nobility of the Polish-Lithuanian commonwealth and the Jewish population in the eighteenth century. The author has drawn on the Sieniawski-Czartoryski archive in Jerusalem. Two questions are the focus of the analysis: what were the spheres of interaction between the Jews and the nobility and what was the significance of the interaction? "My findings document what has therefore been asserted only on an impressionistic basis: that the Jews interacted with the magnates through their commercial, leasing and administrative activities, and magnates wielded great influence over the Jewish community." The chapters are arranged topically discussing first the general position of the magnates of Poland and then turning to two landed nobility families the Sieniawskis and the Czartoryskis. Next the author examines the role of the Jews on these estates and then their several economic positions in Poland. Two appendices are included supplying population data and information on the currency of the early eighteenth century.

677. Shelton, Anita Krystina, **The Democratic Idea in Polish History and Historiography**. Boulder, Colo.: East European Monographs, 1989. ix, 315 p. *East European Monographs, no. 267*, ISBN: 088033161X. Includes bibliographical references.

This work explores the role of historians in shaping social and political views in Poland. "This study is primarily about Franciszek Bujak. If it can be said that historians were influential and important in the formulation and development of opinion and ideologies in independent Poland, Bujak was among those who were responsible for reinterpreting Poland's historical past in a way that brought her democratic heritage not as a wreck but as a living tradition into the twentieth century. Bujak was the creator of social and economic history in Poland." (p. viii)

678. Slowes, Saloman W., **The Road to Katyn: A Soldier's Story,** edited by Wladyslaw T. Bartoszewski, translated by Naftali Greenwood. Oxford: Blackwell Publishers, 1992. xxxii, 234 p. ISBN: 0631179674. Includes index.

As a consequence of the Ribbentrop-Molotov pact the Soviet Union and Germany agreed to "eliminate the stratum of Polish society that was able to lead the resistance against their rule." (p. xiii) The massacre in the Katyn Forest was the result of this heinous policy. This book is the personal narrative of one of the 448 survivors of this massacre in which over 4,000 Poles were killed.

679. Taras, Ray, **Poland, Socialist State, Rebellious Nation**. Boulder, Colo.: Westview Press, 1986. xviii, 200 p. *Westview Profiles. Nations of Contemporary Eastern Europe*, ISBN: 0813301815. Includes bibliographical references and index.

The author's purpose "is to introduce the reader to diverse aspects of contemporary Poland." (p. xv) His approach is topical, with chapters devoted to history, politics, international relations, economics, society, and culture.

680. Tarnstrom, Ronald L., **Poland and the Baltic Republics**. Linsburg: Trogen Books, 1990. 175 p. *50 Centuries of Warfare*, ISBN: 0922037043.

This military history of Poland and the Baltic states traces each country's military history from earliest times, but the most detailed discussion focuses on the twentieth century. The book is divided into four parts, one devoted to each country. Within each section various military actions in which the country has been involved are discussed in individual chapters. Tables giving uniforms and emblems of each country and an index of weapons are included.

681. Tec, Nechama, **In the Lion's Den: The Life of Oswald Rufeisen**. New York: Oxford University Press, 1990. x, 279 p. ISBN: 019503905X.

The story of one of the remarkable people of World War II who saved the lives of many others. Oswald Rufeisen, also known as Father Daniel, is a Jew who converted to Catholicism but this is only one of the many "enigmatic" facets of his life. "A World War II hero turned monk. A Christian who is a Jew. An Israeli who wore the Nazi uniform. A Polish Jew who as an officer with a German police unit organized a ghetto breakout. A fugitive from his erstwhile Nazi colleagues who found refuge with Polish nuns and became Catholic." (p. 3) The book is based on interviews with Rufeisen and others who could corroborate his story. It also describes conditions for the Jews in Poland during the war.

682. Tighe, Carl, **Gdansk: National Identity in the Polish-German Borderlands**. Winchester, Mass.: Pluto Press, 1990. p. ISBN: 0745304745 (pbk); 0745303463. Includes bibliographical references.

While this work is primarily a history of the city of Gdansk, it also has a major theme, "the import of industrialization and capitalism on the formation of national identities and national strategies in East-Central Europe." (p. vii) The fifteen chapters are arranged in three parts: part one covers from 8000 BC to 1918. Part two examines the period 1918-1945 and the final part is concerned with the post-war era.

683. Trzeciakowski, Lech, **The Kulturkampf in Prussian Poland,** translated from the Polish by Katarzyna Kretkowska. New York: Columbia University Press, 1990. vii, 223 p. *East European Monographs, no. 283*, ISBN: 0880331801. Includes bibliography (p. 215-223).

A study of Germanization policy imposed on Poland from 1872 to 1885. The author hopes to present a balanced picture of the controversy by fully analyzing both the government policy and the resistance offered by Polish society. This work is divided into four chapters. The first looks at conditions leading to the establishment of the Kulturkampf. The second examines the role of the church during the Kulturkampf period. The third focuses on the policy in Poland, its implementation and repercussions. Finally the author turns from the Polish resistance to the policy of Germanization. The author demonstrates not only why the policy failed but how it served to mobilize the nationalistic feelings of the society. A scholarly study, this work draws heavily on archival sources.

684. Zawadzki, W. H., **A Man of Honour: Adam Czartoryski as a Statesman of Russia and Poland, 1795-1831**. Oxford: Clarendon Press, 1993. xvi, 374 p. ISBN: 0198203039. Includes bibliographical references and index.

Zawadzki sets forth the life of nineteenth-century Polish statesman Adam Czartoryski, focusing on his attempts to reconcile the Polish and Russian states. "...as we approach the two-hundredth anniversary of the events that led to the annihilation of the old Polish Commonwealth in 1793 and witness at the same time the beginning of a new chapter in Polish-Soviet relations, it does appear a good and opportune moment to reassess Czartoryski's long association with Russia; to scrutinize the nature of this relationship, and the political, ideological, and other considerations that lay behind it." (p. 3) The work is arranged chronologically and includes a genealogy of the Czartoryski family.

685. Zielonka, Jan, **Political Ideas in Contemporary Poland**. Brooksfield, Vt.: Avebury, 1989. ix, 210 p. ISBN: 056607012X. Includes bibliography (p. 189-199) and index.

While many works have appeared recently on Solidarity, none have traced the history of Polish political thought. This book is intended to fill that gap; it is not meant as a history of Solidarity. However, Solidarity is used as a focal point around which Poland's political development is analyzed. The six essays discuss the forerunners of Solidarity; the role of the Catholic Church in politics; the doctrine of Solidarity; the non-violent strategy of Solidarity; the development of political authority in Poland and the relationship between politics and international relations. Each essay presents a somewhat different theoretical view and deals with Polish political development up to 1985.

GOVERNMENT, POLITICS AND LAW

686. **Poland into the 1990s: Economy and Society in Transition,** edited by George Blazyca and Ryszard Rapacki. New York: St. Martin's Press, 1991. x, 148 p.

"The idea behind this book is to bring together, from a former principality in the land of 'darkness and demons', some current thinking in key social, political and economic issues." (p 1) All the contributors are Polish citizens. Topics covered include change and future scenarios of Poland's political system, systemic reforms and economic policy, environment, energy and conservation, agriculture, housing, capital investments, prices, banking, privatization, and foreign trade. Review: *Foreign Affairs* 70, no.4 (Fall 1991): 183.

687. Coutouvidis, John, and Jaime Reynolds, **Poland 1939-1947**. Leicester: Leicester University Press, 1986. xxi, 393 p. *Politics of Liberation Series*, ISBN: 0718512111(cased); 0718512731 (pbk). Includes bibliography (p.372-382) and index.

One volume in the Politics of Liberation series. The series focuses on the liberation of Europe at the end of World War II in light of Stalin's belief that occupying forces could impose their social systems on the countries they controlled. This volume looks at the tragic events in Poland during the German occupation and its subsequent liberation by the Red Army. "While we would not for a moment deny the huge importance of external pressures—arising from Soviet and East-West relations—in shaping the basic pattern and course of Poland's development, we would argue that her own political forces and culture have also had a far greater influence throughout Poland's recent history than is assumed in the West, or indeed by many in Poland." (p. xv) The book is divided into two parts. The first, by John Coutouvidis, draws on primary sources on the Polish government in exile in London from its formation to its dissolution. Part two, by Jaime Reynolds, examines the internal power struggle in Poland during the German occupation and the early years after the war.

688. De Weydenthal, Jan B., **The Communists of Poland: An Historical Outline**. Rev. ed. Stanford, Calif.: Hoover Institution Press, 1986. xvii, 272 p. *Histories of Ruling Communist Parties. Hoover Press Publication, no. 347*, ISBN: 0817984720. Includes bibliography (p. 257-263) and index.

The author traces the history of Polish communists from just after World War I to the present day. "For purposes of analysis the primary emphasis is on evolutionary tendencies within the party's internal organization and changes in the directions and scope of its strategies and operational tactics." (p. xvi)

689. **Polish Paradoxes,** edited by Stanislaw Gomulka and Anthony Polonsky. New York: Routledge, 1990. vii, 274 p. ISBN: 0415043751. Includes index.

A collection of essays that examine some of the paradoxes in Polish social, cultural, political and economic life and their consequences. The volume is based on the premise that the Polish experience can be characterized as one rooted in paradox. The essays are grouped under three headings, "History and Politics"; "Culture and Political Economy"; and "Social Attitudes and Everyday Life." The authors are all scholars in Polish studies. Essays discuss such subjects as the relationship between the Catholic Church and the communist state, the cult of heroic failure, the present economic crisis, the popularity of Solidarity coupled with its repression by the Communist government.

690. Hahn, Werner G., **Democracy in a Communist Party: Poland's Experience Since 1980**. New York: Columbia University Press, 1987. xxv, 368 p. ISBN: 023106540. Includes bibliography (p. 347-350) and index.

"The aim of this book is to throw light on possible future directions for communist parties by examining reform and change in one communist party, a rather unusual, pluralistic party. It presents a detailed history of the evolution of the PZPR and the struggle within its ranks from August 1980 through the martial law regime imposed in December 1981 into the post-marital law system of1986. It also aims to aid the comparative study of communist parties by presenting much of the unprecedented detailed information on intraparty procedures which appeared in the Polish press during renewal." (p. xvi-xvii) Reviews: *Problems of Communism* 39, no.4 (July-August 1990): 84-90. *Foreign Affairs* 66, no.5 (Summer, 1988): 1134.

691. Heinrich, Hans-Georg, and Slawomir Wiatr, **Political Culture in Vienna and Warsaw**. Boulder, Colo.: Westview Press, 1991. xiii, 190 p. ISBN: 0813378184. Includes bibliographical references.

High school students in both Vienna and Warsaw participated in a survey. The data that resulted provided the basis for this study which presents a picture of the political culture in each city. "The authors show that as social bonds become weaker, specific forms of individualism appear. Exploring the role and the place of a capital city within society, as well as the function of urban centers in the development of a society's political culture, the authors analyze the relationship between various aspects of political culture, including elite political culture, mass political culture and the attitudes of individuals toward authority structure." (back cover) The book's four parts begin with a general introduction to the study of political culture. Parts two and three are devoted to the political cultures of Austria and Poland respectively. The final part presents a close comparison of the data. An appendix includes a copy of the questionnaires used in the study.

692. Kaminski, Bartolomiej, **The Collapse of the State Socialism: The Case of Poland**. Princeton, N.J.: Princeton University Press, 1991. xiv, 284 p. ISBN: 0691023352. Includes bibliographical references (p. 247-262) and index.

This book is about the absence of self-recuperating mechanisms in a communist system. "On one level, it is a theoretical inquiry into the characteristics of state socialism, its principles of organization, and its disintegration; on the second level, this book is empirical; it attempts to integrate a theoretical framework of state socialism with an empirical analysis of developments in Poland." (p. 13-14) Two appendices provide additional information on the stages of the post-martial law normalization and the debt trap. Review: *Foreign Affairs* 70, no.5 (Winter 1991-92): 198.

693. Kolankiewicz, George, **Poland: Politics, Economics, and Society**. New York: Pinter Publishers, 1988. xx, 210 p. *Marxist Regime Series*, ISBN: 0861874374 (pbk); 0861874366. Includes bibliography (p.193-204) and index.

This book, one of a series on Marxist regimes around the world, is intended to be a multidisciplinary study of Poland. After a beginning chapter on history and traditions, the author covers social structure and social welfare, structures of political rule, the economics of crisis, power and policy and a chapter on contemporary Poland, bridge or bastion. It also includes a section of basic data, useful for ready reference. Reviews: *Contemporary Sociology* 19, no.3 (May 1990): 358-360. *Canadian-American Slavic Studies* 24, no.3 (Fall 1990): 375-376.

694. Kurczewski, Jacek, **The Resurrection of Rights in Poland**. Oxford: Clarendon Press, 1993. xix, 462 p. ISBN: 019825685X. Includes bibliographical references and index.

"This book deals with the social, political, and normative changes of the last decades in Poland, and aims to synthesize the empirical evidence of the normative aspects, as reflected in attitudes and action, with a theoretical interpretation of this historic process." (p. vii) The author has based some of his analysis on public opinion surveys that were carried out in Poland in the 1980s and from a "nationally representative sample" survey carried out in 1988. Kurczewski is both Dean of the Faculty of Social Problems at the University of Warsaw and at one time was Deputy Speaker of the Polish Sejm.

695. Lamentowicz, Wojciech, Krzysztof Ostrowski, and Maciej Perczynski, **Eastern Europe and Democracy: The Case of Poland**. Boulder, Colo.: Westview Press, 1990. ix, 45 p. *Special Report / Institute for East-West Security Studies*, ISBN: 081338088; 0913449172.

This publication is the text of a paper by three participants of a 1990 conference on East European democracy. The three essays included here discuss democratic evolution and political culture change, the decline of power and its effect on democratization and democratization of the economy.

696. Lepak, Keith John, **Prelude to Solidarity: Poland and the Politics of the Gierek Regime**. New York: Columbia University Press, 1988. xvii, 271 p. Includes bibliography (p.257-264) and index.

"The purpose of this book is to help explain the phenomenon of 'Solidarity' and the crisis of Communism in Poland by examining the development of the Polish political system during Edward Gierek's rule (1970-1980). It argues that errors and contradictions in systemic policymaking generated the political and economic difficulties of the late 1970s. Those difficulties were in turn major factors behind the severe deterioration of Communist party authority and regime legitimacy which began in the summer of 1980" (p. xiv) Reviews: *Studies in Comparative Communism* 23, no.1 (Spring 1990): 101-108. *Orbis* 33, no.3 (Summer 1989): 458-59.

697. Lewis, Paul G., **Political Authority and Party Secretaries in Poland 1975-1986**. New York: Cambridge University Press, 1989. xix, 344 p. *Soviet and East European Studies*, ISBN: 0521363691. Includes bibliography (p. 302-333) and index.

The erosion of the authority of Communist party leaders at a local and central level is described in this study. The author points out that this is not a study of the erosion of the power base of communist rule in Poland. To a large extent the author focuses on the secretaries of provincial committees and their structural location. The book is arranged topically beginning with a general discussion of the nature of authority in Poland then focusing on the provincial party secretaries, the provincial party committees from 1915-1980 and then turning to the deterioration of authority and the attempts to reestablish it. This is a scholarly study with extensive notes. Reviews: *Problems of Communism* 39 no.4 (July-August 1990): 84-90. *American Political Science Review* 84 no.3 (September 1990): 1039-1040.

698. Ludwikowski, Rett R., **The Beginning of the Constitutional Era: A Bicentennial Comparative Analysis of the First Modern Constitutions**, Rett R. Ludwikowski and William F. Fox, Jr. Washington, D.C.: Catholic University of America Press, 1993. viii, 331 p. ISBN: 0813207762. Includes bibliographical references and index.

This book developed as part of the Comparative and International Law Program at the Catholic University of America. "The scope of this book is limited to an intensive examination of the first three written constitutions: the United States Constitution of 1787, the Polish Constitution of May 1791, and the French Constitution of September 1791." (p. 3) The authors discuss many aspects of the development of each constitution: constitutional traditions among the population of the United States, in Poland and in France; the "Interflow of ideas" at the time, particularly due to the Enlightenment; and the formation, and principles of each constitution. The appendices include copies of each constitution and their later incarnations. The French and Polish constitutions are printed in translation.

699. Michta, Andrew A., **The Red Eagle: The Army in Polish Politics 1944-1988**. Stanford, Calif.: Hoover Institution Press, 1990. xiv, 270 p. *Hoover Press Publication, 386*, ISBN: 0817988629 (pbk); 0817988610. Includes bibliographical references (p. 251-261).

"This book describes the military's intervention in Poland's domestic politics from 1944 to the present, with special emphasis of the rise of the officer elite to leadership of the Polish Communist Party in the 1980s." (p. 1) Michta proceeds chronologically, covering the sources of Poland's military tradition, rise of the army in communist Poland, Jaruzelski's tactics through the Bydgoszcz crisis, the army in the 1970s, the army between the ninth Congress and martial law, Jaruzelski's martial laws, the Soviet role in the crisis, and normalization and beyond, 1982-1988.

700. Rensenbrink, John C., **Poland Challenges a Divided World**. Baton Rouge: Louisiana State University Press, 1988. x, 246 p. ISBN: 0807114464. Includes bibliography (p.235-242) and index.

Rensenbrink and his family traveled to Poland for a five-month stay in 1983. His purpose in going was to study economic reform. The memoir of his trip is as much a personal reflection in what he found there as it is an analysis of the Solidarity labor organization and its gathering strength. "The Gdansk Accord" is included in an appendix. Reviews: *Annals of the American Academy of Political and Social Science*, no.511 (September 1990): 194-195. *Orbis* 33, no.2 (Spring 1989): 299-300.

701. Roth, Kenneth, **Repression Disguised as Law: Human Rights in Poland**. New York: Lawyers Committee for Human Rights, 1987. 110 p. ISBN: 0934143153. Includes bibliographical references.

"This report describes the status of human rights in Poland on the fifth anniversary of the declaration of martial law." (p. i) Sections of the report include heightened attacks in the rule of law, official violence, undermining the independent labor movement, curbing press freedom, silencing free speech, restricting academic freedom, restricting political association and assembly, and elections.

702. **Democratization in Poland, 1988-90: Polish Voices,** edited and translated by George Sanford. London: Macmillan, 1992. xv, 203 p.

"The need to understand the reflections of both intelligentsia wings—the communist-reform and the Solidarity-opposition academics—to the Round Table compromise on the causes of the Polish crisis, the nature of the political mechanisms of 1988-1990 which produced the abdication of communist power and the dynamics of the immediate post-communism transition period shaping its future evolution therefore provides the rationale for this volume." (p. viii) The individually authored essays are by well-known Polish scholars.

703. Sanford, George, **Military Rule in Poland: The Rebuilding of Communist Power, 1981-1983**. London: Croom Helm, 1986. 288 p. ISBN: 0709933231. Includes bibliography and index.

"This study seeks to explain why it was possible for the Polish military to take power in December, 1981. It then examines how this was done and with what consequences." (p. 1) In section 1 (ch. 1-3), the author examines various aspects of the rise of the political military in Poland. Section 2 covers the state of war in Poland and military rule.

704. Schatz, Jaff, **The Generation: The Rise and Fall of the Jewish Communists of Poland**. Berkeley: University of California press, 1991. x, 408 p. *Societies and Culture in East-Central Europe 5*, ISBN: 0520071360. Includes bibliographical references (p. 389-405) and index.

The group of Jewish communists described in this book were born around 1910. They became communists in their late teens and early 20s. After serving in World War II in the USSR they returned to Poland to rebuild what they had lost. The basis for much of the book was personal interviews with eyewitnesses.

705. **Transition to Democracy in Poland,** edited by Richard F. Staar. New York: St. Martin's Press, 1993. xiv, 271 p. ISBN: 0312100000. Includes bibliographical references and index.

The contributors to this volume treat Poland as a case study of an emerging democracy. Each paper was critiqued by an expert on the topic in Poland. The essays cover numerous topics including electoral procedures, the parliamentary system, local governmental reform, constitutional reform, privatization, monetary policy, foreign trade, and national security.

706. **Constitutionalism and Human Rights: America, Poland, and France: A Bicentennial Colloquium at the Miller Center,** edited by Kenneth W. Thompson and Rett R. Ludwikowski. Lanham, Md.: White Burkett Miller Center of Public Affairs, University of Virginia, 1991. xv, 185 p. *Miller Center Bicentennial Series on Constitutionalism, v. 6*, ISBN: 0819181528; 081918151X. Includes bibliographical references.

This Bicentennial Colloquium was held at the Miller Center for Public Affairs. The faculty affiliated with the Miller Center have a continuing interest in the study of the U.S. constitutions and its relationship to constitutions in other nations. In this work the contributors look at constitutional development in Poland as it has been affected by the constitutionalism in general. Part two presents several comparative studies between Poland and America and France and America. In part three the role of democracy, freedom and individual liberty in French and American political thought is discussed. Part four gives a historical perspective on human rights in Poland.

707. Toranska, Teresa, **"Them": Stalin's Polish Puppets,** translated from the Polish by Agnieszka Kolakowska, with an introduction by Harry Willetts. New York: Harper & Row, 1987. 384 p. ISBN: 0060156570.

A collection of interviews with prominent individuals from Poland's postwar regime. The interviews convey the mentality of those that supported Soviet intervention in Polish affairs. All of these interviewed were born between 1900-1910. All seemed to see the interview as an opportunity to justify themselves. It provides the reader with a unique insight into the Polish government during the Stalinist and early post-Stalinist period. The interviewer is a journalist closely connected with the Solidarity movement.

708. Walendowski, Edmund, **Combat Motivation of the Polish Forces**. New York: St. Martin's Press, 1988. xii, 154 p. ISBN: 0312016069. Includes bibliography (p. 142-151).

Walendowski's purpose is to investigate the fighting spirit of the Polish armed forces. As a result the focus is primarily on the psycho-sociological aspects rather than on the military hardware and strategy. Individual chapters cover small unit cohesion, ideology, discipline, the general war scenario and combat motivation in perspective. Much of the data upon which his conclusions were based were obtained from interviews with those having first hand knowledge of the Polish military. Review: *Armed Forces & Society* 16, no.3 (Spring 1990): 472-474.

709. Walesa, Lech, **A Way of Hope**. New York: H. Holt, 1987. 325 p. ISBN: 0805006680. Translation of: Un chemin d'espoir. Includes index.

Lech Walesa gives his own account of how and why Poland emerged from under Soviet control. The Polish labor leader and government official does not pretend to have some unifying theory of these events. He does provide a unique perspective and often draws on the archives of his correspondence in recounting these events. The work is presented chronologically. A map and brief chronology of Polish history are included. Reviews: *Foreign Affairs* 66, no.4 (Spring 1988): 885. *Polish Review* 33, no.4 (1988): 487-88. *Orbis* 32, no.2 (Spring 1988): 331-32.

710. Walicki, Andrzej, **The Enlightenment and the Birth of Modern Nationhood: Polish Political Thought from Noble Republicanism to Tadeusz Kosciuszko,** translated by Emma Harris. Notre Dame: University of Notre Dame Press, 1989. xi, 152 p. ISBN: 0268006180. Includes bibliography (p. 133-152).

In this volume Walicki intends to show "that some influential views on nationalism and on the nation building processes in East-Central Europe, views which are almost universally accepted in the United States, are simply wrong and misleading, and that the main reason for this is inadequate knowledge of Polish history." (p. ix) Individual chapters cover noble

Republicanism of the age of enlightenment, the enlightenment concept of the law of nations, Stanislaw Staszic, Hugo Kollataj, and the political thought of Tadeusz Kosciuszko.

711. Wiatr, Jerzy J., **The Soldier and the Nation: The Role of the Military in Polish Politics, 1918-1985**. Boulder, Colo.: Westview Press, 1988. xx, 204 p. ISBN: 0813303583. Includes bibliography (p. 185-188) and index.

The question of why a society turns to its military to solve political problems is explored in this book. The author intends this work to be a "sociological essay" rather than a comprehensive history and has thus avoided lengthy discussions of Polish history. Aside from the problem of examining the role of the military as Poles see it, the author focuses on two other theoretical problems. First he tries to examine the breakdown of a political system in a comparative context. Second the changing nature of the armed forces is considered as a factor in the changing role of the military. The book is divided into two parts. The first covers the role of the military in the Second Polish Republic and draws on Polish and foreign historical studies as sources. The second examines the relationship between the military and the party from 1944 to 1980. Here the author often draws on his own observations and public opinion polls.

712. Zagajewski, Adam, **Solidarity, Solitude: Essays,** translated from the Polish by Lillian Vallee. New York: Ecco Press, 1990. x, 176 p. ISBN: 0880011866. Translation of: Solidarnosc i samotnosc.

These essays reflect the poet's inner struggle to come to terms with several conflicting questions: "What does it mean for me to be involved in a political movement? Which part of myself should be involved? The civic or the poetic? Or both? And I have discovered there is also a 'metaphysical' part of myself that is rather anarchic—not interested in politics or history but in poetry and music." (p. ix) Zagajewski, a native of Krakow, Poland, now lives in Paris. Review: *New York Review of Books* 38, no.14 (August 15, 1991): 17-20.

FOREIGN RELATIONS

713. Bogacki, Anatole C. J., **A Polish Paradox: International and the National Interest in Polish Communist Foreign Policy, 1918-1948**. Boulder, Colo.: East European Monographs, 1991. 320 p. *East European Monographs, no. 303*, ISBN: 088033200X. Includes bibliographical references (p.293-311) and index.

Foreign policy in Poland has often been viewed as an extension of Soviet foreign policy. Anatole Bogacki feels this may have distorted the analysis of Polish foreign policy in the past. In this book he will examine the Polish perspective on living under Soviet rule, and their view of the effect Soviet influence had on policy. The book begins with several chapters of background information. Bogacki then turns to a discussion of Polish Communists and the USSR, state security, territorial security, national prestige and the relation between the perception of state and the role of internationalism in a communist country.

714. Cynkin, Thomas M., **Soviet and American Signalling in the Polish Crisis,** foreword by Robert L. Pfaltzgraff, Jr. Macmillan, 1988. ix, 263 p. ISBN: 0333446925. Includes bibliography (p. 252-254) and index.

Cynkin examines "the patterns of interaction that characterise superpower relations in the case of a crisis such as that which unfolded in Poland reaching its climax in early December 1981 and resulting in the imposition of martial law. Central to the analysis is a comprehensive examination of the crisis management strategies of the USA and the USSR within the context of a variety of signals transmitted between Washington and Moscow." (p. viii) Review: *Slavic Review* 49, no.2 (Summer 1990): 299-300.

715. Pease, Neal, **Poland, the United States, and the Stabilization of Europe, 1919-1933**. New York: Oxford University Press, 1986. 238 p. ISBN: 0195040503. Includes bibliography (p.222-231) and index.

Pease's arguments are these: "that the Polish authorities of mid-1920s recognized the American yearning for stability in Europe and sought to derive political and economic benefit from it, that this theme and its consequences dominated the relationship between the two countries in the fifteen years following World War I and enmeshed it in many of the foremost diplomatic and financial issues of the day, and that the Polish courtship of the United States ultimately failed for reasons largely inherent in the structure of the interwar world." (p. vi) Reviews: *Polish American Studies* 44, no.2 (Autumn 1987): 76-78. *Polish Review* 32, no.3 (1987): 316-19.

716. Prazmowska, Anita, **Britain, Poland, and the Eastern Front, 1989**. New York: Cambridge University Press, 1987. viii, 231 p. *Soviet and East European Studies. Includes index and bibliography (p.220-224).*

The author draws upon her knowledge of Polish sources to explore British-Polish relations in 1938-1939. By showing the tenuous nature of British influence in Poland, she is able to refute "the suggestion that the British espousal of the Polish cause led directly to Poland rejecting German demands in Danzig and thus drew upon Poland the full wrath of German attack." (p. vii)

717. Rachwald, Arthur R., **In Search of Poland: The Superpowers' Response to Solidarity**. Stanford, Ca.: Hoover Institution Press, 1990. xii, 149 p. ISBN: 0817989625 (pbk.: alk. paper); 0817989617 (alk. paper). Includes bibliographical references and index.

Rachwald examines the Soviet Union's resistance to Solidarity, the independent trade union movement in Poland. His "analysis of lengthy encounters between martial law authorities and Solidarity in the years following the 13 December 1981 crackdown on the union portrays Soviet failure to ascertain or reverse the political aspirations of the Polish people." (p. viii) He also examines Polish internal politics and its response to international affairs during this period.

718. **The Soviet Takeover of the Polish Eastern Provinces, 1939-1941,** edited by Keith Sword. New York: St. Martin's Press, 1991. xxiii, 318 p. ISBN: 0312055706. Includes bibliographical references and index.

Polish and Western scholars contributed essays to this volume based on papers delivered at a 1989 conference held at the University of London to mark the fiftieth anniversary of the Soviet takeover of Eastern Poland. The essays cover numerous topics related to the takeover but not all areas or viewpoints are covered. This volume is intended "...both to draw attention to the nature and consequences of the Soviet takeover and to encourage others to look at the events in more detail." (p. xx) Essays are included on the Polish-Soviet War of 1939, the situations of the refugees, sociological, economic and cultural aspects of the takeover. The new openness afforded by Glasnost is evidenced by the contribution of Polish scholars. Three appendices are included, one on world press reaction to the takeover, the second on Soviet accounts of the Red Army in Poland and the last contains numerous documents on mass deportations.

719. Teague, Elizabeth, **Solidarity and the Soviet Worker: The Impact of the Polish Events of 1980 on Soviet Internal Politics**. New York: Croom Helm, 1988. 378 p. ISBN: 0709943504. Includes bibliographical references (p. 347-361) and index.

This is a study of the impact the success the Solidarity movement in Poland had on the Soviet worker. The author has focused on policy in relation to the work force in order to discover how the Soviet leadership viewed and managed the working class. Most source material dates from the pre-Gorbachev era. The author examines official trade unions in the USSR and past attempts to establish unofficial unions. She then turns to methods used to "ward off the 'Polish infection' " (p. 17) in the official trade unions, public opinion, and changes in the priorities of the five-year plans. An examination of unofficial sources follows as the indication of the effect the Polish Union movement had on the general public. Next the author turns to the tightening of internal policies and an examination of the ideological debates initiated by the events in Poland. The final chapter looks to the future under Gorbachev.

720. Wolff, Larry, **The Vatican and Poland in the Age of the Partitions: Diplomatic and Cultural Encounters at the Warsaw Nunciature**. New York: Columbia University Press, 1988. ix, 282 p. *East European Monographs, no. 245*, ISBN: 0880331429. Includes bibliography (p. 271-282) and index.

The strong identity Poles feel between their own national identity and Catholicism is the underlying theme of this study. The author is focusing on the historical events of the late eighteenth century to examine this topic. The partition of Poland in the late eighteenth century helped foster what would become a national identity for Poles and gave the Pope particular interest in the area.

721. Wozniuk, Vladimir, **From Crisis to Crisis: Soviet-Polish Relations in the 1970s**. Ames, Iowa: Iowa State University Press, 1987. 176 p. ISBN: 0813803861. Includes bibliography (p. 163-169) and index.

A study of Russo-Polish relations is by necessity also a study of international socialist relations. Vladimir Wozniuk believes that in order to understand the events of the 1980s between Russia and Poland, it is necessary to understand the history of their relationship. Thus his work is divided into three parts. The first provides a historical description of Soviet-Polish relations during the partitions, Polish independence and the early socialist period, up to 1970. Part II examines the 1970s and Edward Gierek's leadership. Part III focuses on the events of the summer of 1980 and their effect on Soviet-Polish relations and East European communism. "The relationship represented in this study reflect less the Leninist ideal of 'proletarian internationalism' or its corollary 'socialist internationalism' than the cynical but pragmatic Machiavellian understanding of power relationships. As Machiavelli himself might have speculated, a vassal state could strive to play a role in a larger game—in this case, Poland as 'mediator' between East and West in the game of detente—in which case the weaker country could accrue some bargaining strength against the stronger." (p. 8)

ECONOMICS, BUSINESS AND TRADE

722. **Poland: Decentralization and Reform of the State**. Washington, D.C.: World Bank, 1992. vi, 113 p. *World Bank Country Study*, ISBN: 0821322133.

"The primary objective of this report is to take stock of Poland's progress in decentralization to local governments within the context of the Government's transition program, and to make recommendations on how decentralization policy may support, broaden and deepen transition objectives." (p. 1) After an introductory chapter that presents a normative framework for decentralization, the remainder of the report covers the following issues: assignment of public responsibilities by level of government; central/local fiscal relations; financing of local government investments; and local government planning and financial management.

723. **Poland: Economic Management for a New Era**. Washington D.C.: The World Bank, 1990. xx, 117 p. *A World Bank Country Study, 0253-2123*, ISBN: 0821319508. Includes bibliographical references.

Poland faces tremendous obstacles in its attempt to create a market economy. The centralized economic system had failed to make Polish industries internationally competitive, capital and labor were not mobile and there were many other problems. "This report identifies areas where special efforts are needed, such as a firm macroeconomic framework to provide a stable environment, and micro and sectoral reforms to help stimulate a supply response. The report advocates debt and service reduction programs for Poland to allow it to achieve creditworthiness and fully participate in the world economy, and therefore resume growth and improve living standards." (p. iii) The majority of the volume (pp. 41-115) is taken up with statistical data and data on the effect of foreign exchange restraints, shortages and subsides in the Polish auto, color TV and butter markets. The statistical data cover the economic situation in Poland in general and are taken from the Polish statistical yearbook.

724. **Poland: Income Support and the Social Safety Net During the Transition,** compiled by Nicholas Barr. Washington, D.C.: World Bank, 1993. xviii, 144 p. *A World Bank Country Study, 0253-2123*, ISBN: 0821323709. Includes bibliographical references.

Nicholas Barr compiled this report for the World Bank based on information gathered between 1989 and 1992. "This report describes the system of income transfers in Poland, assesses current arrangements, and makes recommendations for improvements. There are two main conclusions. First, current arrangements require reshaping to meet the needs of a market economy: additional expenditure is needed for unemployment compensation and poverty relief, with cuts in excessive spending on some other benefits. Second, the savings from the latter.... will finance most, though possibly not all, the additional costs of the former." (p. xi) Barr details this plan in this brief study. As with other World Bank publications, a wealth of statistical data is provided.

725. **Poland: The Economy in the 1980s,** edited by Roger Clarke; contributors, Andrew Dawson et al. Chicago: St. James Press, 1989. vi, 149 p. *Perspectives on Eastern Europe*, ISBN: 1558620451; 0582044421. Includes bibliographical references.

"The 1980s have been an era of dislocation and discontent in Poland, the upheavals of the Solidarity insurgency and the military clamp-down which followed, leading to years of unresolved political instability set against a background of economic stagnation, shortages and indebtedness. In this new volume leading specialists from Poland and the West analyze the economic record of the past decade, and the implications this has for Poland's future." (back cover) The essays cover reform, wages and incentives, private agriculture in Poland, spatial development and reform, demographic anomalies, and the economic crisis in Poland. The contributors are affiliated either with Warsaw University or the University of Glasgow.

726. Czarniawska-Joerges, Barbara, **Economic Decline and Organizational Control.** New York: Praeger, 1989. xi, 157 p. ISBN: 027593277X. Includes bibliographical references.

Until the publication of this volume no work had dealt with the relationship between organizational control processes and the decline of an economic system. Dr. Czaniawska-Joerges presents an economic model in the first chapter which is developed by the empirical case studies that follow on various aspects of the Polish and Swedish economies. "The cases illustrate the fact that there is only a loose coupling between international control and economic conditions." (p. 23)

727. Kalecki, Michal, **Socialism—Economic Growth and Efficiency of Investment,** edited by Jerzy Osiatynski; translated by Bohdan Jung. England: Clarendon, 1993. xiii, 369 p. *Collected Works of Michal Kalecki; v. 4*, ISBN: 019828666X. Includes indexes.

The essays in this volume of the collected works of Michal Kalecki tend to be more theoretical in nature than those in the previous volumes. While all of his writings have their base in his experience as an economic planner, in these essays Kalecki's theoretical views as an economist come to the fore. The editor has included extensive notes to place the author's work in context.

728. **Creditworthiness and Reform in Poland: Western and Polish Perspectives,** edited by Paul Marer and Wlodzimiercz Siwinski. Bloomington: Indiana University Press, 1988. xxiii, 348 p. ISBN: 0253204771 (pbk); 0253314720. Includes bibliographies.

A case history of the deterioration of the Polish economy under the Communist regime is presented in the form of a collection of essays by Polish and Western scholars. The essays are grouped into six sections. The first provides an overview of the Polish economy examining industry and agriculture in the context of Poland's inability to pay its international debt. The second focuses on the question of reform and the obstacles to it in Polish society and the Polish political system. The third section presents a variety of balance of payments scenarios by Polish experts, while the fourth provides Western views on the same theme. The World Bank and International Monetary Fund and their roles in Poland are subjects of the essays in section five. U.S. policy toward Poland, including a discussion of the effectiveness of trade sanctions, is the subject of the essays in the final section. "The work's thirty-three chapters combine the perspectives of several academic disciplines— economics, business, banking, political science, sociology—with the viewpoints of practitioners, such as bankers, government officials, and staff of the International Monetary Fund (IMF). The book combines the 'big picture' with a wealth of detail and recommendations, some of which break new ground" (p. xvi) Review: *Journal of Comparative Economic* 13, no.2 (June 1989): 352-53.

729. Matey, Maria, **Labor Law and Industrial Relations in Poland**. Boston: Kluwer Law & Taxation publishers, 1988. 180 p. ISBN: 9065444017. Includes bibliographical references and index.

This is a scholarly study of the history, structure and international position of Poland's labor law by one of Poland's foremost experts on the subject. The book is divided into three parts. The first is an introduction providing general information on the history of Poland, its governmental structure, economy, an outline of its labor law and the sources of that law. The next part examines, in depth, the individual employment relationship, looking at employment policy in the mid-1980s in Poland, termination of employment, duties, rewards and liabilities of the worker; hours of work, annual leave, salaries and benefits, job protection and settlement of labor disputes. The last part examines collective labor relations—trade unions, collective agreements, the right to strike and worker's self-management.

730. **Industry in Poland: Structural Adjustment Issues and Policy Options**. Paris: Centre for Co-operation with the European Economies in Transition, 1992. 184 p. ISBN: 9264137556. Includes bibliographical references.

"This report evaluates the need for structural adjustment in Polish industry. It identifies the obstacles: the delay in creating a job market and in developing an efficient financial system, as well as the barriers against Polish exports. The report also examines the options open to the Polish government for speeding up the short-term restructuring of industry and proposes a medium-term framework for enhancing its competitiveness." (back cover) As with the other reports issued by the Centre for Co-operation with European Economies in Transition, extensive statistical data on Polish industry are included in the annex.

731. Osiatvnski, Jerzv, **Michal Kalecki on the Socialist Economy,** translated by Jan Toporowski. New York: St. Martin's Press, 1988. x, 191 p. ISBN: 0312015623. Includes bibliographies and index.

The author of this study is interested in the connection between Michal Kalecki's work on the theory and practice of socialist economy and Kalecki's activities as an expert and adviser to government policy makers. This study will also attempt to bring together various elements of Kalecki's economic theories on the socialist economy. The book is topically arranged and is described as having a narrow analytical quality. The various chapters cover Kalecki's work on the planned economy, worker's self-management, long-term planning, projecting investment and the problems faced in post-war Poland.

732. **Stabilization and Privatization in Poland: An Economic Evaluation of the Shock Therapy Program,** edited by Kazimierz Z. Poznanski. Boston: Kluwer Academic Publishers, 1993. vi, 269 p. *International Studies in Economics and Econometrics; v. 29,* ISBN: 0792393414. Includes bibliographical references.

The essays collected in this volume are the result of the annual U.S.-Polish Economic Roundtable. The four parts of the book group the essays under the headings "Stabilization Program and Economic Recession," "Foreign Trade Sector: Reform and Policies," "Privatization of State Capital Assets" and "Alternative Approaches to Economic Transition." "Post shock recession, lasting at least through 1992, is examined to establish whether a sharp decline in output was caused by excessive demand contraction or lack of accommodating credit policies. The merits of an evolutionary approach and a more proactive state are debated." (back cover) Most essays include brief bibliographies.

733. **Kalecki's Relevance Today,** edited by Mario Sebastiani. New York: St. Martin's, 1989. xvi, 366 p. ISBN: 0312024118. Includes bibliographical references.

This series of essays on the Polish economist is arranged in five parts: reminiscences and comparisons; microfoundations and the theory of distribution; savings, investment and money; trends and the business cycle; and socialism and planning. Review: *Southern Economic Journal* 57, no.1 (July 1990): 265-267.

734. Shen, Raphael, **Economic Reform in Poland and Czechoslovakia: Lessons in Systemic Transformation**. Westport, Conn.: Praeger, 1993. xiv, 268 p. ISBN: 0275943518. Includes bibliographical references (p. 261-264) and index.

Shen has used both documentary sources and field interviews in this comparative economic study of Czechoslovakia and Poland as they each attempt economic reform. He believed that any program of change must take into consideration basic factors—"cultural, social and political as well as economic"—if it is to succeed. Shen also sees the current differences in approach and their success to date in terms of these factors. Thus his book begins with a discussion of differences between Czech and Polish societies. He then turns to more specifically economic problems: fiscal reform, monetary reforms, investment policies, foreign trade policies, privatization, industrial development, labor policies. The book includes a chronology of significant events from 1989-1992 and a list of sources.

735. ———, **The Polish Economy: Legacies from the Past, Prospects for the Future**. New York: Praeger, 1992. xvi, 226 p. ISBN: 0275938867. Includes bibliographical references (p. 217-219) and index.

Poland's reforms have been the most radical of all the East European nations trying to open their markets. This study attempts to focus on the consequences of those economic policies for Poland's future. "For now, it is the studied opinion of this writer that measures and approaches of transforming the Polish economy from the old to the new should be paced over time rather than instituted overnight, and should be moderate rather than radical." (p. xv) After presenting an historical overview of Poland's economic development Shen focuses on specific sectors of the economy such as monetary policy, pricing, labor, privatization, agriculture and foreign investments. A chronology of events from January, 1989 to December, 1990 is included.

736. Stefancic, David R., **Robotnik: A Short History of the Struggle for Worker Self-Management and Free Trade Union in Poland, 1944-1981**. Boulder, Colo.: East European Monographs, 1992. vii, 109 p. *East European Monographs; no. 338*, ISBN: 0880332352.

The rise of the "solidarity" movement has been viewed in various ways by scholars in the past few years. Oddly enough, this workers' union is rarely viewed from the point of view of the Polish worker. David Stefancic sets out to do just that in this brief study. He analyzes the development of the Polish workers' movement since the end of World War II. "To be more specific, I will trace two trends that are evident in the Polish labor movement; one towards autonomous trade unionism and the other centered around the concept of worker self-management." (p. v) Stefancic is also interested in tracing trends in the workers' movement. The author has deemphasized certain periods of political and religious history to make the topic more manageable. A bibliography is included but the book lacks an index.

LANGUAGE

737. Bethin, Christina Y., **Polish Syllables: The Role of Prosody in Phonology and Morphology**. Columbus, Ohio: Slavic Publishers, Inc., 1992. 278 p. ISBN: 0893572349. Includes bibliographical references (p. 269-278).

"This book is an attempt to define the role of the syllable in Polish phonology, thereby providing a comprehensive analysis of Polish phonological structure, a principled basis of comparison with other Slavic languages, and a mechanism for viewing historical developments and language change in progress." (p. 8)

738. **Phonological Investigations,** edited by Jacek Fisiak and Stanislaw Puppel. Amsterdam: John Benjamins Co., 1992. x, 507 p. ISBN: 1556192630. Includes bibliographical references and indexes.

This book is in two parts. Part one focuses entirely on Polish phonology, covering such topics as non-linear palatalisation and vowels, Polish yers and extrasyllabicity, abstract vowels in three dimensional phonology, the beze(cny) family of words and the phonology of Polish prefixation. The second part also concerns phonology, but in a more general, comparative framework, not limited to Polish.

739. Mazur, B. W., **Colloquial Polish**. London: Routledge & Kegan Paul, 1988. xii, 270 p. *Colloquial Series*, ISBN: 07100938X; 0710090307 (pbk).

This introductory Polish grammar is intended for students preparing for exams, a review of basic principles for teachers or an intensive course for new students of the language. "The emphasis right from the start is on a working knowledge, and the introductory section of the book includes a pocketful of 'survival Polish'—a useful selection of those words, phrases and expressions which are essential for communication in any language. The main body of the book consists of twenty carefully graded lessons in which the basics of Polish grammar are introduced and a practical vocabulary built up. In addition there are further reading passages plus an easy-reference grammar. The accompanying cassette—an invaluable optional supplement—contains dialogues from the book recorded by native Polish speakers" (back cover).

740. Pogonowski, Iwo, **Polish Phrasebook and Dictionary: Complete Phonetics for English Speakers: Pronunciation as in Common, Everyday Speech**. 2nd ed. New York: Hippocrene Books, 1993. 165, 103 p. ISBN: 0781801346.

This new phrasebook and dictionary provides the student of Polish with full phonetic pronunciation of each word. The phrasebook is divided into sections on subjects such as "simple conversation," "passport control," "customs," "numbers," "colors," "hotel," "shoes," "fitting clothes," "telephone calls" and many other practical subjects. The dictionary contains brief definitions only.

741. Swan, Oscar E., **Intermediate Polish**. Columbus, Ohio: Slavica Publishers, 1986. xii, 370 p. ISBN: 0893571652.

This is a sequel to the author's *First Year Polish* and is intended to be used in the second and third years of study. Each lesson consists of dialogues and/or readings with accompanying glossaries, explanation of grammatical points, and exercises. At the end of the book the author has included a grammatical appendix and glossary. Reviews: *Modern Language Journal* 71, no.2 (Summer 1987): 229-30. *Canadian Slavonic Papers* 29, no. 2/3 (June/September 1987): 355-56.

LITERATURE

742. Aaron, Frieda W., **Bearing the Unbearable: Yiddish and Polish Poetry in the Ghettos and Concentration Camps**. Albany, NY: State University of New York Press, 1990. xii, 242 p. *SUNY Series in Modern Jewish Literature and Culture*, ISBN: 0791402479. Includes index and bibliography (p.223-233).

An analysis of the poetry of the Holocaust. The author has divided the work into four parts. Part one focuses on documentary poetry. Part two examines those poems that concentrate on the morale of the people. The third part is taken up with the poetry of the resistance. An autobiographical essay comprises part four. The author is concerned with identifying "historical archetypes" for the poetry she examines. "Because Aaron does not limit herself only to the best or most carefully wrought poetic works, the reader can begin to appreciate the multilingual culture of the Jews as defined on its own terms, with its own set of internal symbols, allusions and illusions." (p. x)

743. **Polish Poetry of the Last Two Decades of Communist Rule: Spoiling Cannibals' Fun,** edited and with translations by Stanislaw Bananczak and Clare Cavanagh, with a foreword by Helen Vendler. Evanston, Ill.: North-Western University Press, 1991. xxi, 196 p. ISBN: 0810109824 (paper); 0810109689 (cloth). Includes bibliographical references and index.

This collection of Polish poetry written during Communist rule was largely the product of an understanding culture. Much of it reflects the conditions under which artists survive in a totalitarian state. All forms of modern Polish poetry are represented—lyric, religious and meditative. "The reader will gain a new appreciation of figures like Milosz and Zagajewski within the total context of Polish poetry, while encountering for the first time the work of lesser-known, but not lesser, poets—including a significant selection of poems by women writers." (back cover) Short biographies are provided for the twenty-seven poets whose works are presented in this anthology.

744. Begley, Louis, **Wartime Lies**. New York: Random House, 1991. 197 p. ISBN: 0394400168.

This novel portrays a Polish family and the effects of World War II on it and its neighbors. Review: *New York Times Book Review* (May 5, 1991): 1ff.

745. **Monumenta Polonica: The First Four Centuries of Polish Poetry: A Bilingual Anthology**. Ann Arbor: Michigan Slavic Publications, 1989. 567 p. *Michigan*

Slavic Materials, no. 31 0748-0164, ISBN: 0930042689. Polish text, parallel translation. Includes bibliographical references.

A bilingual anthology of Polish poetry, tracing the development of poetry in that country over four centuries. The works are divided by period into four sections: the middle ages, the renaissance, the baroque and the enlightenment. Each section begins with a brief introduction to establish the historical, cultural and literary context of the period. The collection is intended for the general reader as well as the student of Polish literature. The compilers have attempted to collect the best translations available for this volume.

INDIVIDUAL AUTHORS

746. **The Burning Forest,** translated and edited by Adam Czerniawski. Newcastle-upon-Tyne: Bloodaxe, 1988. 184 p. ISBN: 1852240091 (pbk). Bibliography (p.186).

An anthology of modern Polish poetry from Norwid, Staff, Stoinski, Rozewicz, Karpowicz, Szymborska, Herbert, Darowski, Woroszylski, Bursa, Czaykowski, Kowalska, Czerniawski, Krynicki, Wojaczek, Baranczak, and Maj.

747. **The Mature Laurel: Essays on Modern Polish Poetry,** edited by Adam Czerniawski. Chester Springs, Pa.: Dufour Editions, 1991. 325 p. ISBN: 0802312926. Includes bibliographical references (p. 307-313) and index.

Polish poetry gained a Western audience with the English publication of the work of Zbigniew Herbert in 1965. This collection of critical works on modern Polish poetry is testimony to the sustained interest in this literature. Four types of writers have contributed to this volume: critics working in Poland, Polish scholars working abroad, British specialists in Polish literature and other English language writers with an interest, if not an expertise, in the field. The editor chose this wide range of contributors in order to incorporate works that would appeal to readers with varying levels of expertise and to cover the wide range of topics in the works of writers from Norwid to Zagajewski. A bibliography of works in English on Polish poetry is included.

748. Czerwinski, E. J., **Contemporary Polish Theater and Drama (1956-1984)**. New York: Greenwood Press, 1988. xix, 155 p. *Contributions to the Study of World Literature, no. 26*, ISBN: 0313244022. Includes bibliography (p. 131-144) and index.

The purpose of this book is to introduce a number of Polish dramatists who have produced a significant body of work to the general English-speaking public. Some of the names will be familiar (Mrozek, Rozewicz, Gombrowicz and Witkacy), others may be new (Tymoteusz, Karpowicz, Ireneusz Iredinski and Jerzy Broskiewicz)." (p. xii) The book's chapters are each devoted to the playwrights listed above, with greater emphasis on the more recent, less known authors. As some of the works discussed are not available in English, the author has devoted a chapter to Polish directors and a chronology of Polish drama from 1956 to 1983. The author is a well known scholar of Slavic drama who has written numerous works on the topic. Reviews: *Comparative Drama* 23, no.4 (Winter 1989/90): 381-83. *Slavic and East European Journal* 33, no.4 (Winter 1989): 633-35.

749. Dadlez, Anna R., **Political and Social Issues in Poland as Reflected in the Polish Novel: 1946-85**. New York: Columbia University Press, 1989. x, 288 p. *East European Monographs, no. 269*, ISBN: 0880331888. Includes bibliographical references.

Countries whose literature is subjected to severe censorship often remain something of a mystery to the outside world. "This book will attempt to show how the feelings and thoughts of the Polish population—to whom free expressions of their sentiment was partially denied—found their outlet in the Polish novel in the postwar period (1946-1985); how changing literary themes, characters and conflicts reflected altered ways of living and thinking." (p. vii) Dadlez has chosen novels dealing with contemporary Polish life. The book is divided into two parts, the first covering the period 1946-1969, the second focusing on the years 1970-1985. The themes of the two sections vary reflecting changes in the political, social and cultural life in Poland.

750. Davie, Donald, **Slavic Excursions: Essays on Russian and Polish Literature**. Chicago: University of Chicago Press, 1990. 312 p. ISBN: 0226137597; 0226137589. Includes bibliographical references and index.

Donald Davie is a noted scholar of Slavic literature. He examines Russian and Polish literature as a poet bringing to his study not an extensive knowledge of the language and culture, but an intense feeling for literature and understanding of the creation of poetry. The thirteen essays in this work deal with a range of topics including the Polish Baroque, the works of Mickiewicz as compared with Pushkin and Walter Scott, and the writings of Zbigniew Herbert. Primarily this is a comparative study of the literatures of Russia and Poland.

751. **Four Decades of Polish Essays,** edited by Jan Kott. Evanston, Ill.: Northwestern University Press, 1990. xi, 403 p. ISBN: 0810108631 (pbk).

A collection of some of Poland's best essays by writers whose experiences span the century are gathered in this volume. The compiler has tried to include those works that treat somewhat universal topics. He does note in his introduction that the subject of emigration does arise frequently. Essayists he included here are Jerzy Stempowski, Jozef Wittlin, Zbigniew Herbert, Aleksander Wat, Czeslaw Milosz, and Adam Michnik.

752. Kott, Jan, **The Memory of the Body: Essays on Theater and Death,** with translations by Jadwiga Kosicka, Lillian Vallee, and others. Evanston, Ill.: Northwestern University Press, 1992. ix, 153 p. ISBN: 0810110431. Translated from the Polish. Includes index.

A collection of essays on a wide range of literary topics by Polish writer Jan Kott. The essays are collected into three topical sections. The first section contains Kott's writings on theater in and out of Poland. Sections two and three both include essays on mortality.

753. Witoszek, Nina, **The Theatre of Recollection: A Cultural Study of the Modern Dramatic Tradition in Ireland and Poland**. Stockholm: University of Stockholm, 1988. 220 p. *Acta Universitatis Stockholmiensis, Stockholm Studies in English, 76 0346-6272*, ISBN: 9171463811. Includes bibliography (p. 199-213) and index.

This study compares the dramatic works of the writers of Poland and Ireland as well as their cultural heritages. "The main contention is that within the last 50 years the leading Irish and Polish playwrights (such as Brian Friel, Thomas Kilroy, Thomas Murphy, Witold Gombrowicz and Slawomir Mrozek) have recurrently employed a particular set of signs. This observation is a starting point for the analysis of Irish and Polish cultures as respective cases of Theatrum Mortis and Theatrum Nuptalis." The study falls into two parts. The first presents evidence for the funereal strains in Irish cultural and dramatic traditions and nuptial strains in Polish dramatic and cultural traditions. The second looks at the most significant elements in the symbolism of each country.

754. Benski, Stanislaw, **Missing Pieces: Stories,** translated by Walter Arndt. San Diego: Harcourt Brace Jovanovich, 1990. 160 p.

These stories by Polish author Benski each deal with Holocaust survivors. The stories themselves were originally published by Benski in several short story collections dating from 1979 to 1987.

755. Brandys, Kazimierz, **Paris, New York: 1982-1984**. New York: Farrar, Straus & Giroux, 1989. 265 p. ISBN: 0374252009.

Polish author Kazimierz Brandys recounts the experiences of his emigration in this translation of his diary. The author was born in Lodz, Poland and studied in Warsaw. His first works were published in the 1940s and his writing has won numerous awards. The diary published in this volume covers the first years of his emigration. Review: *New York Review of Books* 37, no.2 (July 19, 1990): 23-34.

756. Gombrowicz, Witold, **The Diary,** translated by Lillian Vallee, Jan Kott, general editor. Evanston, IL: Northwestern University Press, 1988. ISBN: 0810107147. Translation of: Dziennik.

This is the first English translation of Polish author Witold Gombrowicz. Originally published in Paris, the first volume of the diary covers the years 1953-1957. During these years Gombrowicz lived in Argentina, where he had emigrated in 1939. He did not return to Europe until 1963 and was never allowed to return to Poland. However he has had a tremendous effect on Polish literature according to Jan Kott who notes in his "Afterword" to the Diary, "This Polish writer, who left Poland in the thirty-fifth year of his life and never returned, whose writings have been partly or totally banned in his own country, has had an impact on Polish literature unlike any of his contemporaries. In the editions smuggled into Poland from the West, he was read by his own generation and by the two generations that followed." (p. 232) Reviews: *Foreign Affairs* 69, no.2 (Spring 1990): 184. *Choice* (March 1990):1152. *Salmagundi*, no.85-86 (Winter-Spring 1990): 314-325.

757. Baranczak, Stanislaw, **A Fugitive from Utopia: The Poetry of Zbigniew Herbert**. Cambridge, Mass.: Harvard University Press, 1987. 163 p. ISBN: 0674326857. Translation of: Uciekinier z Utopii. Includes bibliography (p. 137-158) and index.

A collection of Baranczak's essays on one of Poland's foremost poets, Zbigniew Herbert. The author believes that all of Herbert's poetry is based on "the confrontation of Western tradition with the experience of an inhabitant of Eastern Europe, of the past with the present age, of cultural myth with the material particulars of life." (p. 8) The author explores Herbert's work as an expression of these contradictions and studies his method of expression in his use of irony and metaphor. The introduction provides biographical background on Zbigniew Herbert's life. Review: *Canadian-American Slavic Studies* 22, no.1-4 (Spring/Summer/Fall/Winter): 446-448.

758. Herbert, Zbigniew, **Selected Poems,** translated by Czeslaw Milosz and Peter Dale Scott, with an introduction by A. Alvarez. New York: Ecco Press, 1986. 138p. ISBN 0880010991.

Herbert has been described as an avant-garde poet whose poetry is unremittingly political. Here a broad selection of his poems has been translated by Nobel Prize winner Czeslaw Milosz.

759. Konwicki, Tadeusz, **New World Avenue and Vicinity,** translated by Walter Arndt, with drawings by the author. New York: Farrar, Straus and Giroux, 1991. 212 p. ISBN: 0374221820. Translation of: Nowy Swiat i okolice.

This autobiographical work by Konwicki is centered in the New World Avenue of Warsaw which the author describes as "my track to a luminous future, on my Golgotha Market by the Stations of my Passion...." (p. 7) Konwicki was born near Vilnius and fought in Eastern Poland in the Resistance during World War II. His experiences during the war often form the basis of his novels. Reviews: *New York Review of Books* 38, no.4 (February 14, 1991): 14-17. *New York Times Book Review* (January 27, 1991): 178. *World Literature Today* 65, no.4 (Autumn 1991): 734. *Foreign Affairs* 70, no.3 (Summer 27, 1991): 178.

760. Lupack, Barbara Tepa, **Plays of Passion, Games of Chance: Jerzy Kosinski and His Fiction**. Bristol, IN: Wyndham Hall Press, 1988. 281 p. *Rhodes-Fulbright International Library*, ISBN: 155605064X (hard); 1556050631 (pbk). Includes bibliographical references (p. 263-279).

The fiction of Jerzy Kosinski is the subject of this study. The author analyzes Kosinski's works as they were published in the United States. She considers them in the context of modern American fiction. The book contains a biography of Kosinski and a bibliography of his writings and critical works on him. Reviews: *Contemporary Literature* 31, no.4 (Winter 1990): 564-570. *Polish Review* 35, no.1 (1990): 91-93. *Modern Fiction Studies* 35, no.4 (Winter 1989): 764-67.

761. Czarnecka, Ewa, and Aleksander Fiut, **Conversations with Czeslaw Milosz,** translated by Richard Lourie. San Diego: Harcourt Brace Jovanovich, 1987. xii, 332 p. ISBN: 0151225915.

This translation of the 1981 and 1983 Polish publication is divided into three parts. The first, chronologically arranged, consists of Milosz' perceptions of the early world that molded him and his work. Part two is divided into sections on individual works by Milosz such as "The Light of Day," "The Seizure of Power" and "The Land of World." The final section is a collection of discussions on philosophy, poetic style, poetry and prose and other topics. A chronology of Milosz' life is included. Reviews: *Commonweal*, 2 June 1989, 339-341. *Parnassus* 15, no.2 (1989): 67-89.

762. Davie, Donald, **Czeslaw Milosz and the Insufficiency of Lyric**. Knoxville: University of Tennessee Press, 1986. xiii, 76 p. *Hodges Lectures*, ISBN: 087049483X. Includes index.

In this "extended essay" critic Donald Davie examines Milosz's poetry and his particular type of poetic discourse. Reviews: *New Republic*, 13-20 (July 1987):40-42. *Slavic Review* 46, no.3/4 (Fall/Winter 1987): 649-51. *American History Review* 92, no.5 (December 1987): 1239-40.

763. Fiut, Aleksander, **The Eternal Moment: The Poetry of Czeslaw Milosz,** translated by Theodosia S. Robertson. California: University of California, 1990. xiv, 226 p. ISBN: 0520066898. Translation of: Moment wieczny.

Fiut describes and analyzes the poetry of Milosz. His purpose is "to sketch at least an initial outline of the fundamental problems in Milosz's poetry, grasp its inner dynamics, and indicate the degree of its complexity." (p. 3) The book includes a chronology of Milosz's life and works.

764. Milosz, Czeslaw, **Beginning With My Streets: Essays and Recollections,** translated by Madeline G. Levine. New York: Farrar, Straus and Giroux, 1991. xii, 288 p. ISBN: 0374110107. Translation of: Zaczynajac od moich ulic. Includes bibliographical references (p. 285-288).

A selection of writings by Polish author Czeslaw Milosz is brought together in this volume. Two of the essays, "Dialogue about Wilno with Tomas Venclova" and "Who Is Gombrowicz" have appeared in English translation elsewhere. Milosz characterizes this volume as "...a travel guide to a certain literary sensibility nourished by 'another,' less known Europe." (p. x) Milosz describes those authors who have influenced his writing such as Stanislaw Vincenz, Gombrowicz and Dostoevsky as well as others who have affected his life in different ways. Thus, the selections here are of interest to anyone studying his writings.

765. ———, **The Collected Poems 1931-1987**. New York: Ecco Press, 1988. ISBN: 0880011734. Translated from Polish.

A collection of many of the poems of the esteemed Polish poet Czeslaw Milosz are gathered in this volume. There were taken primarily from four earlier volumes *Selected Poems*, *Bells in Winter*, *The Separate Notebooks*, and *Unattainable Earth*. Other poems are also included; many appeared for the first time in English. The poems are arranged chronologically. There are no textual analyses in the volume but some notes are included. Reviews: *Salmagundi* no.85-86 (Winter-Spring 1990): 326-343. *Paranassus* 15, no.2 (1989): 67-89. *World Literature Today* 61, no.1 (Winter 1987): 127.

766. **Between Anxiety and Hope: The Poetry and Writing of Czeslaw Milosz,** edited by Edward Mozejko. Edmonton, Alta., Canada: University of Alberta Press, 1988. xviii, 190 p. ISBN: 0888641273. Includes indexes and bibliography (p.175-180).

The Nobel Prize-winning poet Czeslaw Milosz is the subject of the essays collected in this volume. While there was no unifying theme for the contributors, several essays concentrate on the concept of reality in Milosz's poetry. Others focused on the motif of catastrophism which is so much a part of the poet's work. Milosz's political prose is discussed in another essay and still others trace his development through the late forties and fifties. The appendices give information on the poet's visits to Canada in order to provide scholars with some information on how these trips affected the poet. "...this book is a tribute to a poet who managed not only to continue to develop the rich tradition of a national poetry, but also to raise and respond to some fundamental questions of our epoch, to move hearts and feelings wherever his poetic word reached an audience." (p. x) Reviews: *Canadian Review of Comparative Literature* 16, no.1/2 (Mar/June 1989): 492-94. *Canadian-American Slavic Studies* 22, no.1-4 (Spring /Summer/Fall/Winter 1988): 444-45.

767. Nathan, Leonard, and Arthur Quinn, **The Poet's Work: An Introduction to Czeslaw Milosz**. Cambridge, Mass.: Harvard University Press, 1991. xi, 178 p. ISBN: 0674689704 (paper); 0674689690 (cloth). Includes bibliographical references and index.

Two colleagues and translators of Czeslaw Milosz' work set out to provide the first English language, monograph-length, study of his poetry as a whole. The work, which is chronologically arranged, follows Milosz from his home in Poland to the West and back again and traces the development of his poetry. A bibliography of his work is provided.

768. Kosicka, Jadwiga, and Daniel Gerould, **A Life of Solitude: Stanislawa Przybyszewska: A Biographical Study with Selected Letters**. New York: Quartet, 1986. 239 p. ISBN: 0704325977. Includes index.

A biography of Polish dramatist Stanislawa Przybyszewska with extensive selections from her letters, is presented in this volume. The author's tragic life is described in terms of its isolation from family, from the intellectual nurturing one might have expected a young author to have. Przybyszewska's correspondence is a part of her literary achievement along with her plays *The Danton Case* and *Thermidor*. The book contains a chronology of her life and a family tree.

769. Przybyszewska, Stanislawa, **The Danton Case; Thermidor: Two Plays,** translated by Boleslaw Taborski with an introduction by Daniel Gerould. Evanston, Ill.: Northwestern University Press, 1989. 297 p. ISBN: 0810108062; 0810108054. Translation of: Sprawa Dantona and Thermidor. Includes bibliography (p.293-297).

Two plays on the French revolution are presented here in translation. In *The Danton Case* Przybyszewska portrays the struggle between Robespierre and Danton. She takes the position that Robespierre is the most misunderstood figure of the revolution, a statesman struggling to govern France through its most turbulent period. He is besieged by enemies, chief among them Dalton. The five-act play has not often been staged due to its extreme length. The play has a metaphoric style and open form. The second play in the volume, *Thermidor* shows the author's vision of the final days of the Revolution and the downfall of Robespierre. The first act goes behind the scenes of terror showing "the effects of the system on those who have sent so many to the guillotine." The second act focuses on Robespierre's lonely decline. Reviews: *World Literature Today* 64, no.4 (Autumn 1990): 667. *Slavic and East European Journal* 34, no.3 (Fall 1990): 395-397; *Choice* (May 1990): 1509. *Theatre Journal* 42, no.4 (December 1990): 389-390.

770. Schulz, Bruno, **Letters and Drawings of Bruno Schulz: With Selected Prose,** edited by Jerzy Ficowski, translated by Walter Arndt with Victoria Nelson, preface by Adam Zagajewski. New York: Harper & Row, 1988. 256 p. ISBN: 0060158964. Includes bibliographical references and index.

This collection of prose writings, letters and drawings of Bruno Schultz spans twenty years and shows the many facets of his talent. Schultz was a victim of the Nazi drive to destroy the Jews. He grew up in Poland and became a fairly well-known literary figure in his own time. His work has attracted more attention in recent years in part due to his posthumous sponsor, the Polish poet Jerzy Ficowski. As Schulz considered his letters to be a part of his literary work they represent one facet of his talent and also give the reader a glimpse into the times. The book also contains three short prose works: "The Republic of Dreams," "Autumn" and "Fatherland." Numerous illustrations, many reproductions of Schulz's work, are included in this volume. Reviews: *New Republic 2 (January 1989):28-34. New Leader* 20 (February 1989): 20-21. *Wilson Quarterly* 13, no.4 (Autumn 1989): 114. *Choice* (December 1990): 635.

771. Sienkiewicz, Henryk, **With Fire and Sword,** in modern translation by W. S. Kuniczak, foreword by James A. Michener. New York: Hippocrene Books, 1991. 1135 p. ISBN: 0870529749. Translation of: Ogniem i mieczem.

Although this book is not nearly so well-known in the West as *Quo Vadis?* it was for this volume and its two companion works that Sienkiewicz won his Nobel Prize for literature. Written in 1884 this first volume of his trilogy deals with the Hmyelnitzki Rebellion of the Ukrainian cossaks and the Tartar wars of the early 17th century. This new translation is by Polish-American novelist W. S. Kuzniak and makes this classic work more accessible to the modern reader. Reviews: *New York Times Book Review* (June 30, 1991): 3. *World Literature Today* 65, no.3 (Summer 1991): 514-515. *Polish Review* 36, no.4 (1991): 487-494.

772. Karpinski, Maciej, **The Theatre of Andrzej Wajda**. New York: Cambridge University Press, 1989. xviii, 135 p. *Directors in Perspective*, ISBN: 0521322464. Translation of: Andrzej Wajda—teatr. Includes index.

"This book provides the first account and critical evaluation of this Polish director's work for the theatre. Maciej Karpinski examines Wajda's theatrical career focusing especially on such milestone productions as his internationally acclaimed adaptations of Dostoyevsky. Through an analysis of Wajda's aesthetic views and resultant productions, the study also reveals the vital link between his art and contemporary Polish culture. Karpinski is in a unique position to present a study of Wajda. Since 1974 he has collaborated with the director on a number of productions including *The Affair, The Emigrants,* and *Nastasya Filippovna*." (frontispiece) Reviews: *World Literature Today* 64, no.3 (Summer 1990): 489-490. *Slavic Review* 49, no.4 (Winter 1990): 687-688. *Theatre Journal* 42, no.1 (March 1990): 131-132.

773. Wat, Aleksander, **Lucifer Unemployed,** translated by Lillian Vallee, with a foreword by Czeslaw Milosz. Evanston, Ill.: Northwestern University Press, 1990. xii, 123 p. ISBN: 0810108402. Translation of: Bezrobotny Lucyfer.

A collection of nine studies by Polish author Aleksander Wat that portrays life in the chaotic world of internal Europe. Wat explains these stories, published first in 1927, as his attempt to show what drove the intellectuals of the time to totalitarianism. The works of Aleksander Wat give American readers some insight into the development of modern Polish literature, particularly the futurist school.

774. ———, **My Century: The Odyssey of a Polish Intellectual,** edited and translated by Richard Lourie with a foreword by Czeslaw Milosz. Berkeley: University of California Press, 1988. xxx, 407 p. ISBN: 0520044258. Translation of: Moj wiek. Includes index.

While this work could be classified as a biography, it is much more. Transcribed from the taped reminiscences of its poet/author Aleksander Wat, the book chronicles the conversation between him and Czeslaw Milosz from 1964 to 1965. Wat was an unusual figure "...not only was Wat a member of the intelligentsia, but he was also an intellectual, educated in philosophy, and his Jewish origins made for a valuable shading, one that provided him with a certain distance on Polish ways; moreover he was a member of the Writer's Union for many years, and, further, he was a poet." (p. xxiii) Wat saw politics as the central force of his time and communism the shaping force of his century. The book includes a chronology of the author's life, a "foreword" by Czeslaw Milosz and an "Introduction" by Richard Lourie. Reviews: *Polish Review* 35, no.2 (1990): 166-168. *Orbis* 33, no.2 (Spring 1989): 299.

775. ———, **With the Skin,** translated and edited by Czeslaw Milosz and Leonard Nathan. New York: Ecco Press, 1989. 111 p. *Modern European Poetry Series*, ISBN: 0880011831.

A collection of poems by one of Poland's most important poets is presented in this volume. The poems are translated by Czeslaw Milosz and Leonard Nathan. Many of the poems in this volume appeared in a 1977 publication entitled *Mediterranean Poems*.

776. Witkiewicz, Stanislaw Ignacy, **The Witkiewicz Reader,** edited, translated, and with an introduction by Daniel Gerould. Evanston, Ill.: Northwestern University Press, 1992. xiii, 359 p. ISBN: 0810109948. Includes bibliographical references.

"The aim of this collection is to present Stanislaw Ignacy Witkiewicz in the full range of his artistic and intellectual activities; as a playwright, novelist, aesthetician, theorist of the theater, philosopher, cultural critic, experimenter with drugs, painter, portraitist, and photographer. Although in his lifetime he occupied only a marginal position in the cultural life of his country, he was rediscovered after 1956 and became a major force in the second half of the twentieth century." (p. xi) Besides a wide range of works by the author the collection includes a selection of comments by Witkiewicz' contemporaries, a chronology of his life, biographical notes, a select bibliography and numerous illustrations.

777. John Paul II, Pope, **The Collected Plays and Writings on Theater**, Karol Wojtyla, translated with an introduction by Boleslaw Taborski. Berkeley: University of California Press, 1987. x, 395 p. ISBN: 0520052897. Translated from the Polish.

These dramas of Wojtyla written between 1939 and 1964 are "religious without being devotional." (p. 16) In this volume appear translations not only of his plays *Job, Jeremiah, Our God's Brother, The Jeweler's Shop, Radiation of Fatherhood*, and *Reflections of Fatherhood*, but also his writings on theater. An introductory essay by the translator analyzes and describes Wojtyla's development as a playwright and his involvement with the theater in Poland from the end of the 1930s to the end of the 1960s.

THE SOCIETY, SOCIOLOGY

778. **Violations of the Helsinki Accords, Poland: A Report Prepared for the Helsinki Review Conference, Vienna, November 1986,** by the staff of the Helsinki Watch Committee. New York: U.S. Helsinki Watch Committee, 1986. ix, 84 p. *A Helsinki Watch Report*, ISBN: 0938579827. Includes bibliography (p. 84).

This report chronicles human rights violations in Poland. It is arranged topically, covering violations in the areas of arrest and detention, prison conditions, death, police torture and violence, kidnapping, restrictive legislation, academic freedom, freedom of religion, restrictions on lawyers and judges, freedoms of expression and movement, and elections.

779. Curry, Jane Leftwich, **Poland's Journalists: Professionalism and Politics**. Cambridge: Cambridge University Press, 1990. x, 302 p. *Soviet and East European Studies, 66*, ISBN: 0521362016. Includes bibliography (p.289-293) and index.

Curry examines several aspects of journalism in Poland. Her individual chapters cover journalists as professionals in theory and reality; the post war roots of the profession; living and learning journalism; professional associations and professional politics; journalists as political actors; and a concluding chapter on Solidarity and beyond: the critical test of professionals and professionalism. An appendix includes notes concerning her research methodology.

780. Fluek, Toby, **Memories of My Life in a Polish Village, 1930-1949**. London: Hamish Hemilton, 1990. 110 p. ISBN: 0241130204.

"Toby Knobel Fluek was born in the village of Czernica, Poland. In 1939 Soviet forces occupied the village, and in 1942, following the invasion of the Nazis, the Knobel family was forced to leave their home in the Brody ghetto. Toby and her sister escaped from Brody in March 1943, and her mother survived the war..." (back page) This volume contains the author's diary and drawings of those years in Poland.

781. Gildner, Gary, **The Warsaw Sparks**. Iowa City: University of Iowa Press, 1990. xii, 239 p. *Singular Lives*, ISBN: 0877452768 (pbk); 877452709 (alk. paper).

Gildner has written a memoir of his experience in coaching a baseball team in Poland. "The true center of these adventures of Polish (and Cuban) men learning the sport and myths of America, their land of dreams in which Stan Musial is King, is Gildner himself." (p. x) His work not only focuses on the day-to-day details of his team and their adventures, but also on Gildner's own midwest boyhood. Review: *Polish American Studies* 47, no.1 (Spring 1990): 81-83.

782. **The Polish Dilemma: Views from Within,** edited by Lawrence S. Graham and Maria K. Ciechocinska. Boulder, Colorado: Westview Press, 1987. xiv, 258 p. *Westview Studies on the Soviet Union and Eastern Europe, 0163-6057*, ISBN: 0813371600. Includes bibliographies and index.

A collection of essays on contemporary Poland is offered in this volume. This collection was compiled to "provide a balanced assessment of the current situation" and to make accessible to English speaking scholars the views of Polish experts not previously available in translation. The eleven essays are grouped into five sections by subject: politics and state, social structures and attitudes, socioeconomic change and dislocation, sources of tension within the system and a reassessment of Poland's problems. "These chapters have been organized in such a way as to carry the reader through the current Polish policy from its initial structuring to the present. The point of departure is the primacy of politics and the apparatus of power over all other factors, be they social or economic." (p. 4) The reader is provided with numerous illustrations, tables and charts.

783. Huelle, Pawel, **Who Was David Weiser?**, Pawel Huelle; translated by Michael Kandel. 1st U.S. ed. New York: Harcourt Brace Jovanovich, 1992. 304 p. ISBN: 0151962944. Translation of: Weiser Dawidek.

This book is a translation of Pawel Huelle's 1987 publication *Weiser Dawidek*. It chronicles the lives of a few young boys who spend a strange summer together in Gdansk, Poland in 1937. Huelle portrays not only life in Gdansk in the 30s but also tries to give the reader a sense of Poland's recent past and the heritage that remains. Review: *Polish Review* 37, no. 3 (1992): 365-66.

784. Jaworski, Rudolf, **Women in Polish Society**. Boulder, Colo.: East European Monographs, 1992. x, 219 p. *East European Monographs; no. 344*, ISBN: 0880332417. Includes bibliographical references.

This collection of essays is not an attempt at "General History." Rather it is an attempt at analyzing the more basic social and historical questions—labor, mobility, family—using women as the focus of study. "The present anthology proposes to focus the attention of Western readers on an Eastern European country in which women played an especially important role during the last century: partitioned Poland. An examination of the situation and the self-perception of Polish women in the nineteenth century..., not only furnishes us with an important dimension of Polish social history but additionally provides the basis for valuable comparisons in international women's history." (p. v) The essays cover a wide range of topics: the women's underground in nineteenth-century Poland, women in the nationality conflict, and the professional position of Polish women in the nineteenth century. A bibliographic essay is included.

785. Kennedy, Michael D., **Professionals, Power and Solidarity in Poland: A Critical Sociology of Soviet-Type Society**. New York: Cambridge University Press, 1991. xiv, 421 p. *Soviet and East European Studies, 79*, ISBN: 0521390834. Includes bibliographical references (p.391-413) and index.

There is no question about the importance of Solidarity as a catalyst for change in Eastern Europe in the 1980s. Kennedy examines the significance of Solidarity on three levels. "First, he explains the background to and nature of the conflict between Solidarity and the authorities by examining the relation between the distribution of power and movement strategies. Second, he considers the implications of Solidarity's struggle for the theory of the Soviet-type system's reproduction and transformation by offering a critique and synthesis of relevant theories of class and civil society. Third, he examines the internal constitution in terms of gender and in particular, cross-class alliances. In a concluding chapter, he explores the implications of his analysis both for understanding Perestroika in the Soviet Union and more generally for reformulating a critical sociology of Soviet-type societies." (p. i) The study is intended not only for sociologists and Polish specialists but for anyone interested in what motivates change and the effect radical change has on society.

786. **Between East and West: Writings From *Kultura*,** edited by Robert Kostrzewa. New York: Hill and Wang, 1990. xiv, 273 p. ISBN: 0809029375. Translations from the Polish.

Kultura is an important Polish journal that is highly regarded by Polish intellectuals. The articles culled from the journal are arranged in three sections: where we live; what we think; what we write. The compiler hoped "to accomplish two goals: to introduce *Kultura* and its intellectual milieu to a broader audience, and to present several important issues and concerns which the Poles have been trying to cope with in recent years" (p. xiii) Reviews: *Journal of Democracy* 1, no.4 (Fall 1990): 116-119. *New York Times Book Review* (April 1, 1990): 23. *Polish Review* 35, no.3/4 (1990): 355-356. *Orbis* 34, no.3 (Summer 1990): 458-459.

787. Ludwikowski, Rett R., **Continuity and Change in Poland: Conservatism in Polish Political Thought**. Washington, D.C.: Catholic University of America Press, 1991. xv, 313 p. ISBN: 0813207436. Includes bibliographical references and index.

This book is a "study of the tradition of Polish conservative thought." (p. xi) The author begins with the historical background of Poland at the end of the eighteenth century and then moves to the panorama of political thought in the early nineteenth century. Subsequent chapters cover the consolidation of the conservative movement after the November insurrection of 1830, mature conservatism in the period of the insurrection of 1863, neo-conservatism as the decline of the conservative political hegemony, and conservatism in the Polish People's Republic.

788. Nagengast, Carole, **Reluctant Socialists, Rural Entrepreneurs: Class, Culture, and the Polish State**. Boulder, Colo.: Westview Press, 1991. xiv, 239 p. *Studies in the Ethnographic Imagination*, ISBN: 0813380537. Includes bibliographical references (p. 229-238).

An anthropological analysis of Poland's rural society. The author believes that the socialist system imposed on Poland after World War II masked the capitalist structures already in place but did not destroy them. "I elaborate here the argument that the appropriation and accumulation of capital in all its forms continued to be a class phenomenon in rural Poland during the forty-five years of putative communism and that these class relations and consciousness configure contemporary, economic, political, and social relations in unexpected ways." (p. 3) Nagengast draws evidence to support this argument from her field experience as a participant observer in a rural community in Poland at various times between 1977 and 1990. She provides extensive historical evidence for her argument drawn from a wide range of sources. The book includes appendices supplying statistical data on the region. The book should be of interest to anthropologists, sociologists and scholars of Eastern Europe.

789. **Malinowski Between Two Worlds: The Polish Roots of an Anthropological Tradition,** edited by Ellen Roy. New York: Cambridge University Press, 1988. xxv, 261 p. ISBN: 0521345669. Includes bibliography (p. 229-249) and index.

Eight of the ten papers presented here were originally read at a symposium commemorating the centenary of Malinowski's birth. The other two papers were specifically written for this volume. The papers, written by scholars from around the world, deal specifically with Malinowski and his influence. Reviews: *American Anthropologist* 92, no.4 (December 1990): 1090-1091. *Contemporary Sociology* 19, no.5 (September 1990): 764-765. *ISIS* 81, no. 306 (March 1990): 137-138. Polish Review *35, no.2 (1990): 173-175.*

790. **Social Stratification in Poland: Eight Empirical Studies,** edited by Kazimierz M. Slomczynski and Tadeusz K. Krauze, with a foreword by Gerhard Lenski. Armonk, N.Y: M.E. Sharpe, 1986. xii, 191 p.

This series of essays on social stratification is empirically based and deals with such topics as social inequality and social mobility, changes in social structure, occupational states, clan's images, the prestige of education, and value systems among occupational groups. Reviews: *Social Forces* 66, no.1 (September 1987): 279-81. *Polish Review* 32, no.2 (1987): 221-23. *Slavic Review* 46, no.3/4 (Fall/Winter 1987): 632-33.

791. Swick, Thomas, **Unquiet Days: At Home in Poland**. New York: Ticknor and Fields, 1991. 286 p. ISBN: 0395585635.

Thomas Swick was a student in Poland in the 1980s. In this book he describes his experiences living, studying and working in Warsaw during those turbulent years. Review: *Foreign Affairs* 70, no.5 (Winter 1991-92): 200.

792. Swiderski, Bronislaw, **Myth and Scholarship: University Students and Political Development in XIX Century Poland**. Kobenhavn: C.A. Reitzels Forlag, 1987. 150 p. *Kobenhavns Universitets Slaviske Institute*, Studier 13. ISBN: 8774215760. Includes index and bibliographical references (p. 145-50).

Swiderski's aim "is to reconstruct the history of the students of Vilna and Warsaw in the years 1800-1830 in a manner emphasizing that a free choice of ideas and actions is possible at any moment in history." In doing so the author questions several assumptions of Polish historiography, the primary one being that the main goal of the student movement was the realization of national-patriotic intentions. Swiderski believes that they, instead, wanted to express their own political interests and have more local power. The first and last chapter are primarily theoretical, analyzing the scientific and mythical forms of social memory. The three intervening chapters cover free-masonry as a political paradigm, Vilna student activity from 1817 to 1823, and Warsaw students from 1808 to 1830.

793. Walicki, Andrzej, **Russia, Poland, and Universal Regeneration: Studies on Russian and Polish Thought of the Romantic Epoch**. Notre Dame: University of Notre Dame Press, 1991. x, 225 p. ISBN: 0268016410. Includes bibliographical references (p. 185-221) and index.

This volume contains four self-contained essays that complement one another and deal with relations between Russian and Polish thinkers of the romantic era. The individual essays are: Alexander Herzen's "Russian Socialism," as a response to Polish revolutionary Slavophilism; Alexander Herzen, August Cieszkowski, and the philosophy of action; Adam Mickiewicz's Paris lectures and Russian Slavophilism; and Adam Gurowski: Polish Romantic Naturalism, Russian Panslavism and American "Manifest Destiny."

794. ———, **Stanislaw Brzozowski and the Polish Beginnings of "Western Marxism."** New York: Oxford University Press, 1989. viii, 349 p. ISBN: 0198273282. Includes bibliography (p. 339-344) and index.

Brzozowski was a Polish philosopher and literary critic who was born in 1878 and died of tuberculosis in 1911. Brzozowski was a Marxist, but one who diverged from the main currents of Marxist thought of his time and developed his own unique stance, that was "remarkably close to the philosophical outlook of Marx's early writings that have since come to light." (p. 1). Walicki traces the development of Brzozowski and Western philosophy.

795. **The Unplanned Society: Poland During and After Communism,** edited, annotated, and with introductions by Janine R. Wedel. New York, N.Y.: Columbia University Press, 1992. viii, 271 p. ISBN: 0231073720. Includes bibliographical references and index.

This volume contains several essays arranged in five parts dealing with social conditions, communism, social networks, economics and the role of religion. Each essay is in the tradition of task-centered practice. The collection as a whole "develops applications of the model (task-centered practice) for a range of problems frequently encountered by clinical social workers: difficulties of families and children, anxiety, depression, alcohol abuse, inadequate resources, and psycho-social problems associated with mental and physical illness. The focus is on how problems in these areas can be specified and assessed and how strategies consisting of tasks by clients and practitioners can lead to the alleviation of these problems." (p. vii)

796. Wulff, Kenneth R., **Education in Poland: Past, Present, and Future**. Lanham, Md.: University Press of America, 1992. 110 p. ISBN: 0819186155.

This brief introduction to education in Poland begins with an examination of the traditions of Polish education (Part I). The main part of the book is devoted to management and finance, the structure of the educational system, teachers and teacher training, parental views of education, and the Committee for National Education (Part II). In the final two chapters (Part III), Wulff speculates on the future of Polish education.

797. **Crisis and Transition: Polish Society in the 1980s,** edited by Jadwiga Koralewicz, Ireneusz Bialecki and Margaret Watson. New York: St. Martin's Press, 1987. 184 p. ISBN: 0854965254. Includes bibliography (p.177-184) and index.

This collection of essays presents some of the work of the new Polish sociologists who view their society with a more critical eye than their predecessors. "The present volume of essays is the brave product of this younger group of sociologists. It uses sociological theory and sociological techniques to deal with the problems which really face contemporary Poland." (p. 1) The essays discuss the structural nature of the crisis of the 1980s, and problems of legitimizing the social order, property rights, economic reform, the Solidarity movement, social stability. The one theme that runs through all the essays is how people live "in a society in which public behavior is constrained by an alien and unwanted system." (p. 1) The essays are of interest not only to scholars of Polish studies but to anyone with an interest in sociology.

RELIGION

798. Frick, David A., **Polish Sacred Philology in the Reformation and the Counter-Reformation: Chapters in the History of the Controversies (1551-1632).** Berkeley: University of California Press, 1989. xi, 288 p. *University of California Publications in Modern Philology, v.123*, ISBN: 0520097408. Includes bibliography (p.261-277) and index.

Polish Sacred Philosophy in the Reformation and the Counter Reformation attempts to provide what might be termed an external history of Polish Bible translation. It investigates opinion on the translation and interpretation of Holy Scripture in Polish during the age of confessional debate, concentrating on the view of translators of the Polish Bibles and New Testaments printed between 1551 and 1632, as well as views of their supporters, critics, and competitors." (p. ix) The work is also intended as a source book, making some primary source materials more accessible. The study is intended for both Slavists and students of the Reformation and Counter-Reformation. The work is arranged chronologically with each chapter devoted to a different Polish Bible translation beginning with the 1551 translation of the New Testament by Stanislaw Murzynowski and ending with the Gdansk Bible of 1632. Review: *Slavic and East European Journal* 34, no.4 (Winter 1990): 568-570.

799. Michnik, Adam, **The Church and the Left,** edited, translated and with an introduction by David Ost. Chicago: University of Chicago Press, 1993. xvii, 301 p. ISBN: 0226524248. Includes bibliographical references and index.

In this book Polish historian and activist Adam Michnik discusses the relationship between the intelligentsia and the Catholic Church in Poland. The book was written in 1977 when the role of the church in opposing the communist dictatorship then in power was being questioned by Poland's intellectuals. Originally this book, along with the writings of several other authors, was to appear in a special issue of the journal *Aneks*. "Our aim...was to reexamine the complex relationship between the Catholic Church and the secular intelligentsia.... My book was thus situated in a context of encounters and conversations between people far removed from the Church who, in the course of their involvement in the political opposition, were discovering that the Church was itself a source of democratic and humane values." (p. xi) This translation of Michnik's book presents the American reader with an interesting and unusual discussion of the opposition movement in Poland and the role of the Catholic Church in Polish society.

800. Sikorska, Grazyna, **Light and Life: Renewal in Poland, with a Message from Pope John Paul II**. London: Fount Paperbacks, 1989. 156 p. ISBN: 0802803415.

Father Blachnicki was an important spiritual leader in Poland, but has remained relatively unknown in the West. He founded the light-life movement, a Christian renewal program begun in the 1950s. Initially Father Blachnicki organized retreats for children which became popular and spread. This "Oasis" movement encouraged a personal relationship with Christ and commitment to spiritual life. This brief book tells of Father Blachnicki's struggle to establish his renewal program while being persecuted by the Communist regime. The author is a Polish émigré working on the staff of Keston College.

DISSIDENT MOVEMENTS

801. Bernhard, Michael H., **The Origins of Democratization in Poland: Workers, Intellectuals, and Oppositional Politics, 1976-1980**. New York: Columbia University Press, 1993. xv, 298 p. ISBN: 023108093X. Includes bibliographical references (p. 257-283) and index.

Bernhard's book examines the origins of civil society and the opposition in Poland. After devoting two chapters to civil society and democratization in the East Central European context and Poland under Gomulka and Gierek, he focuses in on the price reform and strikes that occurred in Poland in June of 1976. The remaining five chapters are concerned with KOR (the Workers' Defense Committee), the struggle for amnesty of the workers involved in the strikes, other manifestations of oppositional politics, and KOR's significance for Solidarity.

802. Gerrits, Andre W. M., **The Failure of Authoritarian Change: Reform, Opposition, and Geo-Politics in Poland in the 1980s**. Brookfield, Vt., U.S.A.: Dartmouth Pub. Co., 1990. ix, 260 p. ISBN: 1855211335.

What started as a study of the role of non-violent, self-organization shifted its emphasis to become an analysis of three aspects of the Polish power structure. The author examines the interrelationships between the Polish party-state, the Polish opposition and the leadership in the Soviet Union. The author believes that the authoritarian structure of the Communist regime collapsed because it was unable to stabilize a faltering economic and social system through limited changes. The study is divided into three parts. The first looks at "Patterns of authoritarian reform" its origins, the institutional methods of reform and the use of repression. In part two the author looks at Solidarity as an example of self-organization and nonviolent action used for social self-defense. In the last part the role of the Soviet Union is the focus.

803. Goodwyn, Lawrence, **Breaking the Barrier: The Rise of Solidarity in Poland**. New York: Oxford University Press, 1991. 466 p. ISBN: 0195061225. Includes bibliographical references and index.

From the author's point of view this book is "an attempt to pursue what for Poland is a new path of research into the interior of popular insurgency by a proud people who were forever under Leninist confinement." (p. viii) Goodwyn describes and analyzes the events that led to the establishment of Solidarity and its role in the events of 1989. Reviews: *Studies in Comparative Communism* 24, no.3 (September 1991): 313-330. *New York Times Book Review* (June 2, 1991): 12. *New York Review of Books* 38, no.11 (June 13, 1991): 46-58. *Telos,* no.90 (Winter 1991-92): 157-174.

804. **The Birth of Solidarity,** edited by A. Kemp-Welch. New York: St. Martin's Press, 1991. 281 p. ISBN: 0312060211. Includes bibliographical references (p.244-248) and index.

The first edition of this book covered "the negotiations between the Polish government and the Strike Committee at the Gdansk Shipyard in August 1980 which led to the birth of Solidarity." (preface) This second edition has been enlarged to cover the role of experts in Gdansk and the development of Solidarity from 1980-1989. The first part, a translation of the 1980 negotiations, has been slightly amplified as well.

805. Kurski, Jaroslaw, **Lech Walesa: Democrat or Dictator?,** translated by Peter Obst. Boulder: Westview Press, 1993. xx, 178 p. ISBN: 0813317894. Includes bibliographical references (p. 155) and index.

Kurski has written a critical account of Walesa's personal and political style. "Challenging conventional hagiography, Kurski criticizes Walesa's modus operandi, arguing that the leader manipulated or alienated many of his old supporters—including Tadeusz Mazowiecki, the man Walesa had championed as the first postwar non-Communist prime minister of Poland. While crediting Walesa's many accomplishments, the author paints a damning portrait of a man losing touch with both the political situation and the working people who brought him to power." (p. 171) The book also includes an essay by Lech Badkowski entitled "A Man of What Substance" that asks some hard questions of Walesa. In addition, the appendix contains a chronology, a glossary of terms, and list of suggested readings.

806. Lopinski, Maciej, Marcin Moskit, and Mariusz Wilk, **Konspira: Solidarity Underground,** translated by Jane Cave, afterword by Lawrence Weschler. Berkeley: University California Press, 1990. xix, 261 p. *Studies in Society and Culture in East Central Europe,* ISBN: 0520061314.

Written in 1984 this translation of a Polish publication is drawn from interviews with members of Solidarity. The conversations covered specific events and general problems and were held with Bogdan Borusewicz, Zbigniew Bujak, Wladislaw Frasyniuk, Aleksander Hall, Tadeusz Jedynak, Bogdan Lis and Eugeniusz Szumiejko. Besides the interviews, some interpretation by the authors, all Polish journalists from Gdansk, is provided. Reviews: *Foreign Affairs* 69, no.5 (Winter 1990/91): 202. *New York Times Book Review* (June 24, 1990): 12.

807. NSZZ "Solidarnosc," **The Solidarity Congress, 1981: The Great Debate,** edited, translated and introduced by George Sanford. New York: St. Martin's Press, 1990. x, 270 p. ISBN: 0312044909. Includes bibliographical references and index.

This is a translation of the transcript of the proceedings of the Solidarity Congress, held in September and early October of 1981. It covers the free-wheeling and far-ranging debates over their strategy, program, and organizational structures and procedures. It also contains, in appendices, speeches by various non-delegates, sermons, messages sent and received by the Congress, resolutions and declarations passed, committees elected by the Congress, and, elections to the National Council. It is a necessary primary source for studying Solidarity.

808. Ost, David, **Solidarity and the Politics of Anti-Politics: Opposition and Reform in Poland since 1968**. Philadelphia: Temple University Press, 1990. xiv, 279 p. *Labor and Social Change,* ISBN: 0877226555. Includes bibliographical references and index.

Ost was fortunate enough to be in Poland in 1980-81 when Solidarity was born. In this book, based on his dissertation, he begins by offering an explanation of the style of Solidarity, the politics of antipolitics. This is followed by a chapter on the history and significance of civil society, a concept central to the politics of Solidarity. Chapter three provides a historical sketch of the Polish opposition from 1944 to 1970, and four covers some of the "anti-political" texts of the 1920s, as a precursor to Solidarity. The heart of the book is concerned with an analysis of Solidarity's political practice from August 1980 to December 1981. Political developments in Poland following martial law, the international ramifications of the movement and an epilog on the relegalization of Solidarity in April 1989 complete his examination.

809. **Solidarity and Poland: Impacts East and West,** edited by Steve W. Reiquam with the Assistance of Cathie M. Lorenz. Washington, D.C.: Wilson Center Press, 1988. x, 60 p. ISBN: 0943875056.

These seven essays by noted experts on Poland and Eastern Europe were originally presented as papers at a conference held in February 1987 at the Wilson Center. Its purpose was to examine several aspects of the Polish Solidarity movement on the fifth anniversary of its suppression by imposition of martial law. The conference was convened to evaluate the successes, failures, and short-term legacy of Solidarity. Individual essays examine the regime's response to Solidarity, Poland and Solidarity today, Solidarity and the Soviet Union, Solidarity and U.S. foreign policy, the reaction of the left in Western Europe, and its legacy in Eastern Europe. A chronology of events from July 1, 1980 through July 1987 is included as an appendix.

810. Swidlicki, Andrzej, **The Political Trials in Poland, 1981-1986**. New York: Croom Helm, 1988. 426 p. ISBN: 0709944446. Includes index.

Political trials have been used as a mechanism of state terrorism in Soviet-style societies. The author here examines the trials that took place after the imposition of martial law in Poland. He first examines legal changes associated with the introduction of martial law: extraordinary legislation, internment procedures, the use of force and other special procedures used. He then looks at various trials held: those of the 1981 strikers, trials of internees, sedition trials, and the trials of underground Solidarity activists. The book also includes discussions of the basic freedom of the courtroom, the police, the prison system and personal freedoms under the old system. It is a general study of legality and martial law in Poland that is accessible to the general reader and scholar.

811. Wankel, Charles, **Anti-Communist Student Organizations and the Polish Renewal**. New York: St. Martin's Press, 1992. x, 288 p. ISBN: 0312055544. Includes bibliographical references (p. 251-269) and indexes.

Wankel examines the role of anti-communist student organizations in Poland and the role they played in the transition from communism to a democratic society. In particular the author focuses on NZS, Poland's most notable student movement. "Students were found to play a key role in the events leading to the Polish renewal or odnowa. Workers' and students' organizations came to work together towards democracy and justice. Provocations against the NZS seemed crafted to provoke Solidarity, and were correctly viewed by August 1980 as a foreshadowing of the fate of Solidarity itself." (p. 187) Two appendices include a glossary and a description of his methodology.

812. Weber, Wolfgang, **Solidarity in Poland, 1980-1981 and the Perspective of Political Revolution,** translated from the German by Bill Brust. Detroit: Labor Publications, 1989. xiii, 157 p. ISBN: 0929087305. Translation of: Solidarnosc 1980-1981 und die Perspektive der politischen Revolution. Includes bibliographical references and index.

Weber describes and analyzes the history of Solidarity from 1980-1981. Individual chapters cover historical and social origins of struggle, the history and significance of the struggle for an independent trade union, the proclamation of martial law, Jacek Kuron's "open letter to the Party" and the perspectives of the KOR, the betrayal of the working class by the Pabloites, and the betrayal of the political revolution by the renegades Healy, Barda, and

Slaughter. Appendices contain the 21 demands of Gdansk and suggestions for further reading.

813. Zuzowski, Robert, **Political Dissent and Opposition in Poland: The Workers' Defense Committee "KOR."** Westport, Conn.: Praeger, 1992. 293 p. ISBN: 0275941388. Includes bibliographical references (p. 271-280) and index.

KOR (The Workers' Defense Committee) was formed in Poland in 1976 by several intellectuals as a dissident group. It existed until 1981 when Solidarity was formed. Zuzowski's book is about the ideas and activities of this group, its interaction with the Roman Catholic Church, its relations with other dissident organizations, and the significance of KOR. It also includes appendices listing KOR members and an interview with Wlodzimierz Schilling-Siengalewicz, former chairperson of the Seamen's and Deep-Sea Fisherman's Trade Union.

NATIONAL MINORITIES

814. Bartoszewski, Wladyslaw, **The Warsaw Ghetto: A Christian's Testimony,** foreword by Stanislaw Lem. Boston: Beacon Press, 1988. ISBN: 0807056022. Translation of: Das Warschauer Ghetto, wie es wirklich war. Includes index.

Bartoszewski, a Roman Catholic, was one of the few non-Jews who came to the aid of the Jews imprisoned in the Warsaw ghetto. His narrative recounts his activities as a liaison between the Polish underground and the Jewish leadership in the Warsaw ghetto. The book was originally published in German.

815. **The Jews in Warsaw: A History,** edited by Wladyslaw T. Bartoszewski and Antony Polonsky. Oxford, UK: Blackwell, 1991. viii, 392 p. ISBN: 1557862133. Includes bibliographical references and index.

An important chapter in Jewish history is covered by the fifteen essays in this volume. They chronologically survey the history of the Jewish population that was, at one time, so much a part of Warsaw's life. A section on historiography is included.

816. Beller, Ilex, **Life in the Shtetl: Scenes and Recollections 80 Paintings,** translated by Alastair Douglas Pannell. New York: Holms and Meier, 1986. 140 p. ISBN: 0841910952. Translation of: La vie du shtetl. Includes index.

"Beller paints ordinary people working in their shops, studying the Torah and Talmud, celebrating Jewish holidays—and he transforms these people into figures of universal appeal and significance. Accompanying the reproductions are selected poems and prose pieces and Beller's illuminating commentary." (jacket)

817. Bielawski, Shraga Feivel, **The Last Jew from Wegrow: The Memoirs of a Survivor of the Step-by-Step Genocide in Poland,** edited and rewritten by Louis W. Liebovich. New York: Praeger, 1991. x, 165 p. ISBN: 0275938964.

This is a graphic and well-written personal narrative by the author of his experiences in Wegrow Poland from 1939 to 1945.

818. Blady Szwajger, Adina, **I Remember Nothing More: The Warsaw Children's Hospital and the Jewish Resistance,** translated from the Polish by Tasja Darowska and Danusia Stok. London: Collins Harvill, 1990. xv, 184 p. ISBN: 0002720582. Includes bibliographical references (p. 183-184).

The author was a doctor at the Bersohn and Bauman hospital in Warsaw during the war. Her memoir chronicles her life there and her treatment of diseased and dying children who were victims of German genocide.

819. Browning, Christopher R., **Ordinary Men: Reserve Police Battalion 101 and the Final Solution in Poland**. 1st ed. New York: HarperCollins, 1992. xxii, 231 p. ISBN: 0060190132. Includes bibliographical references (p. 193-218) and index.

Browning, basing his story on judicial transcripts and testimony, describes the actions of Reserve Police Battalion 101, a unit of the Order Police, as they became the tool for the final solution in Poland. The focus of his narrative is the spring of 1942 to the spring of 1943, when the majority of Polish Jews were exterminated.

820. **Jews in Eastern Poland and the USSR, 1939-46,** edited by Norman Davies and Antony Polonsky. New York: St. Martin's Press, 1991. xiv, 426 p. ISBN: 0312062001. Includes bibliographical references and index.

The articles in this volume were commissioned "in order to provide a fuller picture of the complex problems raised by the position of the Jews in Eastern Poland, as well as those deported from Poland to the USSR in the period of 1939 to 1946." (p. ix)

821. Doblin, Alfred, **Journey to Poland,** translated by Joachim Neugroschel, edited by Heinz Graber. New York: Paragon, 1991. xxviii, 274 p. *European Sources*, ISBN: 1557782679. Translation of: Reise in Polen. Includes bibliographical references.

This book was first published in German in 1925. Doblin, a physician from Berlin, took a two month trip to Poland in the autumn of 1924. His primary interest was the Jew in Poland and other ethnic relations, as well as the political and social conditions of that country. In addition to his narration, the editor has supplied a map, bibliography and notes.

822. Eisenbach, Artur, **The Emancipation of the Jews in Poland, 1780-1870,** edited by Antony Polonsky, translated by Janina Dorosz. Oxford, UK: B. Blackwell, 1991. xlix, 632 p. *Jewish Society and Culture*, ISBN: 0631178023. Includes bibliographical references (p. 587-594) and index.

"The aim of this book is to set out the development and character of the civic emancipation of the Jews in the Polish territories under the three partitioning powers. [He also intends] to show the changes which took place in the various partitions affecting the Jews' mobility, their social and political position and their cultural level and prestige." (p.1)

823. Engel, David, **Facing a Holocaust: The Polish Government-in-Exile and the Jews, 1943-1945**. Chapel Hill: University of North Carolina Press, 1993. x, 317 p. ISBN: 0807820695. Includes bibliographical references (p. 295-304) and index.

This book is "an examination of the thoughts and actions of the political Polish government-in-exile on matters of primary concern to Jewish citizens of Poland from the end of 1942 until the conclusion of the European chapter of the Second World War in May 1945. ...Like its predecessor, *In the Shadow of Auschwitz*, ...the present study endeavors, ...to uncover the considerations...that influenced Polish policymakers in formulating their responses to those Jewish citizens' expressed needs at a time when both parties...faced the challenge of life or death." (p. 1)

824. **In the Shadow of Auschwitz: The Polish Government in Exile and the Jews, 1939-1942**. Chapel Hill: University of North Carolina Press, 1987. xii, 338 p. ISBN: 0807817376. Includes bibliography (p. 307-319) and index.

The debate about the role of the Poles in the Holocaust has prompted this author to reexamine the question from a different perspective. "The study that follows examines the thinking on Jewish related matters of that segment of the Polish leadership which conducted the struggle for the renewal of Poland's independence within its prewar borders from a position of exile outside the occupied homeland." (p. 7) The book is arranged chronologically and includes a bibliography.

825. Georg, Willy, **In the Warsaw Ghetto: Summer 1941,** photographs by Willy Georg; with passages from Warsaw Ghetto diaries compiled and with an afterword by Rafael F. Scharf. 1st ed. New York: Aperture, 1993. 111 p. ISBN: 0893815268.

Georg was a photographer who was in the German army. In 1941 he was given permission by his superiors to go into the Warsaw Ghetto and take pictures. The result is this book. The afterword by Rafael Scharf gives background information about the ghetto and the fate of the residents there.

826. Hertz, Aleksander, **The Jews in Polish Culture,** translated by Richard Lourie, with a foreword by Czeslaw Milosz. Evanston, IL: Northwestern University Press, 1988. ISBN: 0810107589. Translation of: Zydzi w kulturze polskiej. Includes index.

This twenty-five-year-old work appears here in English for the first time. The author, a renowned Polish scholar, attempts to discern the degree to which Polish and Jewish cultures have interacted and affected one another. The original edition was intended for a Polish or Polish-Jewish audience, with numerous references to historic dates or events. The present edition has been supplied with footnotes to give the reader background where necessary. The book is topically arranged, covering such subjects as the specifics of cultural interaction between Jews and Poles, the role of Jews in Polish society, the basis for the belief that Jews were alien. Hertz discusses the Jews as a caste in the sociological sense but it is this concept that provides a framework for his work. The work still serves as a starting point for studies of Jews in European society and the survival of anti-Semitism. Reviews: *Journal of Church and State* 31, no.3 (Autumn 1989): 566-567. *Orbis* 33, no.3 (Summer 1989): 457-58.

827. Huberband, Shimon, **Kiddush Hashem: Jewish Religious and Cultural Life in Poland During the Holocaust,** translated by David E. Fishman, edited by Jeffrey S. Gurock, Robert S. Hirt. Hoboken, NJ: Ktav Publishing House, 1987. xxxvii, 474 p. *Heritage of Modern European Jewry*, ISBN: 0881251186. Includes index.

This book consists of personal accounts of events in the Polish Ghettos during the Holocaust. The author sought to preserve for posterity an account of the terrible events of those years. This book collects reports of acts of Kiddush Hashem—voluntary self-sacrifice for the sake of an idea. Rabbi Huberband was a young rabbi who devoted himself to maintaining the archive of the Jewish Ghetto until his death at Treblinka in 1942. This work was originally published in Hebrew in 1969. The English language edition was commissioned in 1982. The book is divided into four parts. Section I is comprised of autobiographical material on Rabbi Huberband. Sections II and III contain accounts of daily life in the Warsaw Ghetto and, more generally, Jewish religious life in Nazi occupied areas. Section IV chronicles "the destruction of East European Jewry."

828. Hundert, Gershon David, **The Jews in a Polish Private Town: The Case of Opatow in the Eighteenth Century**. Baltimore: Johns Hopkins University Press, 1992. xvi, 242 p. *Johns Hopkins Jewish Studies*, ISBN: 0801842735. Includes bibliographical references and index.

This study "presents an analytical and, where possible, comparative approach to the social, economic, and political history of the Jews in [Opatow]. More than half of the Jews alive in the world in the 18th century lived in small private towns like Opatow. Because the life of Jews in Opatow has been so richly documented, the author chose Opatow as his focus. The volume also contains two appendices: 1) The Privilege of the Jewish Community of Opatow (document); and 2) measures, weights, and money (tables).

829. Irwin-Zarecka, Iwona, **Neutralizing Memory: The Jew in Contemporary Poland**. New Brunswick, N.J.: Transaction, 1989. ISBN: 0887382274. Includes bibliography and index.

An analysis of "what it means to remember the Jews of Poland today." The author is concerned with what Polish children are being taught about the Jews of that country and why. The study examines the importance attributed to the past in politics, the place of Jews in Poland's past, and discussions of Jews in Polish memory based on interviews.

830. **Hippocrene Insider's Guide to Poland's Jewish Heritage**, Joram Kagan. New York: Hippocrene Books, 1992. 208 p. ISBN: 0870529919. Includes index and bibliography (p. 202-204).

"This guide includes almost 100 maps and photographs showing the location of points of Jewish interest throughout Poland. It offers information on the present organizational and religious structure of the tiny Jewish community, and gives thorough and detailed lists of synagogues, cemeteries and other places of Jewish heritage. The index of towns includes well over 250 communities of significant interest to Jews today." (back cover)

831. Levi, Primo, **Moments of Reprieve,** translated from the Italian by Ruth Feldman. New York: Summit Books, 1986. 172 p. ISBN: 0671605356.

Levi has published two non-fictional accounts of his experiences in Auschwitz and elsewhere during World War II. Collected here are stories based on actual episodes of those times, most of which have been previously published in Italian.

832. **Out of the Inferno: Poles Remember the Holocaust,** edited by Richard C. Lukas. Lexington: University Press of Kentucky, 1989. 201 p. ISBN: 0813116929. Includes bibliographical references (p. 192-193) and index.

This volume contains fifty-nine personal accounts of Poland under German occupation. They were written by Poles, both Christian and Jewish, and chronicle the savage treatment of Poles by Hitler. They also shed some light on what the compiler believes to be the poorly understood Polish-Jewish relations during the war.

833. Pinchuk, Ben-Cion, **Shtetl Jews under the Soviet Rule: Eastern Poland on the Eve of the Holocaust**. Cambridge, Mass.: B. Blackwell, 1990. 186 p. *Jewish Society and Culture*, ISBN: 0631174699. Includes bibliographical references (p. 172-178) and index.

This book "is an attempt to describe the history of the Jewish community in the Polish provinces annexed by the USSR in the autumn of 1939." (foreword) The area examined contained one of the largest pre-Holocaust Jewish communities in Europe. Individual chapters focus on different aspects of the Shtetl and its conflict with Soviet rule.

834. Pinkus, Oscar, **The House of Ashes**, rev. ed. New York: Union College Press, 1990. 272 p. ISBN: 0912712241 (pbk); 0912756233 (cloth).

This is a personal memoir of a Jewish Pole from Eastern Poland from September 1, 1939 to the end of the war.

835. Pogonowski, Iwo, **Jews in Poland: A Documentary History: The Rise of Jews as a Nation from Congressus Judaicus in Poland to the Knesset in Israel,** by Iwo Cyprian Pogonowski. New York: Hippocrene Books, 1993. 402 p. ISBN: 0781801163. Includes bibliographical references (p. 164-181) and index.

This documentary history of the life of Jews in Poland brings together an enormous range of material from the "1264 Statute on Jewish Liberties in Poland" to numerous documents on the annihilation of the Jewish population in Poland during World War II. The volume includes many illustrations and an atlas of Jewish history in Poland. Explanatory texts are included with most of the translations. This is a valuable documentary source for anyone interested in Jewish life in Poland.

836. **'My Brother's Keeper?': Recent Debates on the Holocaust,** edited by Antony Polonsky. London; New York: Routledge for Institute for Polish-Jewish Studies, 1990. 242 p. ISBN: 0415042321. Includes bibliographical references and index.

These essays were all part of a national debate on the Polish Jews during the Holocaust and the moral questions arising from that interaction.

837. Salsitz, Norman, **A Jewish Boyhood in Poland: Remembering Kolbuszowa,** Norman Salsitz as told to Richard Skolnik. 1st ed. Syracuse, NY: Syracuse University Press, 1992. xv, 295 p. ISBN: 0815602626.

This is the story of Jewish life in Poland before World War II as it is remembered by author Norman Salsitz. He was born in the village of Kolbuszowa in 1920 to a prosperous Jewish family. Salsitz recounts a way of life that disappeared with the Holocaust.

838. Szurek, Alexander, **The Shattered Dream,** translated from the Polish by Jacques and Hilda Grunblatt. New York: Columbia University Press, 1989. xiii, 382 p. *East European Monographs, no. 263,* ISBN: 0880331607.

Szurek, a Polish communist, participated in the International Brigades in Republican Spain in the late 1930s. These memoirs cover events from that period, through his internment in a German concentration camp during the war and back in Poland up to 1968-1969, when a fierce Polish anti-Semitic campaign drove him from his homeland. These memoirs, originally written in Polish, were assembled and translated after the author's death in 1978.

839. Werner, Harold, **Fighting Back: A Memoir of Jewish Resistance in World War II;** with a foreword by Martin Gilbert. New York: Columbia University Press, 1992. xxvi, 253 p. ISBN: 023107882X.

Werner was part of a large Jewish fighting force that battled the Germans in Eastern Poland during World War II. In addition to his wartime exploits, Werner also describes "the prewar life of Polish Jewry, when poverty and uncertainty were the daily accompaniments for so many. We see city life and village life, a world in which Jews, however much they were surrounded by antagonistic neighbors, built for themselves a vibrant and exhilarating existence, and sought to better themselves." (p. xiii)

CRASH COURSE IN CAPITALISM

840. **The Polish Road From Socialism: The Economics, Sociology, and Politics of Transition,** edited by Walter Connor and Piotr Ploszajski with Alex Inkeles and Wlodzimierz Wesolowski. Armonk, N.Y.: M.E. Sharpe, 1992. 319 p. ISBN: 0873328868. Includes bibliographical references and index.

The essays in this volume were written by both Polish and American scholars to give some perspective on the accelerating change in Polish politics, society, and the economy. The essays are divided into four parts. Part one covers economic change, privatization, resource allocation and competitiveness. Part two looks at social change, focusing on the transformation of the social order, the bureaucracy, public opinion, and attitudes on everyday life. Part three covers political change, the emerging social and political structure, elections, and political institutions. Part four looks at ideology, the legacy of real socialism, group interests, the search for a new utopia, and class stratification and democracy.

841. **Transforming Economic Systems: The Case of Poland,** edited by Manfred Kremer, Marion Weber; with the cooperation of Feliks Gradalski. Heidelberg:

Physica-Verlag, 1992. xvii, 179 p. *Contributions to Economics*, ISBN: 3790805858. Includes bibliographical references.
This collection of essays differs from many others in that all the essays deal with theoretical rather than existing economic transformations. Each essay is self-contained and all were written by Polish economists. They cover a range of topics from changes in Polish electoral law to privatization. The volume is one in the series Contributions to Economics.

ARTS AND CULTURE

842. Czekanowska-Kuklinska, Anna, **Polish Folk Music: Slavonic Heritage, Polish Tradition, Contemporary Trends**. New York: Cambridge University Press, 1990. xii, 226 p. *Cambridge Studies in Ethnomusicology*, ISBN: 0521300908. Includes bibliographical references (p.216-222) and index.

Anna Czekanowska sees contemporary Poland as a culture characterized by strong national features and an intense desire to maintain its traditions. In this study of Polish folk music, Czekanowska uses the study of music as a vehicle to analyze the more basic processes involved in culture change. "The man objective of this study is to present a vision of Polish folk music as it has developed often along different streams in which past and present coexist side by side. It is also a vision of culture that has been created against a background of varied historical, social and religious traditions while being integrated and transformed into a unique quality which must be identified as being clearly Polish." (p. xii) The book's four sections present an introduction discussing basic concepts and Poland's diversity; a section on topics and trends covering Poland's place in the Slavonic world; Polish tradition and the transformation of Polish culture and music; an analysis and description of Polish folk music; and a discussion of Polish and non-Polish music in Poland. A discography as well as an extensive bibliography are included. This volume is one in the Cambridge Studies in Ethnomusicology.

843. **The Polish Renaissance in Its European Context,** edited by Samuel Fiszman, foreword by Czeslaw Milosz. Bloomington: Indiana University Press, 1988. xxviii, 479 p. ISBN: 0253346274. Includes bibliographical references.

The papers that appear here were originally presented at a conference held at Indiana University in 1982 to commemorate the birth and death of Jan Kochanowski. The papers are arranged in six parts: historical and cultural aspects of the Renaissance in Poland; religion and law in Renaissance Poland; Renaissance Poland and other cultures; art and architecture in Renaissance Poland; and Jan Kochanowski.

844. Flam, Gila, **Singing for Survival: Songs of the Lodz Ghetto, 1940-45**. Urbana: University of Illinois Press, 1992. xv, 207 p. ISBN: 0252018176. Includes bibliographical references and index.

Flam attempts to understand the role of singing in the Lodz, Poland ghetto during the Holocaust. After an introductory chapter that sets the historical context of the Lodz Ghetto and its culture, she devotes separate chapters to Chaim Rumkowski and his songs, Yaakov and the street songs, domestic songs, other contexts for singing, and the role of such songs in the contemporary context, that of commemoration ceremonies. A glossary of terms is included.

845. Heine, Marc E., **Poland**. New York: Hippocrene Books, 1987. 182 p. ISBN: 0870523805. Includes index.

This travel guide of Poland is written by a Westerner for Westerners. The size of the country has forced the author to be selective: "I have concentrated largely on those parts of Poland which a foreign traveler is most likely to visit namely the south-east (i.e. the Warsaw-Lublin-Cracow triangle), which for various historical reasons is particularly rich in fine buildings." (p. vi) The author includes only limited information on hotels, restaurants, passports, etc.

846. **Polish Music Literature (1515-1990): A Selected Annotated Bibliography,** compiled by Kornel Michalowski and revised with additions by Gillian Olechno-Huszcza. Los Angeles: University of Southern California, Friends of Polish Music, 1991. 243 p. *Polish Music History Series, 0741-9945, 4*, ISBN: 0916545008; 0916545040. Includes index.

"The bibliography contains selected books, pamphlets and other separate publications, periodicals, yearbooks, and collective works written by Polish authors and published in Poland or abroad in the Polish language. Some important foreign-language books on Polish music, mainly published abroad after 1975, are included. The subject matter and theme of the bibliography includes all problems of music history, theory and practice, and selected issues in all aspects of Polish musical life and culture." (p. 13)

847. Norseng, Mary Kay, **Dagny: Dagny Juel Przybyszewska, the Woman and the Myth.** Seattle: University of Washington Press, 1991. xix, 219 p. ISBN: 0295969997. Includes bibliography (p.203-209) and index.

A biography of Dagny Juel Przybyszewska, a woman of both the establishment and avant-garde, who lived in Norway and Poland.

848. Osinski, Zbigniew, **Grotowski and His Laboratory,** translated and abridged by Lillian Vallee and Robert Findlay. New York, N.Y.: PAJ Publications, 1986. 185 p. ISBN: 0933826893; 0933826907 (pbk).

This translation is only a part of the original work which appeared in Polish in 1980. That work, entitled *Grotowski i Jego Laboratorium*, contained one part that was a chronological calendar of Grotowski's life and a second part which included essays on his work. The first part has been translated for this publication. "It covers Gratowski's early schooling and influences, his early theatrical experiences, his rise to prominence as a youthful anti-Stalinist political figure in the mid-1950s, and his founding in Opole in 1959 (with critic Ludwik Flaszen) of the theatre group that eventually was to become the world-famous Teatr Laboratorium (or, as it has been traditionally referred to in English, the Polish Laboratory Theatre)." (p. 7) An "afterword" by Robert Findlay and an appendix listing the personnel of the laboratory theatre from 1959 to 1977 are included.

849. Schauss, H. Joachim, **Contemporary Polish Folk Artists**. New York: Hippocrene Books, 1987. 204 p. ISBN: 0870522957.

Twenty-five Polish folk artists are profiled in this work. The author is not an art expert or ethnographer, and makes no claim that these are the most important or finest artists in the genre in Poland. Rather the author wishes to give the reader a sense of the great variety in Polish folk art. Each section is devoted to one artist. Each section includes the artist's own description of his work and his sense of his art, photographs of the artist's work and of the artist. All of the folk artists included in this work have been recipients of awards for their work.

850. Segel, Harold B., **Renaissance Culture in Poland: The Rise of Humanism, 1470-1543**. Ithaca, NY: Cornell University Press, 1989. x, 285 p. ISBN: 0801422868. Includes index and bibliography (p. 263-277).

Segel's purpose is to present the "first comprehensive view of Renaissance humanism in Poland." (p. 9) His ten chapters generally focus on specific individuals and their role in the development of the Renaissance in Poland. Among the individuals studied are Gregory of Sanok, Filippo Buonaccovsi, Copernicus, Pope Leo X, Dantiscus, Clemens Ianicius, Jan Kochanowski and Andrzej Krzycki.

851. Simons, Peter, **Philosophy and Logic in Central Europe From Bolzano to Tarki: Selected Essays**. Dordrecht: Kluwer Academic Publishers, 1992. xiv, 441 p. *Niihoff International Philosophy Series, v. 45*, ISBN: 0792316215. Includes bibliographical references (p. 395-428) and indexes.

"This book views the history of philosophy and logic from 1837 to 1939 from the perspective of the cradle of modern exact philosophy—Central Europe. In a series of case studies, it illuminates the developments in this region, most notably in Austria and Poland, examining thinkers such as Bolzano, Brentano, Meiwong, Husserl, Twardowski, Lesniewski, and Tarski, as well as the logicians like Frege and Russell with whom they bore a close resemblance." (back cover) The essays are framed in a biographical and historical structure and should be of interest to students of Polish culture and politics as well as philosophy. However, the language is often that of formal logic and does require a basic knowledge of the terminology.

852. Smialek, William, **Polish Music: A Research and Information Guide**. New York: Garland Pub., 1989. 260 p. *Music Research and Information Guides, vol. 11, Garland Reference Library of the Humanities, vol. 1093*, ISBN: 0824046145. Includes discography (p. 181-222) and index.

This partially annotated guide to Polish music contains 989 items; 600 of these are annotated citations of books, articles, dissertations and bibliography. In addition to this discography, the book is made up of eight other sections: reference and research materials, history, Polish art Music, ethnomusicology, instruments and voice, pedagogy, music and related disciplines, music and liturgy, and editions of Polish music. Many of the citations are in Polish and other European languages. Abstracts are in English.

Chapter 8
ROMANIA

GENERAL REFERENCE WORKS

853. **Romania, a Country Study**, Federal Research Division, Library of Congress, edited by Ronald D. Bachman. Washington, D.C.: Headquarters, Dept. of the Army, 1991. xxxvi, 356 p. *DA Pam, 550-160, Area handbook Series.* Includes bibliographical references (p. 317-335) and index.

This reference handbook, written by a team of social scientists, describes and analyzes the history, society, economy, politics, and national security of Romania. It also contains a statistical appendix and glossary of frequently used terms. The introduction chronicles the tumultuous events of Ceausescu's fall from power and the political and economic chaos that ensued.

854. Brinkle, Lydle, **Hippocrene Companion Guide to Romania**. New York: Hippocrene Books, 1990. 211 p. ISBN: 0870526340. Includes index.

This guide begins with an introduction to the geographical setting, people, history, and folklore of Romania. Separate chapters are then devoted to Bucharest, major cities and historic sites of Wallachia and Dobruja, of Transylvania, of Moldavia, the monasteries of Bukovina, the Danube River and delta region, health resorts and spas. A concluding chapter covers practical information.

HISTORY

855. Berthelot, Henri Mathias, **General Henri Berthelot and Romania: Memoires et Correspondence 1916-1919,** edited with a biographical introduction by Glenn E. Torrey. New York: Distributed by Columbia University Press, 1987. xlv, 247 p. *East European Monographs, no. 319*, ISBN: 0880331151. Includes bibliography (p. xl-xlv).

General Henri Mathias Berthelot describes his two missions to Romania, October, 1916-May, 1918 and October, 1918-May, 1919, in his extensive memoirs. That portion of his memoirs published here is supplemented with his correspondence to his sister-in-law and nephew to add detail to his sometimes cryptic descriptions. What emerges is of importance "to those interested in Romanian history, to the history of the war on the Eastern Front, in the story of allied intervention in Russia or in the origin of the Romanian occupation of Hungary." (pp v-vi) The volume includes a biographical introduction providing the reader with the details of the general's life and career, a biographical index and list of French personnel on the mission to Romania.

856. Castellan, Georges, **A History of the Romanians,** translated from the French by Nicholas Bradley. New York: Columbia University Press, 1989. 266 p. *East European Monographs, no. 257*, ISBN: 0880331542.

The book covers Romania's historical development from earliest times to the 1960s. Arranged chronologically, the study opens with a discussion of historiography and sources. No index or bibliography is included.

857. Codrescu, Andrei, **The Hole in the Flag: A Romanian Exile's Story of Return and Revolution.** 1st ed. New York: W. Morrow, 1991. 249 p. ISBN: 0688088058. Includes index.

This is a personal narrative of Codrescu's return to Romania after 25 years of exile. The author traveled the country, finding old friends and making new ones during his lengthy visit. Reviews: *New York Book Review* (June 30, 1991): 16. *Freedom Review* 22, no.6 (November-December 1991): 48-49. *Orbis* 35, no.4 (Fall 1991): 623.

858. Fischer-Galati, Stephen A., **Twentieth Century Rumania.** New York: Columbia University Press, 1991. x, 246 p. ISBN: 023107462X (acid-free paper); 0231074638 (pbk). Includes bibliographical references (p. 221-237) and index.

A revised and expanded version of the author's original work published in 1970. The author has included a section on the Ceausescu Regime and its aftermath. He remains optimistic about the future of Romania but more guardedly so than in the past. As with the original edition, this book is largely a political history of Romania through the twentieth century. The "bibliographical notes" provide the reader with English-language sources on Romania.

859. Florescu, Radu, and Raymond T. McNally, **Dracula, Prince of Many Faces: His Life and His Times**. Boston: Little, Brown, 1989. xxiii, 261 ISBN: 0316286559.

This book is the culmination of twenty years of research and three books about Dracula by both authors. "It represents the first comprehensive attempt at putting the life story of Dracula into the broad context of fifteenth century European history in the century of the Renaissance." (p. xvii) After tracing the ruler's life, the authors "follow the growth of the Dracula legend after his death." In a concluding chapter they answer the question "Who was the real Dracula? "

860. Georgescu, Vlad, **The Romanians: A History,** edited by Malei Calinescu, translated by Alexandra Bley-Vroman. Columbus: Ohio State University Press, 1991. xiv, 357 p. *Romanian Literature and Thought in Translation Series.* Includes bibliographical references (p. 325-343) and index.

This is a translation of Georgescu's *Istoria Romanilor,* first published in 1984. The author was in the process of updating the book at the time of his death in 1988. The editors have added an essay by the author entitled "Romania in the 1980s" and an epilogue that describes the events of the Romanian revolution of 1989 and collapse of the communist regime. The author believed in the role of personality in history, indeed he used this as his methodology in this work. This work covers Romanian history from earliest times to 1989. Aside from R. R. Seton-Watson's 1934 history of Romania, this is the only English language publication providing the reader a general history, uncensored. An extensive bibliographical essay is included in the volume.

861. Ioanid, Radu, **The Sword of the Archangel: Fascist Ideology in Romania,** translated by Peter Heinegg. New York: Columbia University Press, 1990. 323 p. *East European Monographs, no. 292,* ISBN: 0880331895.

This study of Romanian fascism is one in the series of East European Monographs. It examines the genesis and trends of Romanian fascism. The book is topically arranged into chapters. Chapter one is an overview of the historiography of Romanian fascism. Chapter two focuses on the development of fascist ideology in Romania touching on socio-economic and political factors leading to fascism. Chapter three turns to the practical means used to spread fascist propaganda. The final chapter looks at those characteristics unique to

Romanian fascism. A chronology of events from 1877 to 1956 is provided along with numerous photographs.

862. Jagendorf, Siegfried, **Jagendorf's Foundry: Memoir of the Romanian Holocaust, 1941-44,** introduction and commentaries by Aron Hirt-Manheimer, foreword by Elie Wiesel. New York: Harper Collins Publishers, 1991. xxix, 209 p. ISBN: 006016106X. Includes bibliographical references (p. 201-202) and index.

This is the story of the man responsible for "the miracle of Moghileu." Siegfried Jagendorf restored a foundry and spare parts factory and in so doing, saved the lives of some 10,000 Romanian Jews. But many questions have been raised about this so called "Miracle" and its role in the Holocaust. Some have claimed that the Jagendorf workforce was productive for a Nazi Government and was, therefore, collaborating with the enemy. Some claim Jagendorf oppressed his own people. The memoir is supplemented with commentaries by Aron Hirt-Manheimer, who attempts to clarify some of the issues included. "Jagendorf portrayed himself as a stern but sympathetic leader who saved his people by outmaneuvering Romanian officials and by converting a bewildered mob into a productive labor force." (p. xiii) Hirt-Manheimer questions this contention but seeks to present a more objective picture of events. Reviews: *Midstream* 37, no.5 (June-July 1991): 42-43. *Holocaust and Genocide Studies* 6, no.4 (1991): 424-426.

863. Lehrer, Milton G., **Transylvania, History and Reality,** edited and with a foreword by David Martin. Silver Spring, Md.: Bartleby Press, 1986. xii, 307 p. ISBN: 0910155046. Translation of: Ardealul, pamint romanesc. Includes bibliography (p. 305-306).

This book was originally written in 1944 by Lehrer and is here edited and annotated by Martin. It intends to explore the history of Transylvania and the historical disputes by Romanians and Hungarians about that territory.

864. Mehedinti, Simion, **What Is Transylvania?** Miami Beach, Fla.: Romanian Historical Studies, 1986. 124 p. *Romanian Historical Studies, 23*, ISBN: 093701902X (hard); 0937019038 (pbk). Translation of: Ce este Transilvania. Includes bibliographical references.

This book is one in a series on the history of Romania. The works in the series attempt to present the English-speaking reader with brief but accurate historical studies of Romania. "This book, written by a distinguished Professor of Geography at the University of Bucharest, offers an overview of the geographic layout and the historical circumstances of the territory occupied by the Romanians which is supported by irrefutable evidence." (p. i) The book's sections discuss Transylvania as the mountainous center of Romania; its climate, its hydrography, ethnography, linguistic and economic characteristics; its history and ethnographic and geopolitical role in the area. The editors of the series include works that argue for a maintenance of modern borders against those who wish a return to Pre-World War I frontiers.

865. **The United States and Romania: American-Romanian Relations in the Twentieth Century,** edited by Paul D. Quinlan. Woodland Hills, Calif.: Sovthian Books, 1988. 180 p. *ARA-American-Romanian Academy of Arts and Sciences-Academia Romano-Americana de Stiinte si Arte, Vol. 6*, ISBN: 0912131071. Includes bibliographies.

This collection of essays is one of the first studies of American-Romanian relations in the twentieth century. Most of the contributions are from historians on a range of subjects and numerous periods such as Romania's role in the development of the Cold War, changes in America's perception of Romania in the post-war years, Romanian Americans and Romania in the Roosevelt Era. A few essays were written by diplomats.

866. Ratesh, Nestor, **Romania: The Entangled Revolution,** foreword by Edward N. Luttwak. New York: Praeger, 1991. xxiv, 179 p. *Washington Papers, 0278-937x, 152*, ISBN: 0275941442; 0275941450. Includes bibliographical references (p. 158-171) and index.

"This volume offers a full documentary account of the December 1989 revolution that toppled the Communist dictatorship of Nicolae Ceausescu in Romania the author explores the economic, social, and human disaster that led to the uprising and then chronicles the seven days of the revolution from its inception in the Western city of Timosoara to its climax in Bucharest in December 22, 1989, when the dictator fled the city." (p. xxiii)

867. Saiu, Liliana, **The Great Powers and Rumania, 1944-1946: A Study of the Early Cold War Era**. Boulder: East European Monographs, 1992. xiii, 290 p. *East European Monographs; no. 335*, ISBN: 0880332328. Includes bibliographical references (p. 271-282) and index.

In this work Liliana Saiu examines the policy of each of the great powers toward Rumania from 1944 to 1946. Saiu is interested in those elements of foreign policy that may have affected Soviet goals in the region. "By observing the activities, aspirations, and potentialities of Rumanian political forces, it also aims at evaluating whether and to what extent, the political situation in Rumania may have influenced the Soviet Union's policy, and what alternatives the Rumanian historical parties could have offered to the Allies." (p. ix) The author's main goal is to determine the importances of the confrontation over Romania as a cause of the Cold War. The book is arranged chronologically.

868. Seisanu, Romulus, **Rumania**. Miami Beach, Fla.: Romanian Historical Studies, 1987. 116 p. *Romanian Historical Studies, 25*, ISBN: 0937019062; 0937019070 (pbk). Includes bibliographical references and index.

This brief history of Romania covers the period from its origins in the Dorian people through the end of World War I and the Treaty of Trianon.

869. Stefanescu-Draganesti, Virgiliu, **Romanian Continuity in Roman Dacia: Linguistic Evidence**. Miami Beach Fla.: Romanian Historical Studies, 1986. 89 p. *Romanian Historical Studies, 24*, ISBN: 0937019046; 0937019054. Includes bibliographical references.

Linguistic evidence can be used to fill the gaps in the historical record. In this work Stefanescu-Draganesti attempts to do just this looking at borrowings in Gothic and its significance for the Romanians, the historical significance of the words "Vacah," "Ruman," and "Ardeal," and the significance of Romanian religious terminology borrowed by the Hungarians before the year 1001. The author hopes to raise some basic issues and questions which can be developed in later research.

870. Tokes, Laszlo, **The Fall of Tyrants: The Incredible Story of One Pastor's Witness, the People of Romania, and the Overthrow of Ceausescu**, Laszlo Tokes with David Porter. Wheaton, Ill: Crossway Books, 1990. xiv, 226 p. ISBN: 0891076247.

This autobiography of the priest Laszlo Tokes is a part of the study of the historic changes that overtook the Romanian Government and Nicolae Ceausescu. Tokes defied the Romanian government by refusing to leave his church when the government tried to evict him.

871. Watts, Larry, **Romanian Cassandra: Ion Antonescu and the Struggle for Reform, 1916-1941**. New York: Columbia University Press, 1993. x, 390 p. ISBN: 0880332557. Includes bibliographical references.

"This is the first work to examine Antonescu's role in contemporary history before September 1940, an examination that is absolutely necessary for understanding Antonescu's later attitudes toward the collaboration with Germany, toward the Western Alliance, and toward the Holocaust." (p. 2) Individual chapters cover Antonescu as a military figure, the General Staff, 1933-1934, the rise and fall of the Iron Guard, the collapse of Romania, 1939-1940, the National Legionary State, and an epilogue, 1941-1944.

GOVERNMENT, POLITICS AND TRADE

872. Behr, Edward, **Kiss the Hand You Cannot Bite: The Rise and Fall of the Ceausescus**. New York: Villard Books, 1991. xxiii, 293 p. ISBN: 0679401288. Includes bibliographical references (p. 279-282) and index.

Behr, a correspondent for *Newsweek*, has written a detailed account of the rise and fall of the Ceausescus. In it he explores their private lives and political careers. The author has interviewed people close to Ceausescu—not only party workers and army colleagues, but also cooks, doctors, bodyguards, and maids. Several photographs of the couple, taken over a span of thirty years, are included. Reviews: *New York Times Book Review* (July 28, 1991): 24. *Orbis* 35, no.4 (Fall 1991): 623-624.

873. Brucan, Silviu, **The Wasted Generation: Memoirs of the Romanian Journey from Capitalism to Socialism and Back**. Boulder, Colo.: Westview Press, 1993. xii, 227 p. ISBN: 0813318335. Includes bibliographical references.

Brucan fought in the antifascist underground movement during World War II and after the war was acting editor of Romania's leading communist daily. After becoming disenchanted with the Ceausescu regime, he became "a prime mobilizer of popular support for reform and subsequently one of the leaders of the National Salvation Front." (p. 227) This book is about the fall of Ceausescu and the events that led up to it.

874. Crowther, William E., **The Political Economy of Romanian Socialism**. New York: Praeger, 1988. ISBN: 0275928403. Includes bibliography and index.

"This study focuses on Romania in the period since World War II as a case study of state-socialist politics. Its primary purpose is to describe the organization of power following the inception of communist party rule, its social basis, and its evolution up to the present time. Its basic hypothesis is simply stated: the current Romanian regime and those of the other state-socialist countries can only be adequately understood when seen as integral elements in coherent political economies and located in the social histories of their particular countries." (p.1) Review: *Orbis* 33, no.1 (Winter 1989): 135.

875. Dima, Nicholas, **Journey to Freedom**. Washington, DC: Selous Foundation Press, 1989. vii, 399 p. ISBN: 0944273041. Includes index.

Dima, a former Romanian political prisoner, presents an autobiographical memoir. "The author breaks new ground in showing a glimpse of life in labor camps. He demonstrates how soldiers are used for the dirty jobs of socialist construction, and how they are treated in many ways as badly as those in prison for crimes against the state. Additionally, he provides insight into the new religious trends in Romania in the past few decades." (p.vii)

876. Fischer, Mary Ellen, **Nicolae Ceausescu: A Study in Political Leadership**. Boulder, Colo.: L. Rienner Publishers, 1989. 325 p. ISBN: 0931477832. Includes bibliography (p. 305-314) and index.

"The focus of this study is Ceausescu himself, his background, his personality and character, the political environment in which he operates, his own political views and techniques, and his methods of leadership and control as he has revealed them publicly in his actions and in the Romanian press." (p. 3) Reviews: *American Political Science Review* 84, no.3 (September 1990): 1032-1033. *Orbis* 34, no.1 (Winter 1990): 142-143.

877. Gilberg, Trond, **Nationalism and Communism in Romania: The Rise and Fall of Ceausescu's Personal Dictatorship**. Boulder, Colo.: Westview Press, 1990. x, 289 p. ISBN: 0813374979. Includes bibliographical references.

The history of Nicolai Ceausescu's dictatorship is the subject of this study. The author takes a topical approach initially discussing dictatorship in Romania in the context of religious belief, nationalism and ethnicity. He also examines the role of the Communist Party as it used and was used by Ceausescu. Other topics discussed include modernization, societal change, international relations, and Perestroika in Romania. A bibliographic essay is included. Reviews: *Foreign Affairs* 69, no.5 (Winter 1990/91): 202. *Current History* 89, no.551 (December 1990): 425ff.

878. International Delegation to the Romanian National Elections, **The May 1990 Elections in Romania**. Washington, DC: National Democratic Institute for International Affairs, 1991. viii, 133 p.

"This is the report of the 60-member international delegation that observed the May 20, 1990 Romanian national elections. It is based on information gathered by the sponsoring organization prior to the elections and by the delegation teams that visited 11 regions of the country during the elections. The report presents a national perspective on the electoral process, including the campaign, voting procedures and the tabulation of the results." (p. iii)

879. **Romania After Tyranny,** edited by Daniel N. Nelson. Boulder, Colo.: Westview Press, 1992. viii, 311 p. ISBN: 0813313481. Includes bibliographical references and index.

Nelson conceived this volume in order to "offer broad assessments of the country's domestic and international conditions in the aftermath of the revolution." The contributors are from the United States, Western Europe and Romania. The essays are arranged in two parts: domestic issues and foreign and defense policies. The editor writes a concluding essay drawing the disparate opinions together.

880. Nelson, Daniel N., **Romanian Politics in the Ceausescu Era**. New York: Gordon and Breach Science Publishers, 1988. xvii, 244 p. ISBN: 2881242618. Includes bibliography (p. 225-235) and index.

Nelson emphasizes elite-mass relations, local politics and Romanian defense and military policies. The eleven chapters are divided into three parts. Part one (chapter 1-4) is entitled "The Rulers and the Ruled" and looks at worker-party conflict, trade unions, and public opinion. Part two (chapters 5-8) focuses on issues in local politics, women and the cult of Ceausescu. Part three (chapters 9-11) examines military and defense policies and political conflict. A postscript describes the party and crises in late 1987.

881. Pacepa, Ion Mihai, **Red Horizons: Chronicles of a Communist Spy Chief**. Washington, DC: Regnery Gateway, 1987. 446 p. ISBN: 0895265702. Includes index.

A former aide to Ceausescu recalls his years in power in Romania. He focuses on several weeks in 1978. The book "contains the story of my day-to-day life with a Communist leader who, during more than 20 years of absolute power, has built the most orthodox Marxist domestic policy in Eastern Europe and has clearly designated capitalism as his number one enemy. A leader who, cleverly using various influence operations, has simultaneously been able to gather enough Western political support and cold cash to keep his moribund, self-serving regime alive, and to build the first true Communist dynasty in history." (pp xvi-xvii) The conversations quoted in the book are from the author's memory. Reviews: *New York Times Book Review*, 3 (January 1988): 73-74. *Orbis* 32, no.3 (Summer 1988): 478-79.

882. Rady, Martyn C., **Romania in Turmoil: A Contemporary History**. London: IB Tauris, 1992. vii, 216 p. ISBN: 1850435006. Includes bibliographical references and index.

"This work attempts to achieve two separate but interrelated purposes: to provide an authoritative account of events in Romania during and after the 1989 revolution; and to place these developments in their broader historical context. As a 'contemporary history' it seeks therefore to unite not only the present and the past but also the different disciplines of historical writing and of contemporary political analysis." (p. vii)

FOREIGN RELATIONS

883. Boia, Eugene, **Romania's Diplomatic Relations with Yugoslavia in the Interwar Period, 1919-1941**. Boulder, Colo.: East European Monographs, 1993. xiii, 501 p. *East European Monographs; no. 356*, ISBN: 0880332530. Includes bibliographical references (p. 428-453) and index.

Boia's book is "the first study in English to cover the entire interwar period. Its purpose is to detail as objectively as possible the events and issues of Romania's relations with Yugoslavia in all their complexities and categories." (p. ix) In conducting his study, Boia has also had access to Romanian archives. The work is arranged in nine chapters. After an introductory chapter covering developments to 1918, he proceeds chronologically through June 1941. Several maps are also included.

884. Dima, Nicholas, **From Moldavia to Moldova: The Soviet-Romanian Territorial Dispute**, 2nd ed. New York: Columbia University Press, 1991. v, 194 p. ISBN: 0880332050. Includes bibliography (p. 187-194).

This volume updates the author's 1982 publication *Bessarabia and Bukovina: The Soviet Romanian Territorial Dispute*. As in that earlier publication "the purpose of this study is to present the succession of events which led to the last Soviet annexation of the Romanian territories in 1940 and 1944; to analyze the socioeconomic and ethno-demographic changes brought about by the Soviet Union in the area and particularly in Moldavia; to analyze the current cultural and linguistic status of the Soviet Romanians; and to describe the present dispute between Bucharest and Moscow and its perspective." (p. 3) The period under study, 1945-1980, has been largely ignored in the Western literature. Those works that have dealt with this topic are included in the author's extensive bibliography.

885. Funderburk, David B., **Pinstripes and Reds: An American Ambassador Caught Between the State Department and the Romanian Communists, 1981-1985**, with a foreword by Congressman Philip M. Crane. Washington D.C: Selous Foundation Press, 1987. xiii, 226 p. ISBN: 0944273017. Includes bibliography (209-220) and index.

Funderburk was U.S. ambassador to Romania from 1981 to 1985. His memoir "explains how one of the most despotic tyrannies of the century deceived the American government into legitimizing Romania's inhumane and anti-religious domestic policies by the continual granting of Most-Favored Nation trading status, while, at the same time, the U.S. ignores the many alarming characteristics of Romania's foreign policy." (p. xiii)

886. Harrington, Joseph F., and Bruce J. Courtney, **Tweaking the Nose of the Russians: Fifty Years of American-Romanian Relations, 1940-1990**. New York: Columbia University Press, 1991. vi, 657 p. *East European Monographs, no. 296*, ISBN: 0880331933. Includes bibliographical references (p. 617-647) and index.

"Following a brief sketch of Romanian-Allied relations from 1940-1947, this book examines post World War II American-Romanian relations within the following context. Whenever documentation is available, the American side considers first, the larger perspective of East-West trade, which at the outset focused on restricting commerce through export controls; second, American's national security policy, which normally addressed the issue of Soviet-American relations; third, America's policy toward Eastern Europe, which at times differed from its approach toward the Soviet Union; and fourth, specific relations with Romania, first as a satellite and later as a nation, somewhat independent of Moscow. Romania's relations with America are considered within the framework of Bucharest-Moscow relations and Romania's internal developments which affect her foreign policy toward Washington." (p. v) Reviews: *Foreign Affairs* 70, no.3 (Summer 1991): 177-178. *Soviet Union/Union Sovietique* 18, no.1-3 (1991): 354-355.

887. Lungu, Dov B., **Romania and the Great Powers, 1933-1940**. Durham, NC: Duke University Press, 1989. xiv, 294 p. ISBN: 0822309157. Includes bibliography (p. 275-286) and index.

"This study is concerned with the role of Romania in the international politics of Europe before and immediately after the outbreak of the Second World War. It is about the attempts of Romania's leaders to preserve the relative independence and the territorial integrity of their enlarged country by maneuvering between the interests of the European Great Powers as well as about the policies of these powers toward Romania during one of the stormiest periods in this century." (p. xi) Review: *Canadian Slavonic Papers* 32, no.4 (December 1990): 513-514.

888. Verona, Sergiu, **Military Occupation and Diplomacy: Soviet Troops in Romania, 1944-1958,** foreword by J.F. Brown. Durham: Duke University Press, 1992. xii, 211 p. ISBN: 0822311712. Includes bibliographical references (p. 171-206) and index.

"This book examines the interrelated pressures of military occupation and diplomacy as they were employed by the Soviet Union from 1944 to 1955, when it made the highly significant decision to withdraw its military forces from Romania. This unique decision challenged the long-established rules of the Soviet empire." (p. 2) In part one Verona examines the sources of Khrushchev's new policy, Soviet-Romanian relations and Soviet-East European relations. Part two discusses Soviet-Romanian relations as they changed and the effect of changing Soviet-Yugoslav relations. The author drew on many documentary sources for this work. The bibliography includes numerous English language references.

ECONOMICS, BUSINESS AND LAW

889. **Romania: An Economic Assessment**. Paris: Centre for Co-operation with the European Economies in Transition, 1993. 122 p. ISBN: 9264139397. Includes bibliographic references.

This volume is one in a series published by the Organization for Economic Co-operation and Development (OECD). Its purpose is to analyze the context in which economic reforms will be implemented in Romania and propose possible policy choices. The authors have taken special note of the way in which reforms have been introduced in the past. "This report argues that a determined effort is now necessary to rapidly complete price liberalisation, stabilize the exchange rate, and accelerate those structural reforms which would improve financial discipline of enterprises. Western assistance will be vital if the balance of payments situation is to be prevented from slowing the needed structural reforms." (p. 3) The book is divided into five sections discussing the background of Romania's economic problems; macroeconomic changes from 1990-1992; structural reforms in business; macroeconomic policy proposal; and general conclusions. Three annexes are included supplying extensive statistical data and information on the Romanian accounting system, agriculture reform and plans for privatization.

890. Turnock, David, **The Romanian Economy in the Twentieth Century**. London: Croom Helm, 1986. 296 p. *Croom Helm Series on the Contemporary Economic History of Europe*, ISBN: 0709901070. Includes index and bibliography (p. 281-85).

In general this series, of which this volume is one part, is designed to provide balanced surveys of the economic development of individual European countries from the end of World War I to the present day. It is to do this, as well as examine problems encountered by these economies, against the background of the economic and political trends of the time. After giving the requisite geographical and historical perspectives and describing the state of the Romanian economy in 1914, Turnock then devotes three chapters to Romania in the interwar years. Here he explores the debate on economic policy, agrarian reform and industrial progress, and the attempts to overhaul the infrastructure. After WWII Romania was placed under the control of the Soviet Union. Turnock examines the results of this political act and the ensuing socialist economic program, collectivization of agriculture, nationalization of industry and patterns of trade, transport and settlement. He concludes by speculating on Romania's economic future. Reviews: *Canadian Slavonic Papers* 29, no.2/3 (June/September 1987): 359-60. *Journal of Economic History* 47, no.4 (December 1987): 1024-26.

LANGUAGE AND LITERATURE

891. Beissinger, Margaret H., **The Art of the Lautar: The Epic Tradition of Romania**. New York: Garland, 1991. xiii, 186 p. *Harvard Dissertations in Folklore and Oral Tradition*, ISBN: 082402897X. Revision of the author's thesis (Ph.D.)—Harvard University, 1984. Includes bibliographical references (p. 173-183) and index.

Lantari are male Gypsy singers who have performed Romanian song and dance music in Romania. This work focuses on the epic songs of these singers, their manner of composition, and the means of that genre's perpetuation. This is a revision of the author's doctoral dissertation that was based on extensive field work in Romania.

892. Mallinson, Graham, **Rumanian**. Dover, NH: Croom Helm, 1986. 371 p. *Croom Helm Descriptive Grammars*, ISBN: 0709935374. Includes bibliography (p. 368-369) and index.

This is a descriptive grammar that follows a widely used theoretical linguistic framework for its exposition. The five main chapters cover syntax, morphology, phonology, ideophones and interjections and lexicon. There are no exercises for the beginning language student. Review: *Language* 63, no.3 (September 1987): 678.

INDIVIDUAL AUTHORS

893. Astalos, Georges, **Contestatory Visions: Five Plays,** translated by Ronald Bogue. Lewisburg: Bucknell University Press, 1991. 207 p. ISBN: 0838751997.

The five plays—"What Will We Do Now Willi's Gone;" "The Apotheosis of the Void;" "Madmoisselle Helsenka;" "Our Daily Tea;" and "The Soldiers Are Coming"—are from both his Romanian and Parisian periods. Mr. Astalos is an internationally acclaimed playwright who has received drama awards.

894. Cassian, Nina, **Life Sentence: Selected Poems,** edited and with an introduction by William Jay Smith. New York: W. W. Norton, 1990. xxiv, 129 p. ISBN: 0393027864.

This volume contains poems translated from Romanian and covers a wide range of lyrical themes.

895. Codrescu, Andrei, **The Disappearance of the Outside: A Manifesto for Escape.** Reading, Mass.: Addison-Wesley, 1990. vii, 216 p. ISBN: 0201121948.

Prolific author Codrescu reflects on the fall of the Iron Curtain in his native Romania. "The thesis of this book, which is both personal and rarely reflected, is that the two former oppositions of East and West will join together in a new electronic globe that is not a good thing for human beings. [He] attempts to show from two simultaneous sides how this future is coming about, and [he] proposes a number of escapes from it through the use of imagination." (p. viii) Review: *Nation* 251 (September 10, 1990): 246-247.

896. Manea, Norman, **October, Eight O'Clock,** translated by Cornelia Golna et al. 1st English-language ed. New York: Grove Weidenfeld, 1992. 216 p. ISBN: 0802112803. Translated from the Romanian.

Like other fiction by Manea, these stories are preoccupied with the trauma of the Holocaust and with daily life in a totalitarian state.

897. Rezzori, Gregor von, **The Snows of Yesteryear: Portraits for an Autobiography,** translated from the German by H. F. Broch de Rotherman. New York: Knopf, 1989. 290 p. ISBN: 0394574427. Translation of: Blumen im Schnee.

Author Gregor von Rezzori creates autobiographical portraits of his family in early twentieth century Bukovina. In doing so he also paints a picture of life at the time in the villages and cities of the Austro-Hungarian empire.

THE SOCIETY, SOCIOLOGY

898. **Romania—Human Resources and the Transition to a Market Economy.** Washington, D.C.: World Bank, 1992. viii, 242 p. *World Bank Country Study*, ISBN: 082132084X.

This volume is another in the World Bank Country Study Series. As with all other volumes in this series, it is particularly valuable for the statistical data it supplies in its appendixes. The text of the volume will be of interest to those studying the social sectors in Romania. "It contains a description of sector policies, programs and institutions, identifies issues both with respect to the transition and medium term sector development, and offers recommendations for government action. These recommendations are based on the situation in Romania in June, 1991." (p. iii) Subjects discussed include labor markets, education, social security, health and population, and family planning.

899. Banc, C., and Alan Dundes, **First Prize, Fifteen Years! An Annotated Collection of Romanian Political Jokes,** compiled by C. Banc and A. Dundes. London: Associated University Presses, 1986. 182 p. ISBN: 0838632459 (alk. paper). Includes bibliography (p. 172-175) and index.

These jokes, collected from a single informant, are arranged in topical order. Each joke is presented, followed by an annotation that includes an explanation, as well as other East European variants and their sources. Reviews: *Folklore Forum* 19, no.2 (1986): 218-19. *Journal of American Folk* 100, no. 397 (July/ September 1987): 376-77.

900. ———, **You Call This Living? A Collection of East European Jokes**. Athens: University of Georgia Press, 1990. 184 p. ISBN: 0820312827. Includes bibliographical references (p. 172-177) and index.

Romanian versions of political jokes common all over Eastern Europe are presented in this volume. The jokes are organized topically with sections on the reign of terror in Romania, the constant shortages in communist society, leaders of the government and other topics. This volume was originally published in 1986 under the title *First Prize Fifteen Years*. Explanations for the material included here are only added where the compilers felt the humor would be lost without it.

901. Giurescu, Dinu C., **The Razing of Romania's Past: International Preservation Report**. Washington, D.C.: U.S. Committee, International Council on Monuments and Sites, 1989. 68 p. ISBN: 0911697047. Includes bibliographical references.

This book describes the Romanian government's destruction of the People's Architectural Heritage. This publication was issued to protest the destruction and to make Western readers aware of this. The book includes extensive bibliographical information but is not, unfortunately, indexed.

902. Kideckel, David A., **The Solitude of Collectivism: Romanian Villagers to the Revolution and Beyond**. Ithaca, NY: Cornell University Press, 1993. xix, 255 p. ISBN: 0801480256. Includes bibliographical references (p. 229-245) and index.

The author proceeds on the premise that in order to understand the successes and failures of socialism, we must examine the "actual lives of the people who lived it, how they did so, and what their daily lives ultimately meant for the larger society." (p. xiii) In order to achieve his goal, he focuses on the social conditions of the people in the Olt Region in Romania. Individual chapters deal with labor, culture, land culture, class, social and cultural system, and the effect of the introduction of socialism. A concluding chapter speculates on the effect of the revolution of 1989 on these people's lives.

903. Kligman, Gail, **The Wedding of the Dead: Ritual, Poetics, and Popular Culture in Transylvania**. Berkeley: University of California Press, 1988. xiii, 410 p. ISBN: 0520060016 (alk. paper). Includes bibliography (p. 377-394) and index.

Kligman's work was based on field work done in the Maramures region of Romania. It "begins with a chapter about contemporary village life in Maramures and emphasizes the basic features of social relations and social organization, past and present. The second, third and fourth chapters are detailed analyses of the life-cycle rituals themselves: weddings, funerals, and death-weddings, respectively. The concluding chapter situates the analysis of ritual in the broader context of the state." (p. 17) Reviews: *Contemporary Sociology* 19 no.1 (January 1990): 113-114. *American Anthropologist* 92, no.3 (September 1990): 784. *Harvard Ukrainian Studies* 15, no.1-2 (July 1990): 232-234. *Canadian American Slavic Studies* 24, no.3 (Fall 1990): 372-374.

904. Manea, Norman, **On Clowns: The Dictator and the Artist: Essays**. New York: Grove Wedenfeld, 1992. xii, 178 p. ISBN: 0802114156. Translated from the Romanian. Includes bibliographical references.

"The present disparate essays—for better or worse subject to a certain journalistic, rhetorical dialectic—are all obsessed with the relationship between the writer and the totalitarian ideology and society in a country where political tradition was never admirable and where the dictatorship of the last several decades was a picturesque mixture of brutality and farce, of opportunism and demagogy." (p. x)

NATIONAL MINORITIES

905. Butnaru, I. C., **The Silent Holocaust: Romania and Its Jews,** foreword by Elie Wiesel. New York: Greenwood Press, 1992. xxv, 236 p. *Contributions to the Study of World History, 0885-9159; no. 31*, ISBN: 0313279853. Includes bibliographical references (p. 223-225) and indexes.

Butnaru traces the history of Jewish persecution in Romania. Chapter one describes the Jewish problem in general and the history up to World War I. Chapter two continues the saga up to the Second World War. Chapter three focuses on the Second World War and the complicity of Romania with the German induced Holocaust. A disturbing photographic essay follows chapter three. Chapter four concludes the story with the post-war situation.

906. ———, **Waiting for Jerusalem: Surviving the Holocaust in Romania.** Westport, Conn.: Greenwood Press, 1993. xiii, 264 p. *Contributions to the Study of World History, 0885-9159; no. 37*, ISBN: 0313287988. Includes bibliographical references (p. 247-251) and indexes.

Butnaru's book is about the Jews in Romania during World War II. He not only focuses on the Holocaust in Romania but also on the rescuing of over 300,000 Romanian Jews during the war.

907. **Violations of the Helsinki Accords, Romania: A Report Prepared for the Helsinki Review Conference, Vienna, November 1986,** by Janet Fleischman. New York: Helsinki Watch Committee, 1986. iv, 47 p. *A Helsinki Watch Report*, ISBN: 0938579835. Includes bibliography (p. 47).

Prepared for the Helsinki Review Conference, this brief report documents the severe human rights abuses that have been associated with the Communist regime under Ceausescu. The reports issued by Helsinki Watch focus on those countries where the violation of human rights have been most severe.

908. Oldson, William O., **A Providential Anti-Semitism: Nationalism and Polity in Nineteenth Century Romania.** Philadelphia: American Philosophical Society, 1991. 177 p. *Memoirs of the American Philosophical Society, v. 193*, ISBN: 0871691930. Includes bibliographical references (p.165-172) and index.

Oldson explores "the birth of modern Romania at the Congress of Berlin in 1878 and the subsequent elaboration of anti-Semitic themes by the Romanian intelligentsia in the period before World War I." (p. 11) After an introduction in which he describes the scope of his study, the author devotes separate chapters to the Congress of Berlin, the price of independence, the voice of the intelligentsia, and the logic and rhetoric of anti-Semitism.

909. Volovici, Leon, **Nationalist Ideology and Antisemitism: The Case of Romanian Intellectuals in the 1930s,** translated from the Romanian by Charles Kormos. New York: Pergamon Press, 1991. x, 213 p. *Studies in Antisemitism*, ISBN: 0080410243. Includes bibliographical references (p. 201-207) and index.

"The focus of this book is confined to the essential and specific element of antisemitism within Romanian nationalism and its considerable repercussions on various frameworks of Romanian society." (p. vii) Volovici examines the decade in which Romania's dictatorship was established. He looks at the work of the intellectuals of the period. Of particular interest to the author is the rise of antisemitism in Romania. This is also one of the most creative periods for Romania's intellectuals. While many of Romania's most well-known intellectuals (Mircea Eliade, Nae Ionescu, for example) have their intellectual roots in Romanian nationalism, the author's stated purpose is not to "indict" them but to study the phenomenon of the rise of nationalism as manifest in a group of intellectuals. The book is arranged topically in five sections: "Nationalism and Antisemitism in Modern Romanian History," "Between Democracy and Dictatorship (1930-1938)," "Ethnocracy, Antisemitism and Legionary Commitment," "Intellectual Antisemitism-Developments and Stereotypes," "Conclusion." The volume includes a section of biographic sketches to assist the reader.

Chapter 9
YUGOSLAVIA

GENERAL REFERENCE WORKS

910. Carter, April, **Marshal Tito: A Bibliography**. Westport, Conn.: Meckler, 1990. ix, 150 p. *Bibliographies of World Leaders, no. 1*, ISBN: 0887363105.

As Carter stated in her preface, "the purpose of this bibliography is to provide a reasonably comprehensive set of references to Tito's life, covering his early career, his political decisions and actions, and his writings and speeches." Most of the 354 annotated references are in English, but the compiler has also included some in German, French, Italian, and Serbo-Croatian. The bibliography is arranged in twelve chapters, each with its own helpful introduction. These chapters cover manuscript and archival sources, personal writings, general biographies, seven chapters covering significant chronological periods in Tito's life and career, his general place in history, and general reference works and bibliographies. Access to the items is facilitated by separate author and subject indexes.

911. **Yugoslavia, a Country Study,** edited by Glenn E. Curtis. 3rd ed. Washington, D.C.: Federal Research Division, Library of Congress, 1992. xiii, 348 p. *Area Handbook Series, 1057-5294*, ISBN: 0844407356. Includes bibliographical references (p. 303-319) and index.

The volume updates an earlier publication of the same title issued in 1982. The tremendous changes in Eastern Europe have provided the impetus for this new edition. The volume begins with a country profile, providing the reader with basic data on the geography, society, economy, transportation, government, and military of Yugoslavia. The text is divided into five chapters which discuss Yugoslavia's history, society, economy, government, and military. A bibliography and glossary of terms as well as a statistical appendix are included.

912. Friedman, Francine, **Yugoslavia: A Comprehensive English-Language Bibliography,** compiled and edited by Francine Friedman. Wilmington, Del.: Scholarly Resources Inc., 1993. xv, 547 p. ISBN: 0842023402. Includes indexes.

Friedman's purpose was "to record as fully as possible those works in the English language that deal with some aspect of Yugoslavia." (p. xiii) The 9,059 items are arranged topically under the following rubrics: reference works and aids, geography, history, economics, politics and government, anthropology, and culture. Within each broad division, the items are further subdivided. Each of the citations, which span from the 17th century to the early 1990s, includes author, title, publication information, journal and page references if applicable and a Library of Congress call number. Items not inspected *de visu* are so indicated with an asterisk. Author and subject indexes facilitate access to the items in the bibliography.

913. McFarlane, Bruce J., **Yugoslavia: Politics, Economics, and Society**. New York: Pinter, 1988. xxii, 240 p. *Marxist Regimes*, ISBN: 0861874536 (pbk); 0861874528. Includes index and bibliography (227-234).

This survey, based on primary sources, outlines "the basic attitudes and mechanisms that have emerged in socialist Yugoslavia, attempts to probe the sources and the results of

Yugoslavia's contrasts." (p. xiii) The author devotes chapters to history, political traditions and social structure, political systems, the economic system and contemporary political issues. Review: *Slavic Review* 49, no.3 (Fall 1990): 489.

914. Mihailovich, Vasa D., **First Supplement to A Comprehensive Bibliography of Yugoslav Literature in English 1981-1985**. Columbus, Ohio: Slavica, 1988. 338 p. ISBN: 0893571881. Includes index.

Although this bibliography formally supplements *A Comprehensive Bibliography of Yugoslav Literature in English 1593-1980* by presenting material published during 1981-85, it also includes items not part of the basic volume. The work is divided into three parts: translations, criticism, and indexes. Each of these parts is further subdivided into relevant sections; for example, criticism has entries on reference works, books and articles, reviews, and dissertations (including masters' theses). Arrangement within these smaller sections is alphabetical by author. Of the four indexes, only three can properly be called that. The "index" to periodicals and newspapers is simply a listing of the periodicals and newspapers cited in the work; no page references are given. The remaining three—English titles of first lines, original titles of first lines, and subject and name—provides adequate access to the contents of the bibliography. This bibliography, like the basic volume covering 1593-1980, fills a definite gap in bibliographical coverage of Yugoslav literature.

915. **Yugoslavia 1945-1985: Statistical Review**, Federal Statistical Office, editor in chief Dusan Miljkovic. Beograd: The Office, 1986. 244 p.

This statistical review is intended to show the course of Yugoslavia's development from an underdeveloped country to industrialized nation. Statistics on population, labor, employment, national income, industry, agriculture, forestry, natural resources, trade, construction, transportation, tourism, education, defense and housing are included. Statistics are those supplied by the communist government. No index is included. Some explanations of the statistics are included.

916. Pavlowitch, Stevan K., **Tito—Yugoslavia's Great Dictator: A Reassessment**. Columbus: Ohio State University Press, 1992. xv, 119 p. ISBN: 0814206018. Includes bibliographical references (p. 111-113) and index.

Tito was demonized after his death in 1980, almost to the extent that he was idealized prior to that date. Pavlowitch attempts to reassess Tito's life and impact on Yugoslavia. His short monograph devotes chapters to separate chronological segments of Tito's life. Two final chapters examine Yugoslavia after Tito and the viability of the Tito myth and the question of Tito, Titoism, and reunification of Yugoslavia.

917. Terry, Garth M., **Yugoslav History: A Bibliographic Index to English-Language Articles,** compiled by Garth M. Terry. England: Astra Press, 1990. xxxii, 165 p. *Astra Soviet and East European Bibliographies, no. 10*, ISBN: 0946134235. Includes indexes.

A revision and expansion of the first edition. "The Index attempts to list all articles on the history—in its broadest sense—of Yugoslavia contained in Festschriften, conference proceedings, collected papers and journals in the English language." (p. xiii) This work complements Prof. Terry's other fine indexes, *East-European Languages and Literatures Covering English Languages Periodical Publications from 1900-1987*. The articles cover diplomatic, political, economic, social, legal, intellectual and religious topics. Two contents listings are supplied. One is general, giving broad subject and chronological divisions. The second supplies all detailed headings used in the body of the bibliography. A table of abbreviations is included at the beginning of the book; a name index, at its conclusion.

HISTORY

918. Alexander, Stella, **The Triple Myth: A Life of Archbishop Alojzije Stepinac**. New York: Columbia University Press, 1987. ix, 257 ISBN: 0880331224. Includes bibliography (p. 240-243) and index.

The author examines the many "myths" that have arisen or been deliberately propagated about Archbishop Stepinac. She traces his life from his youth. The Archbishop's role in the Yugoslav Catholic Church, his support for Croatian nationalism, and opposition to communism are all major themes of this work. The author tries to present an objective view of the archbishop's life.

919. Andric, Ivo, **The Development of Spiritual Life in Bosnia Under the Influence of Turkish Rule**, Zelimir B. Juricic and John F. Loud, editors and translators. Durham, NC: Duke University Press, 1990. xxii, 125 p. ISBN: 0822310635. Translation of: Die Entwicklung des geistigen Lebens in Bosnien unter der Einwirkung der turkischen Herrschaft. Includes bibliography (p.99-113) and index.

Bosnian literary figure Ivo Andric's doctoral dissertation is presented in translation. The dissertation is divided into five chapters. The first looks at Bosnian spiritual life before the Turkish conquest. Chapter two examines the reforms imposed by the Turkish occupiers. In the third chapter social and administrative structures established by the Turks are the focus. Chapter four studies the intellectual life of the Catholic population under the Turks. The status of the Serbian Orthodox Church under the Turks is the subject of the final chapter. The translators feel that the work offers a different view of those topics Andric so often treated in his fiction. A brief supplement on the "hybrid literature of the Bosnian Muslims" is included in the volume.

920. Billows, Richard A., **Antigonos the One-Eye and the Creation of the Hellenistic State**. Berkeley: University of California Press, 1990. ixi, 515 p. *Hellenistic Culture and Society, 4*, ISBN: 0520063783. Includes bibliographical references (p. 470-492).

Antigonos was the greatest of Alexander's successors, even though his life ended in defeat at the battle of Ipsos in 301. Billows reappraises "the aims and significance of Antigonos' activities" and focuses "on his contribution to the process of state building which began to develop the procedures and institutions characteristic of Hellenistic monarchies and of the Selenked Empire especially." (p. 5) The biography is divided into two parts with a total of eight chapters. The first part covers his early life and career and the second appraises his contribution as a ruler of a Hellenistic empire.

921. Bracewell, Catherine Wendy, **The Uskoks of Senj: Piracy, Banditry, and Holy War in the Sixteenth-Century Adriatic**. Ithaca: Cornell University Press, 1992. xiv, 329 p. ISBN: 080142674X. Includes bibliographical references (p. 309-322) and index.

The Uskoks were not only heroes of South Slavic epic songs, but were also a military community still active in the sixteenth century. The author begins by placing the Uskoks in their geographic and social context and then examines the processes that shaped this world and the military community that grew from it. A chronology and glossary are contained in appendices.

922. Cseres, Tibor, **Titoist Atrocities in Vojvodina, 1944-1945: Serbian Vendetta in Bacska**. Buffalo, NY: Hunyadi Pub., 1993. 166 p. ISBN: 1882785010. Bibliographical references: p. 165.

This is a graphic portrayal of the massacre of Hungarian civilians in Bacska at the end of World War II by Titoist forces. The author has also written a novel concerned with these atrocities called *Cold Days.*

923. Cuvalo, Ante, **The Croatian National Movement, 1966-1972**. New York: Distributed by Columbia University Press, 1990. iv, 275 p. *East European Monographs, no. 282,* ISBN: 0880331798. Includes bibliography (p.254-271) and index.

This book is the only monograph on the Croatian National Movement covering the years of the late sixties and early seventies. The author is attempting to take a different approach looking at the movement outside the context of its relation to the stability of Yugoslavia. "The main purpose of this study is, therefore, to understand how the national forces in Croatia from 1966 to 1972 viewed themselves and their nation at that time, and what their vision of Croatia's future was." (p. 4) The work is chronologically arranged.

924. Dedijer, Vladimir, **The War Diaries of Vladimir Dedijer**. Ann Arbor: University of Michigan Press, 1990. ISBN: 0472100912 (v. 1; alk. paper); 0472101099 (v. 2; alk. paper). Translation of: Dnevnik. Includes index.

Dedijer, a prominent Yugoslav intellectual, fought with Tito and his guerrilla forces throughout the war. His war time diary begins in 1941 and ends in September 1943. It has been called "the most detailed and important source about Yugoslavia and the Partisans in World War II." (p. xv) Review: *Journal of Baltic Studies* 22, no.4 (Winter 1991): 371-372.

925. **The Yugoslav Auschwitz and the Vatican: The Croatian Massacre of the Serbs During World War II,** documents selected and compiled by Vladimir Dedijer; translated by Harvey L. Kendall. Buffalo, N.Y.: Prometheus Books, 1992. 444 p. ISBN: 0879757523. Rev. translation of the German version which was translated from the Serbo-Croatian (roman) original: Vatikan i Jasenovac. Includes bibliographical references.

This book is a collection of documents and personal testimonies that attest to the persecution of Serbs by Croats during the Second World War. The twenty-six chapters are divided into five sections: 1) The Balkans as a bulwark against Orthodoxy; 2) Massacres among dissenters in the "Kingdom of God"; 3) The death camp Jasenovac; 4) The Pope's attitude toward the massacres; and 5) The Pope's loyalty to the Utashe even after the collapse of the NDH. The compiler presents evidence to claim that the Vatican authorities were implicated in these atrocities.

926. Djilas, Aleksa, **The Contested Country: Yugoslav Unity and Communist Revolution, 1919-1953**. Cambridge, Mass.: Harvard University Press, 1991. 259 p. *Harvard Historical Studies. V.108; Russian Research Center Studies. 85,* ISBN: 0674166981. Includes bibliographical references and index.

Djilas examines the phenomenon of Yugoslavism from its beginning in 1740 through 1953. Her six chapters proceed in chronological order and cover the origins of Yugoslavism to socialist internationalism, 1740-1918; the Yugoslavism and separatism of the Communist Party of Yugoslavia, 1918-1925; the Communist Party of Yugoslavia and the Popular Front, 1925-1941, national state and genocide: the Utasha movement, 1929-1945; Croatian and Serbian political parties, 1939-1945; and federalism and Yugoslavism, 1943-1953. Reviews: *New Republic* 205, no.15 (October 7, 1991): 29-36. *New York Times Book Review* (May 12, 1991): 23. *Orbis* 35, no.4 (Fall 1991): 622.

927. Ford, Kirk, **OSS and the Yugoslav Resistance, 1943-1945**. College Station; Texas: A & M University Press, 1992. xiii, 249 p. ISBN: 089096517X. Includes bibliographical references and index.

Kirk Ford, a specialist in the history of World War II, turns his attention to the question of the role of the Office of Strategic Service (OSS) in Yugoslavia in this book. He focuses on the operational aspects of the work of the OSS, relying on their operational files, correspondence, interviews with participants and more traditional published sources. "I have attempted to show the kind of work American liaison officers did in Yugoslavia and to assess the extent to which their efforts either advanced or influenced the goals of Allied policy there." (p. x) Kirk found that his access to the operational files, not previously available, gave him a different view of Yugoslavia's Civil War between Tito's Partisans and Mihailovich's Chetniki (Nationalists). He believes that Mihailovich's supporters were not the collaborators they have been previously described to be. Two brief appendixes are included on Serbo-Croatian pronunciation and prominent OSS personalities.

928. Gal, Joseph, **In Death's Fortress,** translated by John F. Csomor. New York: Columbia University Press, 1991. 195 p. *East European Monographs, no. 312*, ISBN: 0880332107.

Joseph Gal's description of the Sixth Battle of Isonzo illustrates many of the broader issues of World War I. The bravery of the troops, the tremendous destructive power of the weapons, and the weakening of the Austro-Hungarian empire as a result of the hatred between minority groups within its borders are all themes pursued in Gal's account. The description deals with the experiences of enlisted men in battle; it is not a tactical analysis. Gal was a 20-year-old man at the time experiencing all the horrors of war.

929. Jancar-Webster, Barbara, **Woman and Revolution in Yugoslavia, 1941-1945.** Denver, Colo.: Arden Press, 1990. xvi, 245 p. *Women and Modern Revolution Series*, ISBN: 0912869100 (pbk); 0912869097. Includes bibliographical references and index.

"The central theme of this study is that the war years do not represent a revolution in the Yugoslav woman's experience but rather a foreshortening of the process of consciousness development. It took over 200 years for American women to make the shift from androcentricity to woman-centeredness as exemplified in the present feminist movement. The second stage, namely the achievement of civil rights and the right of entrance into society on male terms, has not yet been fully completed." (p. 4) In addition to consulting primary source documents, the author also interviewed nineteen leading woman partisans who took part in the war.

930. Jelavich, Charles, **South Slav Nationalisms—Textbook and Yugoslav Union Before 1914**. Columbus: Ohio State University Press, 1990. xvii, 359 p. ISBN: 0814205003. Includes bibliographical references (p. 313-348) and index.

How do the textbooks of primary and secondary school affect feelings of nationalism? This is the question Charles Jelavich tries to answer in this study of pre-World War I Yugoslavia. By examining hundreds of textbooks in use at the time he hopes to discover what children were being taught about each of the national groups of the area and how the knowledge may have contributed to the growth of Yugoslavism, helping to create a unified South Slav state. The first six chapters begin with a general historical background and a discussion of the Serbian, Croatian and Slovenian educational systems. The remaining four chapters discuss various types of textbooks: readers, geography, history and Slovenian texts. An extensive bibliography is included.

931. Laffan, Robert George Dalrymple, **The Serbs: The Guardians of the Gate**. New York: Dorset Press, 1989. 299 p. ISBN: 0880294132. Includes index.

This history of Serbia focuses primarily on the period from the Treaty of Berlin through 1917. It was written by a British soldier stationed in the Balkans with the British Salonika Force in 1917. It includes an appendix giving demographic data "of the Macedonian population."

932. Lees, Michael, **The Rape of Serbia: The British Role in Tito's Grab for Power, 1943-1944**. San Diego: Harcourt Brace Jovanovich, 1990. xvi, 384 p. ISBN: 0151959102. Includes bibliographical references (p. 363-365) and index.

Based on documents of the Public Records Office and his personal experiences, former special forces officer, Michael Lees recounts the events of the Yugoslav civil war. He finds that the official account of the events from 1943-44 are highly at odds with his memories. The "British Yugoslav Establishment View" is supported by those who have sponsored the Tito regime. In this chronological account of the events the author tries to give the world a different picture of the events of those years, one he feels more closely reflects the truth. The volume includes maps, a chronology of events and a bibliography.

933. Lindsay, Franklin, **Beacons in the Night: With the OSS and Tito's Partisans in Wartime Yugoslavia**. Stanford, Calif.: Stanford University Press, 1993. xxii, 383 p. ISBN: 0804721238. Includes bibliographical references (p. 371-374) and index.

This is a memoir of Lindsay, who was an officer with the Office of Strategic Services and who parachuted into Yugoslavia during the Second World War in order to work with the partisans against the Germans. This partisan wartime revolution and the one in neighboring Albania were, Lindsay states, "the only successful Communist revolutions in which a few officers of both the United States and Britain served on the ground with the Partisan forces." (p. ix) His memoir is extremely well written and is packed with suspense. It is based on the author's memory and recently declassified documents from that period.

934. **Divostin and the Neolothic of Central Serbia,** edited by Alan McPherron and Dragoslav Srejovic. Pittsburgh, PA: Department of Anthropology, University of Pittsburgh, 1988. xiv, 492 p. *Ethnology Monographs, no. 10*, ISBN: 0945428006. Includes bibliographies.

"This volume contains the results of the excavations and research that I (Alan McPherron) directed jointly with Professor Dragoslav Srejovic at Neolithic sites in the heart of Serbia's 'Land Forest'—the Sumodija. The major aim was to test hypotheses regarding ways in which farming became established and developed in southeastern Europe." (p.xiii) The project was a joint venture from its inception and planning to the analysis of the find. The results reflect the differing approaches to archaeology taken in the East and West. The twenty essays included in this volume discuss the geographic details of the site at Divostin; Neolithic sites in Central Sumadija, architectural and structural features at the Divostin, descriptions of stone, ceramic, bone and textile artifacts from the site; and human skeletal remains found at Divostin. There are also essays on botanical investigations at Divostin, the Neolithic fauna of the region, a geomagnetic survey of the area and a general discussion of the Balkan neolithic. Numerous illustrations accompany the volume, including a set of site maps showing the precise locations of the finds at Divostin.

935. Pavlowitch, Stevan K., **The Improbable Survivor: Yugoslavia and Its Problems, 1919-1988**. Columbus: Ohio State University Press, 1988. xv, 167 p. ISBN: 0814204864. Includes bibliography (p. 159).

A series of lectures, originally delivered between 1981 and 1986 in Paris, have been reworked and expanded in this publication. The author focuses on the survival of Yugoslavia as a unified nation. He begins his discussion with a description of the circumstances leading to Yugoslavia's creation in 1918. He then gives a general overview of how the country was ruled during Stalin's and Tito's regimes. The book then becomes a topical study of Yugoslavia's problems and its strengths, examining the Albanian problem, the question of religion, and Yugoslavia's place in the world. The author includes a historical chronology beginning in 1918. A short list of English language material is also included. Review: *Journal of Social Political Economic Studies* 14, no.2 (Summer 1989): 251-252.

936. Perry, Duncan M., **The Politics of Terror: The Macedonian Liberation Movements, 1893-1903**. Durham, NC: Duke University Press, 1988. xxii, 257 p. ISBN: 0822308134. Includes bibliography (p.235-248) and index.

This history of the Macedonian Revolutionary Organization is also a case study of Third World terrorism. The book fills a gap covering a subject not previously analyzed in Western literature. At the same time it shows the danger of the use of terrorist organizations in the name of political independence. The book is arranged chronologically and includes appendices on the treaty of Berlin and the organization of the Macedonian Revolutionary Organization. Reviews: *Slavic Review* 49, no.1 (Spring 1990): 143-144. *American Historical Review* 95, no.3 (June 1990): 867. *Modern Greek Studies Yearbook* 5 (1989): 559-561. *International History Review* 11, no.3 (August, 1989): 560-62.

937. Stuard, Susan Mosher, **A State of Deference: Ragusa/ Dubrovnik in the Medieval Centuries**. Philadelphia: University of Philadelphia Press, 1992. viii, 269 p. *Middle Age Series*, ISBN: 0812231783. Includes bibliographical references (p. 241-257) and index.

Ragusa was a South Slav city state that maintained its independence for one thousand years. Susan Stuard believes that the methods available to historians today, that is those historical methods that emphasize social elements of development, are more enlightening when dealing with the history of this region. "That is to say, this may be a story more accurately told by methods of investigation that look to the internal history of family, family networks, and their impact on community life.... If so, this is the proper arena for historical investigation, and it is a contention of this study that through analyzing informal, occasional, and familial systems a new internal chronology, one sometimes congruent with events in the public sphere, sometimes distinct from them, may be constructed. This amended chronology may reveal a picture of intense urban dynamism." (p. 8) Chapters are topically arranged covering the nobility, women, household life, the community, wealth and fame. Appendixes includes a timeline, and a brief discussion of Ragusa's later history.

938. Todorovich, Boris, **Last Words: A Memoir of World War II and the Yugoslav Tragedy,** edited by J. Stryder and Andrew Karp. New York: Walker, 1989. xi, 319 p. ISBN: 0802710670. Includes index.

After Todorovich went into battle against the Germans he was captured and was a prisoner of war for eighteen months. He escaped and continued to elude police agents in French Vichy, Spanish border guards and finally to fight as a guerrilla in occupied Serbia. His memoir covers the years 1941 to 1944.

939. **Selevac, a Neolithic Village in Yugoslavia,** edited by Ruth Tringham, Dusan Krstic. Los Angeles, Calif.: Institute of Archeology, University of California, 1990. xii, 712 p. *Monumenta Archaeologica, v. 15*, ISBN: 0017956680. Includes bibliographical references (p. 617-636) and indexes.

Fifteen hundred years after the first introduction of agriculture into Eastern Europe societal changes had begun. This work is concerned with finding and interpreting evidence of those changes. The Selevac Archeological Project is concerned with finding and interpreting evidence of those changes. The Selevac Archeological Project was a joint study by the U.S. and Yugoslavia which focused on the Selevac-Staro Selo Site located in the Moravo River valley in Serbia. The site was first discovered in 1968 and excavations have been done in three six-week seasons beginning in 1976 and ending in 1978. The original aims of the project were to clarify the chronology and cultural evolution in the area; to study the socioeconomic development of early agricultural societies, focusing on intensification; to analyze the nature and reason for variation in settlement patterns; and to study regional patterns of settlement. "It is hypothesized in this volume that the Vinza-Plocnik phase of the Vinca culture, along with other late neolithic/early neolithic Balkan cultures, represent those stages of the transformation into a new form of agricultural society in southeast

Europe in which permanent and highly organized villages were established." (p. 1) The 15 essays discuss the site, chronology, research methods, faunal environment, archeological remains, ceramics at the site, cultural finds at Selevac, use of stone resources, bone tools, use of copper, and Selevac in European prehistory. Numerous plates and a lengthy bibliography are provided.

GOVERNMENT, POLITICS AND LAW

940. **Yugoslavia in Transition: Choices and Constraints: Essays in Honour of Fred Singleton,** edited by John B. Allcock, John J. Horton and Marko Milivojevic. New York: St. Martin's Press, 1991. xi, 461 p. ISBN: 0854966099. Includes bibliographical references and index.

The purpose of these essays is to describe the choices and constraints that face contemporary Yugoslavia. The essays, by different authors, are arranged in three parts. Part one is an overview of contemporary Yugoslavia in transition and includes essays on the geography, economy, society, and development of Yugoslavia. Part two examines more closely the choices and constraints facing that country, such as external migration, Yugoslav intelligence and security forces, foreign trade, foreign relations, nationalism, health care, ecology, economic development and the press. Part three is a bibliography of the late Frederick Singleton.

941. Banac, Ivo, **With Stalin Against Tito: Cominformist Splits in Yugoslav Communism.** Ithaca, NY: Cornell University Press, 1988. xvi, 294 p. ISBN: 0801421861. Includes bibliography (p. 271-85) and index.

Little scholarship has focused on that segment of Tito's party that supported the Cominform Resolution. Banac seeks here to uncover trace elements that motivated the pro-Soviet force, "whom the Cominformists appealed to and what internal differences (if any) existed within their ranks, to establish whether all persons tarred with the Cominformist brush actually considered themselves to be adherents of the movement (if such it was), and to explain why the *ibeovci* of 1948 failed in their mission." (p. xi) Review: Vladimir Tismaneanu, *Orbis* 33, no.3 (Summer 1989): 459.

942. Cohen, Lenard J., **The Socialist Pyramid: Elites and Power in Yugoslavia.** London: Tri-Service, 1989. 499 p. ISBN: 1854880047 (pbk); 1854880047 (cased). Includes bibliography and index.

Cohen focuses on "the strategic political actors in the upper tiers of a still decidedly hierarchical and stratified society." (p. 4) In particular his analyses is aimed at "the efforts of Belgrade's unusual Marxist regime to surmount the challenging problems of bureaucracy and socio-political inequality." (p. 9) The book's nine chapters are divided into five parts: introduction, elites and ethnonationalism, and choosing Tito's comrades and heirs. Reviews: *Foreign Affairs* 69, no.2 (Spring 1990): 183-184. *Canadian Slavonic Papers* 32, no.1 (March 1990): 110-111.

943. Dragnich, Alex N., **Serbs and Croats: The Struggle in Yugoslavia.** New York: Harcourt Brace Jovanovich, 1992. xxi, 202 p. ISBN: 015810737. Includes bibliographical references (p. 196-198) and index.

Dragnich "was led to write this book primarily by the realization that the journalism produced in the wake of the collapse of the Communist regimes in Eastern Europe, including Yugoslavia, has been not only inadequate, but also often incorrect." (p. x) This short history of ethnic relations in Yugoslavia clarifies the background and context of the current civil war there.

944. Drakulic, Slavenka, **The Balkan Express: Fragments from the Other Side of the War**. 1st American New York: W.W. Norton & Co., 1993. 146 p. ISBN: 0393034968.

The author claims that "this is not the book about the war as we see it every day on our television screens or read about in the newspapers. *Balkan Express* picks up where the news stops; it fits somewhere in between hard facts and analysis and personal stories, because the war is happening not only at the front but everywhere and to us all. I am speaking about the other, less visible side of the war, the way it changes us slowly from within." (p. 3-4)

945. Ferdinand, Peter, **Communist Regimes in Comparative Perspective: The Evolution of the Soviet, Chinese and Yugoslav Systems**. Savage, Md.: Barnes & Noble, 1991. xi, 332 p. ISBN: 0389209759; 0710801750; 0710801807. Includes bibliographical references (p.322-324) and index.

Yugoslavia, China, and the Soviet Union share two basic political characteristics. All three had communist regimes that came to power as the result of domestic revolution. These regimes enjoyed a certain degree of legitimacy that the Polish or Czech Communist regimes did not have. Also, all three were in some sense models for the rest of the communist world. Peter Ferdinand has chosen these three nations as the focus of his study in comparative politics based on these similarities. Beginning with the premises that all regimes go through stages of development and that the development of communist regimes is different from other nations, Ferdinand adopts the theme of diversity within unity. The book is arranged topically beginning with a chapter discussing the origins of each regime and then turning to specific topics: leaders, political institutions, government and economy, nationality policies, workers and peasants, and welfare. He closes with a discussion of the attempts at reform in each nation. This book was originally intended for a politics course and includes a list of suggested readings.

946. Hayden, Robert M., **Social Courts in Theory and Practice: Yugoslav Workers' Courts in Comparative Perspective**. Philadelphia: University of Pennsylvania Press, 1990. xiii, 187 p. *Law in Social Context Series*, ISBN: 0812282590. Includes bibliographical references and index.

Alternative dispute resolution (ADR) has long been a topic of interest in American legal literature. The existence of such a system in the form of the Working Courts gave Robert Hayden the basic premise for this comparative study on law in Yugoslavia, India and the United States. Hayden used his anthropological research data from Belgrade, Yugoslavia in the 1980s as the basis of this study of the Workers' Court in Belgrade. In his final section he compares his data with data others have collected on India and the U.S. This is an unusual study since it also is a study in the anthropology of law. A lengthy bibliography is included.

947. **The Disintegration of Yugoslavia,** edited by Martin van den Heuvel and Jan G. Siccama. Amsterdam: Rodopi, 1992. xii, 218 p. *Yearbook of European Studies; 5*, ISBN: 9051833490. Includes bibliographical references.

The papers published in this volume were originally presented at a symposium held in 1991 in the Netherlands and sponsored by the Netherlands Institute of International Relations. The authors focus on such topics as the origins of the Yugoslav state, nationalities and religion, Titoism, relations between Albanians and Serbs, and the role of the European community.

948. **Yugoslavia in the Age of Democracy: Essays on Economic and Political Reform,** edited by George Macesich; with the assistance of Rikard Lang, Ljubisav Markovic, and Dragomir Vojnic; foreword by Bernard F. Sliger. Westport, Conn.: Praeger, 1992. xii, 237 p. *Contributions to Economics*, ISBN: 0275941752. Includes bibliographical references (p. 213-220) and index.

The authors of this work hope to use the experience of Yugoslavia as a case study for the rest of Eastern Europe. Hopefully, by carefully tracking their experience they can help others to avoid its mistakes and duplicate its economic success. The essays are grouped under three broad topics: "Historical View," "Economic Reforms" and "European Integration."

949. Magas, Branka, **The Destruction of Yugoslavia: Tracking the Break-up 1980-1992**. London: Verso, 1993. xxv, 366 p. ISBN: 0860913767; 086091593X (pbk.). Includes bibliographical references and index.

The author has taken her earlier writings, often published under the pseudonym of Michael Lee, to construct a quasi-documentary account of the breakup of Yugoslavia from 1980-1992. The work is divided into five parts: 1) The Kosovo Watershed and Its Aftermath, 1981-1987; 2) Interregnum (1980-1988); 3) Milosevic Assails the Federal Order (1988-1989); 4) Systemic Collapse (1990-1991); and 5) War (June-December 1991).

950. Ramet, Sabrina P., **Balkan Babel: Politics, Culture, and Religion in Yugoslavia**. Boulder, Colo.: Westview Press, 1992. xvi, 230 p. ISBN: 0813381843. Includes bibliographical references (p. 211-213) and index.

This volume contains a series of essays by Ramet, six of which have been revised and updated. Three of the chapters are new. In collecting these essays together the author hopes "to suggest a vital interconnection and interaction among the political, cultural, and religious spheres and show how changes in one sphere are accompanied by parallel changes in the other spheres." (p. xv)

951. ———, **Nationalism and Federalism in Yugoslavia, 1962-1991**. 2nd ed. Bloomington: Indiana University Press, 1992. xviii, 346 p. ISBN: 0253207037. Includes bibliographical references (p. 331-337) and index.

"This book seeks to demonstrate that, with the multifaceted reform set in motion between 1963 and 1965, the Yugoslav political system acquired, domestically, the basic features of an international balance-of-power system. It will show that these features account for the basic pattern and dynamics of Yugoslav politics to the present day. In this spirit, I will outline, in the pages that follow, a theory that synthesizes the insights of several balance-of-power theorists, including Morton A. Kaplan and Dina A. Zinnes." (p. xvii) The book is divided into three parts. Part one examines the "dynamics of nationalism" and the problems that arise from ethnic nationalism. In part two Ramet describes the role of the autonomous federal unit in the Yugoslav system and how the autonomy of these units has contributed to the rise of nationalism. In part three the hypotheses concerning ethnic nationalism are tested through a variety of case studies that look at the reforms of 1962-1971, the Croatian crisis (1967-72), problems in the economic sector, nationalist tensions from 1968-1990 and the civil war. This book updates Ramet's 1984 publication.

952. **Yugoslavia, a Fractured Federalism,** edited by Dennison Rusinow. Lanham, Md.: Distributed by arrangement with UPA, 1988. xvi, 182 p. *Wilson Center Perspectives*, ISBN: 0943875080; 0943875072 (pbk). Includes bibliography (p. 177).

This group of essays, originally presented at a conference in 1986, covers all major aspects of contemporary Yugoslavia: federal government structure, politics and government, social and economic conditions. "Its assessment of Yugoslavia recognizes that the country's long experience with nonalignment and market socialism sets it formally apart from 'Eastern Europe,' and also that the complexity of the Yugoslav experience often demands single-country study rather than cross- or multi-country comparisons usually favored by the program as promoting better analysis." (p. xiii)

953. Sekelj, Laslo, **Yugoslavia: The Process of Disintegration**. Boulder, Colo.: Social Science Monographs, 1993. xxiv, 234 p. *East European Monographs; no. 359. Atlantic Studies on Society in Change; no. 76*, ISBN: 0880332565. Translated from the Serbo-Croat by Vera Vukelic. Includes bibliographical references (p. 287-305) and indexes.

Sekelj's book traces what the author sees as the inevitable disintegration of the Yugoslav state, a crisis whose causes "were built into the very foundations of the new Yugoslavia." (p. xxii) The argument is divided into four parts: 1) Theory and Practice of Self-management in Yugoslavia, 2) The League of Communists of Yugoslavia, or about Oligarchy; 3) The Crisis; and 4) The Final Disintegration of the Yugoslav State.

954. Seroka, James, and Rados Smiljkovic, **Political Organizations in Socialist Yugoslavia**. Durham, NC: Duke University Press, 1986. xxvi, 321 p. *Duke Press Policy Studies, 0020-6555*, ISBN: 0822305704. Includes bibliography (p.269-299) and index.

Coauthored by an American and Yugoslav professor, this unique study analyzes the structure and operation of the Yugoslav political system. Information on developments and organizational structure is provided for the League of Communists, the Socialist Alliance, the Trade Union Alliance, and the League of Socialist Youth. The authors feel that the feature of Yugoslav sociopolitical organization they describe can be "put into broader perspective" when examining the Yugoslav political system as a whole. "What emerges is a picture of a pluralist and competitive political system (within certain limitations) in which politics rather than mere administration plays a crucial role." (p. xvii)

955. Stokes, Gale, **Politics as Development: The Emergence of Political Parties in Nineteenth Century Serbia**. Durham, N.C.: Duke University Press, 1990. xiv, 400 p. ISBN: 0822310163. Includes bibliography (p.371-387) and index.

Although backward in many areas such as literacy and industrialization, Serbia politically was as advanced as many more economically developed states. "The purpose of this study is to show how this modern political system in Serbia began, how constitutionalism led to the development of a party system—even though Serbia did not enjoy the pluralist socioeconomic system that a party system seems designed to reflect—and how an increasingly emotional nationalism became the standard form of Serbian political discourse." (p. 2) This study focuses on the years 1869 to 1883 and the struggle between the liberals, progressives, radicals and Milan Obrenovic, ruler of Serbia from 1868 on. The chapters are chronologically arranged tracing the development of Serbia's political system to its ultimate test, a peasant revolt brought on by the King's refusal to accept a radical electoral victory.

956. Zimmerman, William, **Open Borders, Nonalignment and the Political Evolution of Yugoslavia**. Princeton N.J.: Princeton University Press, 1987. ix, 158 p. ISBN: 0691077304. Includes bibliography (p. 149-153) and index.

In this work William Zimmerman focuses on the effects the international environment has on a state's development. In particular he concentrates on three central areas. First he examines national-international linkages turning to issues such as influences on foreign policy formulation, strategies for alignment and the like. The second area of concern is the influence of external factors in the Yugoslav economy and Yugoslav institutions and the policy process. Finally he discusses the relation between international and Yugoslav economies and Yugoslav mass-elite relations. The author hopes to examine these problems from a different point of view than has been adopted in the literature on the subject in the past rejecting the idea that Yugoslavia is a part of Eastern Europe and the notion that there has been "negligible" foreign influence on Yugoslav domestic affairs. The book is arranged topically examining the general question of foreign influence and then looking at specific areas that have been affected by the international environment such as politics, migrant workers and the governance of a seventh republic. Reviews: *Perspective: Review of New*

Books 17, no.1 (Winter 1988): 29. *American Political Science Review* 82, no.2 (June 1988): 673-74. *Political Science Quarterly* 103, no.2 (Summer 1988): 376-77.

FOREIGN RELATIONS

957. Heuser, Beatrice, **Western "Containment" Policies in the Cold War: The Yugoslav Case, 1943-53**. London: Routledge, 1989. xx, 304 p. ISBN: 0415013038. Includes bibliography (p. 277-297) and index.

Heuser's purpose is to concentrate on the Tito-Stalin split and the effect this had on Western perceptions of Yugoslavia and the Soviet Union. Using primary sources, the author examines the policies adopted by the United States towards Yugoslavia as a result of this split. Reviews: *Canadian Journal of History* 5, no.2 (August 1990): 293-295. *International History Review* 12, no.2 (May 1990): 410-413. *Diplomatic History* 14, no.4 (Fall 1990): 623-629.

958. Martin, David, **The Web of Disinformation: Churchill's Yugoslav Blunder**. San Diego: Harcourt Brace Jovanovich, 1990. 425 p. ISBN: 0151807043. Includes bibliographical references and index.

Martin attempts to explain the dramatic switch in policy that occurred in Great Britain just before the end of 1943 with respect to Yugoslavia. Britain abandoned General Draza Mihailovic and supported Josip Broz Tito instead. Martin believes that James Klugman, the fifth man of Soviet espionage, was responsible for sabotaging Britain's support of Mihailovic.

959. United States. Congress. Senate. Committee on Foreign Relations. Subcommittee on European Affairs, **Civil Strife in Yugoslavia: The United States Response: Hearing Before the Subcommittee on European Affairs of the Committee on Foreign Relations, United States Senate, One Hundred Second Congress**. Washington: U.S. G.P.O., 1991. 165 p.

These hearings of the Subcommittee on European Affairs of the Committee on Foreign Relations of the U.S. Senate focus solely on events in Yugoslavia. The need for this meeting was created by the unstable situation in Yugoslavia and the changes in the Eastern bloc as a whole. Besides the testimony of many experts on Yugoslav affairs and U.S-Yugoslav relations, the volume includes an appendix with numerous articles, interviews and prepared statements, all intended to clarify the situation in Yugoslavia and suggest the appropriate response to it.

ECONOMICS, BUSINESS AND TRADE

960. Bauwens, Jan G., Nicholas Buento De Mesquita, and Martin Jones, **Industrial Co-operation and Investment in Yugoslavia**. Luxembourg: Office for Official Publications of the European Communities, 1986. viii, 161 p. *Document (Commission of the European Communities)*, ISBN: 928256410X. Bibliography (p. 114).

This book describes business conditions in Yugoslavia in 1986. It is a technical manual issued by the Commission of European Communities providing information on opportunities for investment, legislation on technology transfer, practical problems in establishing joint ventures, taxation of profits and import/export regulations.

961. Dyker, David A., **Yugoslavia: Socialism, Development, and Debt**. New York: Routledge, 1990. xi, 201 p. ISBN: 0415007453. Includes bibliographical references (p. 186-195).

Dyker examines the workings of the Yugoslav economy with a view toward analyzing Yugoslav balance of payments, external debt service and international trade. In the first four chapters the author examines the Yugoslav economy, focusing on the post-war years through the 1970s. Chapters five through nine examine more closely topics such as growth strategy and economic structure, the debt-service crisis of 1982, adjustment policies in the 1980s, external economic relations, and politics and the price of reform.

962. Flakierski, Henryk, **The Economic System & Income Distribution in Yugoslavia**. Armonk, N.Y.: M.E. Sharpe, 1989. viii, 104 p. *Eastern European Economics*, vol. 27, no. 4. ISBN: 0873326059. Includes bibliographical references (p. 89-104).

Flakierski's purpose here is to investigate the relationship between self-government and the income distribution pattern in Yugoslavia. The work consists of five chapters. He first surveys the changes in the Yugoslav economic system since 1945, emphasizing changes in distribution principles and policies. Chapter two consists of a statistical analysis of pay inequalities for the period 1964-1983. Chapters three and four are devoted to defining the relationship between differentials and the socioeconomic characteristics of Yugoslavia's self-management system. In the last chapter he draws his conclusions from the data presented. In part he argues that "pay must be differentiated to a greater degree than it is now in order to motivate better work." (p. 1)

963. Gapinski, James H., **The Economic Structure and Failure of Yugoslavia**. Westport, Conn.: Praeger, 1993. xviii, 212 p. ISBN: 0275946002. Includes bibliographical references (p. 193-202) and index.

The motivating question that drives this book is whether the failure of Yugoslavia could have been prevented. After a brief historical, political and economic introduction, subsequent chapters cover Illyrian theory and its implications for modeling Yugoslavia quantify relationships such as consumption, investment, labor, etc., prices, a macroeconomic simulation and conclusions.

964. Gapinski, James H., Borislav Skegro, and Thomas W. Zuehlke, **Modeling the Economic Performance of Yugoslavia**. New York: Praeger, 1989. 292 p. ISBN: 0275933857. Includes bibliographical references (p. 275-283).

A cooperative venture between the Ekonomski Institut Zagreb and Florida State University produced an economic model for the study of Yugoslavia's economy. The model was a small one involving more than 50 equations. It was policy oriented focusing on improving the existing system and it was based on the main sectors of Yugoslavia's economy: industry, social agriculture, private agriculture and the non-agricultural sectors. The book is structured as a reference source for others exploring the same problem. "Accordingly, Chapters 1 and 2 concentrate on the facts of the Yugoslav economy; they provide background information. Chapters 3 through 6 examine the different components of the economy and review the theoretical basis and the empirical performance of the equations describing those components. Chapter 7 collects the equations to form and test a complete model-building effort. Chapter 8 and 9 then appeal to the mark 1.0 [model] to study remedial policy maneuvers." (p. xv)

965. Lampe, John R., Russell O. Prickett, and Ljubisa S. Adamovic, **Yugoslav-American Economic Relations Since World War II**. Durham, N.C.: Duke University Press, 1990. xi, 249 p. ISBN: 0822310619. Includes bibliographical references (p. 229-235) and index.

A completely new business environment exists today in Eastern Europe: those seeking to establish business in that part of the world will need to draw on all the information and experience available. This volume attempts to present some part of that information by reviewing the history of Yugoslav-American economic relations. "We hoped to provide an objective account of the relationship which, being binational in authorship and available in the languages of both countries, could provide a useful reference and historical review, not only for scholars, but also for professionals in government, business, and banking in both countries. In particular we aimed to provide a basis for encouragement when dealings became difficult, by referring to past problems encountered and in the main successfully resolved." (p. x) The authors present a survey of economic history from 1945 on, discussing among other topics, difficulties that were resolved, connections established, and methods of debt repayment. The study is not comprehensive. The book is arranged chronologically and includes an extensive bibliography.

966. Lydall, Harold, **Yugoslavia in Crisis**. New York: Oxford University Press, 1989. xii, 255 p. ISBN: 0198286953. Includes bibliography (p. 249-250) and index.

Since 1979 the Yugoslav economy has been in a constant state of decline. This book offers an analysis of the underlying causes of the present crisis. After two introductory paragraphs that describe background information about the economy and the political situation, the author describes the causes of the decline and then examines in separate chapters enterprise self-management, enterprise income, taxation and money, foreign trade, and regional politics. Conclusions are presented in a final chapter. Review: *Annals of The American Academy of Political and Social Science* no. 509 (May 1990): 199.

967. **Essays on the Yugoslav Economic Model,** edited by Geroge Macesich with the assistance of Rikard Lang and Dragomir Vojnic. New York: Praeger, 1989. xv, 246 p. ISBN: 0275926702. Includes bibliographical references and index.

The upshot of these essays, written prior to the Yugoslav civil war, is that the Yugoslav economy must resort to a greater reliance on markets, become more export oriented, and move toward a fully convertible currency. After experiencing three-and-one-half decades of healthy growth and a transformation from an agrarian to an industrial economy, the Yugoslav economy at the end of the 1970s began to be faced with high inflation, lulls in production, growing unemployment, a decrease in labor productivity, and excessive foreign debt. The thirteen essays presented here examine various aspects of these problems and offer suggestions for solutions. Most of the authors are collaborators involved with the Long-Term Program of Economic Stabilization and wrote, therefore, not only with an academic, but with a practical, concern for the problems identified.

968. Organization for Economic Co-operation and Development. Environment Committee, **Environmental Policies in Yugoslavia: A Review by the OECD and Its Environment Committee,** undertaken in 1985 at the request of the government of Yugoslavia. Washington, D.C.: OECD Publications and Information Centre, 1986. 160 p. ISBN: 9264128662. Includes bibliographical references.

After an introductory chapter that gives a general overview of Yugoslav environmental policy and its context, other chapters follow that cover specific policies governing the environment of towns and cities, agriculture and soils, forestry, air management, energy, water management, chemical waste, the conservation of nature and monuments, tourism, and international technical cooperation.

969. Plestina, Dijana, **Regional Development in Communist Yugoslavia: Success, Failure, and Consequences**. Boulder, Colo.: Westview Press, 1992. xxix, 223 p. ISBN: 081338186X. Includes bibliographical references (p. 203-215) and index.

Dijana Plestina looks at the longstanding disparities in Yugoslavia as a factor contributing to the recent disintegration of that country. "Basing her argument on longitudinal data and on in-depth interviews with Yugoslav leaders at federal and regional levels...Dijana Plestina examines and assesses the economic inequalities as well as the effects that the leadership's regional policies had on them. She shows that despite the mandate for equalization that was part of socialist doctrine, Yugoslav leaders were at first unwilling, and later unable, to formalize policies that would enhance the economic well-being of the poorest regions." (p. 223) The book is chronologically arranged beginning with a general section on Yugoslavia's history and then devoting individual chapters to each decade from the 1950s through the 1980s. The final chapter reviews the geopolitical, ethnonational and economic problems that led to the current crisis and looks ahead to the possible future outcomes of the war. Several appendixes include background information.

970. Sarkovic, T. Misha, **Direct Foreign Investment in Yugoslavia: A Microeconomic Model**. New York: Praeger, 1986. xvii, 206 p. ISBN: 027592159X. Includes bibliography (p.189-204) and index.

In this volume Sarkovic "focuses on foreign investment in Yugoslavia and specifically on the important issue of joint ventures. The study discusses incentives and barriers for the formation of joint ventures in Yugoslavia. It provides a theoretical microeconomic framework useful for gaining insights that may not be immediately obvious into the complex issues surrounding joint ventures." (p. ix)

971. Schierup, Carl-Ulrik, **Migration, Socialism and the International Division of Labour: The Yugoslavian Experience**. Brookfield, Vt.: Gower Pub. Co., 1990. xii, 339 p. *Research in Ethnic Relations Series*, ISBN: 1856280632. Includes bibliographical references (p. 315-339).

The OECD has envisioned a partnership between countries who receive and send migrant labor. Schierup discusses the development of this partnership "as reflected in Yugoslavia's modern integration into an emerging transnational division of labour." (p. 3) Topics covered include the roots of underdevelopment, migration and immigration policy, migration and the international division of labor, the economic reality of Yugoslavia, and labor under bureaucratic rule.

972. **Yugoslavia in Turmoil: After Self-Management?**, edited by James Simmie and Joze Dekleva. London: Pinter Publishers, 1991. xviii, 167 p. ISBN: 0861871413. Includes bibliographical references and indexes.

"The contributors to this volume analyse the theory of self-management and how it operated in practice. They conclude that this approach did not bring the anticipated benefits, and that inequality not only persisted but actually increased under self-management. The economic situation has therefore been a driving force for political reform." (back cover) The essays are grouped into five parts beginning with an overview of self-management as it developed in Yugoslavia. This is followed by a section on government politics where the affect on the political situation is discussed. Section three analyzes economic growth and change in Yugoslavia. In the fourth section social problems are the focus. The final section discusses the relevance of the Yugoslav experience for other developing nations. Some essays include bibliographical references.

973. Uvalic, Milica, **Investment and Property Rights in Yugoslavia: The Long Transition to a Market Economy**. New York: Cambridge University Press, 1992. xii, 260 p. *Soviet and East European Studies; 86*, ISBN: 052140147X. Includes bibliographical references and index.

"The intention of this book is to evaluate the impact of such 'dualism'—self-management and increasing use of the market on the one hand, and socialist features on the other—on the nature of the Yugoslav system, by focusing on the specific field of investment. The period examined is primarily post-1966, since it is with the reforms of the 1960s that substantial institutional changes were introduced into the economy, in particular in the field of investment." (p. 1) The book is divided into three parts. Part I examines the institutional theoretical framework in which the study takes place. Part II evaluates the empirical evidence on the nature of the Yugoslav system. Part III focuses on the pressure for more radical reforms in Yugoslavia.

974. Yagci, Fahrettin, and Steven Kamin, **Macroeconomic Policies and Adjustment in Yugoslavia: Some Counterfactual Simulations**. Washington, DC: World Bank, 1987. 29 p. *World Bank Discussion Papers, 0259-210X, 16*, ISBN: 0821309382.

This brief study by the World Bank examines ways by which Yugoslavia might have averted the economic crisis it faced in the 1980s. Using models, three conclusions were reached: "First, the balance of payments crisis was attributable to a deterioration in the policy environment, Second, the crisis could have been avoided with alternative macroeconomic policies. Third, Yugoslavia could have achieved external balance and satisfactory growth in investment and output since 1980 had the policy environment been reformed promptly and significantly." (p. 1) After presenting the background to the crisis the authors describe their model, evaluate alternative policies and present a summary of their conclusions.

THE SOCIETY, SOCIOLOGY

975. **Violations of the Helsinki Accords, Yugoslavia: A Report Prepared for the Helsinki Review Conference, Vienna, November 1986**, by Mary Jane Camejo and Catherine Fitzpatrick. New York: Helsinki Watch Committee, 1986. iv, 51 p. *A Helsinki Watch Report*, ISBN: 0938579770. Includes bibliography (p. 51).

This report chronicles human rights violations in Yugoslavia. It is arranged topically, covering violations in the areas of legal and extralegal punishment, the scholars' trials, human rights monitoring, freedom of expression, freedom of the press and publication, prison conditions and torture, unrest in Kosovo, Bosnia-Herzegovina, émigrés and workers abroad, and workers' rights.

976. Davis, James C., **Rise from Want: A Peasant Family in the Machine Age**. Philadelphia: University of Pennsylvania Press, 1986. xv, 165 p. ISBN: 0812280342. Includes bibliography (p. 153-161) and index.

Davis "explores the ways in which a family of poor peasants in the Karst plateau above Trieste, Italy, experienced the effects of industrialization and modernization and lived through that great change, that rise from want." (p.xi)

977. Magid, Alvin, **Private Lives, Public Surfaces: Grassroots Perspectives and the Legitimacy Question in Yugoslavia Socialism**. New York: Columbia University Press, 1991. 617 p. *East European Monographs, no. 314*, ISBN: 0880332123. Includes bibliographical references (p.611-617).

The author presents nineteen profiles of individual lives in Yugoslavia. "Each of the nineteen profiles deals with the interviewee's private life; with Yugoslavia and its public life in his or her own lifetime; and with how one's own affairs and the country's seemed to the interviewee to intersect and amplify each other." (p. x) The book is in three parts. Part one is a long essay on Yugoslav socialism under siege; Part two consists of the profiles; and part three contains the notes and bibliography.

LANGUAGE AND LITERATURE

978. Benson, Morton, **An English-Serbo-Croatian Dictionary**. New York: Cambridge University Press, 1990. 722 p. ISBN: 0521384966. Includes bibliographical references (p. xliv-xlv).

This third edition of Benson's well-regarded dictionary updates previous redactions. This one is distinguished by the addition of computer terminology. The dictionary is based on standard American English but British spelling variants are also given. Each entry indicates the equivalent in Serbo-Croatian, the part of speech of the word, hyphenation, stress, and American Standard pronunciation. A lengthy introduction provides further guidance.

979. **Language Planning in Yugoslavia,** edited by Ranko Bugarski and Celia Hawkesworth. Columbus, Ohio: Slavica Publishers, 1992. 233 p. ISBN: 0893572322. Includes bibliographical references and index.

The papers collected in this volume resulted from a conference held in September of 1989. The picture of language planning it presents was therefore drawn during the Socialist regime. Nevertheless, the essays describe an attempt at intermingling numerous ethnic groups of diverse cultural and political backgrounds. The essays are grouped under three headings: "Language Situation and General Policy," "Planning of Individual Languages" and "Aspects of Change and Variation." An appendix includes a case study on Rusyn language planning. The book was intended for sociolinguists and students of language policy and of Yugoslavia.

980. Elson, Mark J., **A Diachronic Interpretation of Macedonian Verbal Morphology**. New York: E. Mellon Press, 1990. ii, 207 p. *Studies in Slavic Language and Literature, vol.2*, ISBN: 0889462925. Includes bibliographical references.

This is the second of two volumes analyzing Macedonian verbal morphology. It assumes a knowledge of the basic verbal system. This volume "attempts to integrate the facts by establishing: 1) the system which united them in the earliest period of the language; and 2) the changes which relate this system to the contemporary one." (p. i) The first chapter summarizes the contemporary verbal system. The following chapters discuss the evolution of verbal items, dissonance initial vowel, and morphophonemic changes in the stem. The author uses a combination of Praguian and generative theory in his analysis. This is a highly technical linguistic analysis of Macedonian verbal structure. It includes a glossary of verbs and nouns cited and a bibliography. Review: *Slavic and East European Journal* 35, no.2 (Summer 1991): 303-304.

981. Hawkesworth, Celia, **Colloquial Serbo-Croat**. New York: Routledge & Kegan Paul, 1986. xxi, 288 p. *Colloquial Series*, ISBN: 0710099207.

This basic textbook for foreigners presents the main points of Serbo-Croat grammar and introduces a basic vocabulary. Each chapter consists of one or more dialogues, a list of newly introduced vocabulary, explorations of grammatical points covered, and exercises.

982. Holton, Milne, and Vasa D. Mihailovich, **Serbian Poetry from the Beginnings to the Present**. Columbus, OH: Distributed by Slavic Publishers, 1988. xxxi, 435 p. *Yale Russian and East European Publications, no. 11*, ISBN: 0936568117. Includes bibliographical references.

A chronological history of Serbian poetry beginning with the songs of the tribal Serbs and continuing to the contemporary poetry. The two traditions of oral narratives in verse form and the liturgical literature that was secularized and passed to the literature of the bourgeoisie are both represented in this volume. The poems are divided into chapters based on their chronological development. The volume includes poetry from Old Serbia, poetry of the Serbian enlightenment, the Romantic period, and the modern age. Along with the translations is a descriptive text. The bibliography has sections of English language publications of anthologies, individual poems, collection of works of specific poets, critical works, and historical background materials.

983. Jovanovski, Meto, **Faceless Men & Other Macedonian Stories,** by Meto Jovanovski; edited with an introduction by Jeffrey Folks; translated by Jeffrey Folks, Milne Holton and Charles Simic. London: Forest Books, 1992. xiii, 77 p. ISBN: 1856100073.

Meto Jovanovski has written many works and numerous titles have been translated. He is thus known to Western audiences and feels he has been influenced by such American authors as Hemingway and Faulkner. Jovanovski's writings have some common themes such as Macedonia's future and its social and economic conditions. He is an author who draws heavily on his origins, i.e. Macedonian village life, in his writings. "In these stories from Macedonia, Meto Jovanovski writes wittily against urban authorities, whose agents are everywhere and nowhere, and who conduct absurd 'modernizing' campaigns such as shooting all the dogs in the village.... And like John Berger, he persuades us that it is often the villager who is most in touch with the deepest realities of life." (back cover) These writings are meant to introduce him to American audiences who may be unfamiliar with his short stories.

984. Lehiste, Ilse, and Pavle Ivic, **Word and Sentence Prosody in Serbocroatian.** Cambridge, Mass.: MIT Press, 1986. xiii, 329 p. *Current Studies in Linguistics Series, 13,* ISBN: 0262121115. Includes bibliography (p. 297-322) and index.

This work is the result of over twenty years collaborative research by the authors. It deals with "the so-called Neostokavian accentuation, that is, with the prosodic system of the Serbocroatian dialects." (p. l) Specifically, this book "is an investigation of the phonetic (and phonological) nature of the prosodic distinctions and not of their use in other morphophonemics or the lexicon" (p. 1).

985. Magner, Thomas F., **Introduction to the Croatian and Serbian Language.** 4th ed. Philadelphia: Pennsylvania University Press, 1991. xii, 388 p. ISBN: 0271006854. Includes index.

This standard textbook of Serbo-Croatian is now in its fourth edition. Each lesson begins with parallel texts (conversations, expository prose) in both Serbian and Croatian. Then vocabulary, explanations, and exercises follow. While some grammar is contained in each lesson, most is gathered in a separate grammar section.

986. **The Battle of Kosovo,** translated from the Serbian by John Matthias and Vladeta Vuckovic preface by Charles Simic. Ohio: Swallow Press, 1987. 103 p. ISBN: 0804008973 (pbk); 0804008965.

A translation of the Heroic Epics originally written in Serbian that describe the adventures and daring feats of various rebels during the Turkish occupation in the 14th century. This new translation strives to capture the original feel of the poetry.

987. **The Horse Has Six Legs: An Anthology of Serbian Poetry,** edited, translated, and with an introduction by Charles Simic. Saint Paul: Graywolf Press, 1992. 222 p. ISBN: 1555971652. Translated from Serbo-Croatian.

"In *The Horse Has Six Legs,* Pulitzer Prize-winner Charles Simic has brought together revised versions of his translations of over one hundred poems by some of Serbia's greatest post-war poets, including works by Vasko Popa, Ivan Lalic, and Milorad Pavic. This anthology offers an absorbing and timely journey through one of Europe's richest bodies of poetry." (back cover) Brief biographical entries on each poet are included in the text.

988. **The Oxford-Duden Pictorial Serbo-Croat and English Dictionary,** Croatian text edited by Vjekoslav Boban, English text edited by John Pheby, illustrations by Jochen Schmidt. New York: Clarendon Press, 1988. 677 p. ISBN: 0198691653. Includes indexes.

This Serbo-Croat dictionary is the product of a collaborative effort between the Oxford University Press, the Bibliographisches Institut in Mannheim and Cankarjeva Zalozba. The pictorial dictionary provides the user with the additional tool of pictures, in some cases most effective in conveying the meaning of a term. The dictionary is divided into 384 sections which cover many areas of everyday life and scientific activity. An alphabetical index is included at the back of the volume.

INDIVIDUAL AUTHORS

989. Kis, Danilo, **The Encyclopedia of the Dead,** translated by Michael Henry Heim. New York: Farrar Straus Giroux, 1989. 199 p. ISBN: 0374148260. Translation of: Enciklopedija mrtvih.

As Kis states in a postscript: "All the stories in this book, to a greater or lesser extent, come under the sign of a theme I would call metaphysical: ever since the Gilgamesh epic, death has been one of the obsessive themes of literature. If the term 'divan' did not call for brighter hues and clearer tones, the collection might bear the subtitle The West-Easterly Divan for its obvious ironic and parodic undercurrent." (p.191)

990. Bogert, Ralph Baker, **The Writer as Naysayer: Miroslav Krleza and the Aesthetic of Interwar Central Europe.** Columbus, Ohio: Slavica Publishers, 1991. 266 p. *UCLA Slavic Studies, v. 20*, ISBN: 0893572128. Includes bibliographical references (p. 249-257) and index.

Miroslav Krleza is considered the most important author of Croatia and one of the most influential cultural figures of twentieth century Yugoslavia. This study is divided into four chapters that reflect the contexts of Krleza's work: 1) intellectual background, 2) historical setting, 3) theoretical underpinnings, and 4) poetic form. Thus, chapter one examines the social context of Austro-Hungarian cultural life. In chapter two Krleza's role in the two decades of the interwar period is examined, with particular emphasis on his position on the "imposition of social commitment on the practice of art." (p. 17) Chapter three studies the degree to which Krleza defines the theoretical role of art. The final chapter looks at the aesthetic principles behind the Glembay prose and drama cycle. An index of Krleza's works is included.

991. Lalic, Ivan V., **Rollcall of Mirrors: Selected Poems of Ivan V. Lalic,** translated and with an introduction by Charles Simic. Middletown, Conn.: Wesleyan University Press, 1988. 67 p. ISBN: 0819511528 (pbk); 0819521515.

Although seen as a Modernist, Lalic's poetry is often classical. He uses Classical Greek poetry and Romantic visionary poems for his models. Review: *Yale Review* 79, no.3 (Spring 1990): 467-482.

992. Pavic, Milorad, **Dictionary of the Khazars: A Lexicon Novel in 100,000 Words,** translated from the Serbo-Croatian by Christina Pribicevic-Zoric. New York: Knopf, 1988. 338 p. ISBN: 0394571835. Translation of: Hazarski recnik.

This book is a series of essays, letters, and prose poems all having some relation to the Khazar question. The male and female edition differ by one passage, in Dr. Dorothea Schultz's last letter. The comparison of the two editions will enable the book to "fit together as a whole." (p. 335) The male and female comparers will then need this book no longer "for what comes next is their affair alone, and it is with more than any reading." (p. 335, male edition)

993. ———, **Landscape Painted with Tea,** translated from the Serbo-Croatian by Christina Pribicevic-Zoric. New York: Knopf, 1990. 339 p. ISBN: 0394582179. Includes index.

A novel whose main character is Svilar, a brilliant architect whose off-beat designs are never built.

994. Lekic, Anita, **The Quest for Roots: The Poetry of Vasko Popa,** preface by Charles Simic. New York: P. Lang, 1993. xiv, 178 p. *Balkan Studies; v. 2*, ISBN: 0820417777. Includes bibliographical references (p. 163-168) and index.

Anita Lekic has written an analysis of Yugoslav poet Vasko Popa's work focusing on its "principal motifs" and themes. "The chapters that follow focus on the existentialist bent evinced in the early works and the absorption with mythic themes that eventually supplants existentialism in the later works. What is characteristic of Popa's best work is that it manifests a concern with the universal aspects of human existence and readily lends itself, in its artistic complexity, to a wide range of interpretations." (p. 15) The book is thematically arranged discussing Popa's move to existentialism, his fascination with the human need for symbols and myths. A short biographical and bibliographical essay are included.

995. Salamun, Tomaz, **The Selected Poems of Tomaz Salamun,** edited by Charles Simic, with an introduction by Robert Hass. New York: Ecco Press, 1988. xxviii, 93 p. *Modern European Poetry Series*, ISBN: 0880011602.

Salamun, a Slovene writer, came of age in the 1960s. The translations come from two sources: a writers' workshop at the University of Iowa in 1970-1971 and more recent translations by Charles Simic. Reviews: *Slovene Studies* 12, no.1 (1990): 115-116. *Field* no.40 (Spring 1989):60-61.

996. Goldman, Kenneth A., **Formulaic Analysis of Serbocroatian Oral Epic Song: Songs of Avdo Avdic.** New York: Garland, 1990. xxvi, 322 p. *Harvard Dissertations in Folklore and Oral Tradition*, ISBN: 0824028821. Includes bibliographical references (p. 321-322).

Eight of the songs of Avdo Avdic, a singer from Gacko Hercegovina, have been chosen for this study of oral-tradition epic songs. The focus of this analysis is Avdic's use of formula, a common form of composition in the South Slavic tradition. "Goldman's purpose was not only to demonstrate the singer's use of formulas, but also, and highly significantly, in that very process to test the concept and definition of the term 'formula'. Although Goldman's final chapter broaches the subject of themes and the function of formulas and formulaic expression in them, his main contribution lies in the area of formulaic research." (p. vii) This highly technical study is arranged in five chapters. The first provides background on the not-frequent patterns. Chapter three discusses formulaic variations. Chapter four analyzes the synthetic verse paradigm. The final chapter looks at the function of formulas.

ARTS AND CULTURE

997. Milojkovic-Djuric, Jelena, **Tradition and Avant-Garde: Literature and Art in Serbian Culture, 1900-1918.** New York: Distributed by Columbia University Press, 1988. vi, 227 p. *East European Monographs, no. 234*, ISBN: 0880331313. Includes bibliography (p. 194-211) and index.

In a previous volume the author explored the same theme of tradition and the avant-garde in Serbia between the wars. This volume continues that interdisciplinary research for the period 1900-1918. Individual chapters are devoted to the national survival in Serbian cultural history, fine arts, literature, musical arts, theater and cultural progress. Review: *Slavic Review* 48, no.4 (Winter 1989): 698.

DISSIDENT MOVEMENTS

998. Djilas, Milovan, **Of Prisons and Ideas,** translated from the Serbo-Croatian by Michael Boro Petrovich. San Diego: Harcourt Brace Jovanovich, 1986. 166 p. ISBN: 0151679797. Translation of: Tamnica i ideja.

A first-hand account on political repression in Yugoslavia is contained in this volume. The prison system under Tito in the 60s is described in detail. Reviews: *Journal of Croatian Studies* 27, (1986): 148-150. *Orbis* 31, no.1 (Spring 1987): 156-157.

NATIONAL MINORITIES

999. Vukmanovic-Tempo, Svetozar, **Struggle for the Balkans,** translated by Charles Bartlett. London: Merlin Press, 1990. vi, 355 p. ISBN: 0850363470. Translation of: Borba za Balkan. Includes bibliographical references.

Tsola Dragoicheva, a former member of the Bulgarian Communist Party, published her memoirs in 1979. Those memoirs portray a relationship between the Bulgarian and Yugoslav communist parties that Svetozar Vukmanovic believes gives a false impression at best. His strongest objections are to her section on World War II. "Confronted by attempts to distort the truth and falsely portray events in which I actively participated, I decided to write a book in which I would compare what Dragoicheva says with the historical documentary evidence which, fortunately, has been preserved." (pp ii-iii) The author is particularly concerned with the portrayal of the National Liberation Struggle of the Macedonians. The author is not a historian but is attempting to set the record straight and does draw on documentary sources such as the records of the British Military Missions to support his position.

CIVIL WAR

1000. **War Crimes in Bosnia-Hercegovina**. New York: Human Rights Watch, 1992. viii, 359 p. *Helsinki Watch Report*, ISBN: 1564320839.

This detailed report issued by Helsinki Watch calls on the United Nations to intervene in the war in Bosnia-Hercegovina to put an end to the abuses perpetrated there. "The full scale war that has been raging in Bosnia-Hercegovina since early April has been marked by extreme violation of international humanitarian law, also known as the law of war. Indeed, violations of the rules of war are being committed with incredible frequency." (p. 1) A detailed discussion of the positions of the various sides is followed by an extensive listing of the violations of the rules of war. This is followed by a description of the status of refugees and the role of the international community. Appendixes of actions already taken by the U.N. and Helsinki Watch are also included.

1001. **Why Bosnia?: Writings on the Balkan War,** edited by Rabia Ali & Lawrence Lifschultz. Stony Creek, Conn.: Pamphleteer's Press, 1993. lv, 353 p. ISBN: 0963058789. Includes bibliographical references.

This unusual collection of essays attempts to analyze the causes and results of the Bosnian tragedy. The contributors include scholars, journalists and writers from all over the world. "The leitmotif of the collection is multicultural Bosnia—its significance, symbolism and the necessity of its survival in a world increasingly divided against itself. In carefully documented, strongly argued, vividly written accounts, the authors dispel the mist of confusion, misinformation, and propaganda that has obstructed the formulation of a coherent, effective, and just international policy on Bosnia" (back cover).

1002. Cohen, Lenard J., **Broken Bonds: The Disintegration of Yugoslavia**. Boulder: Westview Press, 1993. xvi, 299 p. ISBN: 0813318548. Includes bibliographical references and index.

Cohen's book was one of the first scholarly studies on the disintegration of Yugoslavia. "I begin this book by revisiting the genesis of the 'Yugoslav idea' prior to the creation of the first united South Slav state.... In subsequent chapters I discuss the factors that have fostered and impeded the more recent evolution of the Yugoslav state and political development devoting particular attention to the causes and consequences of the Second Yugoslavia's drift toward disintegration...In the concluding section of the book I consider the serious difficulties connected with the internationalization of 'the Yugoslav crisis' during 1992 and 1993, the savage ethnic and political conflict on the territory of the former Yugoslavia, and also some of the problems facing the successor states to the Yugoslav communist federation." (p. xv) The extensive background supplied by the author makes this a highly readable study of a complex problem.

1003. **The Truth About Yugoslavia: Why Working People Should Oppose Intervention,** edited by George Fyson. 1st ed. New York: Pathfinder, 1993. 89 p. ISBN: 0873487761. Includes bibliographical references and index.

This book presents a Western socialist argument against intervention in Yugoslavia. The essays compiled in this book were originally published in the socialist paper the *Militant*. "This book's authors look into these conflicts, explaining that the would-be capitalists that have emerged from the privileged caste in the former Yugoslavia are responsible for the slaughter taking place today—a slaughter imposed upon working people whose parents and grandparents made a socialist revolution in that country." (p. 17)

1004. Glenny, Misha, **The Fall of Yugoslavia: The Third Balkan War.** 2nd ed. London: Penguin, 1993. xiii, 257 p. ISBN: 0140234152. Includes index.

Misha Glenny has been reporting the war in Yugoslavia for the BBC from its tragic beginnings. "In his penetrating new book, the BBC's celebrated Central Europe correspondent paints incisive pen portraits of the main colorful—and often utterly ruthless—personalities involved. He offers a sobering eyewitness chronicle of the countdown to war.... Above all, he shows us the human realities behind the headlines and puts in its true, historical context one of the most ferocious civil wars of all time." (back cover)

1005. Gow, James, **Legitimacy and the Military: The Yugoslav Crisis**. New York: St. Martin's Press, 1992. 208 p. ISBN: 0312072090. Includes bibliographical references and index.

"In this volume the author analyses the role of the Yugoslav People's Army in the country's crisis, offering an original theoretical framework using concepts of regime legitimacy and military legitimacy. After reviewing the army's position historically within the sociopolitical system, the book concentrates on the period after 1988. Examination of the army's position in the multiple crises is followed by consideration of Slovenia's disputes with the military and Serbia which set the course of disintegration. An evaluation of the impact of crisis on the military's sociopolitical and functional capabilities is followed by analysis of the break-up of the communist party at the beginning of 1990 and the debates which followed—whether Yugoslavia should remain federal, become confederal or cease to be.

The author argues that regime relegitimation was tied to military relegitimation. He concludes that the army's behavior made preservation of Yugoslavia—its priority—increasingly unlikely, whereas at the beginning of 1991, rapid restructuring, depoliticisation and non-intervention might still have saved the country." (back cover)

1006. **The Tragedy of Yugoslavia: The Failure of Democratic Transformation,** edited by Jim Seroka and Vukasin Pavlovic. Armonk, N.Y.: M.E. Sharpe, 1992. xiii, 207 p. ISBN: 1563240351. Includes bibliographical references and index.

These essays were written before the outbreak of hostilities in Yugoslavia in 1991. "The essays in this volume will be of interest to anyone who is seeking an explanation for the failure of Titoist federal and nationality policies and the breakup of the Yugoslav community." (p.xii) The book presents a wide variety of opinion, including two authors each from Croatia, Serbia, and Slovenia.

1007. Sugarman, Martin A., **God Be With You: War in Croatia and Bosnia-Herzegovina: Photographs**. Malibu, Calif.: Sugarman Productions, 1993. ISBN: 1883071003.

This is a brutally honest and extremely well-done photographic record by the author of three separate trips in Croatia and Bosnia-Herzegovina during the last six months of 1992. There is no commentary, just captions for the photographs.

1008. Thompson, Mark, **Paper House: The Ending of Yugoslavia**. London: Hutchinson, 1992. 322 p. ISBN: 0091746191. Includes bibliographical references and index.

Thompson, a journalist for the Slovene magazine *Mladina*, attempts to explain to the Western reader recent events in Yugoslavia and their motivation. It is a personal description of the changes in the political landscape of the experience of the death of one nation, and the birth of another.

Author Index

Reference is to entry number.

Aaron, Frieda W., 742
Abel, Elie, 338
Abondolo, Daniel Mario, 607
Aczel, Richard L., 611
Adam, Jan, 126-127
Adamovic, Ljubisa S., 965
Adelson, Alan, 266
Ajani, Gianmaria, 156
Alcock, Leslie, 14
Alexander, Stella, 918
Ali, Rabia, 1001
Allcock, John B., 940
Allen, Bruce, 502
Allworth, Edward, 257
Alpert, Carl, 272
Alsop, Rachel, 548
Alvarez, A., 758
Aman, Anders, 324
Anderson, Christopher, 542
Andorka, Rudolf, 588
Andric, Ivo, 919
Arad, Yitzhak, 267
Arato, Andrew, 349
Arndt, Walter, 754, 759, 770
Ascherson, Neal, 650
Ash, Timothy Garton, *See* Garton Ash, Timothy
Aslund, Anders, 128, 155
Assetto, Valerie J., 129
Astalos, Georges, 893
Atkinson, A. B., 130
Austin, David, 14

Bachman, Ronald D., 853
Bailey, J. Martin, 15
Bak, Janos M., 566, 621
Baldassarri, Mario, 131
Banac, Ivo, 339, 941
Banc, C., 899-900
Banerjee, Maria Nemcova, 455
Baranczak, Stanislaw, 325, 743, 757
Baranovsky, Vladimir, 78
Barany, George, 606
Barker, Andrew, 520
Barker, Sebastian, 391
Barnard, Frederick M., 110
Barnes, Julian, 326
Barnett, Thomas P. M., 79
Barr, Nicholas, 724
Bartal, Israel, 669
Bartlett, Charles, 999
Bartos, Frantisek Michalek, 404
Bartoszewski, Wladyslaw, 814-815
Batt, Judy, 65, 132-133
Bauman, Janina, 268
Bauwens, Jan G., 960
Baylis, Thomas A., 503

Bazskehazi, Attila, 589
Begley, Louis, 744
Behr, Edward, 872
Beissinger, Margaret H., 891
Beitz, Berthold, 546
Belev, Georgi, 390
Bell, John D., 392
Beller, Ilex, 816
Benjamin, Walter, 523
Benski, Stanislaw, 754
Benson, Morton, 978
Ben-Tzvi, Mordecai, 671
Berend, Ivan T., 16, 590, 636
Berglund, Sten, 340
Bergson, Abram, 134
Bermeo, Nancy, 341
Bernhard, Michael H., 801
Bertalan, Laszlo, 588
Berthelot, Henri Mathias, 855
Bertsch, Gary K., 335
Bethin, Christina Y., 737
Bialecki, Ireneusz, 797
Biberaj, Elez, 365-366
Bibo, Istvan, 622
Bielawski, Shraga Feivel, 817
Billows, Richard A., 920
Bird, Richard Miller, 576
Birnbaum, Marianna D., 327
Biro, Sandor, 17
Biskupski, M. B., 651
Bisztray, George, 608
Blady Szwajger, Adina, 818
Blanchard, Oliver, 135
Blanke, Richard, 652
Blazyca, George, 686
Bleaney, M. F., 136
Blejer, Mario I., 367
Bleyleben, Maximilian, 528
Bley-Vroman, Alexandra, 860
Boehm, Philip, 529
Bogacki, Anatole C. J., 713
Bogdan, Henry, 18
Bogert, Ralph Baker, 990
Bogue, Ronald, 893
Boia, Eugene, 883
Bonnekamp, Uli, 310
Borneman, John, 536
Bornstein, Jerry, 342
Borocz, Jozsef, 588
Boros-Kazai, Andras, 622
Borsody, Stephen, 554
Bossak, Jan, 152
Bourgault, Rosemarie, 215
Boyarin, Jonathan, 251
Boyd, Michael L., 137
Bozoki, Andras, 577, 621

Brabant, Jozef M. van, 138-142
Bracewell, Catherine Wendy, 921
Brada, Josef C., 143-144, 591-592
Bradley, John Francis Nejez, 423, 478
Bradley, Nicholas, 21, 856
Braham, Randolph I., 269
Brandt, Willy, 342
Brandys, Kazimierz, 755
Braun, Aurel, 49
Brent, Jonathan, 459
Breslauer, George W., 343
Bridge, F. R., 19
Brinkle, Lydle, 854
Broch de Rotherman, H. F., 897
Brock, Peter, 252
Brody, Ervin C., 610
Brogan, Patrick, 20
Bromke, Adam, 653
Brook, Stephan, 303
Broun, Janice, 304
Brown, Douglas M., 593
Brown, J. F., 888
Brown, James F., 50, 80, 111, 344
Browning, Christopher, 270-271, 819
Brucan, Silviu, 873
Brus, Wlodzimierz, 145
Brusak, Karel, 405
Brust, Bill, 812
Bryson, Phillip J., 516
Buento De Mesquita, Nicholas, 960
Bugajski, Janusz, 475
Bugarski, Ranko, 979
Burant, Stephen R., 490, 551
Burawoy, Michael, 594
Burleigh, Michael, 654
Burnstone, Deborah, 282
Butnaru, I. C., 905, 906
Byrnes, Robert Francis, 81

Calhoun, Daniel Fairchild, 555
Calinescu, Malei, 860
Callinicos, Alex, 112
Camaj, Martin, 368
Camejo, Mary Jane, 975
Campbell, Dennis, 51
Carlton, Terence R., 238
Carnovale, Marco, 82
Carpenter, Bogdana, 745
Carter, April, 910
Cassian, Nina, 894
Castellan, Georges, 21, 856
Cavanagh, Clare, 743
Cave, Jane, 806
Celan, Paul, 527
Chalfen, Israel, 528
Chamberlain, Lesley, 305
Childs, David, 503
Chirot, Daniel, 146
Chloupek, Jan, 438
Chnoupek, Bohus, 405
Choldin, Marianna Tax, 328
Ciechocinska, Maria K., 782
Cioc, Mark, 497

Cipkowski, Peter, 345
Clague, Christopher, 147
Clarke, James Franklin, 378
Clarke, Roger A., 229, 725
Claudon, Michael P., 148
Clawson, Patrick, 123
Clucas, Lowell, 22
Cochavi, Yehoyakim, 272
Codrescu, Andrei, 857, 895
Cohen, Asher, 272, 632
Cohen, Lenard J., 942, 1002
Cohen, Robert S., 500
Cohen, Yohanan, 46
Colin, Amy D., 239
Collins, Susan Margaret, 149
Coltman, Derek, 371
Comisso, Ellen, 150
Commander, Simon, 151
Congdon, Lee, 623
Connor, Walter, 840
Conquest, Robert, 63
Cook, Kevin, 159
Corbo, Vittorio, 152
Coricelli, Fabrizio, 152
Cornia, Giovanni A., 306
Corrin, Chris, 307
Courtney, Bruce J., 886
Coutouvidis, John, 687
Crampton, R. J., 379
Crane, John O., 406
Crane, Keith, 153
Crane, Philip M., 885
Crane, Sylvia E., 406
Crouch, Colin, 52
Croucher, Murlin, 402
Crowe, David, 253
Crowther, William E., 874
Csaba, Laszlo, 154, 155
Cseres, Tibor, 922
Csomor, John F., 928
Curry, Jane Leftwich, 779
Curtis, Glenn E., 375, 911
Cushing, George F., 240
Cuvalo, Ante, 923
Cviic, Christopher, 53
Cynkin, Thomas M., 714
Czarnecka, Ewa, 761
Czarniawska-Joerges, Barbara, 726
Czekanowska-Kuklinska, Anna, 842
Czerniawski, Adam, 746-747
Czerwinski, E. J., 748

Dadlez, Anna R., 49
Dahrendorf, Ralf, 54
Dallago, Bruno, 156
Daniels, Anthony, 113
Darnton, Robert, 504
Darowska, Tasja, 818
Davie, Donald, 750, 762
Davies, Norman, 820
Davis, James C., 976
Dawisha, Karen, 83
Dawson, Andrew H., 157

De Nevers, Renee, 84
De Weydenthal, Jan B., 688
Deacon, Bob, 308
Deak, George, 595
Dean, Jonathan, 85
DeBardeleben, Joan, 158
Dedijer, Vladimir, 924-925
Dekker, Arie, 55
Dekleva, Joze, 972
Dellenbrant, Jan Ake, 340
Dembinski, Pawel H., 159
Dennis, Mike, 624
Deutsch, Robert, 160
Dewetter, Jaroslav, 473
Dillard, Walter Scott, 28
Dima, Nicholas, 875, 884
Djilas, Aleksa, 926
Djilas, Milovan, 998
Djordjevic, Dimitrije, 29
Doblin, Alfred, 821
Dobozi, Istvan, 591-592
Dobroszycki, Lucjan, 646
Domonkos, Leslie S., 43
Don, Yehuda, 254
Dopfer, Kurt, 161
Dorosz, Janina, 822
Drachkovitch, Milorad M., 6
Dragnich, Alex N., 943
Drakulic, Slavenka 346, 944
Dressen, William, 282
Dubcek, Aleksander, 400, 419, 424
Duignan, Peter, 347
Dundes, Alan, 899-900
Dunn, Dennis J., 114
Dwork, Deborah, 273
Dwyer, Ruth, 330
Dyker, David A., 961
Dyson, Kenneth, 86
Dziedzic, Eugene E., 674

Earle, John S., 162, 165
Earle, Reybold, L., 311
Echikson, William, 348
Eckart, Gabriele, 519
Edelheit, Abraham J., 274
Edelheit, Hershel, 274
Eidlin, Fred, 434
Eisenbach, Artur, 822
Elkins, Thomas H., 493
Elsie, Robert, 369
Elson, Mark J., 980
Enderlyn, Allyn, 163
Engel, David, 823-824
Engel, Pal, 570
Enyedi, Gyorgy, 625
Epstein, Francis, 428
Epstein, Helen, 428
Eri, Gyongyi, 636
Eviatar, Daphne, 393, 541
Eyal, Jonathan, 87

Feher, Ferenc, 27, 349
Fehervary, Istvan, 18

Feldman, Ruth, 831
Felkay, Andrew, 578
Felstiner, John, 528
Fenyes, S., 556
Fenyo, Mario D., 17, 566
Fenyvesi, Charles, 633
Ferdinand, Peter, 945
Fermor, Patrick Leigh, 491
Fickert, Kurt J., 530
Ficowski, Jerzy, 770
Fiddick, Thomas C., 655
Findlay, Robert, 848
Fine, John Van Antwerp, 23
Fink, Ida, 275
Fischer, Mary Ellen, 876
Fischer-Galati, Stephen A., 24, 858
Fishman, David E., 827
Fishman, Sterling, 535
Fisiak, Jacek, 738
Fiszman, Samuel, 843
Fitzpatrick, Catherine, 975
Fiut, Aleksander, 761, 763
Flakierski, Henryk, 164, 962
Flam, Gila, 844
Fleischman, Janet, 626, 907
Florescu, Radu, 859
Fluek, Toby, 780
Fodor, Neil, 56
Folks, Jeffrey, 983
Follinus, Gabor J., 581
Ford, Kirk, 927
Fox, Leonard, 368
Fox, William F., Jr., 698
Frank, Tibor, 569
Freney, Michael A., 543
Frick, David A., 798
Friedman, Francine, 912
Friedman, Ina, 300
Friedman, Saul S., 290
Fries, Sibley Marilyn, 532
Frucht, Richard, 57
Frydman, Roman, 162, 165
Fuegi, John, 524
Fugedi, Erik, 557-558
Fulbrook, Mary, 544
Funderburk, David B., 885
Fust, Milan, 617
Fyson, George, 1003

Gabel, Joseph, 627
Gabrisch, Hubert, 166
Gal, Joseph, 928
Galai, Haya, 300
Galantai, Jozsef, 255
Gann, L. H., 347
Gapinski, James H., 963-964
Garlinski, Jozef, 656
Garrett, Stephen A., 88
Garton Ash, Timothy, 301, 350, 581
Gaskill, Howard, 520
Gaster, Bertha, 611
Gathy, Vera, 625
Gati, Charles, 89, 586

Gawdiak, Ihor Y., 401
Gedmin, Jeffrey, 505
Gelb, Alan H., 167
Gelber, Yoav, 272
Gella, Aleksander, 309
Georg, Willy, 825
Georgescu, Vlad, 860
Gerasimos, Augustinos, 58
Gerevich, Laszlo, 559
Gerould, Daniel, 768-769, 776
Gerrits, Andre W. M., 802
Giersch, Herbert, 168
Gilberg, Trond, 105, 877
Gilbert, Martin, 276, 839
Gildner, Gary, 781
Giron, Arthur, 531
Giurescu, Dinu C., 901
Glaessner, Gert-Joachim, 545
Glenny, Misha, 351, 1004
Gleye, Paul, 506
Goetz-Stankiewicz, Marketa, 439-440
Goldfarb, Aron, 277
Goldman, Kenneth A., 996
Goldman, Minton F., 2
Goldstein, Imre, 619
Golna, Cornelia, 896
Gombrowicz, Witold, 756
Gomulka, Stanislaw, 169, 689
Goncz, Arpad, 618
Goodwyn, Lawrence, 803
Gordon, Lincoln, 90
Gorecki, Piotr, 657
Gorman, G. E., 13
Gotfryd, Bernard, 278
Gotz-Kozierkiewicz, Danuta, 191
Gow, James, 1005
Gowland, D. H., 170
Graber, Heinz, 821
Grade, Chaim, 256
Graham, Lawrence S., 782
Grancelli, Bruno, 156
Grant, Colin B., 545
Granville, Brigitte, 65
Gray, Cheryl W., 167
Greenbaum, Avraham, 257
Greenwood, Naftali, 46
Gribble, Charles E., 386
Griffith, William E., 91
Gromada, Thaddeus V., 659
Groot, Casper de, 609
Gross, Jan Tomasz, 658
Grosschmid, Geza, 43
Groueff, Stephane, 380
Gruber, Ruth E., 258
Grunblatt, Hilda, 838
Grunblatt, Jacques, 838
Gumpel, Werner, 94
Gurock, Jeffrey S., 827
Gutner, Tamar L., 148
Gwertzman, Bernard, 352
Gyorgyey, Clara, 610
Gzowski, Alison, 115

Habova, Dana, 450, 451
Hadjihristev, Argir Kirkov, 398
Hahn, Werner G., 690
Halacsy, Katalin, 639
Hale, Keith, 3
Halecki, Oscar, 659
Hall, Derek R., 171
Hamann, Brigitte, 25
Hamilton, Geoffrey, 172
Hanak, Peter, 569
Hankiss, Elemer, 579
Hanzlicek, C. G., 450
Haraszti, Eva, 628
Haraszti, Miklos, 637
Harbutt, Fraser J., 92
Hardt, P. John, 173
Hare, P. G., 596
Harkins, William, 468
Harper, John Lamberton, 660
Harrington, Joseph F., 886
Harris, Emma, 710
Harteis, Richard, 387
Hartley, Rebecca S., 543
Hass, Robert, 995
Havel, Vaclav, 425, 448, 463, 476, 479
Havlik, Peter, 174
Hawkesworth, Celia, 250, 979, 981
Hayden, Robert M., 946
Hebbert, Charles, 625
Hedberg, Augustin, 310
Hedges, Jane T., 497
Hegedus, Jozsef, 597
Heim, Michael Henry, 453, 989
Hein, Christoph, 529
Heine, Marc E., 845
Heinegg, Peter, 861
Heinrich, Hans-Georg, 552, 691
Held, Joseph, 26
Heller, Agnes, 27
Henley, Kaca Polockova, 466
Herbert, Zbigniew, 758
Hertz, Aleksander, 826
Hester, A., 311
Heuser, Beatrice, 957
Heuvel, Martin van den, 947
Hewett, Ed A., 143
Hibbert, Reginald, 370
Hieronymi, Otto, 598
Hill, Ronald J., 353
Hillman, Arye L., 175
Hirt, Robert S., 827
Hirt-Manheimer, Aron, 862
Hochman, Jiri, 400
Hoensch, Jorg Konrad, 560
Hoffman, Charles, 259
Hoffman, George W., 103
Holan, Vladimir, 450
Holloway, Ronald, 388
Holton, Milne, 982-983
Holub, Miroslav, 451
Holzman, Franklyn D., 176
Horak, Stephan M., 11
Hormats, Robert D., 80

Horton, John J., 940
Horvath, Agnes, 580
Hosking, Geoffrey A., 240
Hoskins, Janina W., 661
Howard, A. E. Dick, 4
Hrabal, Bohumil, 452-453
Hruby, Peter, 441
Huberband, Shimon, 827
Huelle, Pawel, 783
Hundert, Gershon David, 828
Hupchick, Dennis P., 378, 381
Husak, Gustav, 426

Inkeles, Alex, 840
Inotai, Andras, 177
Institute for East-West Studies, 178
International Auschwitz Committee, 279
International Conference of Slavic Librarians, 328
International Delegation to the Romanian National Elections, 878
Ioanid, Radu, 861
Irwin-Zarecka, Iwona, 829
Isaacson, Judith Magyar, 634
Istvan, Bart, 611
Ivic, Pavle, 984

Jagendorf, Siegfried, 862
Jancar-Webster, Barbara, 929
Jaworski, Rudolf, 784
Jeffries, Ian, 179, 517
Jelavich, Barbara, 93
Jelavich, Charles, 930
Jessup, John E., 12
Jobbagyi, Zsuzsa, 636
John Paul II, Pope, 777
Johnson, Paul M., 180
Jonas, George, 561
Jonas, Paul, 181
Jones, Anthony, 312
Jones, James R., 182
Jones, Martin, 960
Jordan, Alexander, 643
Jovanovski, Meto, 983
Jowitt, Kenneth, 116
Jung, Bohdan, 727
Juricic, Zelimir B., 919

Kadare, Ismail, 371
Kadic, Ante, 241
Kaen, Fred R., 183
Kagan, Joram, 830
Kalecki, Michal, 727
Kalib, Goldie Szachter, 280
Kalib, Sylvan, 280
Kaltenthaler, Karl, 542
Kalvoda, Josef, 407
Kamin, Steven, 974
Kaminski, Andrzej Sulima, 662
Kaminski, Bartolomiej, 692
Kandel, Michael, 783
Kane, Martin, 522
Kanka, August Gerald, 644

Kantor, Marvin, 408
Kantorosinski, Zbigniew, 645
Kaplan, Karel, 427, 434
Karady, Victor, 254
Karp, Andrew, 938
Karpinski, Maciej, 772
Kaser, Michael, 184
Kaufman, Michael T., 352
Kavan, Jan, 435
Kavan, Rosemary, 435
Kavan, Zdenek, 481
Keithly, David M., 494, 507
Kemp-Welch, A., 804
Kendall, Harvey L., 925
Kende, Pierre, 313
Kennedy, Michael D., 785
Kennett, David, 185
Keren, Michael, 186
Kerepesi, Karoly, 177
Kern, William S., 187
Kertesz, Imre, 281
Kessler, Jascha, 612
Kideckel, David A., 902
Kiel, Machiel, 329
Kieval, Hillel J., 469
Kiezun, Witold, 188
Kikeri, Sunita, 189
Kim, Dalchoong, 94
Kindermann, Gottfried-Karl, 94
Kiraly, Bela K., 24, 28-29
Kirschbaum, Stanislav J., 45, 409
Kis, Danilo, 989
Kis, Janos, 581
Kisiel, Chester A., 361
Kiss, Katalin E., 613
Kittrie, Nicholas N., 95
Klassen, John M., 404
Klee, Ernst, 282
Kligman, Gail, 903
Klima, Ivan, 454
Klukowski, Andrew, 663
Klukowski, George, 663
Klukowski, Helen, 663
Klukowski, Zygmunt, 663
Knell, Mark, 190
Kodaly, Zoltan, 638
Kolakowska, Agnieszka, 707
Kolankiewicz, George, 693
Kolodko, Grzegorz W., 191
Kolsti, John, 253
Komlos, John, 192
Konrad, George, 617, 637
Konrad, Gyorgy, 619
Konwicki, Tadeusz, 759
Kopacsi, Sandor, 561
Koralewicz, Jadwiga, 797
Korbonski, Stefan, 664
Kormos, Charles, 909
Kornai, Janos, 193, 599-600
Koroseny, Andras, 577
Kosicka, Jadwiga, 752, 768
Kostrzewa, Robert, 786
Kott, Jan, 751-752, 756

Kovacs, Janos Matyas, 194
Kovaly, Heda Margolis, 428
Kovanda, Karel, 427
Kovarikova, Ruzena, 299
Koves, Andras, 195, 203
Kovrig, Bennett, 96
Kovtun, George J., 410
Krall, Hanna, 283
Krauze, Jolanta, 73
Krauze, Tadeusz K., 790
Krejci, Jaroslav, 411
Krekic, Barisa, 314
Kremer, Manfred, 841
Kretkowska, Katarzyna, 683
Kronenwetter, Michael, 196
Krstic, Dusan, 939
Kuhn, Anna Katharina, 533
Kula, Witold, 30
Kulikowski, Mark, 5
Kundera, Milan, 456-457
Kuniczak, W. S., 771
Kurczewski, Jacek, 694
Kurski, Jaroslaw, 805
Kussi, Peter, 457
Kutler, Laurence, 290
Kvam, Wayne, 519

Laffan, Robert George Dalrymple, 931
Lajtha, Laszlo, 639
Lalic, Ivan V., 991
Lamarova, Milena B., 474
Lamentowicz, Wojciech, 695
Lampe, John R., 197, 383, 965
Landesmann, Katalin, 637
Landesmann, Stephen, 637
Lang, Rikard, 948, 967
Lapides, Robert, 266
Laquer, Walter, 475
Larrabee, F. Stephen, 546
Laski, Kazimierz, 145
Lasky, Melvin J., 508
Latawski, Paul, 665
Laufer, Peter, 354
Lavigne, Marie, 198, 235
Lazic, Branko M., 6
Lecomte, Bernard, 355
Lederer, Ivo John, 80
Lederhendler, Eli, 260
Lees, Michael, 932
Leff, Carol Skalnik, 429
Lehiste, Ilse, 984
Lehrer, Milton G., 863
Lekic, Anita, 994
Lem, Stanislaw, 814
Lemke, Christiane, 540
Lemke, Jurgen, 536
Lepak, Keith John, 696
Lerski, George J., 646
Lerski, Halina T., 646
Lesnoff-Caravaglia, Gary, 398
Lesourne, Jacques, 355
Levi, Primo, 831
Leviatin, David, 480

Levin, Nora, 284
Levine, Madeline, 275
Levinstein, Joan, 342
Lewis, Paul G., 697
Liang, Hsi-Huey, 537
Lieberman, Marc, 185
Liebovich, Louis W., 817
Lifschultz, Lawrence, 1001
Lindsay, Franklin, 933
Lindsay, Margie, 199
Liska, George, 59
Loiry, William S., 200
Lomax, Bill, 562
Lopinski, Maciej, 806
Lorenz, Cathie M., 809
Los, Maria, 201
Loud, John F., 919
Lourie, Richard, 761, 774, 826
Love, Myra Norma, 534
Lovenduski, Joni, 60
Ludwikowski, Rett R., 698, 706, 787
Luers, William H., 80
Lukacs, Ilona, 193
Lukacs, Janos, 594
Lukacs, John, 563
Lukas, Richard C., 666, 832
Lungu, Dov B., 887
Lupack, Barbara Tepa, 760
Lustig, Arnost, 458-459
Luthardt, Wofgang, 542
Luttwak, Edward N., 866
Lydall, Harold, 966

MacDonald, C. A., 412
Macesich, George, 202, 948, 967
MacFarlane, L. J., 302
MacGregor, Douglas A., 509
Maciejewicz, Jan, 336
Magas, Branka, 949
Magid, Alvin, 977
Magner, Thomas F., 985
Magocsi, Paul Robert, 413
Mahut, Helen, 648
Malcolm, Neil, 65
Mallinson, Graham, 892
Manchin, Robert, 630
Manea, Norman, 896, 904
Mansbach, Steven A., 640
Mantello, Frank, 570
Marcus, Judith, 242
Marcuse, Peter, 510
Marer, Paul, 203, 601, 728
Markovic, Ljubisav, 948
Marquand, David, 52
Marrese, Michael, 204
Martin, David, 863, 958
Martin, Lothar, 535
Mason, David S., 356
Mastny, Vojtech, 32, 61
Matey, Maria, 729
Mathur, Ike, 183
Matthias, John, 986
Mayer, Arno J., 285

Mazur, B. W., 739
McCagg, William O., 261
McCrate, James, 627
McCulloch, P. C., 559
McDermott, Kevin, 436
McDonald, Jason, 589
McElvoy, Anne, 495
McFarlane, Bruce J., 913
McIntyre, Robert J., 376
McKenna, David, 492
McKinnon, Ronald I., 205
McLaughlin, R. Emmet, 31
McLean, Brian, 628
McMillan, Carl H., 173, 206
McNally, Raymond T., 859
McPherron, Alan, 934
McPherson, Karin, 520
Meador, Daniel John, 511
Mehedinti, Simion, 864
Melzer, Manfred, 516-517
Meredith, William, 387
Mews, Siegfried, 525
Michalowski, Kornel, 846
Michener, James A., 771
Michnik, Adam, 799
Michta, Andrew A., 32, 357, 699
Micklewright, John, 130
Mihailovich, Vasa D., 914, 982
Mihalyi, Peter, 117
Milanovic, Branko, 175
Milisauskas, Sarunas, 667
Milivojevic, Marko, 940
Miljkovic, Dusan, 915
Miller, Chris, 355
Millu, Liana, 286
Milojkovic-Djuric, Jelena, 997
Milosz, Czeslaw, 758, 764-765, 773-775, 826, 843
Misurella, Fred, 442
Mojzes, Paul, 13
Molinari, Christine, 628
Molnar, Miklos, 582
Monkiewicz, Jan, 336
Moore, Deborah Dash, 262
Moore, Richard, 7
Morrison, John, 109, 420
Moser, Charles A., 390
Moskit, Marcin, 806
Moss, Joyce, 315
Mozejko, Edward, 766
Murphy, Kenneth, 118
Murrell, Peter, 207
Myant, Martin R., 485
Myers, Sondra, 292

Nagengast, Carole, 788
Nagy, Karoly, 622
Nahon, Marco, 287
Narkiewicz, Olga A., 33
Nathan, Leonard, 767, 775
Neckerman, Peter Josef, 547
Neher, Andre, 414
Nekvapil, Jiri, 438
Nellis, John, 189

Nelson, Daniel N., 62, 77, 97-98, 879-880
Nelson, Linda, 39
Nelson, Victoria, 770
Nemeth, Lajos, 636
Ners, Krzysztof, 178
Neugroschel, Joachim, 821
Newbery, David M. G., 605
Nilsson, Nils Ake, 243
Nir, Yehuda, 668
Nobel Symposium (62nd: 1985: Stockholm, Sweden), 243
Norseng, Mary Kay, 847
North, Jacqueline Y. Jones, 472
NSZZ "Solidarnosc," 807

Oakley, Ray, 596
Obst, Peter, 805
Ofer, Gur, 186
Office for Official Publications of the European Communities, 486
Okey, Robin, 34
Oldson, William O., 908
Olechno-Huszcza, Gillian, 846
Oliver, Merrill, 331
O'Loughlin, John, 358
Opalski, Magdalena, 669
Organisation for Economic Co-operation and Development, 384, 430, 730, 889, 968
Orszagh, Laszlo, 614
Osiatynski, Jerzy, 731, 727
Osinski, Zbigniew, 848
Osmond, Jonathan, 548
Ost, David, 799, 808
Ostrowski, Krzysztof, 695
Ozinga, James R., 99

Pacepa, Ion Mihail, 881
Pachonski, Jan, 670
Paganetto, Luigi, 131
Palankai, Tibor, 208
Pannell, Alastair Douglas, 816
Paral, Vladimir, 460
Parker, Stephen, 521
Parks, Tim, 298
Parlin, Andrew, 660
Pastor, Peter, 564
Patai, Raphael, 288, 565
Patterson, David, 289
Pavel, Ota, 461
Pavic, Milorad, 992-993
Pavlowitch, Stevan K., 916, 935
Payne, Jerry, 568, 615
Pease, Neal, 715
Pehe, Jiri, 431
Peitsch, Helmut, 521
Pekarova, Iva, 462
Peleg, Miryam, 671
Penkower, Monty Noam, 663
Perczynski, Maciej, 695
Perjes, Geza, 566
Perkowski, Jan Louis, 244
Perlman, Robert, 635
Perry, Duncan M., 394, 936

Peter, Laszlo, 35
Petkov, Krusto, 209
Petkov, Petko M., 395
Petrie, Graham, 330
Petro, Peter, 463
Petrovich, Michael Boro, 998
Petsin, Petur, 391
Pfaltzgraff, Robert L., Jr., 714
Pheby, John, 988
Phelps, Edmund S., 131
Philip, Franklin, 648
Phillips, Ann L., 512
Pickel, Andreas, 518
Pienkos, Angela T., 672
Pienkos, Donald E., 673
Pike, David, 496
Pilon, Juliana Geran, 63
Pinchuk, Ben-Cion, 833
Pinder, John, 210
Pinkus, Oscar, 834
Pinter, Istvan, 567
Pipa, Arshi, 372-373
Plestina, Dijana, 969
Ploss, Sidney I., 100
Ploszajski, Piotr, 840
Pogonowski, Iwo, 647, 740, 835
Polackova-Henley, Kaca, 470
Polisensky, Josef V., 415
Polonsky, Antony, 671, 689, 815, 820, 822, 836
Pomerans, Arnold J., 582
Popovic, Tanya, 245
Porter, David, 870
Potter, William C., 82
Powelstock, David, 462
Poznanski, Kazimierz Z., 732
Pravda, Alex, 101, 211
Prazmowska, Anita, 716
Pribicevic-Zoric, Christina, 992-993
Prickett, Russell O., 965
Prizel, Ilya, 357
Proctor, Robert, 538
Prose, Francine, 275
Prust, Jim, 487
Prybyla, Jan S., 212, 223
Prychitko, David L., 119
Przeworski, Adam, 213
Przybyszewska, Stanislawa, 769
Pula, James S., 651, 674
Puppel, Stanislaw, 738
Pynsent, Robert, 405

Quinlan, Paul D., 865
Quinn, Arthur, 767

Rachwald, Arthur R., 717
Racz, Attila, 67
Radke, Linda F., 641
Rady, Martyn C., 882
Raible, Karl F., 161
Ramet, Pedro, 316-317
Ramet, Sabrina P., 318, 950-951
Ranki, Gyorgyi, 629
Rapacki, Ryszard, 686

Rapaczynski, Andrzej, 162, 165
Rapoport, Roger, 359
Ratesh, Nestor, 866
Rau, Zbigniew, 319
Rausser, Gordon C., 147
Razvigorova, Evka, 214
Read, Francoise, 313
Redlikh, Egon, 290
Redor, Dominique, 215
Rees, H. Louis, 432
Reid, J. H., 539
Reinicke, Wolfgang H., 216
Reiquam, Steve W., 809
Reisinger, William M., 217
Rensenbrink, John C., 700
Revesz, Gabor, 601
Reviczky, Adam, 568
Reynolds, Jaime, 687
Rezzori, Gregor von, 897
Rhode, Barbara, 67
Richet, Xavier, 602
Richter, Sandor, 204, 218
Rider, Christine, 190
Riess, Volker, 282
Riordan, Colin, 521
Riordan, James, 320
Rittner, Carol, 291-292
Roberson Center for the Arts and Sciences, 331
Roberts, Ian W., 102
Robertson, Theodosia S., 763
Rodrik, Dani, 149
Rohr, Janelle, 64
Roland, Charles G., 675
Rollo, J. M. C., 65
Roman, Anne C. R., 409
Rosenberg, Blanca, 293
Rosenblum, Mort, 74
Roskin, Michael G., 66
Rosman, Murray Jay, 676
Rotfeld, Adam D., 513
Roth, John K., 291
Roth, Kenneth, 701
Roth, Philip, 299
Roy, Ellen, 789
Rubach, Jerzy, 443
Ruble, Blair A., 211
Rudin, Catherine, 389
Rudinsky, Norma L., 446
Rueschemeyer, Marilyn, 503, 540
Rusinow, Dennison, 952
Ryavec, Karl W., 571
Ryback, Timothy W., 332
Rybicki, Arkadiuz, 648
Ryznar, Eliska, 402

Saiu, Liliana, 867
Salamun, Tomaz, 995
Salsitz, Norman, 837
Salzmann, Zdenek, 416
Sanders, Ivan, 617
Sanford, George, 702-703, 807
Sapinkopf, Lisa, 390
Sarkovic, T. Misha, 970

Sarmany-Parsons, Ilona, 636
Sarosi, Balint, 639, 642
Satterwhite, James H., 120
Saunders, Christopher T., 219
Schaffer, Heinz, 67
Schapiro, Raya Czerner, 294
Scharf, Rafael F., 825
Schatz, Jaff, 704
Schauss, H. Joachim, 849
Scheufler, Vladimir, 416
Schierup, Carl-Ulrik, 971
Schloss, Roslyn, 299
Schmidt, Jochen, 988
Schopflin, George, 8, 68, 577
Schopflin, Julian, 562
Schulz, Bruno, 770
Schwartz, Lynne Sharon, 286
Scott, Peter Dale, 758
Sebastiani, Mario, 733
Segel, Harold B., 850
Seisanu, Romulus, 868
Sekelj, Laslo, 953
Seligman, A., 69
Senelick, Laurence, 333
Seroka, James, 954, 1006
Sgall, Petr, 444
Shama, Avraham, 360
Shawcross, William, 435
Shelley, Lore, 295
Shelton, Anita Krystina, 677
Shen, Raphael, 734-735
Shevardnadze, Eduard, 78
Shirley, Mary, 189
Short, David, 403
Shoup, Paul S., 103
Shulman, Marshall D., 104
Siccama, Jan G., 947
Sienkiewicz, Henryk, 771
Siklos, Pierre L., 603
Sikorska, Grazyna, 304, 800
Simecka, Martin M., 463
Simek, Milan, 473
Simic, Charles, 983, 986-987, 991, 994-995
Simmie, James, 972
Simmons, P. J., 9
Simocatta, Theophylactus, 36
Simon, Jeffrey, 105
Simonovits, Andras, 220
Simons, Peter, 851
Simons, Thomas W., 37
Sinclair, Craig, 337
Sipkov, Ivan, 70
Sipos, Sandor, 306
Siwinski, Wlodzimiercz, 728
Sjoberg, Orjan, 221
Sked, Alan, 38
Skegro, Borislav, 964
Skilling, Harold Gordon, 321, 477
Skolnik, Richard, 837
Skrzeszewska-Paczek, Elzbieta, 191
Skvorecky, Josef, 458, 464-467
Sliger, Bernard F., 948
Slomczynski, Kazimierz M., 790

Slowes, Saloman W., 678
Smialek, William, 852
Smiljkovic, Rados, 954
Smith, Chris, 222
Smith, William Jay, 894
Sobell, Vladimir, 223
Solecki, Sam, 467
Solimano, Andres, 385
Spanger, Hans-Joachim, 78
Spence, Richard B., 39
Spira, Thomas, 583
Srejovic, Dragoslav, 934
Staar, Richard F., 71, 705
Staniszkis, Jadwiga, 121, 361
Stankiewicz, Edward, 246
Stanley, David, 10
Stefancic, David R., 736
Stefanescu-Draganesti, Virgiliu, 869
Stein, William, M., 627
Steinberg, Jonathan, 296
Steinherr, Alfred, 224
Steininger, Rolf, 497
Stenberg, Peter, 247
Stern, Geoffrey, 122
Stoffman, Daniel, 561
Stoffman, Judy, 561
Stojka, Karl, 297
Stok, Danusia, 818
Stokes, Gale, 47, 955
Stone, Norman, 417
Striedter, Jurij, 445
Strmiska, Zdenek, 313
Strouhal, Eduard, 417
Struyk, Raymond J., 597
Stryder, J., 938
Stuard, Susan Mosher, 937
Stutzle, Walter, 513
Subtelny, Orest, 40
Sugar, Andras, 424
Sugar, Peter F., 569
Sugarman, Martin A., 1007
Sukosd, Miklos, 621
Swain, Nigel, 584
Swan, Oscar E., 741
Swick, Thomas, 791
Swiderski, Bronislaw, 792
Swiderski, Karen, 604
Swidlicki, Andrzej, 810
Sword, Keith, 718
Symposium on Science in Eastern Europe, 337
Szakolczai, Arpad, 580
Szalai, Julia, 308
Szekely, Istvan P., 605
Szelenyi, Ivan, 361, 630
Szell, Gyorgy, 225
Szendrei, T., 559
Szirmai, Viktoria, 625
Szreter, R., 30
Szurek, Alexander, 838

Taborski, Boleslaw, 769, 777
Talbot, Kathrine, 470
Tanner, Marcus, 322

Tanzi, Vito, 226
Taras, Raymond, 72, 362, 679
Tardos, Marton, 194
Targetti, Ferdinando, 227
Tarnstrom, Ronald L., 680
Teague, Elizabeth, 719
Tec, Nechama, 681
Tedeschi Brunelli, Giuliana, 298
Teichova, Alice, 488
Terry, Garth M., 248, 917
Thirkell, John E. M., 209
Thompson, Kenneth W., 706
Thompson, Mark, 1008
Thompson, Paul, 222
Thorpe, Wayne, 621
Thuroczy, Janos, 570
Tighe, Carl, 682
Tismaneanu, Vladimir, 123
Todorovich, Boris, 938
Tokes, Laszlo, 870
Tolnai, Marton, 553
Toma, Peter A., 585
Tomaszewski, Jerzy, 73
Tonchev, Belin, 391
Toporowski, Jan, 731
Toranska, Teresa, 707
Torrey, Glenn E., 855
Tosics, Ivan, 597
Townsend, Charles Edward, 447
Traynor, Kim, 560
Trevor-Roper, Hugh, 282
Tringham, Ruth, 939
Triska, Jan F., 106
Tritt, Rachel, 471
Trzeciakowski, Lech, 683
Turner, Henry Ashby, 498
Turnley, David C., 74
Turnley, Peter, 74
Turnock, David, 41, 42, 890
Tusa, Ann, 499
Tusa, John, 499
Tyson, Laura D'Andrea, 150

United Nations Centre on Transnational Cooporation, 228
United States. Congress. House. Committee on Foreign Relations, 107, 959
Unterberger, Betty Miller, 418
Upward, Christopher, 515
Urbanek, Zdenek, 468
Uvalic, Milica, 973

Vacic, Aleksander M., 184
Vago, Raphael, 587
Valenta, Jiri, 419
Vali, Ferenc A., 571
Vallee, Lillian, 752, 756, 773, 848
Van Ness, Peter, 606
Vardy, Agnes H., 573-574
Vardy, Steven Bela, 43, 572, 573, 574
Vasary, Ildiko, 631
Vas-Zoltan, Peter, 553
Vegesack, Alexander von, 474

Vendler, Helen, 743
Verheyen, Dirk, 549
Verona, Sergiu, 888
Vjekoslav, Boban, 988
Vladislav, Jan, 449
Vogel, Heinrich, 335
Vojnic, Dragomir, 948, 967
Volgyes, Ivan, 75, 95
Volovici, Leon, 909
Volten, Peter M. E., 76
Vondracek, Theodor Jan, 433
Vuckovic, Vladeta, 986
Vukasin, Pavlovic, 1006
Vukmanovic-Tempo, Svetozar, 999

Wachsberger, Ken, 280
Wadekin, Karl-Eugen, 144
Waldenburg, Hermann, 550
Walendowski, Edmund, 708
Walesa, Lech, 648, 709
Walicki, Andrzej, 710, 793, 794
Wallace, William V., 229
Wallich, Christine, 576
Walters, E. Garrison, 44
Wandycz, Piotr Stefan, 108
Wankel, Charles, 811
Ward, Philip, 377, 399
Wasserman, Steve, 637
Wat, Aleksander, 773, 774, 775
Watson, Margaret, 797
Watson, Peggy, 121
Watts, Larry, 871
Webb, Marek, 266
Weber, Marion, 841
Weber, Wolfgang, 812
Wedel, Janine R., 795
Weigel, George, 363
Weil, Jiri, 299
Weinberg, Czerner Helga, 294
Welfens, Paul J. J., 230
Werner, Harold, 839
Wertheimer, Jack, 263
Weschler, Lawrence, 806
Wesolowski, Wlodzimierz, 840
West, Richard V., 640
Wetzler, Monte E., 231
Wheaton, Bernard, 437, 481
Whitby, Mary, 36
Whitby, Michael, 36
White, Stephen, 77, 364
Whitehouse, J. C., 602
Wiatr, Jerzy J., 711
Wiatr, Slawomir, 691
Wielewinski, Bernard, 649
Wiesel, Elie, 862, 905
Wilk, Mariusz, 806
Willetts, Harry, 707
Williams, Thys W., 521
Williamson, John, 232-233
Williamson, Samuel R., 48
Wilson, Christopher C., 281, 618
Wilson, George, 315
Wilson, Katharina M., 281, 618

Wilson, Paul, 425, 448, 452, 464-465, 476-477, 479
Wilson, Reuel K., 670
Winiecki, Jan, 234
Winnifrith, Tom, 264
Winrow, Gareth M., 514
Wistrich, Robert S., 265
Witkiewicz, Stanislaw Ignacy, 776
Witoszek, Nina, 753
Wolchik, Sharon L., 482
Wolf, Thomas A., 143
Wolff, Larry, 720
Wolf-Laudon, Gottfried, 214
Woodall, Jean, 60
Woods, Roger, 515
Woodward, William R., 500
World Bank. Trade Policy Division, 489
World Congress for Soviet and East European Studies, 45, 109, 235, 249-250, 420
Wozniuk, Vladimir, 721
Wright, Elizabeth, 526

Wulff, Kenneth R., 796
Wusten, Herman van der, 358
Wyden, Peter, 501
Wyzan, Michael L., 221

Yagci, Fahrettin, 974
Yahil, Leni, 300
Young, David, 451

Zagajewski, Adam, 712, 770
Zang, Ted, 397
Zawadzki, W. H., 684
Zhivkova, Lyudmila, 396
Zielonka, Jan, 335, 353, 685
Zimanyi, Vera, 575
Zimmerman, William, 956
Zloch-Christy, Iliana, 236
Zsuffa, Joseph, 616
Zuehlke, Thomas W., 964
Zuzowski, Robert, 813
Zwass, Adam, 237
Zymberi, Isa, 374

Subject Index

Reference is to entry number.

accounting, 159
aged
　health and hygiene, 398
agricultural imports, 182
agricultural policy, 136
agriculture, 137
agriculture and state, 160
　communist countries, 144
　Bulgaria, 383
　economic aspects, 144, 486, 788
　Hungary, 630
　Romania, 890
Aktivistak, 640
Albania
　description and travel, 113
　economic conditions, 221, 367
　economic policy, 141, 367
　foreign relations
　　China, 366
　　Great Britain, 370
　history, 365, 371
　　Axis occupation 1939-1944, 370
　religion, 304
Albanian language, 374
　political aspects, 373
Albanian literature
　dictionaries, 369
　history and criticism, 372
alliances
　psychological aspects, 97
allocation of resources, 159
anarchism
　Hungary, 621
Anthropoid (mission), 412
anthropology
　Poland, 789
anti-communist movements
　East Germany, 504
　Poland, 811
Antigonos I, King of Macedonia, 920
antiquities, 14
antisemitism
　Germany, 538
　Poland, 826, 836
　Romania, 905, 908-909
Antonescu, Ion, 871
Antschel, Paul. See Celan, Paul
archeology, medieval, 14
architecture, 324
　modern, 324
　Ottoman, 329
　Romania, 901
　and state, 324
archival resources, 9
armed forces, 28

history, 24
armies, 28
arms race, 159
Aromanians, 264
　Hungary, 636-637, 640
arts
　Bulgaria, 396
　Czechoslovakia, 473
　Serbia, 997
astronomers
　Czechoslovakia, 414
Auschwitz (Poland: Concentration Camp), 287, 295, 634, 831
Auschwitz convent controversy, 291
Austria
　economic conditions, 192
　history, 38
　　1867-1918, 432
Austro-Hungarian Empire, 48
authors
　Hungarian, 616
　Polish, 756, 761
authorship, 904
autonomy, 319
avant-garde
　Hungary, 640
Avdic, Avdo, 996

Bacska (Serbia and Hungary), 922
Bakhmeteff Archive, 1
balance of payments, 140, 176
　Yugoslavia, 961, 974
Balazs, Bela, 616
Balkan Peninsula
　bibliography, 12
　defenses, 87
　description and travel, 3
　economic conditions, 58, 221
　foreign relations, 62, 103
　history, 21, 23, 29, 39
　politics and government, 39, 50, 53, 58, 62
　social conditions, 58
Balkan wars, 48
Baltic States
　history, military, 680
Bandkeramik culture (Poland), 667
banks and banking, 224
　Hungary, 592
baseball
　Poland, 781
Bauman, Janina, 268
Belarus
　ethnic relations, 820, 833
Beller, Ilex, 816
Belzec (Poland: Concentration Camp), 267

239

Benjamin, Walter, 523
Berlin, 493
  description, 537
  emigration and immigration, 501
  history, 494, 499, 504
Berlin Wall, 342, 501, 550
Berthelot, Henri Mathias, 855
Bessarabia
  history, 884
Bialobrzegi (Poland)
  ethnic relations, 277
Bible
  criticism, interpretation, etc., 798
  Polish
    versions, 798
bibliography, 11, 248, 402
Bielawski, Shraga Feivel, 817
Birkenau (Poland: Concentration Camp), 287
Blachnicki, Franciszek, 800
Bodzentyn (Poland)
  biography, 280
Bohemia
  ethnic relations, 469
  history
    Hussite Wars, 1419-1436, 404
    1848-1918, 432
  politics and government, 420
    1848-1918, 432
Boris III, czar of Bulgaria, 1894-1943, 380
Bosnia and Hercegovina, 1000
  history, 1001
    1992-, 1007
  intellectual life, 919
  religious life and customs, 919
Brandys, Kazmierz, 755
Bratislava (Slovakia)
  fiction, 463
Brecht, Bertolt, 525-526
  stage history, 524
Brucan, Silviu, 873
Brzezinka (Poland: Concentration Camp), 286-287, 297-298
Brzozowski, Stanislaw, 794
Buda
  history, 314
Budapest, 625
  biography, 565
  civilization, 563
  description, 303
  fiction, 281
Bujak, Franciszek (1875-1953), 677
Bukovina
  history, 884
  intellectual life, 239
Bulgaria, 375
  civilization, 376, 381
  economic conditions, 209, 221, 382, 383-385
  economic policy, 136, 141, 383-384
  economic reform, 143, 166, 382
  foreign relations
    United States, 395
  historiography, 378
  history, 378-379

Ferdinand I, 1887-1918, 395
1918-1943, 380
politics and government
  1878-1944, 394
religion, 304
social life and customs, 398
statistics, 382
Bulgarian Communist Party, 392
Bulgarian language
  interrogatives, 389
  relative clauses, 389
  syntax, 389
  textbooks, 386
Bulgarian poetry, 387, 390-391
Bulgarians
  interviews, 399
business cycles, 220
business enterprises
  Hungary, 589
  Yugoslavia, 973
business information services, 200
Byzantine empire, 22, 36
Byzantine influence on Eastern Europe, 22

Camaj, Martin, 368, 372
capital flows, 149
capital investment, 220
  communist countries, 117
capital market, 197, 199, 224
capital productivity, 727
capitalism, 161, 185, 196, 202, 213
  China, 606
  Hungary, 594, 599, 606, 630
Cassian, Nina, 894
castles
  Hungary, 557
Catholic Church
  foreign relations, 720
  Yugoslavia, 925
  Poland, 799-800
  Yugoslavia, 925
Ceausescu, Elena, 872
Ceausescu, Nicolae, 79, 872, 876, 880-882
Celan, Paul, 239, 527-528
censorship, 240
  Romania, 904
Central America
  economic reform, 213
Central Europe
  economic conditions, 124
  history, 16, 301
  intellectual life, 990
  social conditions, 309
central planning, 119, 134, 173, 179, 234
  communist countries, 161
  Czechoslovakia, 487
  Hungary, 203, 212, 591, 601-602
  Soviet Union, 234
centrally planned economies, 141, 159
CEPU (Central European Payments Union), 142
Charter 77, 475
child welfare, 306
China

economic liberalization, 203
economic policy, 141, 153, 212, 606
economic reform, 203
foreign relations
   Albania, 366
Christianity, 15
church and state
   bibliography, 13
   communist countries, 316
   Poland, 683
   Soviet Union, 316
church history, 15, 316
Churchill, Winston, 92, 958
Cieszkowski, August, 793
cities and towns, medieval
   Hungary, 559
city and town life, 314
civil law, 70
   Czechoslovakia, 433
civil rights, 810
   Bulgaria, 393, 397
   Czechoslovakia, 422, 471, 475, 477
   East Germany, 541
   Hungary, 302, 626
   Poland, 701, 778
   Romania, 907
   Yugoslavia, 302, 975
civil society, 69, 319
   Poland, 801
civil-military relations
   Poland, 711
   Yugoslavia, 1005
class consciousness
   Hungary, 594
CMEA. *See* Council for Mutual Economic Assistance
code switching (linguistics)
   Czechoslovakia, 444
Codrescu, Andrei, 857, 895
Cold War
   archival resources, 9
collective bargaining
   Poland, 804
collectivism
   Romania, 902
collectivization of agriculture
   Hungary, 631
COMECON. *See* Council for Mutual Economic Assistance
Comintern
   biography, 6
commerce, 163, 207
commercial law, 51
communication
   political aspects, 321
communism, 54, 68, 71-72, 77, 110, 112, 114, 116, 123, 346, 355-356, 364
   1945-, 113, 352
   anecdotes, 899
   Czechoslovakia, 437
   demise, 213
   East Germany, 495, 507-508
   fiction, 529

   history, 122, 361, 945
      20th century, 118, 342, 362
   humor, 900
   Hungary, 580, 582, 594, 627, 630
   Poland, 692, 697, 713, 795, 807
      history, 704, 794
   Romania, 873
   Soviet Union, 945
   Yugoslavia, 941, 945, 983
communism and Christianity, 316, 363
   bibliography, 13
   Poland, 799
   Soviet Union, 316
communism and liberty, 359
communist countries, 198
   description and travel, 113
   economic conditions, 352
   economic planning, 117
   economic policy, 161, 600
   history, 111
   politics and government, 97
Communist Information Bureau, 941
Communist International, 6
communist revisionism, 120
communist state, 72, 116
communists, 6
   Poland, 794
   Romania, 873
   Yugoslavia, 916
comparative economics, 161, 196
comparative education, 535
comparative law, 70
comparative literature
   Russian and Czech, 249
comparative politics, 77
competition, international, 206
computer industry, 334
computer networks, 334
concentration camps
   Poland, 287
Conference on Security and Cooperation in Europe, 86
conflict management, 55
conservatism
   Poland, 787
conspiracies
   Poland, 806
constitutionalism, 4
convents
   Poland, 291
cookery, Hungarian, 641
corporations, 183
cosmography
   history, 414
Council for Mutual Economic Assistance, 94, 139, 141-142, 150, 160, 166, 174, 182, 198, 223, 229, 237, 336
   economic reform, 143
Council for Mutual European Assistance, 138
court Jews
   Poland, 676
Croatia
   church history, 925

Croatia (*cont.*)
  history, 923, 1007
Croats, 943
Cuba
  description and travel, 113
  economic policy, 141
  as subordinate state, 106
cubism
  Czechoslovakia, 474
currency convertibility, 174, 183, 232
Czartoryski, Adam Jerzy, 684
Czech drama, 440
Czech language
  dialects, 447
  spoken Czech, 447
  variation, 438
Czech literature, 249, 441, 445
Czechoslovakia, 424
  bibliography, 403
  church history, 408
  economic conditions, 192, 401, 482, 484, 488, 734
    1945-1992, 483, 485, 487
  economic policy, 136, 141, 734
    1945-1992, 133, 485
    1965-1992, 132, 483, 487
    1989-, 483
  economic reform, 127, 143, 166
  ethnic relations, 290, 420, 429, 470
  foreign economic relations, 489
  foreign relations, 419
    France, 108
  history, 46, 401, 407, 415, 418-419, 431, 482
    1918-, 417
    1945-1992, 400
  intellectual life, 473, 475-476
  national security, 401
  political events, 411
  politics and government, 401, 406, 426, 428, 431, 435, 475, 478, 482
    1945-, 423
    1968-1989, 477, 481
    1989-, 132
    1989-1992, 425, 481
    20th century, 420, 429
  relations
    United States, 410
  religion, 304
  rural conditions, 416
  social conditions, 401, 482

Dalmatia (Croatia)
  history, military, 921
dance music
  Hungary, 639
Danube River Valley
  description and travel, 491
debt crisis, 150
debts, external, 236
  Yugoslavia, 961
decentralization in government
  Poland, 722
Dedijer, Vladimir, 924

democracy, 202, 213
  Poland, 705
democratic institutions, 4
deportation in literature, 247
description and travel, 7, 10, 258, 305, 322, 354
detente, 86
devaluation
  Hungary, 143
developing countries
  foreign relations
    East Germany, 79
    Romania, 79
Dima, Nicholas, 875
diplomacy, 57
disarmament, 85
  Russia, 85
dissenters
  Czechoslovakia, 477
  East Germany, 502
  Poland, 813
dissertations, academic
  bibliography, 649
Doblin, Alfred, 821
Dracula, 244
Dubcek, Alexander, 400
Dubrovnik
  civilization, 937
  history, 314
Dvorak, Antonin, 464

East European literature, 325
East Germany, 492
  economic conditions, 490, 503, 517-518, 624
  economic development, 150
  economic policy, 136, 141, 516-517
  economic reform, 143
  foreign relations
    developing countries, 79
    Soviet Union, 505
  history, 490, 495, 498
  literature, 521
  military policy, 509
  national security, 490
  politics and government, 490, 496, 502, 505-507, 510, 513, 515, 544, 624
    1989-1990, 504
  religion, 304
  social conditions, 490, 503, 540, 624
  social life and customs, 506
Eastern Europe, 2, 74
  relations
    Soviet Union, 101
Eastern question, 93
East-West German relations, 94
East-West trade, 154, 204, 229, 335
  1945-, 206, 214
economic assistance
  Czech and Slovak Federal Republic, 178
  Hungary, 178
  Poland, 178
economic assistance, European, 216

economic conditions, 91, 124-125, 128, 130, 134, 140, 146, 149, 151, 165, 167, 180, 195, 213, 218-219, 237, 306
    1945-, 60, 169
    1989-, 65, 148, 190, 194, 230, 360-361, 364
economic development, 165, 181, 727
economic growth, 136
economic history, 136
economic integration, 139, 140, 181, 208, 229, 235, 237
economic planning. *See* economic policy
economic policy, 64, 135, 151, 155, 157, 159, 162, 167-168, 173, 179-181, 187, 195-197, 216, 218-219, 223, 234, 237
    1969-, 186
    1989-, 148, 185, 190, 194, 230
economic stabilization, 135, 151
    case studies, 191
    Hungary, 603
    Poland, 732
    Yugoslavia, 967
economics, 193, 733
    Bulgaria, 174
    Czechoslovakia, 174
    Hungary, 174
    Poland, 174
    Romania, 174
    Soviet Union, 174
    Yugoslavia, 174
economy convertibility, 181
education
    Germany, 535
    Poland, 796
    Yugoslavia, 930
education and state
    Poland, 796
efficiency, industrial
    Hungary, 592
Egypt
    history, 555
elections
    Romania, 878
Elisabeth, Empress, consort of Franz Joseph, 25
elite
    Poland, 785
embroideries, 331
emigration and imigration, 1
employees
    Yugoslavia, 962
energy industries, 217
energy resources, 174
English language
    dictionaries
        Hungarian, 614
enterprises, 159
environmental policy, 158
    Yugoslavia, 968
environmental protection, 158
epic poetry,
    Romanian, 891
    Serbian, 986
    South Slavic, 245
equality, 313

escapes
    Germany, 938
ethnic relations, 253, 258-260, 262
ethnology, 315
    Slovakia, 413
    Soviet Union, 315
Europe
    civilization, 629
    politics and government, 52
    1945-1989, 83, 90
European Economic Community
    Hungary, 208
European Economic Community countries
    economic conditions, 355
    foreign economic relations, 210
European federation, 64
excavations (archeology)
    Poland, 667
exchange notes, 174
experimental literature, 243
exports, 234

fascism
    Romania, 861
federal government
    Yugoslavia, 952
feminism in literature, 533
Fenyvesi, Charles family, 633
feudalism
    Poland, 657
field grains, 182
finance, 138, 170, 176
    Hungary, 604
financial markets, 131
fiscal policy, 226
folk art
    Poland, 849
folk music
    Hungary, 638, 642
    Poland, 842
folk poetry
    Romania, 903
folk songs, Hungarian, 638 Romanian, 891
food supply, 160
foreign economic relations, 94, 174, 184, 210, 233, 235
    communist countries, 198
foreign exchange, 182, 236
foreign relations, 61, 78, 80-83, 88-89, 91, 94-95, 106-107, 109, 217, 586, 655, 885
    1945-1989, 90
    Africa, 104, 514
    Asia, 104
    Balkan Peninsula, 93
    East Germany, 512
    Hungary, 102, 578
    Latin America, 104, 106
    Middle East, 104
    Poland, 717, 718
    Soviet Union, 81, 84, 86, 100, 512
    United States, 81, 90, 96, 104, 106, 714, 717
foreign trade, 131, 159, 166
    Bulgaria, 383

foreign trade (*cont.*)
  Poland, 143
  Soviet Union, 143
Former Soviet Republics
  economic policy, 186
France
  constitutional history, 698
  foreign relations
    Czechoslovakia, 108
    Poland, 108
free enterprise, 185, 205
Free masonry
  Poland, 792
free ports and zones, 228
  Soviet Union, 228
freedom of information, 321
freedom of the press, 311
French in Slovakia, 405
friendship in children
  Poland, 783
Funderbunk, David B., 885
Fust, Milan, 617

Gal, Joseph, 928
Galicia, Eastern
  ethnic relations, 820
Gans, David ben Solomon, 414
Garlinski, Jozef, 656
GATT (General Agreement on Trade and Tariffs), 141, 143
gay men
  East Germany, 536
gays
  Balkan Peninsula, 3
Gdansk
  history, 682
geopolitics
  Yugoslavia, 957
German authors, 523
German fiction, 247
German literature, 522
  20th century, 520, 539
German question, 343
German reunification question (1949-1990), 64, 148, 497, 542, 545-549
Germans in Hungary, 583
Germans in Poland, 652
Germany
  ethnic relations, 300
  exiles, 623
  foreign relations
    Soviet Union, 497
  history, 498
  politics and government, 503, 508, 542, 544
    1933-1945, 412
    1945-, 537
    1990-, 548
  relations
    United States, 543
Gerschenkron effect, 181
Gierek, Edward, 1913-, 696
Gildner, Gary, 781
Gleye, Paul, 506

gods, Slavic
  bibliography, 5
Goldfarb, Aron, 277
Gombrowicz, Witold, 756
Goncz, Arpad, 618
Gorbachev, Michael S., 83, 505
governmental structures, 77
governments and trading, 51
Grade, Chaim, 256
graffitti
  Berlin, 550
Great Britain
  foreign relations
    Albania, 370
    Poland, 716
    Yugoslavia, 958
Greece
  history
    Macedonian hegemony, 323-281 B.C., 920
Grotowski, Jerzy, 1933-, 848
guerrillas
  United States, 933
  Yugoslavia, 924, 933
Gurowski, Adam, 793
Gypsies, 253
  Bulgaria, 397
  Czechoslovakia, 471
  ethnic identity, 397

Habsburg, House of, 38
Haiti
  history, 670
Hale, Keith
  journeys, 3
handbooks, manuals, etc., 8
harvest failures, 182
Haskalah, 260
Havel, Olga, 448
Havel, Vaclav, 448-449, 476, 479
heads of state
  Romania, 871
Helsinki Final Act, 86
Herbert, Zbigniew, 757
Herzen, Alexander, 793
Heydrich, Reinhard, 412
historiography, 45
history, 16, 18, 20, 28, 33-34, 41-42, 44-45, 47, 111, 344, 347, 350
  19th century, 252
  20th century, 26
  1867-1918, 19
  1945-, 37
  1945-1989, 27
  1989-, 63, 354, 357, 359
  sources, 1
hitchhiking
  Czechoslovakia
    fiction, 462
Holan, Vladimir, 450
Holocaust, Jewish, 247, 259, 267, 269, 272-273, 276, 278, 284-285, 295, 298, 300
  in art, 297
  Balkan Peninsula, 296

causes, 270
chronology, 274
Czechoslovakia, 290, 294
in fiction, 275, 281, 299
historiography, 270
Hungary, 632, 634
in literature, 239, 289, 742
personal narratives, 286
Poland, 266, 280, 283, 293, 664, 671, 675, 681, 814, 817, 819-820, 823-824, 827, 832, 836, 839, 844
  Bialobrzegi, 277
  Warsaw, 818, 825
Romania, 861-862, 905-906
sources, 282
World War II, 839
Yugoslavia, 271
Holocaust memorials
  Poland, 291
Holocaust survivors
  France, 251
  history, 258
  Poland, 664, 829
    fiction, 754
Holub, Miroslav, 451
Holzman, Franklin D.
  bibliography, 143
Honecker, Erich, 79
housing policy
  Hungary, 597
Hrabal, Bohumil, 452, 453
human experimentation in medicine
  Poland, 279
human rights
  France, 706
  Poland, 706
  United States, 706
human services, 308
humanism
  Poland, 850
humanists
  Croatia, 327
  Hungary, 327
  Poland, 850
Hungarian drama
  20th century, 610
Hungarian language
  dictionaries
    English, 614
  grammar, 609
  grammar, generative, 613
  inflection, 607
  predicate, 609
  syntax, 613
  textbooks for foreign speakers, 615
Hungarian literature, 240
  Canada, 608
Hungarian poetry, 612
Hungarian prose literature, 611
Hungarian-Americans
  history, 572
Hungarians, 587
  Czechoslovakia, 554

foreign countries, 255
Romania, 554
Soviet Union, 554
Yugoslavia, 554
Hungary, 551
  civilization, 573, 574, 629
  description and travel, 3, 491
  economic conditions, 192, 575, 591, 620
    20th century, 595
    1918-1945, 603
    1945-, 552, 590, 593
    1945-1989, 588
    1968-1989, 193, 585, 590, 594
    1989-, 594, 598-599, 605
  economic development, 150
  economic policy, 136, 141, 164, 212, 584, 600-602, 604
    1945-, 133, 590
    1968-1989, 145, 153, 590, 592, 606
    1989-, 126, 132, 598, 599, 605
  economic reform, 127, 143, 166, 203
  ethnic relations, 17, 635
  fiction, 611, 619
  foreign economic relations, 598
  foreign relations, 586-587
  history, 102, 556, 558-560, 562, 564, 566, 568-570, 573-574, 581
    1000-1699, 557
    Turkish occupation, 1528-1699, 575
    1867-1918, 17
    1918-1945, 632
    revolution, 555, 561
  politics and government, 554, 577-578, 581, 583, 620
    1945-1989, 552, 579-580, 585, 588
    1989-, 132
    20th century, 595
  religion, 304
  rural conditions, 630, 631
  second economy, 201
  social conditions, 575, 620
    1945-1989, 552, 579, 585, 588, 622
  social life and customs, 558
Hussites, 404

IBRD (International Bank for Reconstruction and Development), 141
IMF (International Monetary Fund), 129, 141, 143
immigrants
  United States, 262, 635
imports, 234
incentives in industry
  Hungary, 592
income distribution, 130, 215, 313
  Hungary, 164
  Poland, 164
  Yugoslavia, 962
independence movements
  Crimean Tartars, 319
  Estonia, 319
  Poland, 319
  Ukraine, 319

individualism in literature, 530
industrial efficiency
   Hungary, 594
industrial management, 172
industrial policy, 143
   Czechoslovakia, 127
   Hungary, 127
   Poland, 127
   Soviet Union, 127
industrial relations, 131, 222, 225
   Poland, 729
industry, 234
   Bulgaria, 383
   Romania, 890
inflation
   Bulgaria, 385
inflation, 151
   case studies, 191
   Hungary, 603
informal sector (economics), 201
   Poland, 795
intellectual life, 325
intellectuals
   Austria, 623
   Czechoslovakia, 480
   Germany, 623
   Hungary, 623
   Romania, 909
intelligence officers
   Romania, 881
international business enterprises, 172
   Yugoslavia, 970
international division of labor, 177, 971
international economic integration, 177
international economic relations, 141, 149, 172
   Yugoslavia, 967
international law, 70
International Monetary Fund. *See* IMF
international trade
   econometric models, 207
interstructural trade, 181
invasion by Warsaw Pact Countries, 424
investments
   developing countries, 206
   Yugoslavia, 967
investments, foreign, 214
   Czechoslovakia, 484
   Hungary, 589
   law and legislation, 960
   Yugoslavia, 970, 973
Isaacson, Judith Magyar, 634
Israel
   economic liberalization, 203

Jadwiga, Queen, consort, 659
Jagendorf, Siegfried, 862
Japan
   economic liberalization, 203
Jasenovac, Croatia (Concentration Camp), 925
Jaszi, Oscar, 621
Jelavich, Barbara, 57
Jelavich, Charles, 57
Jewish children, 273

Poland, 783
Jewish communists, 838
   Poland, 704
Jewish fiction, 289
Jews, 247, 254, 257, 259-260,
   in art, 816
   Austria, 261, 265
   Belarus, 820, 833
   bibliography, 646
   Czechoslovakia, 294, 469-470
   economic conditions, 676
   Germany, 300
   history, 258, 262-263
   Hungary, 254, 261, 632-633, 635
      Budapest, 288
      Kaposvar, 634
   in literature, 669
   intellectual life, 523
   music, 844
   Palestine, 288
   Poland, 266, 268, 293, 668, 671, 676, 815,
      820-821, 824, 826-827, 829-830, 834-
      835, 839
      Bialobrzegi, 277
      Bodzentyn, 280
      emancipation, 822
      Gdansk, 272
      history, 822, 832-833
      Lodz, 844
      Opatow, 828
      politics and government. 704, 823
      social life and customs, 816
      Warsaw, 814, 818, 825
      Wegrow, 817
   Romania, 905-906
   Soviet Union, 820
   Yugoslavia, 271
Jews, Polish
   France, 251
Johnson, Uwe, 530
joint ventures, 166, 181, 214, 235
   Soviet Union, 214
   Yugoslavia, 970
journalism
   Poland, 779
journalistic ethics
   Poland, 779
journalists
   Poland, 779
Judaism
   history (425-1789), 414
Juel, Dagny, 847

Kadar, Janos, 578
Kalecki, Michal, 731, 733
Kalib, Goldie Szachter, 280
Kaposvar (Hungary)
   ethnic relations, 634
Karadzic, Vuk, 984
Karst Region
   economic conditions, 976
   social conditions, 976
Katyn Forest massacre, 1940, 678

Khazars
  fiction, 992
Kiev, 314
Kis, Danilo, 989
Klima, Ivan, 454
Klugman, James, 958
Klukowski, Zygmunt, 663
Kochanowski, Jan, 843
Kolbuszowa
  biography, 837
Kollataj, Hugo, 710
Komitet Obrony Robotnikov, 813
Kommunistische Partei Deutschlands, 496
Komunisticka Partija Jugoslavije, 926
Komunisticka Strana Ceskoslovenska, 434
Konstantin Pavlovich, Grand Duke of Russia
    1779-1831, 672
Konwicki, Tadeusz, 759
Kopacsi, Sandor, 561
KOR (Workers' Defense Committee), 801, 813
Korea
  economic liberalization, 203
Kosciuszko, Tadeusz, 710
Kosinski, Jerzy, 760
Kossuth, Lajos, 628
Kott, Jan, 752
Kovaly, Heda, 428
Krakow, 314
Krakulic, Slavenka, 944
Krleza, Miroslav, 990
Kultura (journal), 786
Kundera, Milan, 442, 455-457

labor
  Hungary, 594
labor law and legislation
  Poland, 729
labor policy
  Poland, 804
  Yugoslavia, 971
labor unions
  China, 211
  Yugoslavia, 211
Lalic, Ivan V., 991
language and culture, 247
language planning
  Yugoslavia, 979
Laos
  economic policy, 141
Latin America
  economic reform, 213
Latin language
  Croatia, 327
  Hungary, 327
Lautar, 891
law, 4
  Germany, 511
  sources, 67
  study and teaching, 511
lawyers
  Germany, 511
Le Chambon-sur-Lignon (France), 292
leadership, 98

Levi, Primo, 831
Liang, Hsi-Huey, 537
libraries
  history, 402
library resources, 328
Lindsay, Franklin, 933
literature, 250
literature and society
  Poland, 749
  Romania, 904
literature and state
  Czechoslovakia, 441
literature, comparative
  Russian and Polish, 750
livestock production, 182
loans, 129
local finance
  Hungary, 576
  Poland, 722
local government
  Hungary, 576
local politics
  Poland, 98
  role of women, 98
  Romania, 98
local revenue
  Hungary, 576
logic, modern, 851
longevity, 398
Louis I, King of Hungary and Poland, 1326-
    1382, 43
Lukacs, Gyorgy, 242
Lustig, Arnost, 458, 459

Macedonia
  history, 936
    Diadochi, 323-276 B.C., 920
  independence movements, 936
Macedonian language
  morphology, 980
  verb, 980
Macedonian question, 999
macroeconomics, 234
Magyar Kommunista Part, 567
Malinowski, Bronislaw, 789
management, 188, 225
  communist countries, 188
  Soviet Union, 188
  Yugoslavia, 962, 966
Manea, Norman, 896, 904
Mann, Thomas, 242
Mannheim, Karl, 627
manuscripts
  catalogs, 1
Maramures (Romania)
  social life and customs, 903
Marcuse, Peter, 510
marketing, 163
  Yugoslavia, 967
Marko, Prince of Serbia, 245
Marshall Plan, 142
marshals
  Romania, 871

martial law
  Poland, 808
Marx, Karl, 119
marxian economics, 193
Marxism, 159
Masaryk, T. G., 410, 421
Masing, Leonard, 984
mass media
  Poland, 779
  political aspects, 311
massacres
  Yugoslavia, 922
medicine
  political aspects
    Germany, 538
Mexico
  economic liberalization, 203
  as subordinate state, 106
Mickiewicz, Adam, 793
Mihailovic, Draza, 932, 958
military policy, 56, 509
military relations
  East Germany, 509
military weapons
  economic aspects
    China, 153
    Hungary, 153
    Poland, 153
Milosz, Czeslaw, 761-767
Milton, John, 240
minorities, 255, 257
  ethnicity, 252
  Hungary, 556, 587
  legal status, laws, etc., 255
mixed economy, 128, 145, 147, 151
  Czechoslovakia, 487
  East Germany, 518
  Hungary, 593
modernism, 243
Moldova
  boundaries
    Romania, 884
  languages, 884
monetary policy, 138, 151, 205, 232
  case studies, 191
  Hungary, 592, 603
money and banking, 159, 166, 174, 232
Mongolia
  economic policy, 141
morale, 708
mortality, 752
Moscow
  description, 523
  history, 314
Moscow
  social conditions, 523
motion picture actors and actresses
  Bulgaria, 388
motion picture producers and directors
  Bulgaria, 388
motion pictures, 330
  Bulgaria, 388
MPE (modified planned economy), 142

municipal finance
  Hungary, 576
municipal law, 70
mural painting and decoration
  Germany, 550
music
  Poland
    bibliography, 846, 852

Nahon, Marco, 287
national security, 105
  Czechoslovakia, 32
  Hungary, 32
  Poland, 32
national socialism, 538
  moral and ethical aspects, 279
nationalism, 76, 105, 114
  Balkan peninsula, 50, 53
  Czechoslovakia, 429
  history, 57, 252
  Poland, 710
  religious aspects, 317
  Romania, 63, 909
  Yugoslavia, 926, 930
nationalism and communism, 587
  Romania, 877
Nationalsozialistische Deutsche Arbeiter
    Partei, 412
  Reservepolizeibataillon 1, 819
natural resources
  Yugoslavia, 968
natural security
  Europe, 546
needlework, 331
new economic mechanism (Hungary), 136
Newly Industrialized Countries, 150
  economic policy, 203
Nicholas I, Tsar of Russia, 102
Nir, Yehuda 1930, 668
nobility, 40
North Korea
  description and travel, 113
  economic policy, 141
North-South Korean relations, 94
Novgorod
  history, 314
NSZZ "Solidarnosc," 211, 694, 700, 709, 717, 736, 802, 806-810, 812
  history, 648, 785, 803, 804
nuclear weapons, 85
  Russia, 85
nuclear-weapon-free zones
  Central Europe, 99

OECD, 150
Olszanica site (Poland), 667
Olt Region (Romania)
  social conditions, 902
Opatow, Poland
  ethnic relations, 828
opposition
  East Germany, 515
  Poland, 801, 813

oral formulaic analysis, 891
oral tradition
  Yugoslavia, 996
Organization for Economic Cooperation and Development. *See* OECD
organizational behavior, 726
Orthodox Eastern Church
  Bulgaria, 381
Ostpolitik, 86

Paral, Vladimir, 460
participative management
  Yugoslavia, 962
party politics, 77
Patai family, 288
Patai, Raphael, 288, 565
Pavel, Ota, 461
Pavic, Milorad, 993
peasantry
  Hungary, 630
  Karst, 976
  Slovenia, 976
Peoples' Republic of China. *See* China
perestroika, 343, 360
  East Germany, 505
perfume bottles
  collectors and collecting, 472
persecution
  bibliography, 13
PET (planned economy in transition), 142
Philomatus, 792
philosophy
  Czechoslovakia, 439
philosophy, Polish
  20th century, 851
phonology, 738
physicians
  Germany
    political activity, 538
physicians, Jewish
  Poland, 818
picture dictionaries, Serbo-Croatian, 988
Pinkus, Oscar, 834
pluralism, 110
poets, Polish
  20th century, 764
Poland
  armed forces, 708
  bibliography, 644-645, 649
  business cycles, 726
  church history, 795
  civilization, 689, 850
  constitutional history, 698
  description and travel, 643, 791, 821, 845
  economic conditions, 679, 686, 693, 723, 725, 734-735
  economic development, 150
  economic policy, 136, 141, 164, 724, 726, 731-732, 734-735, 841
    1981-, 126, 132, 153, 722, 730
  economic reform, 127, 143, 166, 203
  ethnic relations, 272, 646, 704, 820-822, 830, 832, 835-836

foreign economic relations, 728
foreign relations, 662, 707, 713, 721, 802
  France, 108
  Great Britain, 716
  United States, 715
genealogy, 661
heraldry, 661
historical geography, 647
historiography, 653, 677
history, 670, 673, 679, 771
  16th century, 651, 843
  1745-1830, 672
  1795-1830, 684
  1864-1918, 683
  German occupation, 1914-1918, 665
  1918-1945, 665
  occupation, 1939-1945, 46, 658, 666, 823, 833
  1945-, 796
  20th century, 650
history, military, 680
intellectual life, 786
  to 1795, 710
  19th century, 793
  1945-, 712
moral conditions, 795
political activity, 812
politics and government, 100, 651, 679, 685-686, 695, 697, 705, 707, 709, 711, 713-714, 785, 797
  1763-1796, 698, 710
  1919-1945, 715
  1945-, 692, 694, 803, 813
  1945-1980, 688, 696, 699, 801
  1980-1989, 648, 688, 690, 693, 699-700, 702-703, 712, 807-809
  1989-, 132, 648, 702, 805, 840
Polskie Sily Zbroina. Armia Kraiowa, 699
relations
  Europe, 843
  Germany, 654
  United States, 673
  Vatican City, 720
religion, 304
religious life and customs, 800
rural conditions, 780, 788
second economy, 201
social classes, 788
social conditions, 657, 679, 781-782, 785, 797
  1945-, 694, 795
  1980-, 693, 795, 840
social stratification, 790
as subordinate state, 106
Poles
  New York, 674
policy outcomes, 77
policy powers, 77
Polish Americans, 673
Polish authors
  20th century, 768, 773
Polish crisis, 100
Polish drama
  20th century, 748, 753

Polish essays, 751
Polish language
 conversation and phrase books, 740
 dictionaries, 740
 grammar, 739
 morphemics, 737
 phonology, 737, 738
 prosodic analysis, 737
 spoken Polish, 739
 syllabication, 737
 textbooks for foreign speakers, 741
Polish literature, 240
 19th century, 669
 20th century, 776
 history and criticism, 750
Polish periodicals
 bibliography, 645
Polish poetry, 745-746
 20th century, 743
 history and criticism, 747
 Jewish authors, 742
 translations into English, 745
Polish question, 660, 672
political alienation, 98
political culture
 communist countries, 116
 Poland, 691, 787
political ethics, 425
political geography, 358
political participation
 Czechoslovakia, 477
political parties, 340
 history, 955
 Yugoslavia, 954
political posters, 323
political prisoners
 Czechoslovakia, 448
 Romania, 875
 Yugoslavia, 998
political satire, Romanian, 899-900
political science, 72
politicians
 fiction, 326
 Romania, 873
politics and government, 40, 49, 52, 54, 59, 66, 68, 73, 75-76, 95, 110, 112, 115, 118, 121, 146, 180, 319, 325, 338-339, 340-341, 348-349, 351, 358, 363
 19th century, 57, 252
 20th century, 57
 1918-1945, 687
 1945-1989, 101
 1945-, 323, 346, 356
 1945-1989, 60, 71-72, 84, 321, 324, 342, 353, 362, 579-580
 1989-, 64-65, 311, 345, 360-362, 364
politics and literature, 250, 325
Polska Zjednoczona Partia Robotnicza, 688, 690
Popa, Vasko, 994
post-communism, 68, 76, 123, 162, 186-187, 190, 219
 Former Soviet Republics, 186

Hungary, 577
Romania, 898, 902
postmodernism, 526
Prague
 biography, 428
 description, 303
 ethnic relations, 294
 fiction, 468
 intellectual life, 480
PRC. *See* China
presidents
 Czechoslovakia, 421
 Poland, 805
price systems, 181
prices, 159, 234
prisoners of war
 Germany, 938
 Italy, 831
 Poland, 279, 831
 Yugoslavia, 938
private international law, 70
private plot agriculture
 Hungary, 631
privatization, 123, 131, 135, 148, 152, 156, 162, 175, 185, 189, 227
 Bulgaria, 142
 Central Asia, 189
 Central Europe, 152
 Czechoslovakia, 142
 East Germany, 142
 Hungary, 142
 joint ventures, 231
 law and legislation, 156
 Poland, 142, 732, 841
 Romania, 142
 Soviet Union, 142
produce trade, 160
production, 159
professions
 Czechoslovakia, 312
 Poland, 312
 Soviet Union, 312
property
 Yugoslavia, 973
property rights, 142
prostitution
 Czechoslovakia, 462
Przybyszewska, Stanislawa, 768, 769
public opinion, 98, 719
 East Germany, 536
public opinion
 Israel, 272
 Poland, 669, 836
public welfare
 Hungary, 126
 Poland, 126
 Soviet Union, 126
publishers and publishing
 Czechoslovakia, 402

Quadrapartite Agreement on Berlin (1971), 494

Rapacki plan, 99
reconstruction
  Yugoslavia, 965
Redlikh, Egon, 290
reformation
  biography, 31
Reformed Church
  Romania, 870
refugees, Jewish, 256
regional cooperation, 142
religion, 114
religion and state, 304, 317
Renaissance
  Poland, 843, 850
Rensenbrik, John C., 700
rent subsidies
  Hungary, 597
research, 337
  Czechoslovakia, 430
  Hungary, 553
research institutes
  Hungary, 553
return migration
  Yugoslavia, 971
reunification question, 343
Reviczky, Imre, 568
revolution, 1989, 310
revolutionaires
  Poland, 838
Rezzori, Gregor von
  biography, 897
righteous gentiles in the Holocaust, 292
rites and ceremonies
  Romania, 903
rock music
  communist countries, 332
Rohr, Janelle, 64
Romania
  boundaries
    Moldova, 884
  Departmentul de Informatii Externe, 881
  description and travel, 113, 491, 854
  economic conditions, 221, 853, 889
    1945-, 874
  economic history, 890
  economic policy, 136, 141, 150, 889-890
  ethnic relations, 17, 905, 906
  foreign relations, 867, 885, 888
    1914-1944, 883, 887
    developing countries, 79
    United States, 886
    Yugoslavia, 883
  history, 853, 856, 858, 860, 866-868
    19th century, 908
    1914-1944, 17, 871
    1944-, 872
    revolution, 1989, 63, 857, 873, 879, 882
  intellectual life, 895
  national security, 853
  politics and government, 853, 861, 870, 877-878
    19th century. 908
    1914-1944, 871
    1944-, 904
    1944-1989, 874-876, 880, 882
    1989-, 882
  relations with United States, 865
  religion, 304
  second economy, 201
  social conditions, 853, 898, 902
Romanian Americans, 895
Romanian language
  foreign elements, 869
  grammar, 892
Romanian literature, 240
romanticism
  influcnce, 520
  Poland, 793
  Russia, 793
Rosenberg, Blanca, 293
RPE (reformed planned economy), 142
Rufeisen, Oswald, 681
Russia
  bibliography, 11
  foreign relations, 662
  history
    Alexander I, 1801-1825, 684
    Nicholas I, 1825-1855, 102
  intellectual life, 793
Russian literature, 240, 249
Russo-Polish War, 1919-1920, 655
Rzeczpospolita Polska (government in exile), 823

Salamun, Tomaz, 995
Salsitz, Norman, 837
samizdat literature, 321
scholarship
  Poland, 792
Schulz, Bruno, 770
Schwenckfeld, Caspar, 31
science
  East Germany, 500
science and state, 337
  Czechoslovakia, 430
second economy, 201
secondary economies, 181
Selevac Site, 939
Serbia
  antiquities, 934
  constitutional history, 955
  ethnic relations. 271
  history
    1804-1918, 931
  intellectual life, 997
Serbian poetry
  20th century, 987
  history and criticism, 982
  translations into English, 982
Serbo Croatian language, 978
  accents and accentuation, 984
  grammar, 985
  intonation, 984
  prosodic analysis, 984
  textbooks for foreign speaker, 981

Serbs, 943
 folklore, 996
Sik, Ota, 161
Simecka, Martin M., 463
Sino-Soviet relations, 94
Skvorecky, Josef, 465-467
Slancikova, Bozena. *See* Timrava
Slavic languages, 246
 phonology, 238
Slavic literature, 241, 243
Slavophilism, 793
Slavs
 religion, 5
Slovak language
 grammar, generative, 443
 phonology, 443
Slovak Republic
 history, 409
 politics and government, 420
Slovakia
 history
  1944 uprising, 405
Slowes, Salomen, 678
Smeral, Bohumir, 437
Sobibor (Poland: Concentration Camp), 267
social classes
 Central Europe, 309
 history, 309
social conditions, 60, 309-310, 318, 579
social courts
 Yugoslavia, 946
social life and customs, 315
social networks
 Poland, 795
social policy, 308
 Yugoslavia, 967
social problems
 fiction, 529
social security, 174
 Poland, 724
socialism, 121, 145, 196, 213
 Balkan Pennisula, 221
 Hungary, 584-585, 620-621
 Poland, 840
 Romania, 874
 Yugoslavia, 119, 977
socialism and literature, 533
 East Germany, 522
 Romania, 904
socialism and society, 593, 902
socialism and the arts
 Hungary, 637
socialism and youth, 115
socialist realism and architecture, 324
socialist realism in literature, 372
sociolinguistics, 247
 Czechoslovakia, 438, 444
sociology
 Austria, 623
 Germany, 623
 Hungary, 623
Sofia (Bulgaria)
 guidebooks, 377

history, 377
soldiers
 Poland, 656
Solidarity. *See* NSZZ "Solidarnosc"
songs
 Poland, 844
South Slavic Literature, 241
Soviet industrialization debate, 181
Soviet Union, 2
 bibliography, 11
 economic conditions, 169, 185, 194, 360
 economic history, 136
 economic policy, 136, 185
  1986- 126, 194
 economic reform, 127, 143, 166
 foreign relations
  East Germany, 505
  Eastern Europe, 84
 politics and government, 49, 118
  1945-1991, 72
  1985-1991, 360
 relations
  Eastern Europe, 101
 second economy, 201
 social life and customs, 315
Soviet-Far Eastern relations, 94
Spain
 economic liberalization, 203
sports and state, 320
Stalin, Joseph, 941
Stambolov, Stefan, 394
Staszic, Stanislaw, 710
statesmen
 Bulgaria, 394
 Poland, 684
 Russia, 684
statutes
 Europe, 67
Stein, Edith, 531
Stepinac, Alojzije, 918
Stojka, Karl, 297
street art
 Germany, 550
strikes, 808
structural adjustment
 Poland, 730
student movements
 Poland, 792, 811
synagogues
 Poland, 830
syndicalism
 Hungary, 621
Szabo, Ervin, 621
Szurek, Alexander, 838

Taiwan
 economic liberalization, 203
taxation, 181
Teatr Laboratorium (Wroclaw, Poland), 848
technology
 Hungary, 596
technology and state, 337
 Czechoslovakia, 430

technology transfer, 234-235, 336
  economic aspects, 335
teenagers, 115
Terezin (Concentration Camp), 290
theater, 752
  Czechoslovakia, 333
  Denmark, 333
  Hungary, 333
  Norway, 333
  Poland, 333, 748, 777
  Romania, 333
  Russia, 333
  Sweden, 333
theatrical producers and directors
  Germany, 524
Timrava, 446
Tito, Josip Broz, 916, 932, 941
  bibliography, 910
Todorovich, Boris, 938
Tokes, Laszlo, 870
totalitarianism, 468
tourist trade, 171
trade, 149
  China, 182
  United States, 182
trade regulation
  Czechoslovakia, 489
  Poland, 841
  Romania, 890
trade unions
  Czechoslovakia, 211, 436
  East Germany, 211
  Hungary, 211
  Poland, 211, 736, 812
  Romania, 211
  Soviet Union, 211
trade unions and communism
  Czechoslovakia, 436
trading companies, 200
transborder data flows, 334
transition problem, 343
transportation
  Romania, 890
Transylvania, 864
  description and travel, 491
  ethnic relations, 17, 863
  historiography, 35
  history, 17, 35, 863
Treblinka (Poland: Concentration Camp), 267
trials (political crimes and offenses)
  fiction, 326
  Poland, 810
  Prague, 427
Trianon, Treaty, 868
Turkey
  description and travel, 3

Ukrainians
  Slovakia, 413
underground literature, 321
  Czechoslovakia, 439
  Poland, 645
unemployment, 174

United States
  constitutional history, 698
  economic policy, 196
  foreign relations, 885
    1945-, 92
    Bulgaria, 395
    Eastern Europe, 96
    Poland, 715
    Romania, 886
    Yugoslavia, 957, 959
  history
    1913-1921, 395
    Office of Strategic Services, 933
  relations
    Germany, 543
universities and colleges
  Hungary, 553
urban policy, 55
urban renewal
  Romania, 901
Uskoks, 921
utopias in literature, 533

Vali, Ferenc, 571
valuation, 183
vampires, 244
Vanek, Ferdinand, 440
Velvet revolution, 74
Vienna
  description, 303
  politics and government, 691
Vietnam
  description and travel, 113
  economic policy, 141
Vilnius, 792
Vinca culture
  Yugoslavia, 934, 939
Vlachs, 264
Vlad III, Prince of Wallachia, 1430-1476, 859
Voltaire, 240

wages, 215
Wajda, Andrzej, 772
Walesa, Lech, 648, 805
Wallachia
  kings and rulers, 859
war
  history, 24
war crimes, 1000
war criminals
  Germany, 819
Warsaw, 792
Warsaw
  ethnic relations, 675, 814-815, 825
  history, 283, 656, 814
  politics and government, 691
Warsaw Children's Hospital, 818
Warsaw Sparks (baseball team), 781
Warsaw Treaty Organization, 32, 56, 97
  armed forces, 87
Wat, Aleksander, 773-775
Wegrow (Poland)
  ethnic relations, 817

weights and measures, 30
werewolf, 244
Werner, Harold, 839
Western and Northern territories (Poland)
  ethnic relations, 652
Witkiewicz, Stanislaw Ignacy, 776
Wojtyla, Karol, 777
Wolf, Christa, 532-534
woman and the military
  Yugoslavia, 929
women
  Poland, 784
  social conditions, 307
  Soviet Union, 307
  Yugoslavia, 929
work councils
  Hungary, 562
working class, 719
World Bank, 129, 143, 382
world politics, 86
  1945-1955, 92, 957
World War I
  campaigns, Yugoslavia, 928
  causes, 48
  peace, 255
  Romania, 855
  Serbia, 931
  territorial questions, 255
World War II
  Albania, 370
  atrocities, 279, 666, 819, 922, 925
  Bacska (Serbia and Hungary), 922
  Balkan Peninsula, 999
  causes, 716
  children, 273
  chronology, 274
  Czechoslovakia, 46
  diplomatic history, 296, 660, 716
  finance, 603
  governments in exile, 823
  Gypsies, 297
  Hungary, 567, 571
  Jews, 292, 906
  medical care, 279
  personal narratives, 658, 678, 832, 834
    German, 819
    Italian, 831
    Polish, 663
    Serbian, 938
  Poland, 46, 278, 666, 718, 832
    fiction, 744
    Zamosc, 663
  prisoners and prisons, 938
  secret service
    United States, 933
  underground movements, 924, 927
    Czechoslovakia, 412
    Hungary, 632
    Poland, 272, 656, 818, 839
    Yugoslavia, 925, 929, 932-933, 938

Yiddish fiction, 247
Yugoslav literature
  bibliography, 914
Yugoslav War, 1991-, 1000-1001, 1003-1004
Yugoslavia, 911
  armed forces
    political activity, 1005
  bibliography, 910, 912
  church history, 918
  civilization, 950
  economic conditions, 221, 948, 952, 964,
      966, 969
    1945-, 913, 940, 961, 963, 971
  economic development, 150
  economic policy, 136, 212, 967, 969, 974
    1945-, 145, 961, 963, 973
  economic reform, 143
  ethnic relations, 943, 952, 1002, 1005
  foreign relations, 932, 952
    1918-1945, 883
    Great Britain, 958
    Romania, 883
    United States, 957
  history, 932, 935, 1002
    Axis occupation, 1941-1945, 924, 927,
        929, 933
    1945-1980, 916
    1980-, 953, 1008
    civil war, 1991-, 944
    periodicals, 917
  languages, 979
  literature, 983
  migrant workers, 956
  nonalignment, 956
  politics and government, 941, 943, 947-949,
      951-952, 954, 956, 959, 972
    1918-1945, 926, 958
    1945-, 913, 926, 942, 966, 1005
    1980-, 940, 953, 1006
  religion, 304
  social conditions, 913
  social policy, 972
  statistics, 915
  strategic aspects, 957

Zamosc Voivodeship, 663
Zdowska Organizacja Bojowa, 818
Zionism
  Czechoslovakia, 469
Zizka, Jan, 404
Zuzek family, 976